Neil J. Sterritt, Susan Marsden,
Robert Galois, Peter R. Grant, and
Richard Overstall

Tribal Boundaries in the
Nass Watershed

UBCPress / Vancouver

Printed in Canada on acid-free paper ∞
ISBN 0-7748-0660-5

_____

Canadian Cataloguing in Publication Data

Main entry under title:

Tribal boundaries in the Nass Watershed

　　Includes bibliographical references and index.
　　ISBN 0-7748-0660-5

　　1. Kitksan Indians – Claims.　　2. Niska Indians – Claims.
3. Kitksan Indians – Land tenure.　　4. Niska Indians – Land tenure.
5. Nass River Watershed (B.C.) – History.　　I. Sterritt, Neil J.

E78.B9T75 1998　　　　332.2′089′9741　　　C98-910465-6

_____

UBC Press gratefully acknowledges the ongoing support to its publishing program from the Canada Council for the Arts, the British Columbia Arts Council, and the Department of Canadian Heritage of the Government of Canada.

UBC Press
University of British Columbia
6344 Memorial Road
Vancouver, BC V6T 1Z2
(604) 822-5959
Fax: 1-800-668-0821
E-mail: orders@ubcpress.ubc.ca
http://www.ubcpress.ubc.ca

To the Simgiiget yet with us – and to those departed: awakened before fires were lit at dawn to be taught their adaaw<u>k</u>, they share in turn their own proud legacy in the Nass watershed; their words and deeds inspire the generations. Ever vigilant, they too have made their mark.

Contents

Maps

Acknowledgments

A work of this nature is not an individual affair, and it cannot be completed without the active support of a great number of people. In the first place, this work would not have been possible without the unceasing efforts of generations of Gitanyow, Kispiox, Kuldo, and Kisgaga'as persons who presented their truths in various forums without once having the satisfaction of knowing that they were heard. They number in the hundreds. The English names of many appear in the pages of this book. Many never had English names, but held the names of their ancestors, names that their descendants hold today.

Others who must be thanked include the Tahltan Nation, in particular the elders in the village of Iskut who explained their genealogies and histories in the upper Nass, Skeena, Klappan, and Stikine watersheds. Many of the Iskut people have a Gitksan origin. Their contribution has been significant.

We would like to thank the Gitanyow and Gitksan Treaty Offices, and Glen Williams and Don Ryan in particular, for supporting the need for an in-depth approach to the issue of competing claims. Thanks go also to Dr. Peter Williams (1900-95), Gugwihl Gyoo, president of the Kitwancool for more than half a century, who practised and taught that reason would prevail in the pursuit of justice for Aboriginal people.

Those persons who assisted in the early stages of the report include Joanne McDonald, Georgiana Ball, and Theresa Crosgrey. Gordon Wilson and Russell Collier were of immense assistance throughout the various stages of this project, and their help is appreciated. Our appreciation also goes to Kathy Holland, archivist at the Gitksan Treaty Office library, whose efficiency in providing materials on request was invaluable, as was that of the British Columbia Archives and the National Archives of Canada. Eric Leinberger must be recognized and thanked for his work on the maps in this book. Our appreciation is also extended to Cole Harris and the

Department of Geography at UBC for the generous donation of some of the cartographic work.

Financial assistance toward printing costs was graciously provided by the Gitksan Government Commission, the Gitanyow Treaty Office, and the law firm of Hutchins, Soroka, and Grant.

As authors, we have worked with so many people, many now gone, some still living, chiefs and house members, who have entrusted us for so many years with their personal experiences on the land and with their knowledge of their histories and territories. They had faith that it would be recorded for the benefit of future generations. They are the true authors of this work.

Neil J. Sterritt
January 1998

Abbreviations

BCA	British Columbia Archives (Victoria)
BCPM	British Columbia Provincial Museum
CNR	Canadian National Railways
CMC	Canadian Museum of Civilization (Ottawa)
COT	Collins Overland Telegraph
DIA	Department of Indian Affairs
DSGIA	Deputy Superintendent General of Indian Affairs
FIBC	Friends of the Indians of British Columbia
GA	Gitksan Archives (Hazelton)
GSC	Geological Survey of Canada
GTO	Gitksan Treaty Office
GWTC	Gitksan Wet'suwet'en Tribal Council (formerly Gitksan-Carrier Tribal Council, GCTC)
HBCA	Hudson's Bay Company Archives (Winnipeg)
MMRC	Canada and British Columbia, Royal Commission on Indian Affairs, 1913-16 (commonly known as the McKenna-McBride Royal Commission)
NAC	National Archives of Canada (Ottawa)
NTC	Nisga'a Tribal Council
SGIA	Superintendent General of Indian Affairs
UBCMAA	University of British Columbia, Museum of Anthropology Archives (Vancouver)
UBCSC	University of British Columbia Library, Special Collections (Vancouver)
UNGM	Unnamed on government maps

Tribal Boundaries in the Nass Watershed

1
Introduction

Tribal Boundaries in the Nass Watershed was originally written as part of the negotiations between the Gitksan and the Nisga'a in preparation for the Nisga'a settlement of their territorial claim with the federal and provincial governments. It concerns four nations – the Gitksan, including the Gitanyow, the Nisga'a, the Tahltan, and the Tsetsaut – whose territorial claims of ownership and jurisdiction include overlapping portions of the upper Nass River.

The Gitksan considered it necessary to produce such a report because the process of negotiations laid out by the Nisga'a and the federal and provincial governments had failed to resolve the issue of an ever-expanding Nisga'a claim to Gitksan territory. The Gitksan objective in producing a report was to initiate substantive discussion between them and the Nisga'a by examining and evaluating the available evidence pertaining to the competing claims. In so doing, the authors drew on both the Gitksan tradition, in which evidence of territorial ownership is formally validated, and the Euro-Canadian academic tradition, in which evidence from documentary sources is researched and analyzed.

Publication of the report is an extension of its original purpose. After its limited release, the report failed to generate the intended dialogue concerning the Gitksan-Nisga'a boundary, with either the Nisga'a or the federal and provincial governments. Given the role of the academic tradition in Euro-Canadian law and politics,[1] the Gitksan and Gitanyow have chosen to make the information in this report available to a wider readership, especially to anthropologists, legal experts, geographers, and historians. As such, this book is part of a long tradition that began in 1884, in which the Gitksan and Gitanyow have taken every opportunity to educate Euro-Canadians, especially those in the political arena, concerning their society, on the assumption that an understanding of indigenous systems would lead to justice for Aboriginal peoples.[2] For the purpose of this publication, the introduction has been rewritten, but only minor editorial changes have been made in the report itself.

This book, although specific in its intended purpose, also addresses an issue of considerable importance, that of Aboriginal land tenure in general. Until recently, discussion of indigenous systems of land tenure has been greatly underrepresented in the academic literature. It is difficult not to conclude, given the volumes of information from which to draw, that the political implications of such a discussion have played a role in steering researchers to less controversial subjects.

The absence of scholarly study on the subject of indigenous systems of land tenure has serious implications for current political processes in British Columbia. The federal and provincial governments, in their ignorance of the ancient political and legal systems of First Nations, are frequently participants in processes that defy indigenous law, the very law that underlies the treaty process itself, and, in the case of their treatment of the "overlap issue," they risk becoming unwitting pawns of individual First Nations that pursue territorial expansion at the expense of their neighbours.

The serious study of indigenous systems of land tenure is also a prerequisite for any consideration of First Nations history since contact. First Nations efforts to have their social and political institutions recognized and their systems of land ownership acknowledged have dominated their own politics, and their lives, for over two centuries and have played a major role in the political life of British Columbia.

The pursuit of recognition of Aboriginal title, commonly known as land claims, began as soon as Europeans first established a presence within the territories of Northwest Coast First Nations. It has taken the form of petitions, meetings, and delegations; it has gone underground when deemed against the law and reemerged as legal suits in the Canadian courts. Since 1973, it has been a formal political process with federal-Nisga'a negotiations and now provincewide treaty negotiations.

It will become evident in the chapters that follow that the Gitksan, Gitanyow, Nisga'a, Tahltan, and Tsetsaut have their own systems of territorial ownership, including processes by which ownership is established, boundaries recognized, and disputes resolved. It will also become apparent that there is a wealth of documentation identifying the boundaries between these nations. Finally, it will become clear that, in the process of pursuing their land claim, the Nisga'a, first at the negotiation table, have used this privileged position to claim territories in excess of twice their legitimate territory.

As this book also shows, the Gitksan and Gitanyow, since the inception of colonialism, have repeatedly and consistently reiterated their claim to their territories and have resisted colonialist encroachment and the efforts of their First Nations neighbours, under the wings of church and state, to expand their territory at the Gitksan's expense.

Geography

The histories and territories of several First Nations – the Gitksan with the Gitanyow, the Nisga'a, the Tsetsaut, and the Tahltan – are the subject of this publication. The Gitksan and Nisga'a, with their neighbours the Tsimshian, form a distinct Northwest Coast group of closely related nations who share a common culture, society, and language. Their territories encompass the Skeena River watershed and almost the entire Nass River. There are, however, significant differences between these three nations. In some ways, the Gitksan more closely resemble the Tsimshian, while in others they have more in common with the Nisga'a, but they all share a common legal system that defines ownership of territory and access rights.

The Tahltan and Tsetsaut are Athapaskan nations that speak entirely different languages than those of the Tsimshian, Nisga'a, and Gitksan, and they organize their societies along quite different lines. These nations, however, also have a legal system that includes inalienable rights to the territories. Their territories encompass most of the Stikine River watershed and a portion of the upper Nass River (see Appendix 1).

The tribes, or villages, of the Gitksan nation are Gitwangak (Gitwingax, Kitwanga), Gitanyow (Kitwancool), Kitsegyukla (Gitksigyukla), Gitanmaax (Hazelton), Kispiox, Kuldo, and Kisgaga'as (Kisgagas). Those tribes with territories on the upper Nass River are Gitanyow, Kuldo, Kisgaga'as, and Kispiox. The Gitanyow are distinct among the Gitksan in that they have maintained an independence from centralized tribal organizations. As will be evident in the chapters that follow, they have long pursued resolution of the land question issue on their own. The term "Gitksan" as used in this publication includes the Gitanyow, and all general references to the Gitksan in this book include the Gitanyow.

The Nass River watershed is a major river system that flows southwest through the rugged Coast Range mountains of the Northwest Coast. The river is 384 kilometres long from its source at Nass Lake to tidewater just below the Nisga'a community of Greenville, and it encompasses an area of 21,150 square kilometres, including several important tributaries: the Blackwater, Kwinageese, Cranberry, and Tseax Rivers, and the Bowser and Meziadin Lakes watersheds (see Map 1).

The portion of the Nass River that is the subject of competing claims from the Nisga'a on the one hand and the Gitksan, including the Gitanyow, on the other hand extends from a short distance above Aiyansh to its headwaters. The Nisga'a currently claim the entire Nass watershed from mouth to source. The Gitksan claim from the confluence of the

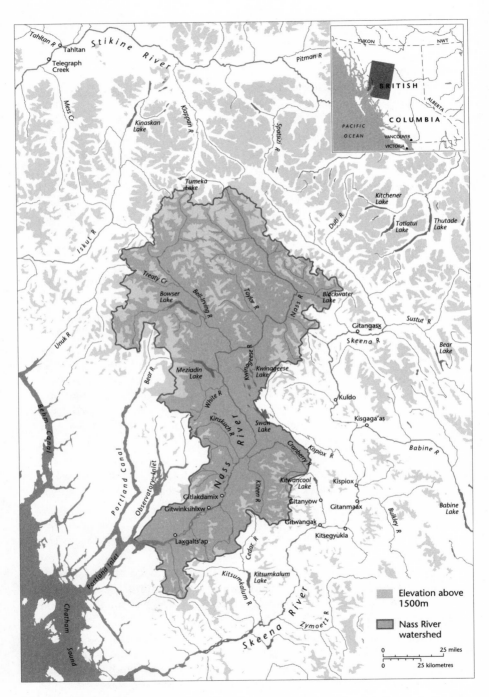

Map 1   Location map

Tchitin and Nass Rivers almost to the headwaters of the Nass. Of this, the Gitanyow claim the lower portion, including Meziadin Lake, and the Kisgaga'as, Kuldo, and Kispiox claim the area beyond Meziadin to the headwaters area of the Nass (see Map 2).

In this book, several geographic features are important and will be referred to many times. Moving upriver from Gitlakdamix (Aiyansh), they are Gitxsits'uuts'xwt and Geltsalo'obit and Gitangyahlxw, which are located on opposite sides of the Nass River at the confluence of the Tchitin River, the Kiteen and Kinskuch Rivers, Meziadin Lake, Surveyors and Treaty Creeks in the Bell-Irving system, and Konigus Creek at the head-waters of the Nass River (see Maps 1 and 36).

In analyzing the historical documents and statements of the Gitksan and Nisga'a, it is important to identify the area indicated by general terms such as "upper and lower Nass." The terms are most often relative to the identity and location of the speaker and need to be understood in each context.

Competing Claims in the Nass Watershed

Competing claims between First Nations have existed since time imme-morial, and indigenous legal systems on the Northwest Coast allow for a number of forms of dispute resolution, most commonly the formation of kinship ties through clan adoption or intermarriage. Until recently, in the absence of such interaction, issues of encroachment were resolved in battle and a subsequent peace ceremony.[3]

These competing claims are qualitatively different from those that have resulted from the formal process of land claims resolution initiated by Canada. In the absence of federal and provincial policy acknowledging Aboriginal land tenure, no process has been established in which First Nations are required to validate ownership of the territory that they claim within the context of their own legal systems.

The consequences of this position, combined with the privileged nego-tiating position of the neighbouring Nisga'a, have been serious for the Gitksan, especially for the Gitanyow, placing them in probably the worst negotiating position of any Aboriginal nation in British Columbia. The Nisga'a claim to Gitksan and Gitanyow territory has eventually grown from a small, specific area at the Gitanyow-Nisga'a boundary on the mid-dle Nass River to encompass the Nass watershed.

The issue of the Nisga'a-Gitksan competing claims first arose in the Euro-Canadian legal and political arena in the Nisga'a Petition of 1913, when they claimed a large portion of Gitanyow territory, including Meziadin Lake. The Gitanyow, in response, formally withdrew their sup-port for this petition. In the *Calder* v. *Attorney General of British Columbia* case in 1968, the Nisga'a intended to introduce their 1913 petition into

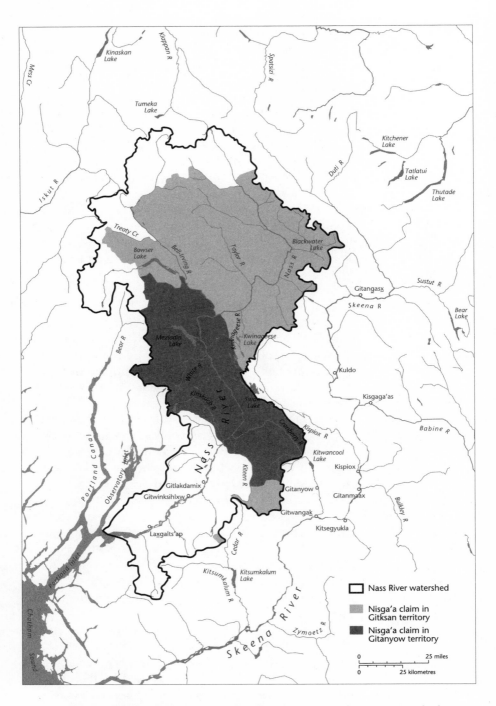

Map 2   Nisga'a claims in Gitksan and Gitanyow territories in the Nass watershed

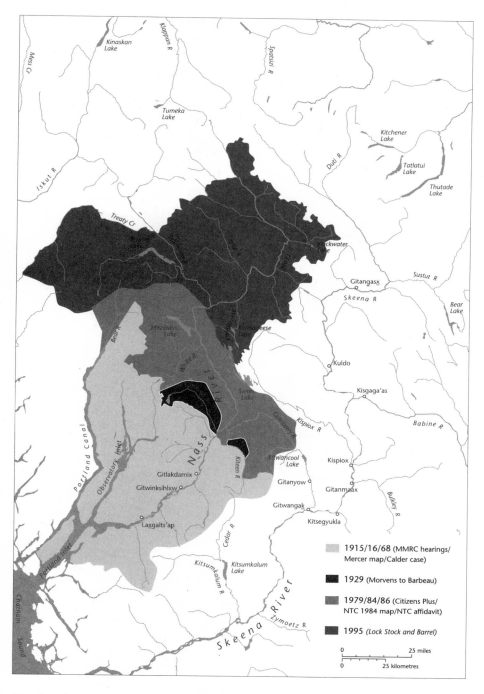

Map 3 Nisga'a claim in the Nass watershed: Changes between 1915 and 1995

court. When the Gitanyow objected again, the Nisga'a decided to eliminate any competing claims with a map showing a reduced territorial boundary. Although the Nisga'a, during recent meetings with the Gitksan, have sometimes characterized the territory defined on this map as being less than their traditional territory, it is evident from the historical record that it was meant to represent, from a Nisga'a perspective, that portion of the Nisga'a claim that can be substantiated within indigenous law. After the *Calder* v. *Attorney General of British Columbia* case was completed in 1973, the Nisga'a reasserted their claim to the larger area, including Meziadin Lake (see Appendix 2).[4]

In 1977 the Nisga'a began a process that led to yet another extension of their claim, this time to include the headwaters of the Bell-Irving and Nass Rivers. At a meeting that year between the Tahltan and the Nisga'a to discuss their territorial boundaries, the Nisga'a realized that the Tahltan were only claiming Nass River territory north of Treaty Creek. A formal declaration of their boundary was made by signing a map indicating their boundary. Unfortunately, at this meeting the issue of whose territory it was on the south side of the boundary was never properly clarified or validated by the Tahltan (see Appendices 3 and 6).

The Tahltan leadership had conducted extensive research into their boundaries and knew that they had a border at Treaty Creek in the Bowser Lake area with peoples whom they called the Nathka, Naasga, and sometimes "Nass Men" and whom they assumed to be Nisga'a. The Gitksan had also researched their territories and knew that the treaty that took place at Treaty Creek was between specific houses from the Gitksan village of Galdo'o and a Tsetsaut group that later joined the Tahltan.

The Gitanyow claim to their territory in the Nass watershed has been consistent since the arrival of Euro-Canadians. It has been validated repeatedly in the context of the indigenous legal system and has been supported by a 120-year cartographic legacy. The documentary record will show that Gitanyow chiefs have restated their claim unchanged for decades.

The Gitksan presented the results of their territorial research to the federal government in 1977 (see Appendix 4). In 1983 it became obvious that there was little or no political will on the part of the federal or provincial government to negotiate seriously with the Nisga'a and that the negotiations would be protracted. It was then that the Gitksan and their neighbours, the Wet'suwet'en, decided to take the issue of ownership and jurisdiction to court in the case of *Delgamuukw* v. *The Queen.*

By this time, although extensive territorial research had been conducted, the work needed to be reviewed to be admissible in court, and meetings had to be held with neighbours, especially with the Nisga'a, who had serious competing claims with the Gitksan in the Nass watershed. A series of formal meetings, intended to resolve the issues in accordance with indigenous law, were initiated by the Gitksan between 1983 and 1986, but the Nisga'a failed to present evidence consistent with this law in support of their claims (see Appendix 5). Between 1987 and 1990, the Gitksan presented their legal position on the ownership of their territories in *Delgamuukw* v. *The Queen*.

As the Nisga'a neared an agreement in principle in their negotiations with the federal government, they were required to meet with neighbouring nations to ensure the resolution of any conflicting claims. It was at this time that they began claiming the entire Nass watershed.

Data and Methodology

In this book, we present the documentation required by Gitksan law to prove the Gitanyow and Gitksan ownership of territories being claimed by the Nisga'a. At the same time, we have made every effort to examine all sources that might also present a case for Nisga'a ownership of these territories. There may be documentary sources that we have not discovered or contemporary research not accessible to us. However, from the extensive literature that we were able to research for this book, a case could not be made within indigenous law for Nisga'a ownership of the territories in question. A brief overview of the chapters that follow indicates the organization of this book according to the data and methodology required by Gitksan law.

At the foundation of both Gitksan and Nisga'a society lies the inalienable and exclusive title of each house[5] to its territories and resources. This title is entrenched in a complex legal system that validates the acquisition and inheritance of house territories and regulates rights of access and resource use.

Membership in a house is inherited through the matrilineage, with all members of the house inheriting rights of access and resource use in the house territories. Membership in a house is formalized in a yukw, or feast, by the taking of a name. With a name, one acquires rights to use specific areas in the house territories; these areas are allocated by the chief and announced by him in the feast. The chief manages or governs all aspects of the territory and is responsible for ensuring both the well-being of the house and the health of the territory.[6]

Gitksan law requires that those who speak to the ownership of Gitksan territories be the chiefs responsible for those territories or be authorized by those chiefs to speak on their behalf. The chiefs who first asserted the Gitanyow and Gitksan rights of ownership and jurisdiction to Euro-Canadians, the Gitanyow chiefs who went to jail for destroying the equipment of surveyors intending to lay out reserves, the chiefs who initiated *Delgamuukw* v. *The Queen*, and the chiefs who initiated and approved this publication – all were and are matrilineal descendants of the generations of chiefs before them who, over many generations, acquired, managed, and defended the territories of their houses. Their words as presented in this publication are also the words of their ancestors before them.

The acquisition of Gitksan and Nisga'a territories is described in their adaaw<u>k</u>, or oral histories. The adaaw<u>k</u> describe the ancient migrations of the house, its acquisition and defence of its territory,[7] and major events in the life of the house, such as natural disasters, epidemics, war, the arrival of new peoples, the establishment of trade alliances, and major shifts in power. The adaaw<u>k</u> also contain limx'oy, ancient songs that refer to events in which the people endured great hardship or loss.[8] The ayuuks, or crests, depicted on poles[9] and on ceremonial regalia also arise out of events in the history of the house as described in the adaaw<u>k</u>.

Every generation of Gitksan chiefs is responsible for ensuring the full transmission to the next generation of the adaaw<u>k</u> and associated prerogatives of their houses through a series of feasts at which these prerogatives are made public and validated by other chiefs. Before the final feast, the chief of the house raises a pole on which are carved the ayuuks of the house. Once erected, the pole represents and validates the history of the house and its territorial rights.

In the feast that follows erection of the pole, formal narration of a house's adaaw<u>k</u> is followed by acknowledgment of the guest houses that confirm the veracity of the history and the house's title to its territory and the validity of the pole as its visual record. The very existence of Gitksan adaaw<u>k</u>, songs, and poles proves that the Gitksan have declared their territories and their rights in the feast over countless generations and that they have been acknowledged by the other houses in their communities and in neighbouring nations.

Many of these adaaw<u>k</u> have been transcribed and can be found in a number of documentary sources. Others were recorded by the Gitksan Wet'suwet'en Tribal Council in a series of research projects and in the preparation of evidence for *Delgamuukw* v. *The Queen*. Since proof of land tenure among the Gitksan requires knowledge of the adaaw<u>k</u>, as well as the associated crests, songs, and personal names, that refer to these historical events, this information is set out in Chapter 2.

For the Gitksan and other Northwest Coast nations, the process of claiming territory is described as "walking the land" or "surveying" it and includes naming mountains, rivers, lakes, and other areas. These names are highly descriptive and reflect a detailed knowledge of the landscape. Once the land was surveyed, the house hosted a feast and announced its claim to the territory and its names. The guests of the host, the chiefs of the other houses, acknowledged the claim to the territory, thereby validating the house's ownership of the territory and completing the process of establishing land tenure.

Knowledge of the names of geographical features within the territories and of their historical origins is therefore an element in the proof of ownership within the indigenous legal system. The Gitksan and Nisga'a have described their territory many times, naming its places and identifying its resources to anthropologists, government agents, judges, and royal commissions on Aboriginal matters. As well, they have developed their own documentary record around a variety of petitions, maps, and claims for presentation to government.

In addition, both the Gitksan and the Nisga'a have conducted major projects to research and analyze this documentary record in preparation for court cases and land claims efforts. The Gitksan have also extensively recorded additional information concerning their territories – hundreds of place names and a detailed record of the Gitksan's economic and spiritual relationship to their territories. This aspect of proof of territorial ownership within Gitksan law is dealt with in Chapters 3 to 5.

Once acquired, rights to territory are inalienable unless the house is unable to produce sufficient wealth to perform its ceremonial responsibilities, or is required to relinquish part of its territory as compensation, or xsiisxw. If a house dies out, another house considered "close" by virtue of sharing a common ancient heritage and common clan and village membership takes full responsibility for the names, history, and territory of the house. If this house eventually becomes too large, it will divide into two again and reestablish the other house for which it took responsibility. If a house is depopulated to the extent that its members can no longer afford to "bury" their dead, then a related house will do so and in return take over the control and use of part of the house's territory. When the house is repopulated and has repaid the other house in a feast, the territory is returned.

Xsiisxw is the Gitksan term that describes the system of compensation in which one house relinquishes wealth, names, crests, or territory to repay a crime committed against another house. Compensation for the accidental death of an individual might involve a gift of material wealth; for the murder of an important chief, it might involve the transfer of territory for the lifetime of the immediate family of the deceased; and for a series of unprovoked attacks on a neighbouring nation, it might involve the permanent transfer of territory to the innocent party.

As with all other legal transactions within Gitksan society, these transfers of territory are formally presented and acknowledged in the feast. Thereafter they form part of the adaawk of the houses involved. Transactions that have directly impacted on the territories of the Gitksan are described in Chapters 2 through 5.

In the Gitksan legal system, additional weight is given to the assertion of title to a territory when the house can document the presence on the territory of individuals from the house, either a current member or an immediate ancestor. The journals of a number of Euro-Canadian explorers who travelled through the territory are witness to the presence of Gitksan and Nisga'a on their territories. Some of their journals also contain key geographic and historical information directly related to this study. The accounts of these explorers are set out in Chapter 6.

Tribal boundaries do exist in the Nass watershed, and they are based on real events described in the adaaw<u>k</u>. The Gitksan and Nisga'a themselves provide a strong voice for identifying the location of these boundaries. However, there is a competing claim limited to a small area at the border, near the Kiteen and Kinskuch Rivers, that existed for centuries before contact. There is a wealth of data pertaining to the issue of tribal boundaries of the Nisga'a and the Gitksan. It should provide the basis for an unequivocal evaluation of the questions at issue.

2
The Adaawḵ Record and Tribal Boundaries in the Nass Watershed

Introduction

In their adaawḵ, Gitksan houses tell the history of their ancestors beginning in time immemorial and continuing through the ages to the present. For generations these histories have been memorized and passed on by succeeding chiefs, and in each generation they have been retold by these chiefs and witnessed by others in the public forum of the feast.

Several historical periods emerge from the collective history of the Northwest Coast nations. In the earliest period, the adaawḵ describe the migration of a number of different peoples into unoccupied lands. In their explorations over great distances, they discovered a treeless and unstable landscape where they experienced flooding, earthquakes, and volcanoes. As those who survived moved through coastal and interior regions, they eventually reached stable areas where they established their early villages. Some remained in these villages, while others continued to explore and later settled elsewhere. Everywhere they settled, they "walked the land" and established their territories. These adaawḵ probably date to the geological upheaval of the early postglacial period between 12000 BP on the coast and 9000 BP in the interior.[1]

According to the adaawḵ, the northern reaches of the Nass were first settled by Raven and Wolf Clan peoples. The People of the Raven migrated southward through deglaciated northern areas and arrived at the headwaters of the Nass, Skeena, and Stikine Rivers. Some settled in this region, while others established themselves in ice-free areas along these river valleys and on the coast. In the same period, a group of coastal Wolf Clan people moved up the Skeena River and settled in a number of regions as far north as the Stikine and Yukon Rivers, where they were later joined by other Wolf Clan peoples from the north.

As these peoples formed early communities, they established their territories in what was still a changing landscape. Little is known about the geography of the interior during the first 5,000 years after deglaciation, but on the coast the shifts in sea level were considerable during this time, and throughout the region the climate and vegetation were undergoing significant change.

The adaaw<u>k</u> presented in this chapter are those of the Gitanyow (Git-winhlgu'l, Kitwancool), <u>G</u>aldo'o, Kispiox, and Kisgaga'as, whose territories are on the Nass River, specifically those adaaw<u>k</u> that relate the historical events surrounding the acquisition and defence of their territories. The adaaw<u>k</u> begin in the early postglacial period and continue to the late 1800s.

The Original Northern Gitksan (Period One)

Gitangas<u>x</u>, Gitwinhlt'uutsxwhl'aks, and Ts'imanluuskee<u>x</u>s

All the houses of the Kisgaga'as and <u>G</u>aldo'o, as well as certain houses of the Gitanyow, trace their ancestry to early Raven and Wolf Clan peoples and ascribe the origins of their present territories on the Nass and Skeena Rivers to the period when their ancestors first established their villages and territories there. One of the earliest of these settlements in the northern Gitksan region was Gitangas<u>x</u>, on the Skeena River just south of the extreme headwaters of the Nass, Skeena, and Stikine Rivers.

Charles Martin, Wiila<u>x</u>ha of the House of Wii<u>k</u>'aax, referred to the antiquity of this village when he described the origins of his house:[2] "This House comes from La<u>x</u>gitangas<u>x</u> (On People of Wild Rice), an old village on the river Skeena up the river. At this place we still see some caches underground, holes in the ground. The flat is still open there. They were there at Gitangas<u>x</u> thousands of years ago, even before they came to Temlaxamit. This family never went to Temlaxam."[3]

The Gitksan who discussed Gitangas<u>x</u> with Lt. George Emmons[4] between 1907 and 1909 also referred to the antiquity of the site: "Kit an gash 'People of the Place That Tastes Bad,' said to have ante-dated most of the other villages, once on the divide between the headwaters of the Nass and the Skeena just this side of the Groundhog country."[5]

The name Gitangas<u>x</u>, like Temlaxam, refers to both a specific village site and a general area in which there were a number of village sites. Temlaxam is said to have stretched from Kispiox to Gitsegyukla, while Gitangas<u>x</u> often refers to a general region that includes Gitwinhlt'uutsxwhl'aks and Ts'imanluuskee<u>x</u>s.

Many Gitksan houses originated at Gitangas<u>x</u>, Gitwinhlt'uutsxwhl'aks, and Ts'imanluuskee<u>x</u>s; some of these houses established themselves further south along the Skeena River in ancient settlements such as Temlaxam and Xsigwinlikstaa't[6] and later helped to found the more recent Gitksan villages. Of those that remained in the north, some founded the villages of Kisgaga'as and <u>G</u>aldo'o while maintaining their ownership of

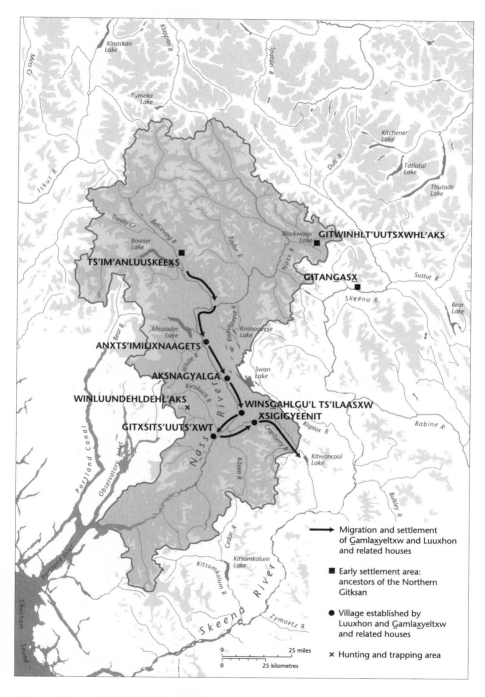

Map 4   The original Northern Gitksan (period one)

their original territories. In recent times, in response to continued attacks by the neighbouring Tsetsaut, Gitangasx and Gitwinhlt'uutsxwhl'aks were abandoned as village sites in favour of more defensible areas.

As the following table indicates, all the Lax Gibuu (Wolf Clan) houses of the Kisgaga'as and Galdo'o trace their origins to the early Wolf Clan at Gitangasx.

Gitangasx

House	Clan	Village
Niik'yap	Lax Gibuu	Kisgaga'as
Wiik'aax	Lax Gibuu	Kisgaga'as
Baskyalaxha	Lax Gibuu	Kisgaga'as
Gwininitxw	Lax Gibuu	Kisgaga'as
K'yoluget	Lax Gibuu	Galdo'o
Kwa'amhon	Lax Gibuu	Galdo'o
Luus	Lax Gibuu	Galdo'o
'Niist	Lax Gibuu	Galdo'o

All the Lax Ganeda (Raven/Frog Clan) houses at Kisgaga'as also trace their origins to Gitangasx, specifically to the early Raven Clan at Gitwinhlt'-uutsxwhl'aks.[7]

Gitwinhlt'uutsxwhl'aks

House	Clan	Village
Meluulak	Lax Ganeda	Kisgaga'as
Ksemgitgigyeenix	Lax Ganeda	Kisgaga'as
'Wiiminoosikx	Lax Ganeda	Kisgaga'as
Alaayst	Lax Ganeda	Kisgaga'as
Wist'is	Lax Ganeda	Kisgaga'as

Ts'imanluuskeexs

The village of Ts'imanluuskeexs was located near Bowser Lake and was closely associated with the villages of Gitangasx and Gitwinhlt'uutsxwhl-'aks. The people there also had close ties with their Raven Clan relatives among the Tsetsaut at Meziadin Lake. Ts'imanluuskeexs is described in the adaawk of Gamlaxyeltxw (Raven Clan, Gitanyow): "Gamlaxyeltxw (head chief of the present Gitwinhlgu'l tribe) had a village, before the Deluge, at Ts'imanluuskeexs, in the Groundhog country. This was a great village, very populous. It was their original home. The men of this family were great hunters and on this territory they hunted many animals. It was rich in game and furs."[8] Gamlaxyeltxw's power, and that of his Raven Clan brothers, Luuxhon, Gamts'iwa', Sindihl, Gyabask, Hlewa'nst, and Hlamii,[9] had been established there through their acquisition of a number of crests in the immediate vicinity and the raising of a xwtsaan (pole) called Ha'niilaahlgaak. Sgawil, Gamlaxyeltxw's Raven Clan relative, also lived at Ts'imanluuskeexs. When Gamlaxyeltxw gave a feast, the guests at the feast were people from Gitwinhlt'uutsxwhl'aks and the neighbouring villages of the Stikine and the Tsetsaut.

Gamlaxyeltxw and Luuxhon later abandoned their village and territories in this northern region and eventually helped to establish Gitanyow. Those who remained at Ts'imanluuskeexs retained their territories and ultimately established their main village at Galdo'o.[10]

Ts'imanluuskeexs

House	Clan	Village
Xskiigmlaxha	Lax Ganeda	Galdo'o
Wa'a (Ts'iwa'a)	Lax Ganeda	Galdo'o
Ksemguneekxw	Lax Ganeda	Galdo'o
Sgawil	Lax Ganeda	Galdo'o
Gamlaxyeltxw[11]	Lax Ganeda	Gitanyow
Sindihl	Lax Ganeda	Gitanyow
Luuxhon	Lax Ganeda	Gitanyow

The Gitksan and the Tsetsaut

Several adaawk refer to the fact that these Raven Clan ancestors of the northern Gitksan were Tsetsaut. The word Tsetsaut refers to people of the interior and is used by the Tsimshian, Nisga'a, and Gitksan when referring to their inland neighbours. The Tlingit have a similar term, Gunana, for the Athapaskan peoples bordering their territory. Tsetsaut therefore describes a number of Athapaskan peoples who have occupied the territory in and around the headwaters of the Nass, Skeena, and Stikine Rivers, at Meziadin Lake, and on the Unuk River, Observatory Inlet, Portland Canal, and Behm Canal.

As a specific term, however, Tsetsaut refers primarily to one of these peoples, the Tsetsaut "proper," also called the Portland Canal Tsetsaut or Western Tsetsaut.[12] These people occupied a core area on Portland Canal and Observatory Inlet and, at various times over the centuries, extended as far west as Behm Canal, as far north as the Unuk River, and as far east as Meziadin Lake. During their history, they were attacked by the Nisga'a, the Tlingit, and the Eastern Tsetsaut, and eventually, during the postcontact period, they became amalgamated with the Nisga'a and the Tlingit, among whom their descendants now reside. The Nisga'a claims to Portland Canal are founded on this amalgamation.

The term Tsetsaut refers as well to the Eastern Tsetsaut, also called the Laxwiiyip and the Stikine.[13] They occupied areas at the headwaters of the Nass, Skeena, and Stikine Rivers and at Meziadin Lake. The Eastern

Tsetsaut were a more heterogeneous people in the earliest times and may have absorbed several other Athapaskan groups over time. Many of the early Eastern Tsetsaut adopted the Gitksan language and culture and became Gitksan. Those who remained Tsetsaut were the northern neighbours of the Gitksan and traded extensively with them. There were also periods of war between the Gitksan and the Eastern Tsetsaut, as well as periods in which extensive intermarriage fostered peaceful relations. The specific Eastern Tsetsaut peoples relevant to this study will be referred to in more detail below.

Anxts'imilixnaagets, Winsgahlgu'l, Gitxsits'uuts'xwt, and Xsigigyeenit

The adaawk of Gamlaxyeltxw and Luuxhon relates how Gamlaxyeltxw and his people split off from the interrelated Gitksan and Tsetsaut villages at the headwaters of the Nass and Skeena Rivers. Gamlaxyeltxw and a number of his clan brothers, Luuxhon, Gamts'iwa', Sindihl, Gyabask, Hlewa'nst, and Hlamii, all members of the Raven Clan group at Ts'imanluuskeexs, left their northern homeland when one of this group killed their clan relative, Sgawil. Although they were related to 'Wiiminoosikx at Gitwinhlt'uutsxwhl'aks, and the Tsetsaut Raven Clan chiefs at Meziadin, Gamlaxyeltxw could not seek refuge in either of these villages, because they were also clan relatives of Sgawil.

The adaawk of Gamlaxyeltxw and Luuxhon describe this group's migration from their homeland at Ts'imanluuskeexs down the Nass River and the establishment of their villages in unoccupied areas along the Nass. As they prepared to leave, Gamlaxyeltxw was filled with sadness at his impending separation from his relatives and his land. He and his family climbed a mountain, and looking out over the land he sang: "I am thinking of Ts'imanluuskeexs, the village we have flown from." Hlamii also sang a limx'oy as he resigned himself to the loss of his territory: "My heart is sore, as I look upon Sga'nism Habasxw."[14] The gravity of the loss, or relinquishment, of territory is shown in the profound sadness expressed in these limx'oy. When the songs are sung in the feast, they remind those present that this land, although no longer belonging to their house, remains a part of their ancestry.

Gamlaxyeltxw and Luuxhon travelled south along the Nass River looking for a new and unoccupied area that would sustain them. Over many generations, they established new villages at Anxts'imilixnaagets and Aksnagyalga and laid claim to the surrounding lands. Finally, they settled, after a number of generations, at Winsgahlgu'l and Gitxsits'uuts'xwt and established formal ties with the people of Gitwilaxgyap, an ancient village near what was later Gitlaxdamixs (Gitlakdamix), on the Nass River. The people there were a different people and spoke another language.

Both Gamlaxyeltxw and Luuxhon gave major feasts at which they identified themselves to these people and formalized ties of friendship. The
adaawk of Gamlaxyeltxw and Luuxhon details these events:

> After living here [at Aksnagyalga] for some time, they left and came close
> to a Nisga'a village, at a place named Winsgahlgu'l Ts'ilaasxw (Place of
> Narrow Canyon). They built their houses at a spot named Sgathlao (in
> Tsimsyan). This is the name of the house type. It became the crest of the
> house, a special type with posts leaning inward and supporting big beams.
> Here they settled. They erected four houses, those of 1. Gamlaxyeltxw,
> 2. Singewin, 3. Ts'iigwa, and 4. Luuxhon.
>
> Luuxhon did not want to stay there. He preferred to roam about. So
> he went across the river to the opposite shore and down the river ... He
> travelled until he came to a pretty big river down the Nass and he went
> up its course until he stopped at a large waterfall. There were plenty of
> beaver here, in the spring of the year. He was very impressed with the
> river, as the game abounded ...
>
> While he was preparing bear meat and the meat of the beaver he had
> killed someone appeared in front of him. He called this place Winluun-
> dehldehl'aks, Where Meets Water (Where Two Rivers Meet). Those he
> suddenly met there were his own phratric [clan] brothers ... They wept
> and one of them told them, "You will now become my real brothers. I
> have taken this river to be mine alone, while my brother Gamlaxyeltxw
> has already erected a village farther up the river at Winsgahlgu'l" ... At
> a distance on this river towards the mouth, Luuxhon erected a house at
> a place called Gitxsits'uuts'xw, People Water Birds or Place of Many
> Birds.[15]

This encounter is recorded in Gamlaxyeltxw's adaawk because it represents a historic event in the lives of this people: their first meeting with
a foreign group since their departure from their homeland. The practice
of feasting to establish formal relations was clearly well developed by this
time, and the establishment of peaceful relations was accompanied by a
full display of naxnox, or spirit powers, and ayuuks.

> When he began this house, one of his brothers came to him and said,
> "We have discovered a village down below us on the main river (the Nass)
> and the people that live there are fighters and warriors." The Gitksan
> Luuxhon was now speaking Tsetsaut. He and the rest of the Ganhada
> at that time were speaking the Tsetsaut tongue. This man said, "These
> people at the village do not speak the same language as ourselves, but
> theirs is a foreign tongue."
>
> The younger man and his party prepared themselves to go down to

this new village, Gamlaxyeltxw, Hlewa'nst and Tsigwe ... They went down to this village, with the exception of Luuxhon, who stayed in this newly acquired fishing village. Gamlaxyeltxw was going to this new village to invite them to his yukw and announce the establishment of his new village of Winsgahlgu'l. They went to the people who afterwards were known as Gitlaxdamixs, the Gitwilaxgyap. It was those people whom Gamlaxyeltxw invited, and they went to his yukw at Winsgahlgu'l. In front of those that had come up from this Nass village they placed gifts of bear skins ...

Before the guests had arrived they had painted the front of the houses with a design known as Kawax or Kawangaak, Raven-House-front Paint-ing. It was a single raven and two smaller ravens under each wing. This he exhibited to his guests and he dramatized his name of Gamlaxyeltxw, meaning a person backwards to and backwards, representing his journeys from one place to another.

Luuxhon at that time was working on his own house at Gitxsits'-uuts'xw. The rest of the Ganedas at Winsgahlgu'l went down to assist him. Luuxhon made a crest that he exhibited, known as [Gan'ala (Smoke-hole Ladder)] and Lademxsimgyet, Ladder of People, a ladder like an entrance through a being: two huge frogs which were surrounded by many human-like beings. Then he made a huge wooden frog, inlaid with abalone pearl and placed it on the rear platform of the house. Around the edge of this frog were caribou hoofs. He called this Ganaaw'm Laxptaw', Frog On Partition. After that he carved a being wearing a lanemgayt (like that on the pole at the present Gitwinhlgu'l)[16] with four layers.

He was now determined to give a yukw, inviting the people of 'Wiilax-gyap (Gitlaxdamixs), to exhibit his own exclusive crests. He took his guests to his village, but for two days he asked them to fast, as he was also to exhibit a naxnox called Tigyet. As his guests arrived before the yukw proper, he had a halayt at which he distributed raw foods, and meats. When his own yukw was finished, and he had distributed garments of goats and other animals, his guests departed for their own village.[17]

After years of rebuilding their population and their wealth, Gamlaxyeltxw and Luuxhon had now established their new territories and their bound-aries with the Gitwilaxgyap. This relationship with a previously unknown people was formalized at a yukw in which elaborate crests, their histories, and their naxnox established their power and their right to ownership. The presence of the Gitwilaxgyap at these feasts represents their acknowl-edgment of Gamlaxyeltxw and Luuxhon's ownership of the lands that they had claimed.

In telling the adaawk associated with the xwtsaan Ha'niilaahlgaak,

G̱amgax̱minmuuxw (Walter Derrick) also described the establishment of G̱amlax̱yeltxw, Luuxhon, Sindihl, G̱amts'iwa', Gyabask, Hlewa'nst, and Hlamii in these Nass River villages and on these territories. He also related the adaawk̲ account of the establishment of Xsigigyeenit and the eventual establishment of the power of these houses at Gitanyow.

> They reached another river which they named Xsigigyeenit, meaning "river above." It was a good salmon fishing river in a good country; they built a permanent village here and put their mark on the river, thus claiming ownership of it ... Once more they moved, leaving their power and mark which made this country theirs. Still travelling they arrived here at Gitanyow ... by following what is now the Cranberry River (Xsiyag̱asgiit – "river that descends gradually"). When they arrived, the clan of the Wolves was already here. The Frog clan decided to build a house close to that of Gwashlaa'm; it was built in the same style as the first house they had built at Ts'imanluuskeex̱s ("place of wading"), and was given that name as a house name ...
>
> The chiefs established themselves at Gitanyow and raised their poles. The poles gave them their power or coat of arms and gave them the right of ownership of all the lands, mountains, lakes and streams they had passed through or over and camped or built villages in. The power of these poles goes unto the lands they had discovered and taken as their own. The power from the house of this chief and his council goes as far as Gitxsits'uuts'xwt, the place of the seagull hunter [Singewin], and includes Xsigigyeenit, the "upper fishing station." The power of the pole still goes on and belongs to Sindihl. Belonging to him also, as a gift, is Winsgahlgu'l ("narrow place").[18]

George Derrick also referred to their establishment at Gitanyow: "After many years of wandering, they arrived at the present site of Gitwinhlgu'l. I am not sure myself who were the first to come there, whether it was 'Wiix̱a or G̱amlax̱yeltxw. At that time they had not left their own village on the Nass, but they had wandered around, until they ended at Gitwinhlgu'l. Some of them stayed at Gitwinhlgu'l and others went back and forth to other Nass villages."[19]

G̱amlax̱yeltxw's Raven Clan relatives remained in the north at Ts'imanluuskeex̱s and Gitwinhlt'uutsxwhl'aks and were allied through marriage with the Wolf Clan peoples at Gitangasx̱ (with whom G̱amlax̱yeltxw's people also continued to intermarry). The Raven Clan at Meziadin remained Tsetsaut, however, allying themselves with other Athapaskan groups farther north on the Stikine and Dease Rivers. They nevertheless retained their close ties with their Gitksan relatives, as Walter Derrick related:

Every year the neighbouring villages used to come to Gitxsits'uuts'xwt and they would laugh and dance. The visitors were Tsetsaut people, and when they got to the hill nearby, they would dance and yell to see if they were welcome. Then Singewin a head chief in the village would go up a ladder on to the roof near the smokehole. He wore a headdress filled with eagle down which represented peace and friendship. He would send out a lot of eagle down on his visitors. Then they exchanged presents, the Tsetsaut people giving furs in exchange for food, which was very scarce with them. This custom was kept up for many years.[20]

Tahltan and Tsetsaut Migrations into Gitksan Territories (Period Two)

Several adaaw<u>k</u> describe a period of migration from the headwaters of the Stikine into the territory of the Gitksan, Nisga'a, and Tsimshian. Whether these peoples were Tahltan or Tsetsaut is not entirely clear, especially because, in the north, strong ties between members of the same clan made interaction over a wide area reasonably common. These migrations took place considerably later than those in early postglacial times, in which the lands settled were uninhabited and unclaimed.[21] By the time of these migrations, large populations were well established throughout the Northwest Coast, and few peoples had sufficient territory to sustain greater numbers. As a result, only a few of those migrating into the region were able to establish themselves among each of these nations. The adaaw<u>k</u> indicate that large areas of unclaimed land were rare, and a sudden influx of people threatened to deplete resources.

Some of the peoples migrating at this time travelled down the Stikine River, while others went overland to the headwaters of the Nass and Skeena Rivers. K'ee<u>x</u>kw,[22] Matthew Gurney of Gitlakdamix, of the Wolf Clan, described the migration of his ancestors through Gitksan territory:

The La<u>x</u> Gibuu group that originally came from the headwaters of the Stikine River, instead of travelling down the river to the coast as did the other Wolf groups, went into the hills and overland and reached the headwaters of the Skeena River around the vicinity of what is now Kisga-ga'as. They stayed here for a time and having no exclusive territory for their own large band, they followed the Skeena downstream. Among them was the large group of Kyeexw. Together with them were the Ganeda spouses of the La<u>x</u> Gibuu men, and some of these, when at Kisgaga'as, went farther inland to what is called "Wilt'uutsxwhl'aks": Where Black Water.

When this La<u>x</u> Gibuu band came to a spot just above the present Kispiox village, they established a village at what they called T'a'ootsip (Fort). As they could find no open territory of their own they had to

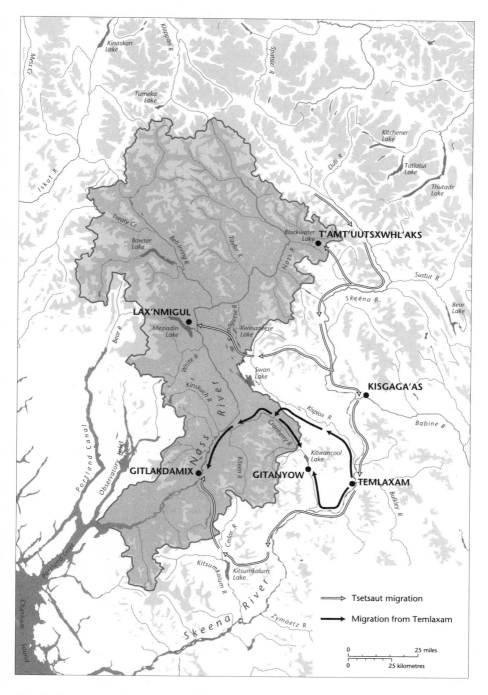

Map 5   Tsetsaut migrations into Northern Gitksan territories and migration from Temlaxam (period two)

suffer continual rebukes and taunts from the other tribes. So they went down the river and established themselves at a point just below where Gitwingax̲ is now. Again the real owners of the hunting and fishing areas they were using began to taunt them as being people without origin. Tok̲ and his people built themselves four large rafts and on these rafts they put all their belongings and themselves and Tok̲ said, "We will cast ourselves adrift and wherever this river takes us, we will not guide the rafts, but wherever the first raft lands, there we will all stay." They sang their dirge song and then pushed the rafts to mid-stream and began to float down the river.

They drifted until they landed in a large bend, and here they became firmly stuck to the beach. "Our supernatural aide has guided us to this. We will now look this country over and here we will be located." They unloaded their effects and went into the hills, and from a rapid survey which Tok̲ made, he said, "We have passed no village nor canoes. There seems to be no people in this country. We will examine it. It seems to have been given to us." Next day, Tok̲ together with his leading men went up into a small valley which they called "Ansgaxs," to climb up, now Lorne Creek ... They knew now that this was the land they had been searching for, one that had all the necessities in food and fish and furs ... They now established their village which they called Lax̲'anmihl, "On-Where-Dry-Plateau."

This group explored the surrounding area and discovered the Gitsemkalum territory, which was already inhabited, and the Nass River territory, which was inhabited by "those that had lived with them on the Tahltan and had also taken to flight when they had fought with the Raven group at Tahltan ... They were very well established and had much territory of their own."[23]

In the Raven Clan adaawk̲ that tell of these events, James Adams, 'Ax̲tiwiluugoodi of Gitlakdamix, gave the following account:

At the headwaters of the Stikine river, at Tahltan, the Ganeda (Raven-Frog) and the Lax̲ Gibuu had fought. The Lax Gibuu had fled from the Ganeda, and some of the Ganeda had followed them in an endeavour to catch them. A group of these Ganeda was led by Ksemxsan, who also had as his aides his nephews, Ax̲tiwiluugoodii and Txanlax̲hatk. These men were great leaders and their followers were in large numbers. Finally those that went overland to the headwaters of the Skeena came upon the Lax̲ Gibuu on whose tracks they were following. But these had already established themselves with the Kisgagas ... and they had already made good alliances with the Lax̲ Gibuu of Kisgagas. So when this Ganeda group came, it also stayed at Kisgagas.

Not very long after, a feeling arose among the people that the new-comers were intruders, as they had no hunting, fishing or berry tracts of their own exclusive property. They only went to the other Ganeda terri-tory by sufferance, which permission was now being grudgingly granted. This greatly embarrassed those people. Some of the Ganeda group had already married among the Gitksan people and become part of their spouse's families. Ksemxsan was not satisfied with these conditions. Call-ing his brother 'Axtiwil, they both built a huge raft and agreed wherever the raft would land them there they would establish their permanent village. This Ganeda group had as their spouses most of the Lax Gibuu family of Kyeexw, with whom they were in flight and were now separated. They had left Wilt'uutsxwhl'aks, (Blackwater River) and were now at Kisga-gas. And now they were going to set out. Some of this Ganeda group stayed behind and became leaders among the Gitksan. These were Galsid-ipxaat, a younger brother of Ksemxsan, Axtiwiluugoodii and Gudeex ...

Three of these brothers and their followers were travelling down the Skeena River until they could find a place which would be their exclu-sive property. They built a large raft and floated it down the Skeena. They passed many villages on their way down and finally the raft landed at a point just above the Gits'ilaasxw Canyon. This was known as Tsemnae'usk (Usk). It seemed to be the mouth of the valley. Here they moored the raft. Some of the young hunters went up the head of a small creek which ran into the Skeena. After travelling many days they came to a large plateau. There they found many lakes, with many with beaver dams. The surrounding country abounded with berries. This was the country they had been looking for. The hunters returned and told Ksemxsan of their discovery and they all set out to journey to these new lands and lakes. When Ksemxsan and his group settled here, they found that Kyeexw, the Lax Gibuu (Wolf), and Tok had already settled on the outside of the lake.[24]

Another version of the adaawk of this Raven Clan group relates that Lax'nmelgul, near Meziadin, was an additional region through which these migrations took place:

Two clans of the Ganeda Ravens on the upper Nass river originated at the headwaters of the Stikine (Staegyin) River. One of them came to Lax'nmelgul [Lax'nmigul] in the vicinity of Lake Meziadin. The other, that of Ksemxsan, went to Blackwater Lake, and later went on down the Skeena River, and we find them at Kisgagas. He stayed there until they fell into difficulties with the Lax Gibuu (Wolf) group. They got on a large raft and drifted down the Skeena. They came first to Kispiox and kept on travelling down the river. Finally, they landed above the Gits'ilaasxw Canyon, and there they made their village.[25]

These migrating peoples were thus dispersed among the northern Gitksan at Kisgaga'as and Gitwinhlt'uutsxwhl'aks, among the Eastern Tsetsaut at Meziadin Lake, and among the Nisga'a in the Sii'aks River region.

Those in this migration who remained among the northern Gitksan were given access to the territories of their clan relatives and became chiefs under their jurisdiction, as detailed in the following table.

House	Clan	Village
Ksemxsan (Ksemgitgigyeenix)	Lax Ganeda	Kisgaga'as
Axtiwiluugoodii (Ksemgitgigyeenix)	Lax Ganeda	Kisgaga'as
Galsidipxaat (Ksemgitgigyeenix)	Lax Ganeda	Kisgaga'as
Kyeexw ('Wiik'aax)	Lax Gibuu	Kisgaga'as (later Gitanmaax)

However, most of those who reached the Skeena and Nass Rivers finally settled on the middle Nass above Gitwinksihlxw. The resources there were sufficiently plentiful to sustain both the Raven and Wolf Clan peoples. In fact, there were so many new Lax Gibuu that they greatly outnumbered the other clans and had to be divided into two distinct groups between which intermarriage and reciprocal feasting were then possible.

As Matthew Gurney and Emma Wright explained,

> [One] band had come down the Stikine from Tahltan under the leadership of Niskinwatk and Niisyok ... The other group of Lax Gibuu led by Tok made their village on the opposite side of the river and there were now two villages of Lax Gibuu. Though they were of the same origin, having come from Tahltan at the headwaters of the Stikine river, and having taken flight from the Raven Clan, they had taken different routes in their flights, one group going down the Stikine river, and the other, over the hills to the headwaters of the Skeena river. Thus, these two groups, while of the same origin, became on the Nass, two distinct groups ... They did not intermarry or contribute to each other's potlatches ... When the funeral feast was on, the other Lax Gibuu were guests along with the other clans (Lax Xskiik and Ganeda) and received gifts as guests.[26]

This migration is placed during the Temlaxam era in a comment on the origins of K'eexkw and Tok: "Origin of this House was from Lax'angasx, up to the headwaters of the Nass River. It was near a river which the waters of was black and here they got the name (Blackwater River). They came from here to Temlaxam ... and went to all directions some to the mouth of the Ksan, others went away across the hills and came to Lisems. This group of Lax Gibuu went among these."[27]

Gwinuu, Hayts'imsxw, and Malii Join Gitanyow

A number of adaawk indicate that a movement out of Temlaxam by some groups probably followed closely after that of these northern peoples. Among those who left Temlaxam were the Houses of Gwinuu and Hayts'imsxw, which joined Gwashlaa'm and Gamlaxyeltxw at Gitanyow. The adaawk of the House of Hayts'imsxw describes these events and concludes as follows:

> After they came down the mountain at Gaksbaxsgiit, they went towards the present Gitwinhlgu'l about six miles. There they met their own people that had separated away from the Temlaxam, also Haiwen. He told them that Gwinuu [a Lax Ganeda chief] had found a place where to catch salmon, that was Gitwinhlgu'l. Gwinuu was the first one who reached Gitwinhlgu'l. So they followed him there. By this time Gwinuu and his family had already climbed all the mountains in the vicinity. But still they were willing to have Hayts'imsxw come and live with them. They wanted somebody to associate with. It was then that they pointed out a mountain near Gitwinhlgu'l that would be Hayts'imsxw's mountain, called Ksit'akxwt, Dirty Water ... [The adaawk goes on to list the other territories that Hayts'imsxw was allowed to take along the Kitwancool River watershed and as far north as Kitwancool Lake.][28]

Malii, from the House of Spookw at Temlaxam, also migrated to Gitanyow. This house, however, had left Temlaxam prior to the others and had made villages at Gitsk'ansnat[29] and Gitangwalkw at the head of the Kispiox River. Their territory included areas from Gitangwalkw to Gwinhagiistxw. From Gitangwalkw, as their adaawk relates, they established themselves at Gitanyow.

> Then Malii called two young men and told them to climb the mountain, Gahahlahlmatx [Chest of the Goat – K'uhlxmatx?], to look over the land and see what was at the back of the mountain. When they reached the top of the mountain they looked down and saw a river, and smoke coming from houses away down below. When it was getting dark, they went down and came to the village of Gwashlaa'm ... They went into the House, and Gwashlaa'm gave them seats and food. They told them that they had been sent by Chief Malii to see what they could see in the way of other lands. Then Gwashlaa'm remembered the words of Spookw: "If you happen to see any of my people, call them to you." That is the reason he called these two young men.
>
> So Gwashlaa'm sent back word to Malii to come and stay with him. When the word came, they at once packed up and went to where Gwashlaa'm was living, a place called Gaksbaxsgiit ... He told the newcomers

that he had a large permanent village at Gitanyow and invited them to join him there. The whole village then went, and when they arrived at Gitanyow, Gwashlaa'm showed Malii where to build his house, beside his own, on the east side. They built the house there. They were very grateful to Gwashlaa'm for his kindness in asking them to come and live with them as brothers.

After the house was built, they decided to have a feast ... The feast was to show all the surrounding tribes that the House of Malii now belonged to Gitanyow. Chief Gwashlaa'm got up and told the assembled people that the House of Malii was now accepted by him and that all were now Gitanyow people.[30]

Gwinuu and Hayts'imsxw were now established in the valley of the Kitwancool River with Gwashlaa'm and 'Wiixa. Gamlaxyeltxw and Luuxhon had their villages and territory to the north in the Nass watershed, beside that of Malii. They all wintered in a common village in the vicinity of Kitwancool Lake. It was the wars that were to follow that would more closely unite the Gitwinhlgu'l.

Tsetsaut Attacks on the Gitanyow

After the establishment of Gwinuu and Hayts'imsxw and Malii at Gitanyow, hostilities developed between the Tsetsaut Raven Clan to the north and their Gitksan clan relative, Gamlaxyeltxw. The hostilities could have been the result of a trade dispute, but territorial encroachment is also referred to in the adaawk. The specific issue that sparked the hostilities, however, was the infidelity of Gyabask's wife with his brother Luuxhon. Gyabask was in Gamlaxyeltxw's house, and his wife was from Galdo'o. Gyabask went to Gitxsits'uuts'xwt and killed his brother Luuxhon in revenge; then he returned with his wife toward Winsgahlgu'l. The adaawk of Gamlaxyeltxw describes the events that followed:

When they got at the edge of the canyon ... [he] broke out into his first outcry of grief, bemoaning his having killed his brother. He sang a dirge ... This song means that he was holding the woman responsible for the death of his brother, that she was rapacious, that she had bewitched him ... The wife of Gyabask belonged to the Wolf phratry, Tiba[31] was one of her brothers and she was of Galdo'o origin.[32]

When Luuxhon's clan brothers among the Tsetsaut came to visit him on their annual trading trip, they found him dead:

The Tsetsaut brothers came upon the village of Luuxhon [Gitxsits'-uuts'xwt] who had been murdered. There was a hill near his smokehouse, which he called An'uksgimiluxw, Place-of dancing (outside), because they used to dance here before entering the house. It was a reunion dance. Luuxhon would come through the smokehole of his smoke house wearing his Lanemgayt (Hat of Layers) and welcome his Tsetsaut brothers. They shouted before coming near the smokehouse, so that they knew the guests were approaching. When this time they came, it was shortly after the murder. They shouted, but they saw nothing come through the smoke hole.

The Tsetsaut discovered that Luuxhon had been murdered and immediately set out to exact revenge, but they found Winsgahlgu'l deserted and burned to the ground:

> After many years, the Tsetsaut prepared to avenge their mother and the murder of Luuxhon, their brother. They gathered other Tsetsaut from all the surrounding tribes. The murderer Gyabask had gone out unmolested to the hunting grounds of the murdered brother. On one of Gyabask's trips to his hunting territory named Wun'nisk'angyamdit, Place-of-bushes-berries [saskatoons], he met there with the Tsetsaut. He was then preparing to go back to his own village, Gitwinhlgu'l. He invited them as his guests. They had on a headdress of bear cub skins upon which were attached many miniature copper shields and ts'iik shells; the eyes were of abalone pearl. When the food and salmon were placed in front of the Tsetsaut, they presented him with a large vessel full of water which he was to drink, knowing that if he did not, he would be killed. There was a warrior standing by with a war club. While they were trying to make Gyabask drink the water, he upset the vessel, covering himself with water. He then struck the Tsetsaut [leader] twice with his club warhkyanaw – arhkyanaw – Across the river opposite, his warriors were awaiting ... Gyabask then took this Tsetsaut whom he had killed and threw his body down the hill. This the Tsetsaut raiders beyond the river saw.

Gyabask's limxseegit (war song) called Limx'wu'nisk'angyamdit (The Song of Wun'nisk'angyamdit) arises from these events.[33]

> Further incensed by Gyabask's actions, the Tsetsaut once again prepared for revenge, this time against the people of Gitanyow (Gitwinhlgu'l). The Gitanyow always went out for the caribou in the moon of Gutkuhloxs [November]. The Gitwingax were also preparing to go to their hunting grounds. During that time, the Tsetsaut were getting ready to retaliate upon the village of Gitanyow. They were on the mountain of 'Wilax-habasxw. The village of Gitanyow at that time extended from the head of the lake to [almost] the end of this south side. The Lax Gibuu [Wolf] folk

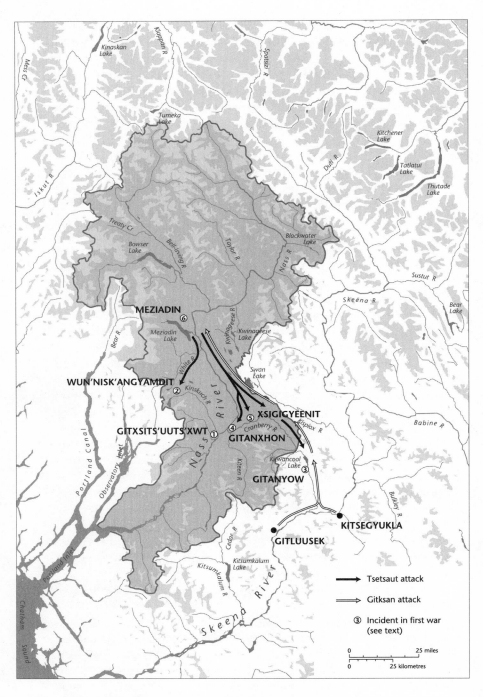

Map 6   First war between Gitanyow and the Tsetsaut

lived near the mountain of 'Wilaxhabasxw towards the shore, and the Ganeda were at the other end, Ksagants'iikxw, Water-of-shellfish (money).

While the Gitanyow were preparing to move on, they looked at the other side of the lake and saw two wolves. Three of their best hunters went after the wolves. When the young hunters got up towards dusk, the people saw the wolves come out. This time, four hunters went for them. The wolves again ran back into the woods. But they reappeared for the third time. The hunters went out for them, thinking that probably the wolves had killed caribou there. When it was just about dark, the people saw three wolves on an island in the lake. There were three of them now. The hunters did not bother to go out after them, expecting to hunt for them early in the morning, thinking that by that time the wolves would have killed many caribous. Meanwhile the Tsetsaut raiders came and surrounded the village, planning to capture it just before daylight. The people of Gitanyow went to sleep early, in order to go out for the wolves and whatever game they had slaughtered. The raiders attacked the village just before daybreak and massacred the entire village.

There were [now] only old people left in the village of Gitanyow. They began singing in lamentation[34] ... about the destruction of the village of Gitanyow and the absence of the young hunters. [This lament] is used now by the households of Gamlaxyeltxw, Luuxhon and Ts'iigwa. It was composed by the old folk who had been left behind in the village.

The Gitanyow were greatly reduced in numbers by this war, and many of those still alive moved to the Gitwingax (Gitwangak) area, probably to Gitsulk on the Kitwancool River, where they were not as vulnerable as they had been farther north. Over time they rebuilt their population and returned to their northern villages. Others assisted in this; Haxpegwootxw, chief of the Fireweed Clan in Gitsegyukla (Kitsegyukla), was married to a woman in Luuxhon's house. He moved out to Gwinsgox and used the territory there. Meanwhile Luuxhon's successor built a permanent house at Gitanxon, but he was attacked there and killed by the Tsetsaut. Gamlaxyeltxw established himself at Xsigigyeenit, where he also was killed. The Tsetsaut were "continually giving trouble, trespassing on Gitanyow hunting grounds."[35]

When Luuxhon was killed, Gwinuu, his clan brother, cremated and commemorated him. Gwinuu's compensation for this was the hunting ground of Luuxhon known as Gitanxon. Gwinuu then made plans to retaliate. He used his kinship ties with members of the Gitwingax Raven Clan dating back to their days at Temlaxam and Luuxhon's marriage ties with the Wolf Clan House of T'enimgyet to foster alliances that would allow him to retaliate in full force against the Tsetsaut. The adaawk describes his preparations:

In order to muster greater strength and assistance from the other villages, he took four women members of his house and married them in each village, at Gitsegyukla and at Gitwingax, four nieces to each, eight altogether. It was his way to bind them as allies. When Gwinuu planned to attack the Tsetsaut, he called upon these outside villages for volunteers, and many came to his aid. All those warriors gathered at Gitwinhlgu'l between Gwinuu and Wud'nsxw. They supplied all the warriors with moccasins made from moose hides. The Gitsegyukla had as their chief Ksu, of the house of Guxsan. He was brave. Then they started off to go and retaliate on the Tsetsaut for the murder of Luuxhon.

Ksu was accompanied by his two sons, who were both warriors. They went along until they came to a river named Xsimaaxwsxwt, Water-white [clear] at the headwaters of the Nass. They were roaming at random, for they did not know in what direction the Tsetsaut village was. The two sons of Ksu always led the others. They went ahead as scouts. Kwihltagooget, Person-going-forward or ahead, and Seski'ilt, were the terms applied to scouts like them. When they arrived at Meziadin Lake, the two scouts saw, at the end, the smoke rising in the direction of the sunset.

They returned and began to prepare themselves for an attack. Before getting to their party, they took charcoal and blackened their hands, and smeared their faces from the forehead down the cheeks, marking black streaks with their fingers. They tied a tuft of their hair on the top of the head with hemlock needles sticking up. When Ksu saw his two sons approaching the camp, he rose up from among the people and called out in Hagwilget, as at that time the Gitsegyukla tribe spoke Hagwilget and Gitksan both. Here is what he said, "My children have killed all the Grizzlies." (He said this on account of their strange appearance.) Then the scouts informed the people that they had found where the Tsetsaut were camping, at the head of the lake (Meziadin). So they prepared then to go and raid them.

They went round to the Tsetsaut village and got ready to capture it by surrounding it. They were now waiting for the night to come before attacking, while watching the movements of the Tsetsaut very closely. The raiders attacked just before dawn ... As the Tsetsaut were being attacked, they began their halayt songs of lamentation. This halayt leader in the songs was Ginigla'i, (dreaming, a Tsetsaut naxnox). Around the Tsetsaut village was a huge network to which were attached deer or caribou hooves, which made a clattering noise when being touched. The halayt had already been singing way before the raid foretelling this attack. But no one took note of him.

Before they were ready to attack the Tsetsaut village, Anax'aus touched the network [of deer hooves]. Although the moment had not yet arrived, he attacked. The raiders slaughtered all of the Tsetsaut warriors. The only man they could not kill was the halayt. As soon as (he was) wounded, he at once healed up on account of his powers. So they captured him on the ice. After torturing him they finally killed him right there.[36]

With this battle, the Gitanyow, assisted by their other Gitksan allies, successfully defended their Nass River territories. The Eastern Tsetsaut once again were restricted to their original territories at Meziadin Lake. The participation of the other Gitksan villages in the defeat of the Tsetsaut strengthened the ties of the Gitanyow with the other Gitksan to the south. The alliances forged through intermarriage continued after these wars and gave the more southern groups a legitimate presence on the territories of their more northern allies. This was especially true of the great warrior Ksu, who was given access to Luuxhon's land on the Nass River.

A note on the dating of this war: Gitluusek, which is mentioned as one of the towns with which the Gitanyow intermarried, and from which people were recruited for the war against the Tsetsaut, was abandoned when the people there (the Gitwingax) moved to Battle Hill around 400 years ago. This indicates that the wars ended, at the latest, several centuries before contact. The hostilities themselves took place over several generations and thus push the time back further. It is also important to note that these hostilities, which began between members of the Raven Clan among the Gitksan and Tsetsaut, are quite distinct and probably separated by many centuries from the later Kitwancool-Tsetsaut wars, which involved the Nisga'a and the Tsetsaut primarily and took place between Wolf Clan groups among the Tsetsaut and Gitksan in the post-contact era.

Tsetsaut/Tahltan Attacks on Gitangasx and Galdo'o (Period Three)

Relations on the Gitksan's northern frontier remained peaceful until 200 or 300 years ago,[37] when the Ts'imlaxyip[38] began hunting groundhogs on Gitangasx territories. The identity of these strangers is not entirely clear. When their village was eventually discovered, it was within Tahltan territory, and it was the Stikine (Tahltan)[39] that later assisted the Ts'imlaxyip in their wars with the Gitksan. On the other hand, the Ts'imlaxyip lived in a type of house never seen before by the Gitksan and did not eat fish, indicating that they may have been recent arrivals in the region, only later amalgamating with the Tahltan. This would account for their designation as Tsetsaut, using the term in its general sense as one of several Eastern Tsetsaut peoples.

The Gitangasx responded to the acts of trespass on the part of the Ts'imlaxyip by killing them whenever they were discovered within their territory. The Ts'imlaxyip retaliated by attacking isolated Gitksan hunting parties. Hostilities intensified until the murder of Gayee'is (House of K'y-oluget, Lax̱ Gibuu, G̱aldo'o) and his son sparked major reprisals by the Gitksan.

The adaawḵ of Suwiiguus, of K'yoluget's house, details the discovery of the murder of Gayee'is and the resulting hostilities. Simon Gunanoot, G̱amanuut (House of G̱eel, Giskaast, Kispiox), told this account:

> The G̱aldo'o Indians were out hunting groundhogs a long time ago. They travelled along to the point past the present 4th Cabin. It is the route they took. They crossed at K'alaa'nhlgiist, at the headwaters of the Skeena. The other side of the headwaters, there are mountains, and these are the mountains they reached. A G̱aldo'o man and his son were hunting groundhogs. And they were attacked by the Tsetsaut Indians. The father of this young man was a very good shot with a bow and arrow. There were no guns at that time. And he had a very good supply of arrows in his arrow bag. When the Tsetsaut killed his son, he took his canoe, and placed it as a kind of screen and stood at the back of it, and shot the Tsetsaut from behind. Those in the camp were anxiously waiting for the return of father and son. And they had set a date for their return. That date had long past and they had not returned. His House-brother was beginning to be very anxious, wondering what had happened to his brother and nephew.
>
> He could not stand the anxiety any longer. So he went out with some other young men. They started out as a search party. He guided the search party. His brother's name that they had shot was Gayee'is. The search party started out and looked for tracks. They found the tracks and followed them. And in their search, they came upon the dead bodies of some Tsetsaut Indians. Then they found the body of their dead brother. The uncle was so grief-stricken at the sight of the dead body of his nephew that he picked it up and held it in his arms. And there was a great number of the arrows, those of the Tsetsaut, near the bodies of the brother and nephew.
>
> Then they went over to see on the other side, and they found as many Tsetsaut dead, and an equally large number of arrows from the dead brother. And they also found some of the dead Tsetsaut in the lake; their own companions had taken them to the water. The brother took his dead brother's body and brought it back to the camp. And the nephew too, he brought his body back. And they cremated them, burnt them all as they always did in the old time. That was the custom in the past, always to cremate the dead. After this was done, they went back to their village.[40]

Soon after these events, the Ts'imlax̱yip raided Gitangasx̱, killed a number of people, and captured a Gitksan woman and two of her children,

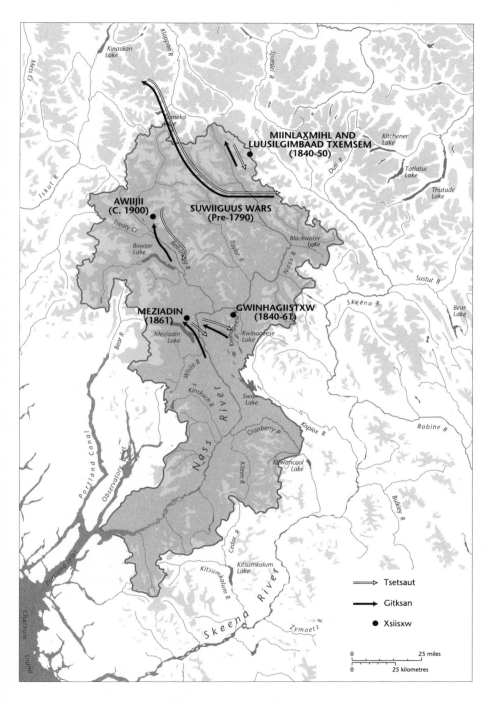

Map 7   Recent conflicts at the Gitksan northern border (period three)

taking them to their underground village. When she escaped, she travelled to the headwaters of the Nass and then downriver to Gitangasx. The adaawk as told by Isaac Tens describes these events. Here the Ts'imlaxyip are identified as Tsetsaut.

> They had no food with them and were starving. They had now reached the headwaters of the Nass. When they got there, they could not cross over to the other shore. One of the daughters got sick and died. They buried her at the foot of a big tree and left her body there. They walked down the river, until they came to where there were many logs adrift. They crossed from one side of the river to the other. They kept on travelling, until they arrived at Gitangasx. They were very thin then, from having no food. She told the people of Gitangasx what she had been through, and where the Tsetsaut lived.[41]

Suwiiguus, a nephew of K'yoluget and a brave warrior, prepared to retaliate on the Ts'imlaxyip. He conscripted warriors from the villages of Kisgaga'as and Kispiox. The war party was said to number over 100 persons[42] and included K'yoluget, Gwininitxw, Niik'yap, Kwa'amhon, Luus, Xgwooyemtxw, Ksemgaakhl, Gutgwinuxs, Laats, Ts'iiwa, and Gwilaagantxw. The warriors began by preparing themselves for the war by ritual purifications, called sesatx, or making oneself clean. Simon Gunanoot described these events:

> Then they started in to eat the bark of the devil's club, and washed themselves, seeking better success. They were doing this in their hearts, that they may be able to conquer and defeat more Tsetsaut. They were a whole year preparing themselves for the war against the Tsetsaut. Then, a large number of all the relatives of the village of Galdo'o started out. They travelled on, and found the place where the battle had taken place. They travelled up and reached the top of the mountain. There they looked down into the valley below them. Looking down into the valley, they saw smoke. By the smoke they knew that there was a large gathering of people down there. So many fires were burning. They looked down and they could not make up their minds as to who must go down into there. As they were still looking down, they saw a great number of people coming to this camp where they saw the smoke ...
> Suwiiguus, who then had prepared himself for this war for a year by eating bark, was so sure of success that, without fear, he entered the camp, and they began to slaughter the Tsetsaut. They attacked six camps before the rest were aroused. Those who tried to escape out of the camp were killed in their attempt to escape by those who surrounded them. Everybody in the camp was killed. There was not a soul left, except the

children. These they used as guides to show them where the other villages were, that is, where they were from. It was a great big piece of country. There were no houses there. But the people lived underground. The
smoke came from out of the ground. They could not get at them.

Suwiiguus said, "Who will go and kill some grizzly bears first?" So they
killed grizzly bears and skinned them. Then they gathered a lot of pitch.
After this, they covered the grizzly bear skins with pitch. They got sand,
and rubbed sand in it. They took a grizzly bear skin and put a man inside
of it, and sewed it all up. As he was walking about the Tsetsaut would
shoot at it, but the arrows had no effect. They could not penetrate the
skin, the gum and gravel. The arrows could not have any effect on the
grizzly bear skins. The attackers placed themselves all round the underground camp and sent the grizzly bear walking round and inside the
circle.

When the people in the holes saw the grizzly bear, they immediately
all came out of their holes to attack this grizzly bear. Everytime they
would shoot at this grizzly bear, the arrows would break. Then they called
out to the rest in the holes, to all come out. They were determined to
kill this grizzly bear. As they had sharp spears, they began to chase the
grizzly with their spears. The grizzly bear enticed them on, and they kept
following him, right near where the Galdo'o kept in hiding. They could
not make out what was wrong with the grizzly bear as the spearing and
the arrows had no effect on him. As they got right near where the people were in hiding, these raiders sprang at them, and killed them as they
were unaware of an attack. There was no means for them for escaping.
They were surrounded and killed.

After the Galdo'o had killed all the men, they went down into the
holes where the people had come out of, and found the children down
in the huts. The young women they took as prisoners, and made the
stronger children pack the small ones. The Galdo'o Indians were quite
surprised and interested to find out what kind of dwelling the Tsetsaut
had lived in. It looked like the burrows of ground-squirrels.[43]

The successful defence of the Gitangasx territories was commemorated
by ayuuks (crests) depicted on totem poles, housefronts, and regalia. The
ayuuks refer to spirit powers acquired on the warriors' journey to the village of the Ts'imlaxyip[44] and to the grizzly bear armour used in the victory against the Ts'imlaxyip. These ayuuks were shared between the
warriors and are now owned by the Houses of Gwininitxw, Kwa'amhon,
K'yoluget, Gutgwinuxs, Guuhadakxw, Niik'yap, Xgwooyemtxw, and
Ksemgaakhl.

This victory, however, did not end the ongoing incursions by various
Tsetsaut groups into the territory of the northern Gitksan. The Tsetsaut

retaliated by attacking Gitangasx, eventually forcing the people there to move to Galdo'o and Kisgaga'as, where they could better defend themselves against attack.

> After this was over, they went back to their own village, Galdo'o. The Tsetsaut children could not eat the dry fish. It sickened them. Those that were able to, got out and killed rabbits which they could eat. The rabbit meat was the right food for them. And as they grew up and became stronger, they ran away from the Galdo'o and went back to their own country of the Tsetsaut, towards the Stikine country. After these children had run back to their own country, the Galdo'o village was attacked by the Stikine.
>
> The Galdo'o village at one time was a very large one. The Stikine retaliated. They almost cleaned the Galdo'o out. They left just a few. Then they figured that they would have peace, as they had both had destructive raids on each other's villages.[45]

Although Simon Gunanoot refers to the people of Galdo'o, other versions indicate that these events began when they were still living at Gitangasx and ended after they had moved to Galdo'o. John Brown, Kwiiyeehl (Giskaast, Kispiox), tells of the move of many of the Gitangasx to more southerly villages as a result of the threat of Tsetsaut attacks:

> Then they planned that they should move from Gitangasx, as they were too close to the Tsetsaut people. 'Wiiminoosikx then said, "I will go to Kisgaga'as to live." And Niik'yap said the same thing. And so did 'Wiik'aax. These went together. K'yoluget moved down towards the mouth of the river at a place called 'Angayts'es, "Taking-a-short-cut." And here he made his new home. This was the foundation of what is now Galdo'o. All the people of Gitangasx came down to this village following K'yoluget. The first to come down after K'yoluget was Kwa'amhon and then Luus, then 'Niist, then Wa'a (a Lax Se'el), Ksemguneekxw (also a Lax Se'el). They made their home here then. After they had settled here they lived peacefully and undertook no more raids. Suwiiguus had died. The house of K'yoluget is practically the same as that of Suwiiguus. K'yoluget is now its name. They founded another place which they used as a fishing station below the present village, about ten miles below the village. This they called Tsilaasxwmganksit, "The Canyon-that-looks-like-nothing-but-trees," or "The canyon-of-trees." They lived right on, down to the time when civilization came to them.[46]

It was probably also at this time that Amagyet and Ksemgaakhl moved to Kispiox and joined the House of Xhliimlaxha there.

The move of these Gitangas<u>x</u> houses to Kisgaga'as and Kispiox gave certain houses in these villages access to Gitangas<u>x</u> territories while, at the same time, providing the Gitangas<u>x</u> with assistance in defending their northern territories. Some houses remained at Gitangas<u>x</u>, however, and only abandoned it in recent times. Among them were Xgwooyemtxw and Niik'yap, who left about four generations ago, probably in the early 1800s.

Tsetsaut Attacks on the Gitksan during the Fur Trade (Period Four)

During the fur trade period, beginning in the early 1800s, the northern relatives of the Gitksan, the Eastern Tsetsaut, the Tahltan, and others who joined both the Tsetsaut and the Tahltan[47] from the east, pushed down into Gitksan territory. War was clearly not the only solution for the Gitksan when faced with these border pressures. Efforts were made to maintain peaceful relations by strengthening ties based on common clan identity and intermarriage. It was when these alliances, formed in an effort to accommodate all parties, did not achieve the desired effect that major hostilities took place, and the adaaw<u>k</u> record these events.

The La<u>x</u>wiiyip

In the early 1800s, the Eastern Tsetsaut were dominated by the powerful Wolf Clan chief Saniik and came to be known most commonly as the La<u>x</u>wiiyip. The name La<u>x</u>wiiyip is said to derive from their territory, alternatively described as being at Meziadin Lake and at the headwaters of the Stikine River, both accounts being accurate since the territory of the Eastern Tsetsaut extended at that time from Meziadin Lake across the headwaters of the Nass and Skeena Rivers to the headwaters of the Stikine. Levi (Dangeli), a Western Tsetsaut, described the situation at that time. There were "three closely related tribes whose languages are different though mutually intelligible: the Tahltan ... of Stikeen and Iskoot Rivers; the Laq'uyip [La<u>x</u>wiiyip], or Naqkyina, of the headwaters of the Stikeen; and the Ts'ets'aut [the Tahltan, Eastern Tsetsaut (or La<u>x</u>wiiyip), and Western Tsetsaut respectively]."[48]

It is difficult to determine whether Saniik and his Wolf Clan group were recent arrivals in the region that took over the Eastern Tsetsaut or were simply a group that had risen to prominence among them. It was around this time that some of the Sekani moved west from the prairies and started to appear in the territories of the Eastern Tsetsaut, and Saniik and his people may have been among them. Whatever their origins, it is clear that, by the early 1800s, Saniik and his Wolf Clan people had replaced the Raven Clan as the leading group among the Eastern Tsetsaut (La<u>x</u>wiiyip) and that Saniik had become their leading chief. During this period, peaceful relations between the La<u>x</u>wiiyip and the Gitksan were once again interspersed with hostilities, and in a number of cases acts of aggression resulted in the transfer of land.

The Laxwiiyip and Laats at Luusilgimbaad Txemsem

Laats, a Wolf Clan chief at Kisgaga'as, met a member of Saniik's group at Laats' territory at T'amsaabayaa on the western headwaters of the Nass River. The following events took place around 1840 and culminated in the transfer of names and territory from the Laxwiiyip to the House of Laats.

> Long ago the Stikine [Laxwiiyip] lived in the area north of Ninth cabin. Laats (a close family member of 'Niist) owned the ground at Dam Sabaiya [T'am Saabayaa]. When Laats and the Stikine, whose name was Taas Aguun, first met, they couldn't talk to each other. But after a while they were able to communicate and became friends. They each knew where their boundaries were. Once Laats sent his nephew to an area towards Taas Aguun's territory but he didn't return.
>
> Laats went searching for him and found him dead. He knew Taas Aguun had done it, and he went in search of him. When he caught up to Taas Aguun, he was about to kill him, but Taas Aguun explained what had happened. Taas Aguun said he didn't know who this person was on his hunting ground, so he killed him – which was the law. Only then did he learn that the person he had killed was Laats' nephew.
>
> Taas Aguun said, "Here is what I'll do. I will give you my name[49] to use as your own, and I will give you part of my territory – this too will be yours." Taas Aguun described an area in a semi-circle around the mountains north of Ninth Cabin [Luusilgimbaad Txemsem] which was to be Laats' territory.[50]

In addition to the name Taas Aguun, the name Saniik was given to Laats. Mary Johnson, Antgulilibiksxw (Giskaast, Kispiox), commented on the passage of this name since the xsiisxw: "The Stikine gave a compensation to Walter Laats' family – they gave land and a name. The name was Saniik.[51] Mary Blackwater gave this name to Wallace Johnson a long time ago, and after he got more chief's names, he gave it to one of Jessie Green's sons – the older one – Murphy Green. Walter Laats held this name too – that's why Mary Blackwater gave it. That's another Stikine name in compensation – it's xsiisxw. They gave this name to Laats and others [names] after the killing."[52]

The Laxwiiyip and Xhliimlaxha at Miinlaxmihl

Adjacent to the territory of Laats is that of the Wolf Clan House of Xhliim-laxha, where a similar series of events ended in a xsiisxw. Although it is not clear which Laxwiiyip (Eastern Tsetsaut) group was involved in the events that led to the transfer of the Miinlaxmihl territory to the House of Xhliimlaxha, it is likely that it was either Saniik's people or a closely related group, because the events probably took place about the same time[53] and in the immediate area of T'amsaabayaa. The House of Amagyet, originally from Gitangasx and closely related to K'yoluget, had moved to Kispiox, probably after the wars with the Ts'imlaxyip. At Kispiox Amagyet formed an alliance with the House of Xhliimlaxha, giving Xhliimlaxha access to Amagyet's northern territories and strengthening the Gitksan position there.

The House of Xhliimlaxha and the Laxwiiyip were continuing the long-standing Eastern Tsetsaut/Gitksan tradition of intermarriage when Xhliimlaxha's sister married a Stikine (Laxwiiyip) whose territory bordered that of Xhliimlaxha (Amagyet). There was a dispute over territory, however, and the woman and her baby were killed and their bodies stuffed in a groundhog hole. The Kispiox people went up to avenge the murders and found the Stikine (Laxwiiyip) people half-starved. Instead of killing them in revenge, they fed them oolichan soup. Later, when their strength had returned, the Laxwiiyip attended a peace ceremony at Xsa'angyahlasxw near the Kispiox village.

> The northern territory was given at a gawaganii at Xsa'angyahlasxw, the Stikine [Laxwiiyip] people on one side and the Kispiox on the other. A messenger coming from Stikine came with mixk'aax [eagle down] in the left hand and a rifle in the right hand. Among the Kispiox, Xhliimlaxha sat with the other three chiefs on either side. They knew the Stikine messenger was coming and they were ready with their mixk'aax and rifles. If Xhliimlaxha brushed the feathers from his head, then the Stikine would shoot Xhliimlaxha. This was the Xhliimlaxha prior to Paul Xhliimlaxha.
>
> The chief from the Stikine named Malee arose and turned over that land, the hunting ground, and also gave over "Malee" (the name) to Xhliimlaxha. Our forefathers called it xsiisxw when they did the gawaganii. The Stikine killed Xhliimlaxha's sister and stuck her in a groundhog hole. She still had her baby on her back. This was what Xhliimlaxha found out. The xsiisxw is when they turned the ansilinisxw [hunting ground] over to Xhliimlaxha. It is a settlement for killing and shedding the blood of Xhliimlaxha's sister. Xsa'angyahlasxw is at 17 mile. David Brown from Telegraph Creek knows everything about this. It was a fight over land because of intermarriage.[54]

The Laxwiiyip and the Western Tsetsaut

That the Laxwiiyip were aggressive in their efforts to gain access to new territories is indicated by their advance into the territory of the Western

Tsetsaut. The Western Tsetsaut were strategically located during the fur trade between the trading ships on the coast and the rich fur country of the interior. Both the Nisga'a and the Tlingit wanted the furs that passed through their hands, but it was the Nisga'a House of Saga'wan that controlled the trade in furs from the Western Tsetsaut. "Before [the Hudson's Bay Co. had established their trading post at Crabapple-Tree-Point] the trading ships had come to the Nass River, and these traded with many different tribes of people. Saga'wan [Chief Mountain] took advantage of this and went to the Lax Gibuu (Wolf) village of Smailx [at Portland Canal] ... These people [the Western Tsetsaut] always had a large quantity of furs, and these brought in great returns from the traders. These furs were obtained from the Lax Gibuu for almost nothing. The trading had been going on for a while."[55]

Saniik and the Laxwiiyip hoped to eliminate the intermediary trading position of the Western Tsetsaut, and they were aggressive in their efforts to trade directly with the coastal peoples. These efforts had led to hostilities between them and the Western Tsetsaut, which, as Levi (Dangeli) described, continued with a failed effort to make peace at Portland Inlet.

> At another time while Levi was a boy, the Tsetsaut had a war with the Laxwiiyip. At that time Levi's sister had just married a man named Nagusts'ikatsa. They were hunting north of the upper reaches of the Nass River. When they returned to Portland Inlet, a party of Laxwiiyip came there accompanying a [Western] Tsetsaut hunter. The Tsetsaut had one gun among them and were about to shoot at the Laxwiiyip, when their countryman asked them to desist, as the Laxwiiyip had come to make peace and to pay for those who had been killed in previous wars. The Tsetsaut allowed them to approach and gave them [food] to eat. When they were about to go to bed, they showed the Laxwiiyip their gun. One of the Laxwiiyip kept it, and in the ensuing quarrel, he shot two of the Tsetsaut.[56]

The Laxwiiyip and the Gitanyow at Meziadin

The efforts of Saniik and the Laxwiiyip to establish a key role for themselves in the fur trade at Portland Canal came to a sudden end around 1852, when a Nisga'a chief, Hlidax, and his relative Ganuxeex, killed Saniik, and his son Aminta, at Smailx. The death of Saniik initiated a far-reaching series of events that ended in a xsiisxw in 1861 and the transfer by the Tsetsaut of their Meziadin Lake territory to the Gitanyow.

Hlidax and Ganuxeex, of the Wolf Clan of the Gitxatin, had access to Portland Canal through the territory of Hlidax's father. Seeing the wealth that flowed to the eagle clan chief Saga'wan from his exclusive Western Tsetsaut allies, Hlidax attempted to form his own trading alliance with a

Tsetsaut group. On one of his hunting trips, he and his relatives encountered Saniik and his son, Aminta, at Smailx and attempted to establish trading relations. However, mutual suspicion prevented successful trading, and Hlidax shot Saniik and his son.

> The Tsetsaut war of Laxwiiyip began with Ganuxeex, a Wolf of the Angida village, on the Nass River. Not so long ago he started out to go hunting in the winter and went up Portland Canal. It is in this district that he and his party met with three Laxwiiyip hunters of the Stikine Prairie. The names of those two Prairie people were Aminta and Saniik. There were besides a third man and Ganuxeex's wife ... The Tsetsaut asked the Nisga'a to what tribe they belonged. Ganuxeex answered that he was Lax Gibuu (Wolf). The Laxwiiyip declared that they too were Lax Gibuus. They were relatives, sewakx, Wolves also. The two Tsetsaut Wolves invited their Nass relatives in the canoe to come to their hut, and the Nisga'a followed them and they were well-received and fed and given to smoke ...
>
> Ganuxeex, during the night, told his wife ... not to sleep, or they slept in turns, for they were not sure whether they were safe with these wicked men – for the Tsetsaut (Laxwiiyip) were reputed to be treacherous. Every time the Tsetsaut made an attempt to kill them, during the night, Ganuxeex would spit. The Tsetsaut lay down and failed just then in their purpose ... [The next day] the Tsetsaut asked the Nisga'a to take them to a certain place, which they did. While they were going ashore, one of them attacked Hlidax, a Wolf chief of the Nass. When Hlidax found himself in danger, he told one of his men who had a gun to shoot the Tsetsaut. He did. Another Tsetsaut rushed upon Ganuxeex with his spear. Ganuxeex shot him with his gun before he had come close enough to spear him.
>
> [The Tsetsaut relatives] knew that Ganuxeex had destroyed Saniik and Aminta, and they were aware of where they belonged, the Nisga'a. That is why they meant to slaughter any Nisga'a Wolves, whenever they had a chance ... To avoid any risk of retaliation, the Gitxatin tribe of the Nass did not go up, that year, to the salmon streams in Observatory Inlet, that is to Kitsoohl, to Ksewan (Hastings) and to Kalaen (Stewart and Hyder) thereby giving their enemies no chance.[57]

'Wiilitsxw (Lax Gibuu, Gitanyow) told the missionary Reverend J.B. McCullagh an account of these events in which he referred directly to the fact that Hlidax and Saniik were engaged in trade: "The time goes back 50, 60, 70 years ago, perhaps 60 will reach it, when Hlidax of Gitxatin, the leading chief of the Nisga'as used to go up to the head of what is now called Portland Canal to trade with the Tennes (Denes) whose territory reached that limit. On one occasion Hlidax bartered a musket

and some ammunition with Saniik a Tenne chief." As McCullagh concluded, the killings would inevitably lead to revenge: "As for Hlidax he
kept the matter a profound secret from the Nisga'a people, a mean thing
to do because according to Indian law, the lives of two Nisga'a chiefs were
now forfeit."[58] Sometime later the Tsetsaut found an opportunity to
retaliate.

> The Gitwinhlgu'l and the Gitlaxdamixs[59] have always traded with the
> Lax̱'wiiyip (On the Prairie tribe) on certain places at the head of the Nass,
> at Meziadin Lake. It is where they always met. The Tsetsauts lived there
> in the summer. The Gitwinhlgu'l started for this place, also Gyalge, the
> chief of the Gitlaxdamixs, together with Galdudao (Pearl's father) and
> Kwunaxhat and his slave No'nes. They went to this place on Meziadin.
> Other Gitwinhlgu'l whose names I have forgotten were already there, in
> particular 'Wiilitsxw. They got to this camp and they traded. The Tset-
> saut asked them about Ganuxeex. Gyalge answered, he is my son-in-law.
> Then the Tsetsaut were very kind to them, and bought from them all
> they had to sell, all the ammunition. They paid a big price for all they
> got. It was then that the Tsetsaut must have planned to kill them.[60]

The Tsetsaut, who had no quarrel with the Gitwinhlgu'l, tried to warn
them to leave the trading place ahead of the Nisga'a because of their
intention to retaliate on the relatives of Hlidax. However, the Nisga'a and
the Gitwinhlgu'l camped together and were attacked the next morning
as they left camp.

> [The Lax̱wiiyip] concealed themselves, and shot their guns, and killed
> some Gitksan ... Some other people were hidden beyond, and they shot
> them too ... Four in all were running away from the Tsetsaut. All the
> other people were killed by the Tsetsaut ... 'Wiilitsxw [who had hidden]
> tried to look up to see who was firing the gun at them. And the men
> firing saw him and shot him. The bullet went right through his chin and
> pierced it. His chin was split in halves. The men who were in hiding then
> tried to shoot some of the Tsetsaut and they killed some of them too.
>   There were in all two Gitwinhlgu'l and two Nass men [chiefs] killed.
> The Nass men were Gyalge[61] and Txaldedaw. Tx̱awoḵ and Ligigalwil were
> of the Gitwinhlgu'l.[62]

The Tsetsaut later attempted to make peace with the Gitwinhlgu'l, but
they wanted them to travel with them to Awiijii, where they were then
established. The Gitwinhlgu'l were reluctant but agreed to send emissaries
if they could keep one Tsetsaut chief, and the Tsetsaut women in the
party, at their camp. On the trail, the Gitwinhlgu'l emissaries suspected

treachery and, rather than complete the journey, killed their Tsetsaut guides. On their return to the Gitwinhlgu'l camp, the Tsetsaut chief was also killed and the women taken prisoner and sold as slaves.

Robert Pearl concluded the adaawk concerning this entire sequence of events with an account of the final outcome:

> The Gitwinhlgu'l got even with the Lax'wiiyip for what they had done. But the Gitlaxdamixs did not. Nothing was done, nothing given to the Gitlaxdamixs.
>
> Gahl'o is another place. The people there were the Tsetsaut of the Nass. Their family on Portland Canal was nearly ruined by the Lax Seel of the Gidaganits (Tlingit) and by the Laxwiiyip Tsetsaut, who murdered many of them. They did not retaliate. So they, the Gitlaxdamixs, have the right to take whatever rights the Laxwiiyip Tsetsaut had at Meziadin and the other hunting grounds of the Tsetsaut, near the head of the Nass, for the killing of Gyalge and Txaldedao, who were both Lax Gibuu. In fact they took those territories as compensation. Now they are in the possession of the Gitlaxdamixs. As the trouble had arisen through Ganuxeex's killing Saniik and Aminta, the Gitwinhlgu'l for that same reason have the right to Meziadin, and they still are there.[63]

Robert Pearl[64] appears to be articulating the Nisga'a claim to Meziadin on two grounds. One is that the Laxwiiyip (Eastern Tsetsaut) killed some of the Western Tsetsaut (the Gahl'o of Portland Canal). Since some of these Western Tsetsaut eventually joined the Nisga'a, the Nisga'a claimed compensation on their behalf. However, there is no record of a xsiisxw in which Meziadin was given to the Portland Canal Tsetsaut by the Laxwiiyip. The law does not allow for the transfer of land as compensation without a properly witnessed xsiisxw. The other ground for the claim appears to be that the Nisga'a had not retaliated against the Tsetsaut. However, it was the killing of Saniik and Aminta by the Nisga'a that initiated the events in the first place and for which the Tsetsaut were themselves retaliating. The Gitwinhlgu'l, however, as Pearl points out, were the innocent party, having been drawn into events that were initiated by the Nisga'a. There is also no record of Meziadin having been given to the Nisga'a in a xsiisxw. As Pearl also states, "nothing was given to the Gitlaxdamixs."

On the other hand, there is extensive evidence that the Laxwiiyip handed Meziadin over to 'Wiilitsxw and Txawok of the Gitanyow in a xsiisxw that took place in 1861 at Meziadin Lake. In the adaawk told to Reverend McCullagh by 'Wiilitsxw, there is a lengthy account of this peace ceremony, of which this is an excerpt: "It may have been six or seven years after the massacre that, one summer, news reached the village of

Gitwinhlgu'l to the effect that the whole Tenne tribe was again in their old camp at Meziadin Falls. A runner was therefore at once despatched to Gitlaxdamixs to invite the tribe to join with the Gitwinhlgu'l in an expedition against the Tennes on La<u>x</u>wiiyip, and so both sides proceeded in force to the head waters of the Naas on the war-path." When the war party arrived, the La<u>x</u>wiiyip decided against war, and Aminta began a ceremony of peace that concluded with the handing over of the Meziadin territory to the Gitanyow.

> When the Tennes heard the herald sing, they all came together by Aminta's house ... in their ceremonial robes, paint and feathers, and began to dance and sing before their enemies. The Tennes then brought the war party over in their canoes, no longer invaders but guests. In a clearing among the pines a large fire was built, around which the assembled warriors were seated in three sides of a square. The Tenne chiefs and ladies, in their robes and ornaments, danced before their guests and sang again the gawaganii song.
>
> A salmon beautifully carved in wood and a hook were then brought to the chief Saniik who holding them forth began to sing the song of the Falls ... Then the whole tribe sang a leave-taking lament, after which Saniik laid the salmon and hook at the war captain's feet ... The same evening the Tennes left for the Stikine, and have never since set eyes on ... Meziadin.[65]

Reverend McCullagh was told the adaaw<u>k</u> of these events at Meziadin Lake, where 'Wiilitsxw then lived with his family. In his summary of the outcome of the xsiisxw, he wrote of having stood on the very site of the attack:

> [We] rested beneath a large spruce tree, where a party of Stickine Indians (those comprising our late mission at Telegraph Creek) massacred a party of Gitwingols and Gitlakdamiks. This country (the LAK-WI-YIP) once belonged to the Stickines, and the Falls – where I am camping tonight – used to be their summer camp, where they caught and dried all their salmon, and did some trading with the Gitlakdamiks and Gitwingols – those now comprising the Aiyansh mission; but after the massacre just mentioned, the Stickine Indians made reparation to the Gitwingols by handing over to them the whole of LAK-WI-YIP, and have come here no more. WI-LIZQU (Blue-grouse) a chief of the Gitwingols has a smoke-house here at the Falls.[66]

Later in his visit, they sat by the fire, with 'Wiilitsxw "narrating the history of Meziadin Lake and the country of Lak-wi-yip, and teaching me the Tenne song of expiation, the tune and vocables of which I managed to learn."[67] Not only was the memory of a properly witnessed xsiisxw kept alive in adaawk and song by those to whom the land was transferred, but the adaawk and song were also witnessed and committed to memory by Reverend McCullagh.

Richard Benson, Gla'eeyu of the House of Luus, Lax Gibuu, and Fred Johnson, Lelt, of the Ganeda of Gitwingax, were also witnesses to the adaawk. Richard Benson, whose grandfather was 'Wiilitsxw, remembered his father telling him about the Stikine (Laxwiiyip) at Meziadin:

> They keep on fighting. The Stikine had all their smokehouses at the falls at Meziaden. My father knows the song of the Stikines. He learned it from his father. When all the Stikine stood around the smokehouses with the Kitwancool. The Stikine said, "no use to kill us off. We give up the land." The Stikine sang a song. My father knows it. They took the gaff hooks and gave them. We going to leave. We give them to you 'Wiilitsxw and they handed them the gaffs and fish. My father said they never saw any Nisga'a there. It was only the Stikine. He was there. The Stikine marched in and they miiluuxwd [danced] coming in. They smoked a great big pipe. They got smoke (tobacco) from the mountain and smoked it.[68]

Fred Johnson was the son of 'Wiilitsxw, who told the adaawk to McCullagh at Meziadin. Johnson spent his early years with his father at Meziadin and was a young man there when McCullagh visited. Johnson was also told the history of the area by his father. In his testimony in *Delgamuukw* v. *The Queen*, he related his knowledge of the adaawk and the song:

Q Mr. Johnson, how did your father, 'Wiilitsxw, how did he get the territory up there? Do you know why? ...
A They left, they walked, they will find the Stikine people. They travel. They wanted the revenge. Good strong men. They got ready, they got organized, they had eagle down. They had sons. They ... wanted to meet the war party from the Stikine. The Stikine people finally came to the falls up Meziadin ... The Stikine person, the chief, came out. He talked from a ways. The Gitksan people called the Stikine people to come over. And chief 'Wiilitsxw ... called them over, come over, don't be afraid of anything. Then they came over, they had fairly big bullets that they used for guns in those days. They had bullets ready in their mouth just in case ... They came, the Stikine people. The Stikine people had a house and they seated the people properly. They took the guns and they placed them quite a ways from where they

were meeting, and the same with the Stikine people, they placed their guns quite a way from where they were gathering. The Stikine people started to sing. (WITNESS SINGS SONG) That's just one of the songs.

Q Was that a peace song?

A That is when they're beginning to recognize the peace.

Q Was this sung by the Stikine person?

A Yes, Stikine.

Q What happened after the song was sung?

A They started to smoke. The Stikine was cutting up the cigarettes. Big blocks of smoke. As they were smoking the Stikine person would be blowing the eagle down indicating peace.

Q When the Stikine sang the song was he doing anything? Did he have anything in his hands?

A That's when he took a wing.

Q What kind of wing?

A A goose wing. The birds of Meziadin. And there's a big chief that did this. And he waved it, there will be peace. This will be your land, this was the big chief talking. We will not return – we will return to our own village, there will be no more wars, xsiisxw. They compensated for the killing of Txawok and Ligigalwil ...

Q Who did the Stikine chief give the land over to? Who received this land from the Kitwancool?

A 'Wiilitsxw and his brother was along with him, his name was Axtsoon and their nephews.

Q What were the names of the Stikine chiefs?

A Atxwmseex and Gela[69] ...

Q Were the Stikine people, were they Tahltan people?

A Tsetsaut.

Q What did the Tsetsaut do that brought about this peace? was there a fight?

A When they killed Txawok and Ligigalwil, they want to fight, they wanted revenge ... That's when the peace was established and they would – will not fight again. There will be peace in our village, said the Stikine person. That's why we will not return to this, we will give it to you, 'Wiilitsxw and Txawok.[70]

Johnson then told the story of the attack at Meziadin that had preceded this peace ceremony and concluded with these comments: "And then Stikine person talked, we broke law when we killed these two people. It was terrible. This will be your song. (WITNESS SINGS SONG) People up know this. Then the Stikine person waved his hand, this will be your land. This will be your land. Waved his hand some more. This was the big chief doing this. And he blew eagle down all over floating around."[71]

Later, in his testimony, Johnson returned to the subject of the xsiisxw at Meziadin and to the attempts of the Nisga'a to claim Meziadin:

Q Now, I wanted to ask about the Meziadin territory again. Did your father tell the Nisga'a people how they got the – how the war with the Stikine and how 'Wiilitsxw got the territory?

A Yes, there was a xsiisxw with the Stikine. It was transferred from the Stikine because of the killing of Txawok and Ligigalwil. They waved the wing out, and this is the song for it. (WITNESS SINGS SONG)

Q Did 'Wiilitsxw tell the Nisga'a about this?

A Yes, they summoned my father. Council from the Nisga'a, Mister McCulough, he was the Indian agent.

Q How did they summon your father?

A They wrote on blue paper and there was blood on the paper. This is the law. They talked Gitksanemx. That's when the court started.

Q Did the Nisga'a want your father's land?

A Yes, they tried to claim it.

Q Is that why they summoned him over the Nass?

A Yes, he was arrested by the council. (In English) Indian agent was the judge and judged him.

Q What happened over there?

A They had court. My father spoke. This was the land that was given by the Stikine, and he sang the song. My father brought the wing that he got from the Stikine and he showed it, and the Indian agent took it. The Indian agent said this is what happens during the war, on the battle fields. This is what happens in the battle fields, this is the sign, this is the symbol of battle. That is why 'Wiilitsxw owns the territory ...

Q Did 'Wiilitsxw have anyone else speak for him?

A Yes, somebody else talked. This is what the chief of the Stikine person gave. One Nisga'a was very angry. He was very angry. That was the person that arranged the summons with Mr. McCullough. It was Aiyansh. The Indian agent realized that 'Wiilitsxw was travel, that is who will be spokesman of the land, and he is not the only one that speaks for the land up there.

Q Did the Indian agent confirm 'Wiilitsxw's right to the ownership of the territory?

A Yes, there's a paper on it. Game warden took – maybe in the office in Terrace ...

Q Mr. Johnson, did any of the Nisga'a people speak before Mr. McCullough?

A No. They spoke – some of them spoke but they didn't have anything to show. They didn't have any sign. They didn't have any symbol. They're still talking about it today.

Q Were there lots of Nisga'a people present at the time this happened?

A Yes, there's lots. That's the tradition of our people. There were lots and they just stand around.

Q Were there other Kitwancool chiefs present there at the time?

A Yes, that's what happened.

Q Did Mr. McCullough speak the Gitksan language?

A (In English) Yes, that's right. Yes, he spoke Gitksan.

Q Were you there when this happened?

A I was very small. I knew the time that the summons actually came to my father. They wanted 'Wiilitsxw to go quickly to the court. He was just on his way out trapping again. He left right away with his brother, after the court, they continued to live there. The Indian agent or Indian office in Hazelton would always give us – they would confirm that we could live there. They recognized that we lived there.

Q Mr. Johnson, did the Nisga'a bother your father again after this court case?

A No they had – they didn't. They couldn't.

Q Did the Nisga'a accept the decision that was made there?

A No, they were very angry. They bit them. 'Wiilitsxw.

Q Did 'Wiilitsxw use the land after that? After that decision?

A Yes. Yes, they always used it and his brother and his nephews.

Q Did his brother and his nephews and his children, did they use it after 'Wiilitsxw died?

A Yes. And the other 'Wiilitsxw that is in Kitwancool now, John Robinson, and others.

Q Does John Robinson use 'Wiilitsxw's territory today?

A Yes, and if he couldn't – if he was unable to use the land he would select somebody who would use the land. Sometimes he would ask me.[72]

In conclusion, the Gitanyow were the innocent party; once attacked, they successfully defended themselves in the ensuing hostilities, and in the end they received the territory at Meziadin in a xsiisxw. The Gitanyow have told the adaawk and sung the associated limx'oy many times, and in a number of formal situations in which the ownership of Meziadin was at issue, and they have lived and camped at Meziadin since the territory became theirs. It should also be remembered that the Gitanyow have owned the Nass River territory from Gitxsits'uutsxwt north to Xsimaaxwsxwt (White River) for millennia and that the Nisga'a only passed through it with the Gitanyow's permission and in their company. The xsiisxw at Meziadin transferred only the territory from Xsimaaxwsxwt north to Gisa'am'maldit (Surveyors Creek), thus adding this to the Gitanyow's preexisting Nass River territories. The Nisga'a, on the other hand, appear to claim that the entire area from Gitxsits'uuts'xwt to

Meziadin was given to them by the Tsetsaut. No record supporting this contention has come to light.

The Laxwiiyip and Delgamuukw and Malii at Gwinhagiistxw

Three territories traditionally came together at Gwinhagiistxw, those of Malii of Gitanyow, Delgamuukw of Kispiox, and the Tsetsaut of Meziadin Lake. Probably shortly after the hostilities at Meziadin, the previously peaceful relations between the Tsetsaut and Delgamuukw broke down. The adaawk refer to these Tsetsaut as the Stikine. The name of the person directly involved was Atsehltaa, who may have been one of the Raven Clan people who were among the original Tsetsaut owners of Meziadin, or one of the Wolf Clan people led at this time by Saniik.

At the time of the incidents related below, Atsehltaa and Delgamuukw both used parts of the Gwinhagiistxw area and were on friendly terms. As well, it appears that there was intermarriage between the Kispiox and the neighbouring Gitanyow, because one of the women involved in this incident was Gitanyow. Conflicts over beaver trapping, perhaps resulting from the escalating demand for beaver in the land-based fur trade, led to the death of Dakhlemges (from Delgamuukw's house) and to the eventual relinquishment by Atsehltaa of any rights to his teritory in the region.

My grandfather, Dakhlemges (House of Hage, same group as Delgamuukw) went out about now to Gwinhagiistxw. They used nets at night for beaver. So the Stikine came and claimed the ground. At night time he was ready ... The Stikine went to check his net and found a net there. He pulled it out and put in his own net. Then he went to Dakhlemges' camp (at the little lake, Wilgidiksit'ax) and shot him.

A young man, Ganaawmsitak, heard the shot ... The young man knew the mountain. He ran away and climbed the mountain (K'alaa'nhl Xsi'angaxda). The young man was up on the mountain – the wind blew really hard. He broke his gun, then he went down to Galdo'o. He looked back and saw the man running all over, because he couldn't see tracks in blowing snow. The young man hid by a tree. After a while the Stikine fired a shot to show he left. The young man went down Xsi'angaxda to Gawalmihl. When he got to Gawalmihl he told them what the Stikine did to Dakhlemges. This was Axmatxwmwil's nephew. They rest one day, then they went to Kisgaga'as. The Tsetsaut always came to Kisgaga'as in fall around August.

Axmatxwmwil's household prepared a place for Atsehltaa. They sent a message to Wii'a'lax to come to Kisgaga'as because the murderer was there. When he heard the message, he grabbed his spear and went. Then the young man told Axmatxwmwil Wii'a'lax was there. Then when everyone was ready Wii'a'lax pushed the door open with his spear and jumped in front of Atsehltaa. Wii'a'lax said, "So you are the one who killed my nephew." So then Atsehltaa fell back and said, "It's no use to kill me. I'll give you the mountain and the hunting ground. I'll give you the mountain. It's called Lipsganisit [Mt. Madely]. And I'll give you all the hunting ground." This included Txaslax'wiiyip because the Stikine were there too ... The young man who ran to Gawalmihl is Ganaaw'msitak (Giskaast), Axmatxwmwil's nephew. The mountain he climbed with the gun was K'alaa'n Xsi'angaxda [at NW Galdo'o Creek]. He broke the gun here and the Stikine saw it.[73]

One of the three people killed at Wilgidiksit'ax was a woman from Kitwancool. This accounts for the fact that part of the land relinquished by Atsehltaa, Mt. Madely and part of Txaslaxwiiyip, is owned by the Kitwancool. "The Kitwancool own ... less than half of the Gwinhagiistxw area, and own the top of Txaslaxwiiyip, with Malii on the west and Kispiox on the east."[74] Percy Sterritt also referred to the boundary between the territory of Delgamuukw and Malii after the xsiisxw with the Tsetsaut: "Our camp was near Wilgidiksit'ax. My grandfather said, 'You can start from the top (west) side of T'am Gwinhagiistxw and run your marten line up to the brow of the hill at Txaslaxwiiyip, but don't go over the other side. That's Kitwancool on the other side' ... My grandfather said they used to make arrangements with the Kitwancool people and go and meet them just over the brow of the hill. They would have a big dinner of Saakx (eulachons)."[75]

The Laxwiiyip and the Long Grass People in the Groundhog Country

After their defeat throughout their territories, some of the Eastern Tsetsaut (Laxwiiyip) had established a village at Awiijii. Others continued to intermarry with the Gitksan of Galdo'o and Kispiox and with the Sekani on their eastern borders. This latter group came to be known as the T'lotona or "Long Grass band of the Sekani, whose home lay in the Groundhog country at the headwaters of the Skeena, Nass and Stikine rivers."[76] Diamond Jenness learned of these people from a Gitksan woman who spent most of her life among them:

I was born at Kispiox about seventy years ago [c. 1854]. My father belonged to the Wolf phratry in that village, my mother to the owl [Giskaast] phratry, so they gave me the name Luskayok, which means "Cry of the baldheaded eagle," the eagle being the crest of my father's phratry. One of my father's sisters married an Indian of the Long Grass band and went to live in his country. When I was eleven years old a fight occurred between these Long Grass Indians and the Kispiox people.

Several Kispiox men were slain and five Long Grass Indians, among them my aunt's brother-in-law, who was killed by my mother's brother. The two peoples then settled their quarrel by holding a feast together in the Groundhog country, and my parents, lacking a son, sent me to live with my aunt as a mark of good will.

The Long Grass people treated me very kindly, and when I was fourteen years old married me to a young chief named Kaiyeish, whose grandmother had been a Kispiox woman also. We were very happy for many years, and had six children, four of whom are buried beside my husband in a big cemetery in the Groundhog Country ... From early spring until nearly Christmas, we wandered in and around the Klappan mountains hunting and trapping, then we travelled south to Bear Lake, or less often, northward to Telegraph Creek to trade our furs. Occasionally we visited Bear Lake during the summer also, in order to see my people; but we never went to Telegraph Creek during the summer because the Long Grass Indians are not allowed to fish in Stikine river.

When my husband died in 1907 his brother wanted to marry me, according to the usual custom; but I refused him, because my husband had told me to return to my people. So the Long Grass people took me down to Bear Lake and restored me to my family, who came up from Kispiox to receive me.[77]

Luuskayok does not give the reason for the original hostilities. According to Constance Cox, Luuskayok's mother's brother, from the House of Geel, initiated the hostilities when he "shot a Sekani Indian whom he found hunting on his hunting ground. Their hunting grounds were a very sacred thing to them and have belonged to the Indians for hundreds of years."[78] Geel's hunting grounds are on the upper Skeena adjacent to those of Xhliimlaxha.

In this account, Luuskayok's husband of the Long Grass people is called Kaiyeish (Gayee'is),[79] and his grandmother is said to have been a Kispiox woman. Gayee'is is a name in the House of K'yoluget, a house closely related to Amagyet and in more recent times to Xhliimlaxha. Luuskayok's husband may have received it from his grandmother from Kispiox or from a Laxwiiyip relative who had previously received it from the Galdo'o or Kispiox. As well, the name Gitkayees is attributed to one of the Laxwiiyip in an account of their war with the Gitanyow.

The passage of this name, however it may have moved from one group to another, is evidence for the ongoing intermarriage between the Eastern Tsetsaut and the Gitksan at Galdo'o and Kispiox, and these ties continue to this day. Many of the elders at the Tahltan village of Iskut are descendants of the Laxwiiyip, Sekani, and Gitksan who made up the Long Grass band, and many of the residents of Iskut have Gitksan names.[80]

The La̲xwiiyip and the Territory of X̲skiigmla̲xha at Awiijii

To the south of the La̲xwiiyip at Awiijii, after the xsiisxw in 1861, was the Gitanyow House of 'Wiilitsxw, with whom they had an uneasy peace, and to the east the G̲aldo'o House of X̲skiigmla̲xha (Sgawil), with whom they had always been on friendly terms. With the rise to prominence of Saniik, the role of the Raven Clan relatives of X̲skiigmla̲xha among the Eastern Tsetsaut had been diminished, but X̲skiigmla̲xha continued to have peaceful relations with these neighbours.

As David Gunanoot explained, X̲skiigmla̲xha always joined with "the Stikine [Eastern Tsetsaut] people and he was a kind of friend for him, that he [the Tsetsaut] was coming into G̲aldo'o and they look for that X̲skiigmla̲xha and spend the night with him and off again ... [X̲skiigmla̲xha] used to do some trapping around here [Awiijii] but they don't break any [beaver] houses."[81] However, a Kispiox man had been trapping beaver in the La̲xwiiyip territories and had made holes in the tops of the beaver houses:

> Over a hundred years there were good relations between X̲skiigmla̲xha and the Tahltans [Eastern Tsetsaut]. However, a Kispiox Indian used to come over the mountains and into this area hunting and trapping. The Stikine owners told this hunter not to trespass, but he continued for several years. Finally the Stikine were fed up with this man and decided to kill him for trespassing. When the Stikine discovered the man, they shot him with a gun with hammers but when the Stikine chief went and turned the body over, they discovered they had killed the wrong man. It was X̲skiigmla̲xha.
>
> A G̲aldo'o man was with the Stikines ... He returned to G̲aldo'o. The men from Kispiox and G̲aldo'o went up and picked up the body and took it to G̲aldo'o. After a year they went to avenge the murder. A half-breed woman was being trained to shoot. They lined up targets on a log and she shot them all. The Stikine knew she was with the people. The Stikine's wife spotted someone when she was getting wood. She warned the chief. He came out of the cabin with a little loin cloth and his hands spread. His wife got skins (moose, bear, goat) and lined them [up] around the cabin. The woman called the people in. She had a big beaver swinging in front of the fire. When it was cooked, she butchered [it] and fed them. No blood in the meat – if there was, it means there would be more killing.
>
> When they were finally through talking, Haa Na'ess [elsewhere said to be Tashuuts] took down a big caribou hide about three feet square. He reached into it and pulled out a red feather. He said: "This is the one I will give you for your trouble, so we won't have no more trouble. You can carry this around. If you have trouble, show this that you have the feather of Gawagaani (a great peace)."

He gave it to the nephew of X̱skiigmlax̱ha, the new X̱skiigmlax̱ha. The Stikines had all kinds of gifts for the Gitksan and they moved out. The Stikine moved out and said they wouldn't come in.[82]

Among the gifts was a feather: "That's the main part of it ... they took that big red feather, kind of silky one, and grab it – 'here take this and don't lose it, don't give it away. If it is any trouble for you, you better take this one and show that [to] who try and get you into trouble.' Old Sgawil take that feather and put it away ... I heard that Jessie Sterritt was looking after that ... they call it T'iye'itxwm Gawaganii."

Those present at the peace ceremony were members of the war party that Nagan and Sgawil had organized to avenge the death of their uncle: "Solomon Dick and Tom Sampson and Dan Skawil – yes Dan Skawil and I forgot who is the other. There's more. And there's that woman. I forgot his name – her name too. The one that has been trained as – to handle those [rifles] like thirty-three or forty-four."[83] Walter Laats was also there, and in 1934 he and Tom Sampson were called upon as witnesses to these events, and at that time they made a statutory declaration about their participation at the xsiisxw at Awiijii:

> That about 35 years ago we were present at Camping Ground near Bowser Lake, in the Province of British Columbia, that we were present at that time and met the Stikine Indians who were at that time claiming the trapping grounds held by Simon Gun-A-Noot's father.
>
> That we saw and heard the remarks from both sides and that we are witnesses to the terms of peace.
>
> That the Stikine Indians stated their settlement as being satisfied that Simon Gun-A-Noot and his father were the rightful ones to take possession of these grounds and trap there. Both sides, that is, the Stikine Indians and Simon's father and Simon Gun-A-Noot, exchanged presents and left as good friends.[84]

In 1885, the last of the Western Tsetsaut joined the new mission at Kincolith and amalgamated with the Nisga'a. The Long Grass people eventually joined the Tahltan, and many of them, including the Gitksan among them, now live at Iskut. The remaining Eastern Tsetsaut, or Lax̱wiiyip, also joined the Tahltan, and after they left Awiijii in the early 1900s, they moved permanently to Telegraph Creek.

Conclusion

These adaawḵ clearly show that the Gitksan, including the Gitanyow, have been established in their territories on the upper Nass and Skeena Rivers since the earliest times. Those who left abandoned their territories, while those who migrated in were either absorbed into preexisting groups or continued their migrations to other areas. When the Gitksan were attacked by the Tsetsaut and forced out of their villages, they retaliated, in each case successfully defending their territories. In some cases, they have expanded their territories as a result of a xsiisxw.

The Gitksan have acquired and validated their ownership of their territories within the Gitksan system of land tenure for millennia, through naming, adaaw<u>k</u>, limx'oy, xwtsaan, and feasting. Their defence of their territories continues into the contemporary period.

3

The Gitksan Documentary Record: Gitanyow

Introduction

In the postcontact era, in reaction to the influx of settlers and government efforts to establish reserves, Gitanyow leaders declared their ownership of their ancestral lands in a variety of forums. They stated their position to visiting surveyors, officials, and commissions, providing them in some cases with detailed hand-drawn maps, and they repeatedly petitioned government leaders to address the issue of their title.

Their assertion of Aboriginal title and the associated naming of territories constituted the Gitanyow's initial defence of their territory in response to the incursions of Euro-Canadians. In the process, the Gitanyow repeatedly detailed the extent of their territories and explained the nature of their system of land tenure. They also repeatedly made their position clear: their territorial ownership was not negotiable.

The documentary record of the Gitanyow is extraordinary for the consistency of the territories claimed, the unrelenting commitment to their system of land tenure, and the sophisticated fashioning of Euro-Canadian law to suit their ends, as, for example, in the registration of the bulk of their territory as a single "Kitwancool" trapline. Their cartographic legacy is also unparalleled. Their maps show an intimate knowledge of the geographic features in their territories, their territorial boundaries, and the locations of their fishing, camping, and hunting sites and their many ancient villages. In doing so, they also provide an invaluable historical record of ancestral lands and tribal boundaries in the Nass and Skeena watersheds.

As the provincial government moved to impose reserves, the Gitanyow also defended their territory on the ground. In 1927, several of their chiefs were jailed for their organized resistance to government surveyors. As early as 1910, when farmers attempted to settle in their territories, they were chased away, and beginning in the 1920s when loggers entered their territories, they frequently found the Gitanyow had barricaded their roads.

The Gitanyow also presented statements concerning their Aboriginal title in the academic arena. In the 1920s they described their territories to Marius Barbeau and Willam Beynon, and in the 1950s they worked with Wilson Duff with the express intent of providing "authentic information on their history, traditions, social organization and laws to properly qualified persons."[1] The British Columbia Provincial Museum supported the Gitanyow in this, in its publication of *Histories, Territories and Laws of the Kitwancool*.[2] From the 1970s to the present, the Gitanyow have pursued their own territorial research, working with chiefs and elders to add further geographic and historical information to the already extensive written record.

For several decades, the threat of Nisga'a encroachment has presented a further challenge to the Gitanyow. The historical record shows, however, that in the face of all attempts to deny their Aboriginal title, the Gitanyow have continued to present the documentation of their ownership of their territories in every possible forum, as they do in this publication, and to defend their territory on the ground. In the process they have produced a record of resistance unique in British Columbia. In fact, the history of the Gitanyow since the late 1800s is one of protest deeply rooted in indigenous law.

Gitanyow Ownership Statements: Gitanyow Meetings with Alfred Green (1910)

During the first decade of the twentieth century, with white settlement increasing in their territories and a transcontinental railway under construction along the Skeena, the Gitksan participated extensively in protests about the land question. These efforts were taken on their own initiative and as part of a wider pattern of protest. A petition was sent to the prime minister in 1908, and in 1909, following a series of confrontations, the Stewart-Vowell Commission was sent by the federal government to inquire into Gitksan grievances.

This was the background to a series of Gitanyow protests beginning in 1910. On 6 July, Chief Samuel Douse, Biiyoosxw, sent a telegram to Prime Minister Laurier on behalf of the Gitanyow people. Douse stated that the whole country belonged to them but "our land at Kitwancool surveyed for whiteman."[3] In the next two weeks, there was an exchange of letters and telegrams between the Department of Indian Affairs (DIA) and A.H. Green, who was in the upper Skeena region and was instructed to visit Gitanyow.

When Green's party reached Gitanyow, Green called a meeting to explain the purpose of his visit, only to be informed that "they did not want me, that the whole of the country belonged to them, and that they had been advised by a Toronto lawyer named Clark, not to accept reserves until the 'Petition' had been answered. This answer they expected before the snow came. When their claims were settled the white men could come in."[4] The reference here is to the Cowichan Petition, which had been drafted by Clark and forwarded to London in March 1909 with the hope of securing a referral to the Judicial Committee of the Privy Council. Chief Simediik of Kitwanga had contacted Clark about the petition, apparently in support of the initiative.[5] Thus, the Gitanyow were aware, in broad terms, of the Royal Proclamation of 1763 and its potential implications for the assertion of Aboriginal title in British Columbia.

In addition to his letters and reports, Green kept some notes of his meeting at Gitanyow. He recorded statements of Gitanyow chiefs concerning their territories and their position on the issue of reserves. The following is a full transcription of these notes:

Conversation with Indians at Kitwancool, Aug. 15, 1910
...

Beyosqu[6]
We did not thank you for coming before. We sent a petition to Ottawa we want our land back so we do not want a reserve, we want our land back, it belongs to us. Mr. Vowell and Mr. Stewart were here last spring and wanted to give us a reserve but we would not have it. If a reserve was given to us we know our hunting ground is not in it. We do not want a reserve now. Do you think it is right that the white man should buy land before our law suit is settled (our rights defined).

Gamlakyeltqu (woman)[7]
All our hopes were that you would help us, but now we are in hard times. I would ask you if you heard anything about our petition. There is one hunting house and four houses in different places on the other side of the lake on a tributary of the Nass. Singewin[8] is their name. Our land extends beyond that posts. We cannot get a living on the reserves they are too small. We do not want reserves we are not so foolish. We know the land belongs to us and we will hold it till we die. Our hunting grounds are our bank. The white men take gold out of our creeks. It is hard on us that we cannot do anything on our land after we have reserves. The Gov. takes the key of our bank. The bear come down to the river in the fall and we do not want fences to keep them away as we trap them there. How much has the Gov. spent on our land. The Gov. did not tell us the surveyors were coming here or tell us that Mr. Vowell was coming here in 18-[sic].[9]

Richard Douse[10]
Did anyone tell you to come here. Did they tell you to make reserve.
Have you authority to place a post at our grandfathers land mark. We
want you to put a post at our grandfathers land mark. We want an answer
to our petition. It is not our grandfathers rule (custom) that we have so
little land. If a man of another tribe comes over our hunting land there
is trouble. We want the whole of the land that belongs to us

Albert Williams[11]
I know the Lord gave my grandfather this land and have lived on it ever
since, so we don't want our land to go to anyone else because the Lord
has given us the land. Our fathers left us this land when they died, so
we do not want our grandfathers post to be removed so long as we do
not agree to it and we want it all. So we ask you to hold that land till
we get settled with the Govermt. The Gov has no right to stop our work
on our land before they have settled with us. We do not want any white
men on our land before our claims are settled. Settle our claims and then
the white men can come

Stephen[12]
I know that you have no authority to give what the chiefs are asking for.
We know that posts have to be in our grandfathers landmarks before
long. We find that our grandfathers law is the same as your grandfathers
law in King George III reign [i.e., Royal Proclamation of 1763]. All the
chiefs will be satisfied if you will put a post at our grandfathers land
mark. I want to ask you if you think the white men will clear their claims.
The white man can take up our land at once while we have to wait for
an answer to our petition.

We hope there will be no trouble after this. What shall we do if the whites
clear their land. We object because they are not allowed to do anything
on our grandfathers land. Our lawsuit will come on before winter and
we do not wish the whites to come before it is settled.[13]

Gitanyow Ownership Statements: A Cartographic Legacy

Samuel Douse Map (1910)
This meeting, with its impressive set of statements to Green, seems to
have inspired Samuel Douse to produce a map of Gitanyow territories.
Two weeks later, he presented such a map to a second DIA visitor to the
upper Skeena. John McDougall had been hired by the DIA to proceed "to
the Skeena River and look into matters relating to Indian reserves and
occupations along this river." More precisely, he was to ascertain the

extent of any "Native holdings" outside reserves and report on any cases in which "Natives" had been dispossessed by white settlers.[14]

At "several points," McDougall met "representatives, chiefs and headmen in gatherings and in small groups and also as individuals." In Gitksan territory, he is known to have held meetings at Kispiox (17 August), Hazelton and Hagwilget (19-22 August), Old Kitsegyukla (25 August), and Kitwanga at about the same time.[15]

At Kitwanga, Biyoosxw, Samuel Douse, representing the village of Gitanyow and "all the Indians in the vicinity," put forward a territorial claim and told McDougall that because of this claim "the Indians of Andimaul and Kitwancool refused to allow the survey of reserves this season."[16]

More significantly, Douse supported the claim with the first recorded map[17] of the Gitanyow territory. McDougall appreciated the significance of this map and took it back to Ottawa, where he wrote a report. After a copy of the map was drafted,[18] the original was returned to Gitanyow.[19] This map does not appear to have survived, but it was likely similar (or perhaps identical) to later maps provided by the Gitanyow to the McKenna-McBride Royal Commission hearings in 1915, Louis Shotridge in 1918, and W.E. Ditchburn in 1920. Fortunately, the Shotridge and Ditchburn maps have survived.

Gitanyow Territorial Map: McKenna-McBride Royal Commission Hearings (Babine Agency, 1915)

The Gitanyow reasserted their position at the McKenna-McBride Royal Commission hearings (MMRC), a joint federal/provincial enquiry into "Native lands" in British Columbia. Its terms of reference specifically prohibited consideration of Aboriginal title; instead, the commission was to seek a "final" adjustment of the size and number of reserves. Between 1913 and 1915, the commission held hearings around the province seeking information from "Native" peoples.

The commission met with the Gitanyow in hearings on 18 April 1915, held at Kitwanga. Albert Williams acted as spokesperson for the Gitanyow band. The commissioners endeavoured to obtain specific information about lands for reserves, but Williams kept raising the broader issue of Aboriginal title. During one exchange, he produced a map to substantiate his claim:

> It is all good land all the way up to the [Kitwancool] lake and also on the west side of the lake. (Producing a map of his own)[20] All different families live where these little red spots are, and that is the reason we signed the petition to get this land back for our own people.

> Q Who was it made this map?
> A A man by the name of Sam Dowes.

Q Was he a surveyor?

A He is supposed to be a man that belongs to Kitwancool. He is an Indian and knows all about the land there.

...

A The reason I am going to give it [the map] to you – I am not going to let anyone have this, but the reason I am going to give it to you is because we signed the petition to get this land back.

...

A We want the whole country within that black line.

...

A One trail from the Indian village runs along the east side right to the Nass river, and it is all good grazing land.

...

A All around the north side of the lake right up to the Nass river is good for grazing and we keep it for grazing, and where the wax spots are (on his map) we have cultivated there.

...

Q Are people living at all these places where they are marked with red wax on your map?

A Yes

Q How many people live at the lowest point marked on the Nass river, on this map, close to the boundary marked "A"?

A There is a big family lives there.[21]

It is clear that the last question refers to the Gitanyow-Nisga'a border on the lower Nass River. This is entirely consistent with all other evidence (Gitanyow and Nisga'a) in the MMRC hearings and, as will be seen in the Shotridge and Ditchburn maps, locates the southern Gitanyow boundary in the vicinity of Gitxsits'uuts'xwt near the confluence of the Tchitin River.

Q How many people live at the place marked "an Indian village" – marked "B" on map?

A There is a lot of people live there ... the family of Chief Alexander lives there.

Q With regard to the place marked "A" – how long have they been living there?

A No one knows it, but since the world was made.

...

Q How about the place marked "B" – has anyone surveyed it?

A Yes, that is surveyed already.

Q Has anyone gone to live there?

A I have trapped up there and I have often seen white men there, but they have never interfered with us.

...

Q Now you say where each and every one of these wax marks show you swear that there are Indian families living at each one of these places?
A Yes I will take my oath to that.
Q And they have been living there for some time?
A Yes.

...

Q Have you some cultivation in all those places that are marked in red wax?
A Those places are chiefly our hunting places, and what we have culti- vated is chiefly around Kitwancool village.[22]

In May 1988, Gamlaxyeltxw, Solomon Marsden (born 1909), gave evi- dence about the Samuel Douse map under cross-examination by counsel for British Columbia:

Q Mr. Marsden, have you ever heard of a map – an old map made by Mr. Sam Douse?
A Yes. He is one of the persons that – that was trying to outline the ter- ritory of the Kitwancool.
Q At page 29 of Exhibit 439 there is a photograph of a map of the Kit- wancool territories stated to be 1918, "Drawn by Samuel Douse of Kitwancool, photographed by Louis Shotridge. Courtesy of the Uni- versity Museum, University of Pennsylvania." Mr. Marsden, have you ever seen the original of Mr. Sam Douse's map?
A No, I didn't seen it.
Q But you know there is such a map?
A Yes. He – he was making the maps for the territory of the chiefs.[23]

Thus, the Douse map has survived in the form of a 1918 photograph by Louis Shotridge.

Gitanyow Territorial Map (Shotridge Photograph, 1918)
In 1918 Gitanyow leaders met with Alaska Tlingit Louis Shotridge (then studying at the University of Pennsylvania), who was travelling through- out the upper Skeena region. He published an account of his trip the following year and referred to his meeting with Gitanyow leaders:

Some of the older men talked over this land question to me and on one occasion one of the leaders showed me a map, cleverly drawn with pen and black ink on a sheet of wrapping paper, indicating a tract of land which the chief claimed had been theirs from time immemorial. He stated that his ancestors had fought hard to retain this possession, and that

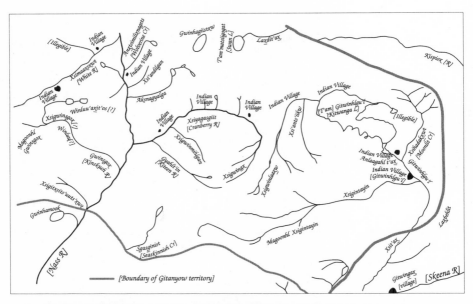

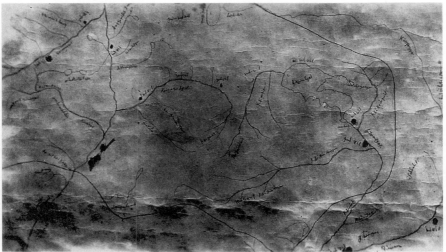

Map 8   Gitanyow territorial map, Shotridge photograph (1918).

every member of the group is taught at childhood to hold on to it. I could not obtain the drawing which I thought would offer a good sample of an Indian idea of map making but I photographed it. This is the first group of Indians I have ever met in the Northwest who foresaw the value of land and who are making efforts to provide some kind of a foothold on behalf of the generation to come.

The chief told me that before Git-wentl-qool [Kitwancool] was founded his forefathers were forced from the Naas River direction further into the interior, during one of the wars over the land which they now claim, and were compelled to build a fortified town which in later years was named Git-inyewo [Gitanyow] and which is now non-existent. This was located on a high hill, about nine miles north of the present town.

The people in this community appear to have fixed habits and their wanderings, until very recently, were in the nature of temporary excursions to established points resorted to from time almost unknown.[24]

The photograph shows the map referred to by Shotridge.[25] It does not show the entire Gitanyow territory, but most features on it can be identified. It shows a solid black line (the Gitanyow external boundary) that encompasses internal features, such as villages, creeks, and lakes. This boundary line crosses the Nass River below Xsiyagasgiit (Cranberry River) at the confluence of an unidentified creek (likely the Tchitin River) and continues west from there. Another feature, a creek (likely Kwinamuck Creek), flows from a nearby lake (Kwinamuck Lake) into the Nass River below the Gitanyow border (see Map 8).

Because it is probable that the map given to the MMRC in 1915, the Ditchburn blueprint of 1920, below, was based on the Samuel Douse map of 1910, the Shotridge photograph is probably of this map as well.

Gitanyow Territorial Map (Ditchburn Blueprint, 1920)

The next important cartographic record is the "Kitwancool" blueprint that resulted from a meeting that W.E. Ditchburn, Inspector of Indian Agencies, Deputy Superintendent General of Indian Affairs (DSGIA), held at Gitanyow in March 1920. In a subsequent letter to the DSGIA (22 March 1920), Ditchburn gave an account of the meeting with the Gitanyow about the denial of access to their territories. Ditchburn enclosed three blueprints, one of which was

made from a map drawn by one of the Kitwancool Indians, showing the land which they claim as their own. This territory is approximately 60 miles wide by 100 miles long and shows the old hunting lodges and fisheries from a few miles above the Kitwangar into the territory of the Upper Nass River as far as Meziadin Lake. Mr. Green improved upon the Indian's original map by marking in the Nass River reserves, those for the Kitwangar, Andimaul, Hazelton, Kiskegas and Kuldo Indians. The three reserves recommended in 1910 are also shown on this blue-print. From this blue-print it will be observed that the great bulk of the places marked Indian villages are a long distance above Kitwancool Lake.[26]

Ditchburn, in a letter to Indian Agent W.E. Collison, 7 May 1920, gave instructions to the latter about a visit to Gitanyow and enclosed a copy of the map (see Map 9) described in the letter of 22 March 1920: "On this blue-print will be seen a large territory of the country which the Indians claim as their own by virtue of their being the original occupiers of, together with a large number of places which they call Indian villages, though I am inclined to think they are really their hunting lodges. This territory extends from a few miles above Kitwangar right over into the Nass River country."[27] This is a remarkable map, and it clearly defines the whole of Gitanyow territory, including the Gitanyow-Nisga'a border on the Nass River. On this map, it appears downriver from, rather than at, the Tchitin River confluence.

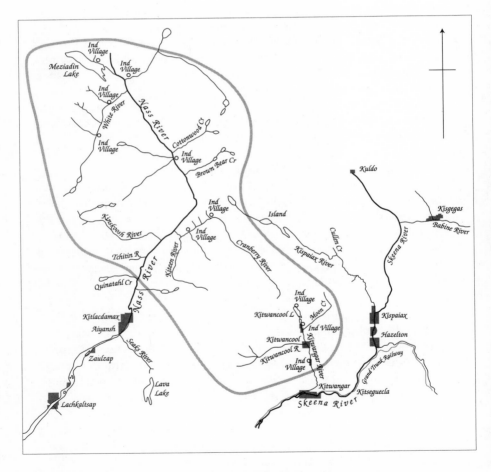

Map 9   Gitanyow territorial map (from Ditchburn blueprint, 1920)

Michael Inspring Bright Map (1926)

Even more remarkable than the Gitanyow blueprint of 1920 is a map produced by Ts'imgwanks, Michael Inspring Bright. He was a Gitanyow living at Grease Harbour when he spoke before the MMRC (see below). Although this map first appears in the Barbeau file in 1926, its purpose became clear in 1939 when Bright approached William Beynon with his map and a desire "to make a statement that this territory and houses and creeks as designated on these maps as recorded are property of the Gitwin-lkul [Kitwancool] as conquered over the Tsetsaut of Meziadin."[28] This impressive map is of the utmost significance in determining the precise limits of Gitanyow and Nisga'a territories. It shows the place names and names of chiefs associated with most of the sites, and it clearly indicates the border between the Gitksan and the Nisga'a.

Of particular importance is Gitxsits'uuts'xwt, frequently mentioned by Nisga'a witnesses in the MMRC hearings. It appears on Bright's 1926 map on the west bank of the Nass at the Tchitin River confluence as "Gitksizuzqu gitksedzo'otsk' (people of birds, of Sqatin)."[29] This indicates that the site is the property of Sgat'iin and therefore belongs to the Nisga'a. Bright also shows "Anbaklhon" on the same side of the Nass, above Gitxsits'uuts'xwt, as being "of Sqatin." However, the Kinskuch River appears on the map as "Kinsqoik Kinsg.o'ix (of lux,on)."[30] "Lux,on" is Luuxhon, the Gitanyow chief. Moreover, the place names along both sides of the Nass River above the Kinskuch River confluence all appear with Gitanyow chiefs' names. Thus, the Gitanyow-Nisga'a border must lie within the few kilometres between the Tchitin and the Kinskuch Rivers.

Bright's hand-drawn map makes this point (see Map 10b). However, his objective is made with greater impact in a modern rendition of the original in the map prepared for this publication (see Maps 10a and 10b).

Bright identified numerous other names on the Nass River up to Meziadin Lake and on the Cranberry River, and he gave the name of the Gitksan owner for most of them. Clearly, his map is of Gitanyow territories, place names, and fishing sites, and where necessary for clarity he listed the Nisga'a owner, as he did with Sgat'iin.

In conclusion, the Gitanyow have a remarkable cartographic record, spanning at least two decades, that clearly places their boundary with the Nisga'a at Gitxsits'uuts'xwt near the confluence of the Tchitin River. As will be seen, the cartographic record was corroborated by Gitanyow and Nisga'a statements to the MMRC.

Gitanyow Ownership Statements: McKenna-McBride Royal Commission Hearings (Nass Agency, 1915)

Albert Williams was not the only Gitanyow chief to appear before the MMRC in 1915. Several other chiefs spoke, but at hearings for the Nass

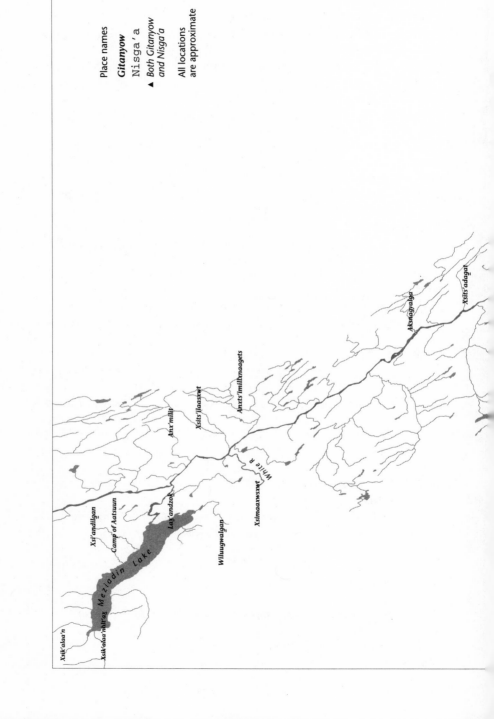

Place names

Gitanyow
Nisga'a

▲ *Both Gitanyow
and Nisga'a*

All locations
are approximate

Xsik'alaa'n

Xsik'alaa'milit'ax   *Meziadin Lake*

Xsi'andligan

Camp of Aatsuun

Laxandzok

Wiluugwalgap

Xsimaaxswxwt   *White R*

Amx'mitit

Xsits'iilaasxwt

Anxts'imiltbmaagets

Aksnagyalga

Xsits'adagat

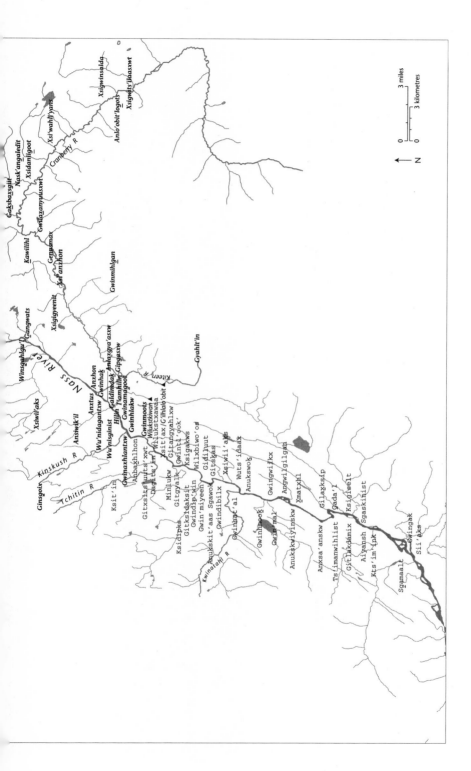

Map 10a   Michael Inspring Bright map (GTO, 1995)

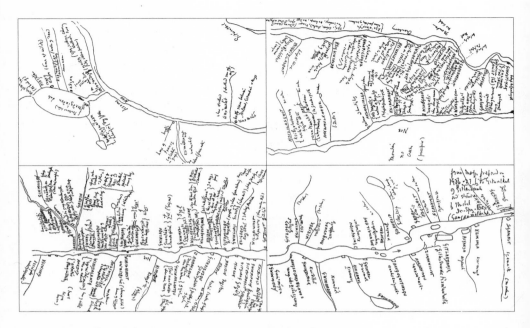

Map 10b Michael Inspring Bright's original hand-drawn map

Agency held at Aiyansh. While the comments of these chiefs are of interest, equally significant is the reason that they attended the hearings at
Aiyansh rather than at Kitwanga. Behind their presence at the Nass
Agency hearings lay a series of developments that has generated a good
deal of confusion about the ownership of the territory above Aiyansh. A
clear understanding of these events is crucial.

   In the late nineteenth century, a number of Gitksan relocated to Nisga'a villages. Trading patterns centred on the oolichan, and marriage
alliances had long ensured a modest movement of population between
the two areas, but this was something new. Some Gitksan sought economic opportunities, especially employment in the salmon canneries at
the mouth of the Nass. Probably more important was the prior development of missionary settlements and schools on the Nass River: Kincolith,
Greenville, and Aiyansh. Missionaries had a vested interest in promoting
relocations to these new "model" settlements.

   The largest group of Gitksan to move to the lower Nass area came from
Gitanyow. Of course, the Gitanyow, more than any other Gitksan group,
were familiar with the Nass – having lived on the upper part of the river
since time immemorial – and the territories and fishing sites above
Aiyansh. By 1900 some 115 Gitanyow were reported to be living in
Nisga'a villages. As a result of these late-nineteenth-century relocations,

a good many contemporary Gitksan have relatives on the Nass. The name Gedimgaldo'o, the leading chief of Gitanmaax (Hazelton), for example, is also held by a descendant of Albert Allen at Kincolith. The crucial point, however, is that these migrants did not take ownership of territories with them. On this point, both Gitksan and Nisga'a law are unequivocal. Those who relocate may retain privileges to use their ancestral lands: they do not carry title to their adoptive nation.

Wilson Duff recognized this when he wrote, in his draft manuscript (undated), that this migration led to the Nisga'a claim to territory on the upper Nass River: "The Niska do not have clear claims to the Nass above this point [Kinskuch River], in recent times the upper Nass was under Kitwancool domination. (For a period between about 1890 and – nearly all of the Kitwancool people lived on the Nass – this contributed to the notion that the upper Nass was Niska territory)."[31] In *Histories, Territories and Laws of the Kitwancool*, Duff and the Gitanyow wrote: "In the 1880's and 1890's many of the tribe decided to move to the Lower Nass, where missionaries had established new settlements ... In recent years, however, the number in the village has grown rapidly, from 90 in 1939 to 173 in 1958. To-day Kitwancool is a vigorous community with a day-school, village hall, and church, and a reputation of industry and independence."[32] They referred to the Gitksan origin of these people: "Their closest relatives, however, are the people of the Upper Skeena, and the Kitwancool are usually classified with them to form the Gitksan (git – 'people of,' ksan – 'Skeena River') division of the Tsimshian."[33]

Dr. Peter Williams, president of the Kitwancool (Gitanyow), made the point clearly in a report written in 1978: "To this day many of the Nass people who are descended from Kitwancool possess ancestral rights in Kitwancool. However, the land remains in Kitwancool territory; it cannot be moved elsewhere; and its ownership remains in the name of those who hold the seats of authority in Kitwancool, the chiefs of the Frog and Wolf clans."[34] In other words, the movement of Gitanyow people to Nisga'a villages cannot be used to validate Nisga'a claims to Gitanyow territory, anymore than the relocation of Nisga'a people to Gitksan villages validates a Gitksan claim to Nisga'a land.

Some specific examples will help to illustrate the context and content of these important developments. Wiilaxha, Charles Martin (1866-1938), a member of the House of Wiik'aax of Kisgaga'as, relocated from Metlakatla to Aiyansh about 1887: "Then I was preparing to return to Hazelton, and I came up the Nass river. And there was no trail. It was winter time and there was lot[s] of snow. There was no trail for me to come to Hazelton, so I went to the village of Ayans. It was a Christian village."[35] Here he met the missionary J.B. McCullagh, who befriended him and provided a house for him to live in. After two years, McCullagh encouraged Martin to marry a local Nisga'a woman. However, when this marriage did not work out, the ensuing friction between McCullagh and Martin prompted the latter to return to Hazelton.

As mentioned above, a member of the Gedimgaldo'o family relocated as well, as Barbeau writes: "Albert Allen, or Geetemraldo,[36] of Kincolith, at the mouth of the Nass, was a sophisticated half-breed, about sixty years old in 1927, who traced his ancestry on his mother's side to the Geeten-maks[37] tribe (now Hazelton) of the Gitksan."[38]

Michael Bright relocated from Gitanyow first to Grease Harbour and then to Aiyansh, after the turn of the century. When Commissioner McDowall of the MMRC came to Bright's house at Grease Harbour in October 1915, the following exchange took place between the commissioner, Bright, and Daniel Guno:

Michael Inspring:
I will first put a question to you Commissioners – I want to know what mission you have come on here whether of peace or trouble?

McDowall:
We have come here in the interests of the Government and to all good men whether they be white men or Indians it is a matter of importance to have good government.
...
Q Are you a member of the Aiyansh Band of Indians?
A I am a member of that Band and also a member of the Naas River people.
Q Since you have been up here have you lived on the reserve most of the time – how much of the time have you lived on this piece of land which is now a Government Reserve?
A I spend most of my time here [at Grease Harbour] but now and again I walk down to Aiyansh.
...
Q Have you a house at Aiyansh or at any other village on the river?
A I have a house at Aiyansh.
...
Q How wide a frontage on the river do you claim?
A I claim the whole frontage – it was used by the Indians before me.
Q How many yards of frontage on the river do you want?
A I just fall in with the request of the other Chiefs that spoke to you from Aiyansh and Gitladamiks, and I myself speak for this piece of land.
...

Daniel Guno [also of Gitanyow] made a statement:

A It is now 9 years and 6 months since we first came to live here. I lived here for five years without hearing a word from anybody. After the five years a surveyor came along.

...

Q Do you know who made the gardens that were here when you came?

A A man by the name of KAKQUE[39] and another man by the name of Philip Ward.

Q Were they white men?

A Timothy Derrick's uncle was KAKQUE and my father's uncle is Philip Ward.

Q So they were both Indians?

A Yes.[40]

Bright's "Naas River people" must include the Gitanyow, because so much of their territory is in the Nass watershed. Also, by this time Bright had lived on the Nass for about thirty years and identified himself with the Nass. His map makes it clear that he considered the Gitanyow to own territory on the Nass eleven years later in 1926. Bright's status as a "member" of the Aiyansh Band is explained in the Aiyansh "Constitution," which deals with the settlement of Aiyansh as a mission village: "'The People of Aiyansh' are ... those who have come from other villages on the Lower Nass or Skeena River, and who, having joined themselves to the Aiyansh community, either through marriage or from a desire to lead a new life, have been admitted to membership in the Band by the general assent of all the Members in Council assembled."[41] In later articles of the Constitution, membership involved administrative obligations and privileges connected with "membership in the Aiyansh Band" consistent with the Indian Act: obligations and privileges that cannot be construed to imply membership in the Nisga'a Nation (see Aiyansh Constitution, discussed in Chapter 5).

Bright's cartographic efforts deal with this issue, and Bright went to great lengths to assert his status as a Gitanyow hereditary chief. His Gitanyow origin was not in doubt when Mrs. Agnes Manesk said: "Michael Bright is of the family of Wixe ['Wiix̲a] (Gitwinkul). In fact he was sometime heir to that name. A tall splendid fellow (relative of Robert Pearl)."[42] 'Wiix̲a is a leading chief from Gitanyow. Similarly, the Gitksan considered Bright a member of Gitanyow, as Niishlaganoos, Fred Good said many years later: "Michael Bright of Gitlakdamiks is a Kitwancool man. He sends his hunters up Kinskuch."[43] Bright himself described the Gitanyow, the largest group of Gitksan to move to Nisga'a villages, to Marius Barbeau: "These are the names of the Gitwinlkul ... that have come to the Nass. Many of them are dead ... 132 altogether including all those in

the lower villages. All these have retained the rights of going to Medziadon. Those of Gitwinlkul now try to retain the exclusive privileges. We
make no objection to them coming but want to retain our own privileges."[44] Bright, a resident of Grease Harbour in 1915, described how the
Gitanyow people were organized within their territory on the Nass:

> In former days there were two divisions of [Gitanyow] people: the people
> of up above and the people below. The people above were the Gitwinlkul
> of the interior. The people below were the people of the lower river. Dur-
> ing the severe weather of the winter months the people of the lower river
> would move to Gitwinlkul with the people of the upper. And often the
> people of the upper division would come to the lower that is to the Nass,
> the Nisg.e. All became habitated there. Then when they would meet the
> missionaries the interior Gitwinlkul came and lived here entirely becom-
> ing Christians. And all those from up above still retain their property
> rights came down here. Many of these Gitwinlkul have come here and
> others down further to Aiyansh. All those that would have assumed the
> rank of chief there have died here and have been adopted here as well
> as the chief women. They went as far as Kincolith.[45]

The MMRC arrived on the Nass River in the fall of 1915 and held hearings at Aiyansh on 9 October. Here five Gitanyow chiefs made statements
to the commissioners and before ten Nisga'a chiefs. The presence of the
latter was significant: they made no objections to the territorial statements of the Gitanyow chiefs. This hearing occurred two years after the
Nisga'a Petition had been written, at a time when territorial claims were
of great significance to both the Gitksan and the Nisga'a.

Nevertheless, three Gitanyow fishing stations were "reserved" to the
Nisga'a by the MMRC in 1915, partly as a consequence of the Gitanyow
presence in Nisga'a communities, as Peter Williams wrote in a land claims
research presentation in 1978: "To explain why the New Aiyansh Reserves
[Reserves 52, 53, and 54] fall within Kitwancool territory, it is necessary
to look at the Royal Commission Reports of the meeting held October 8,
1915 at Aiyansh. For at this meeting five out of the fifteen who gave evidence were from Kitwancool."[46] The Gitanyow submission also explains
the family backgrounds of the Gitanyow persons who made ownership
statements to the MMRC on the Nass:

> **William Gogak or Gu-Ḡaak** was a leading member in the house of
> Gu-'nuu [Gwinuu] of the Frog Clan of Kitwancool. He lived in Aiyansh
> for awhile, but later returned to Kitwancool where he is buried. Two of
> his children live in Kitwancool today – Miles Gogag and Mrs. Lottie
> Douse. The land which Gogak describes, refers to the land at the end of

Kitwancool Lake, called Wilp-am-'tuuts, "house of charred logs," owned by Chief Gu-'nuu ...

Walter Dasque or A<u>x</u>-gun desxw [A<u>x</u>gwindesxw] was a leading member of the house of 'Malii, of the Wolf Clan of Kitwancool. His name is presently held by Bob Bright. Today, Fred Good (chief Niis-hla<u>k</u>-<u>G</u>an-us [Niishlaganoos]) of Kitwancool, the nephew of Walter Dasque is an important elder of the Wolf Clan. The houses of 'Malii and Hai-jimsxw of Kitwancool own the eastern portion of the Kitwancool territory, much of which drains into the Kispiox River system.

Richard Derrick [House of <u>G</u>amla<u>x</u>yeltxw] relates to the Commissioners that his family is living at a place called Ks-gi-geenit. His brother lives at Ksi-mihl-etxwit (Derrick Creek), where he gets his berries and fish. On the map he marked from Win-s<u>k</u>a-hlguu'l, on the upper Nass down to and including the Gin-<u>G</u>uux [Kinskuch] River.

Arthur Derrick eventually occupied the seat of K'am-la<u>x</u>-yeltxw, leading chief of the Frog-Raven clan in Kitwancool. The older Richard Derrick was also a high-ranking member of the same house. Another brother, Thomas Derrick, (Wii-hlemii [Wiihlamii]), lived his entire life at Kitwancool. He is the father of Walter Derrick. Other close relatives include the late Ambrose Derrick (Chief Luu-<u>x</u>hoon), and George Derrick ('Tsii-wa), of the house of Luu-<u>x</u>hoon both of whom always lived at Kitwancool, and never moved to the Nass. However, Timothy L. Derrick of Aiyansh, who spoke before the Commission is not related to the Derricks of Kitwancool.

Another Kitwancool who spoke at the Aiyansh meeting was **Robert Pearl, Chief 'Wii-<u>x</u>a'a** of the Wolf clan. He is the grandfather of Walter Derrick, current Chief 'Wii-<u>x</u>a'a. Pearl was for a short time chief Councillor at New Aiyansh, but late [sic] returned to his former village.[47]

Gitanyow chief William Gogak [Guuga<u>k</u>][48] described his territories as extending upstream from Gitangyahlxw and Gitxsits'uuts'xwt to Meziadin, without break: "I also come from one of these places and I want to speak to you about the hunting-grounds at Kitanqaoqu and Kitsizozquiot.[49] From these two places up belong to my family and from the last two mentioned places there was no space whatever; not even the space of one inch right up to the lake of Maziadin."[50] Gitangyahlxw and Gitxsits'uuts'xwt are located on opposite sides of the Nass at the Tchitin River confluence. Later, after others had spoken, Gogak added: "I want to speak a few words about a piece I have already given to Mr. Perry – I have given him a sketch of it and I would like to get it ... There is another place marked on the sketch known as Anlaubiglozatz.[51] This will belong to my nephew – another one of our camps is called Ginhaq[52] and on here I want another of my nephews to camp. I want to know if it would be agreeable if I were to live on the land which formerly belonged to my grandfathers."[53]

In this way, Gogak described his territories between Gitxsits'uuts'xwt and Meziadin and along the Cranberry River northwest of the village of Gitanyow. He described them in accordance with Gitksan and Nisga'a laws by naming the places on those territories. He went further, however, producing a sketch map that described the territories to which he was referring, and this was done in the presence of Nisga'a witnesses, all members of the Nisga'a Land Committee (see Map 11). It showed, especially, his house territories as extending up the extent of the Kiteen River with the notation – "this is my hunting ground" – written over his name. It also showed his territory north of the Kinskuch-Nass confluence, with an arrow pointing to Meziadin Lake, similarly annotated: "another hunting ground [of mine? (illegible)]" over the initials "W.G."

Richard Derrick[54] (House of G̲amlax̲yeltxw) described his territory, including the Kinskuch River and up the Nass River to Winsgahlgu'l:

You heard the list of names given to you by Chief Peter [Niisyok] yesterday, the names of which are Gunsguk and Aukdaus.[55] These creeks run for twenty miles back of the hill, which are now occupied by white

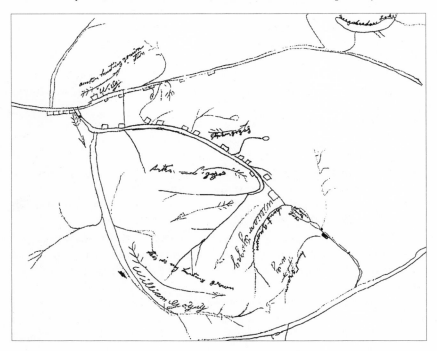

Map 11   Map of William Gogak house territories (1915)

people. There are over fifty people to which these creeks belong. Crossing over the river we also have two more creeks called Gitankam, Gwinsak and Gwilgol, which flow from the Kitwancool side – our families are living up there at a place called Ksgigienit – there is another place known as Ksimilatgut.[56] I also have a brother there in camp ... now. He has gardens there and he gets berries from there, also fish. A little way up these creeks which is a great place for salmon I marked up to a place which is known as Winsgalgol[57] and from that point down on the river.[58]

Gitanyow chief, Walter Dasque, Axgwindesxw (House of Malii), described his territories:

> You have heard the bosses of these different pieces of land and their grievances, and I am also boss of a piece of land known as Gaksbaksit[59] – I am just asking for these pieces that will be large enough for me and my family of which there are over twenty. I have a house and also a garden there ...
>   This parcel of land was used by my grandfathers for hunting purposes and what they used to call garden used to be the beaver dams and beaver lakes, and from this point there are three trails; one running to Kispiox on the Skeena, one to Maziadin Lake and the third one runs to Kitwancool.[60]

Arthur Derrick (House of Gamlaxyeltxw), nephew of Richard Derrick, described his uncle's territories on the Kinskuch River:

> As you see for yourselves Richard Derrick is getting to be an old man and he is just speaking as a spokesman for our family and I, as it were, stand behind him and, as it were, second everything that he says because at any time he might die because he is an old man and I am here to stand in his place.
>   Ginsgok [Kinskuch] Creek is the one we want as that is the nearest to us here. It is over thirty years since we started living here in this village and all this time we have [been] going to this creek to get food for ourselves. That is the reason why I say I am able to stand behind him and I shall continue to use it until the final settlement. As my brother told you he has land further on for hunting, berries, fishing, etc., and I am very glad to have been able to tell you this.[61]

Arthur Derrick is referring to the Kinskuch River, a major stream included in all maps produced by the Gitanyow. It parallels the Tchitin River and enters the Nass River a few kilometres above Gitxsits'uuts'xwt.
   In conclusion, the Gitanyow who spoke at the MMRC hearings in

Aiyansh described Gitanyow territories in the Nass watershed to Meziadin Lake and, in the process, located yet again the Gitanyow-Nisga'a border at Gitxsits'uuts'xwt. On the basis of this information, the border between the Gitksan of Gitanyow and the Nisga'a should be located on the east bank of the Nass River at Geltsalo'obit (Gil'hla'lo'obit) and just above Gitxsits'uuts'xwt on its west bank.

Statements Concerning Territory to Marius Barbeau and William Beynon (c. 1924)

Given the events in the early 1900s, it is not surprising that the Gitksan seized the opportunity to describe the full scope of their territories for the written record. Although early ethnographers often showed little interest in territorial information, the Gitksan were able to convey the extent of their territories to Marius Barbeau and William Beynon. These two ethnographers were unusual in that they specifically sought this information, although the time allotted to the process was brief. Beynon, a Tsimshian, knew the Tsimshian language and system. He was the grandson of Arthur Wellington Clah, who is quoted at length in Chapter 6.

In a 1924 interview with Beynon and Barbeau, Niisyaalexs, Albert Williams, described the territories of Malii, Wiixa', Hayts'imsxw, and 'Wiilitsxw (see Map 12):

House of Malii
Cranberry river above the 50 mile post. Along the trail from the Cranberry River on the Kispayaks there was a fishing station ... On the Kispayaks there was a fishing station at Gitangwalk (Person of Dry) on the north side of the Kispayaks a long way up, 2 miles (days?) steady walking from Kispayaks. (The name is derived from the fact that after the people have taken of the salmon that is caught there, they are quite dry and thirsty. Their thirst is unquenchable.) Their is a river on this territory called Mag.angis (place of among/mussel [freshwater]). The territory is named Txaxslaxwiyip[62] (along on top/on/large territory). The mountain top of this territory on the Kispayaks north is Lipe.'itxut[63] (by itself/standing [the mountain]). They have only one cabin at Gitangwalk where they get salmon and they also have a cabin on the 50 mile post of the trail on the Cranberry, Qakspaxskit[64] (just newly/upwards/lies [trail goes upwards]). They have a lake in the same territory T'am.ag.angi.s[65] (above). They get beaver there and the salmon and trout get right into the lake sockeye, melit, coho. This is all for them. There are many lakes in this territory Ndelo.det[66] (to each one [from one lake to another]/swim) (beaver or salmon). (There is a little connecting tributary between the two lakes.) Anlag.amsto'ks[67] (place/to one side). The tributary comes to one side of the lake, runs into it.

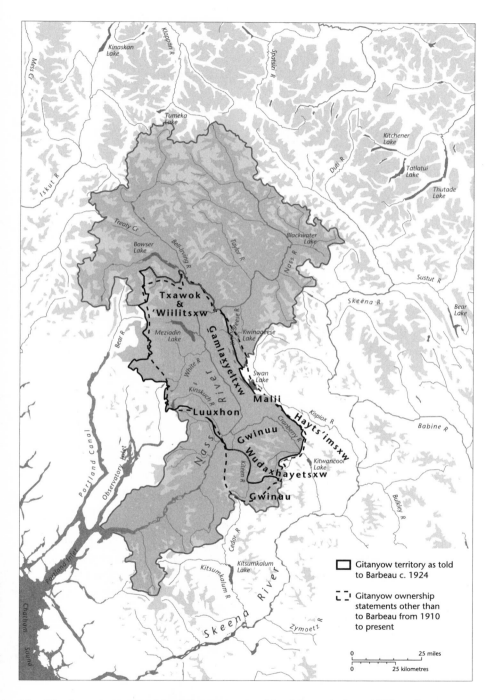

Map 12   Area encompassed by Gitanyow ownership statements from 1910 to the present

House of Malii and 'Wiilitsxw
Besides this ['Wiixa's territory to the south of the Nass River] the laxkibu
have hunting territories among the Tsetsaut towards the Nass and Meziadin Lake. That is Mali and Wilits and all the laxkibu. And they claim that
region surrounding Medziadin. They had a battle with the Tsetsaut at that
place and that is the reason why they claim it. But there is controversy
with the laxsel about it. At one time a laxkibu woman was killed who was
the wife of a former Gamlaxyelk. And the Tsetsaut took as a captive a
sister of the mali house. The woman's name of 'akstox (meaning ?). And
after the Tsetsaut had taken her as captive they never returned her or any
of the family from her to the laxkibu Gitwinlkul and as compensation the
laxkibu have retained this territory. All the laxkibu Gitwinkul.

House of Hayts'imsxw
On the upper Cranberry – Ksadanig.o.t[68] (water/Tahltan?/heart) is the
name of the territory. Runs from 50 miles post upward the river on the
north side.

House of 'Wiilitsxw and Txawok
They have no territory at all in this neighbourhood but their territories
are around Medziadin lake.[69]

In a second interview, Albert Williams described the Frog-Raven Clan
territories:

House of Wudaxhayetsxw
On the Nass tributary name Gilt'in[70] falling into the Cranberry River from
the mouth of the river near to the source. Gihlt'in (fishtrap) is the name
of the territory. On this territory there is another on the upper part which
is called Gwunstim'on[71] (meaning ? [where like]/humpback [salmon]) –
hunt beaver and general hunting. Also melit (Steelhead) and trout and
coho. The spring and sockeye do not run this river there is no lake for
them. House: G.epg.isu[72] at the junction of the two rivers. They have a
fish fence with which they block the river across Cranberry from which
they derive the name of G.epg.isu (barricade [fish]). The Cranberry is
named Ksiyag.askit[73] (water/down along/laying) – three days walking on
this territory from lower end to upper end. It includes the entire valley
of the Gihltin and the mountain tops nearby. Neighbours: Yaxyaq,[74]
neighbour towards the Nass. And further down the Nass people. Neighbour up the Cranberry: Luxon[75] and G.amlaxyelk.[76]

House of Gamlaxyeltxw
Starting from [the territory of] Wudaxayets on the Cranberry River (confluence of Nass) up to the fifty mile post from here (Gitwanga) on the

western side of the Cranberry only (that is downward the Nass). Next to Wudaxayets up to the fifty mile post. Gihlmihlg.en [Gwinmihlgan] (half/burned/wood) is the name of the river or creek on this territory falling into the Cranberry. They have no general name for the territory. One big fishing station at the mouth of Gihlmihlgen. They have a t'in right in the rapids and canyon there. All kinds of game on this territory. Also bears. Other territory ... including the ground between the Cranberry to the Nass upwards up to Anxtsimelixnagets[77] (place/eat/beaver/ wolverine). They had one salmon station at 'Wunsg.ahlku'l (where narrows) near the Stewart trail where it meets the Nass. Wunsg.ahlku'n. The beaver on this territory to be had on the lakes all along.

House of Ya<u>x</u>ya<u>k</u>
General hunting ground. T'amginepdza.ux [?] (lake of/?) is the lake on this territory and also salmon fishing station on the other side of the river on Nass and Cranberry Kunkse.'l [?] (meaning ?).

House of Lu<u>x</u>oon
All the river Kinsg.o.ix (place of fording [transporting]) (split Kinskuch) north of the Nass. Right to the source and also all the creeks falling into it. All the laxse'el of Gitwinkul have their territories together here but separated from each other. They get beaver here and all other animals and berries. No salmon station. No salmon ran that river. Trout. No other territory.[78]

James Hayts'imsxw also spoke to Barbeau and Beynon in 1924 concerning his own territory and that of Gwinuu:

Houses of Gwinuu and Tigewin
They have the same hunting grounds ... mountain range away from this side of the Nass at the mouth of the Gihltin. To the north shore Laxg.adihl(t?)[79] (meaning ? [Tsetsaut name]) is the name of the hunting ground. Another hunting ground at the headwaters of the Gihlt'in – a mountain ... Wunbaxtahlkibu[80] (where up sits the wolf) a mountain ... Anmaxslo'p[81] (where grow rocks) another mountain – It extends from the Gitwinhlkul village to this point. Tsim'anmaqhl[82] (in where the trail leads up). It is a mountain territory. From this territory there is a creek (river) falling into the headwaters of the Gihltin [Gyahlt'in]. It is known as Ksa'anaxtemi.t[83] and the river is the property of Kwinu on the north side only. Hlegwax [Hlengwa<u>x</u>] owns the other side. And all the little tributaries to this side belong to Kwinu [Gwinuu].

House of Hayts'imsxw
Qakspaxskit (just up laid). It includes mountains and many (3) lakes. Beaver and marten and general hunting and bear and caribou ... They

have a fishing station on the Nass. Kwunhaqx (place of geese) Kwung-ibu[84] (where boils [swift waters]) is another fishing station.[85]

The record of Barbeau and Beynon shows the ability of the Gitanyow chiefs (and, as will be seen later, the Gitksan and Nisga'a chiefs) to identify specific geographic features within their territories; it demonstrates powerfully their detailed knowledge of the territory and the history of the names on the territory. What better proof exists under Aboriginal law (or, for that matter, under any oral legal system) than intimate identification of place names, names tied to the history of the acquisition of that territory and site. The evidence recorded by both Barbeau and Beynon in the 1920s from the Gitksan and the Nisga'a in this respect displays these Aboriginal nations' knowledge of their own territories.

Other Gitanyow Protests and Territorial Claims (1919-36)

Between 1919 and 1936, the Gitanyow undertook a considerable array of protest activity addressing the question of their ownership and control of their territories. The following excerpts from documents are limited to statements in which there is direct reference to the extent or location of Gitanyow territories. The accompanying map (see Map 12) shows the area referred to by Gitanyow spokespersons below.

E.L. Davies, a rancher at Kitwanga, was turned back by the Gitanyow in September 1919 when he attempted to travel in their valley. In describing the incident, he stated: "Further I wish to state that the Indians [Gitanyow] claim all the country 60 miles wide and 115 miles long, starting at 10 mile post on the road running into the [Kitwanga] valley. They further said that they would not allow any white man to settle in this valley beyond 10 mile.[86]

The statement of H. du Vernet, another rancher at Kitwanga, in November 1919 shows that the Gitanyow had long been defending their territories: "I have lived here since July 27th, 1910, and have seen many men come into our district with a view to establishing stock ranches, but in every case they have been turned back by the natives of the Kitwancool villages. These natives claim the whole of the Kitwancool Valley, from five miles to the Nass River. They have at different times refused to have any established reserves."[87]

Indian Agent W.E. Collison wrote a letter to Ditchburn dated 31 May 1920 and transmitted a report on the situation at Gitanyow.[88] Much of the document is concerned with land for potential reserves and its use by the Gitanyow – hence only with the area as far as Gitanyow Lake. But Collison adds: "It was apparent from the outset of our investigation [at Gitanyow in May] that the question of Aboriginal Title was uppermost in the minds of the Kitwancool Indians and that no real settlement would be acceptable to them until this vexed question is disposed of."[89] Collison, in a letter to Ditchburn on 7 February 1922, blamed outside agitators for the situation at Gitanyow: "This small band of Indians ... [are] victims of a propaganda which has taken full advantage of their ignorance. They have been informed from time to time that their case is now before the Privy Council and that if they hold out long enough, their claim to the whole of the Kitwancool valley and the territory as far as the Medziaden lake on the upper Nass River will be granted."[90]

A.P. Horne, a forestry engineer from Hazelton, made a trip up the Kitwanga valley in the summer of 1924. On reaching Gitanyow, he was prevented from proceeding any farther. At the meeting with the Gitanyow chiefs, he was informed: "'We beg to state that it was the wish of our ancestors, as it is our wish, that all the products on that area north of the nine-mile pole in this [Kitwanga] valley, and for the distance in that direction of 115 miles by 60 miles east and west, remain ours.' The claims of the Indians may or may not be reasonable in this instance, but I am thoroughly convinced that they solemnly – very solemnly – believe that they are protecting their rights."[91]

H.H. Jebson, of the RCMP, in a letter to his superior dated 9 September 1924, describes a trip to Gitanyow with Indian Agent Edward Hyde. This trip followed more incidents of denial of access. At the meeting, Ebid Palmer of Gitanyow stated: "Our forefathers handed down to us land extending 125 miles north from Kitwanga, and 65 miles wide, and we refuse to accept this offer [of reserves] made to us by the Government."[92]

Ditchburn, in a letter to Inspector McMullin of the provincial police dated 1 October 1924, discussed the above incidents and reported: "The action of these Indians is, in my opinion, on account of the desire to have some action taken with regard to their claims for the extinguishment of the Aboriginal Title, as you will observe that they claim tribal ownership over an area alleged to be 65 miles wide and 125 miles long extending from about 9 miles North of Kitwangah into the upper Nass Valley which would make a total of 8,125 square miles or 5,199,900 acres." Ditchburn recommended that "the Kitwancool Valley should be policed by the Provincial Government sufficiently to ensure free access, ingress or occupation of the Valley by travellers or intending settlers of lands, other than those set apart as Indian Reserves or on which Indians may have their hunting lodges, for I believe there are a considerable number of these in the area above Kitwancool Lake up to the headwaters of the Nass River."[93]

In 1927, five Gitanyow leaders protested DIA attempts to survey reserves allotted to the Gitanyow by confiscating the surveyors' equipment and insisting that they leave. The leaders were arrested, and all but one were imprisoned. V. Schjelderup, one of the surveyors, described the circumstances in a letter to J.D. McLean: "I have to report that I have been held up in preceding [sic] with my work in the Kitwancool Valley owing to the hostility of the Indians claiming this valley. The R.C.M. Police to whom I applied for assistance arrested five of the leaders on Wednesday the 24th inst. and the whole party including myself had to withdraw from the valley as we all were wanted as witnesses. The camp and equipment was left in the valley."[94] The arrest and imprisonment of the Gitanyow leaders were reported in the *Province* newspaper on 3 September 1927: "Five Kitwancool Indians were convicted at Smithers by Magistrate Hoskins of assaulting public officers and obstructing Dominion Government surveyors. With the exception of Richard Douse, who was let off on suspended sentence, jail terms of from one to three months were imposed on Bert (Albert) Williams, Peter Williams, Samuel Douse and Walter Derrick."[95] The Gitanyow thereafter called the Gitanyow Indian Reserve the "Oakalla Prison Reserve" because of this incident.[96]

Protests continued after this incident in spite of the prison terms. In 1928 Albert Williams, on behalf of the Gitanyow people, wrote to the local RCMP: "Think it over about our land. God gave this land to our forefathers generations, that why we know this is our own Kitwancool land. Because all the village knows about this. Also the Alask natif [Alaska native] people know about our land. Almight God give this land to our forefather. White people know about our land the Kitwancool land 60 × 150 mile."[97] Williams also wrote to the provincial minister of lands denying any connection with "the questions and complaints or claims whatsoever of the so-called THE INDIAN ALLIED TRIBES." This is a reference to the hearings and report of the Special Joint Committee of the House and Senate, which rejected claims to Aboriginal title. Williams continued by defining the territory claimed by the Gitanyow: "We, hereby, mention the size of our lands of Kitwancool, commencing at the nine (9) mile post north of Kitwanga, approximately one (1) hundred and fifty miles in length northerly, and approximately sixty miles in broad at the widest area." He also referred to a report sent to the attorney general of British Columbia on 5 September 1927 and to a petition recently sent to the governor general.[98]

Williams, on behalf of the Gitanyow Land Committee, wrote to the provincial government on 2 December 1929 to protest white encroachment: "The Committee has been informed that white men are settling at 50 miles Post, and at 55 mile Post near Nass and that Road are being build through the Kitwancool land along Nass River starting into the Kitwancool lands at 15 mile Post east of Gitlakdamiks village Nass River B.C. This we desire to be deferred for some time until we, and the Provincial Government Reach final arrangement."[99]

C.C. Perry of the Department of Indian Affairs, in a letter to Agent Mortimer dated 19 February 1934, discussed a petition sent by the Gitanyow to the governor general. The petition, dated 25 February 1932, was accompanied by a letter from Peter Williams, son of Albert Williams. It was referred to the SGIA.

In 1936 the Gitanyow Land Committee sought to bring a case to the Exchequer Court of Canada. In a letter to the local Indian agent, Peter Williams, on behalf of the committee, sought DIA assistance to pursue this objective: "That the exchequer court of Canada may determine the extent, validity, and the nature of the Kitwancool land rights or the Indian Land rights of the Kitwancool."[100] No reply was received from the agent, and the request was then sent to the Department of Indian Affairs in Ottawa.

What these protests and claims have in common is the continued assertion of ownership of territory, by Gitanyow hereditary chiefs, to and beyond the Nass River. The claim was widely publicized, and it would be ludicrous to suggest that the Nisga'a were not aware of the scope of the Gitanyow territory on the Nass.

The Gitanyow Trapline (c. 1930)

The Gitanyow trapline is unique. Unlike most Aboriginal groups, the Gitanyow had registered a "block" trapline over most of their ancestral territory by 1930. 'Wiilitsxw had registered nearly his entire territory in and around Meziadin Lake in 1926.[101] Although established by 1930, it suddenly became of concern to the Nisga'a in 1961. The following discussion deals with the origin of the Gitanyow trapline and the Nisga'a reaction in 1961.

In 1926 the provincial government decided to institute a system of registered traplines as a form of wildlife management. This was a source of great discontent among the people of the Nass and Skeena Rivers, as well as Aboriginal people throughout the province. One problem was the requirement that an Indian person, or company (group of persons), could only hold one trapline at a time, while under the Gitksan and Nisga'a systems, if the house held more than one territory, the hereditary chief managed all the territories belonging to the house.

Another problem was that the Indian agent and the provincial conservation officer, who were jointly responsible for registering and managing traplines, did not appreciate or understand the matrilineal inheritance system of the Gitksan and Nisga'a. As a result, some traplines, on the death of the holder, were passed on to the male holder's son, rather than to a nephew or niece. Thus, in order to determine the "correct" ownership of a trapline, it is necessary to establish which house or clan held the trapline at the time of first registration.

Most chiefs in Gitksan and Nisga'a territories registered their hunting grounds individually. However, the Gitanyow people rejected this approach and registered a single trapline over most of their territories.[102] Peter Williams, then president of Gitanyow, and a member of the Land Claims Committee, summarized the origin and evolution of the Kitwancool (Gitanyow) trapline for the benefit of the Gitksan Land Claims Advisory Committee on 1 February 1979:

Kitwancool hold a single registry over their entire territory. This area is registered as the trapping and hunting grounds of the Kitwancool.

The Kitwancool people decided to form a union to hold their grounds rather than register individually as was done elsewhere. This was done in the 1920's.

Originally the land was registered under one simoighet [chief] – Gwasslam (Walter Douse) but later 2 simoighets [chiefs] from each pdek [clan] became the governors over the entire Ansilenisxw [territory] on behalf of all Kitwancool people ...

The advantage of this is that the history of each house holds good as the basis for authority and rights on the hunting and trapping grounds.

Each house respects the rights and laws of the other two houses.

At the time of this registration, some non-Indians were registering in Kitwancool territory. The Kitwancool appealed to the ... game dept and the non-Indians withdrew.

All Kitwancool descendants have the right to use their respectful lands, and can do so by consulting with the capital (Kitwancool) first.

Kitwancool will respect its neighbours if the blanket registered area inadvertently over-lapped the neighbours land.[103]

In short the "Kitwancool" trapline, which includes territory from the village of Gitanyow to beyond Meziadin Lake, represents in part the Gitanyow ancestral claim (see Map 23).

The Nisga'a leadership allege that they only became aware of the Gitanyow trapline in 1961, even though it was common knowledge that traplines had been registered throughout the Nass Valley about three decades earlier (c. 1930). It is also on record that, soon after the Nisga'a Tribal Council was organized in the 1950s, and while lobbying provincial politicians in Victoria on their land claim, a Nisga'a delegation expressed concern about Michael Bright's role in registering the Gitanyow trapline. According to Frank Calder, the delegation[104] "confronted" Wilson Duff, provincial ethnologist of the Royal British Columbia Museum at Victoria, about the memoir that he published on Gitanyow history and territoriality in 1959 (see below), which "included a map which outlined the traplines in the Nass Valley that were registered in the names of several Kitwancool trappers – a map which, according to Mr. Duff, originated with Chief Michael Inspring Bright of Aiyansh."[105]

It is difficult to know how the Nisga'a could construe the map of Gitanyow territory in their 1959 publication *Histories, Territories and Laws of the Kitwancool* as an outline of "traplines in the Nass Valley" (see Appendix 8). Nevertheless, the Nisga'a returned to the Nass Valley and organized a "special convention at Aiyansh, in November 1961 to confront Bright with accusations of conspiracy with the Gitanyow. During the 'packed assembly' Bright allegedly admitted that he 'drafted the trapline map which eventually reached the office of Mr. Wilson Duff in Victoria.'"[106]

There are two issues here: first, that Bright drew a trapline map; and second, that it was the basis for the map in Duff's memoir. The first point may be true, but if such a map exists, it has yet to surface. The second point is not true. Gitanyow chiefs based at the village of Gitanyow provided Duff with the information needed to produce the map outlining Gitanyow territory (see below). Furthermore, if Duff was aware of Bright's map, it was likely because he had first encountered it during his work with the Barbeau-Beynon files in Ottawa some years earlier.

Perhaps the Nisga'a leadership wish to imply that Bright's 1926 map of Gitanyow (and Nisga'a) place names, fishing sites, and associated chiefs is the basis for Duff's map. This may be true in part, but as the documentary record clearly demonstrates, the chiefs resident at their ancestral village, Gitanyow, had been drawing maps even more detailed than the memoir map for at least fifty years. More significantly, Duff's work with Fred Good, Walter Douse, Peter Williams, and other Gitanyow leaders is well documented in his files and shows that their knowledge of Gitanyow history and geography was immense.[107]

To continue with Calder's account of the Aiyansh assembly, Bright apparently admitted that "he had allocated and registered the names of a number of his friends and relatives from Kitwancool to certain traplines from the Kinskuch River northward to the Bell Irving River in the Nass River Valley."[108] In this instance, the issues must be separated: Bright's involvement in registering traplines, his role in the Gitanyow trapline, and Gitanyow territoriality. As a Gitanyow chief, Bright had a right to register his "friends and relatives from Kitwancool" to traplines, although his role in the Gitanyow trapline is not known. Regardless of his role in registering traplines, the territory involved belonged to the Gitanyow, and Bright knew it. This should be no surprise to anyone, least of all the Nisga'a. The Gitanyow and Nisga'a documentary record is clear. Perhaps the new leaders were not aware in 1961 that prominent Nisga'a and Gitanyow chiefs had affirmed the Nisga'a boundary at Gitxsits'uuts'xwt on the Nass River nearly fifty years earlier during the MMRC hearings (see Chapter 5) and in other forums.

According to Calder, "Bright admitted" that he "registered those traplines contrary to the advice of B.C. Indian leaders in 1927."[109] Perhaps

Calder is not aware that the Nisga'a also registered traplines in 1926.[110] Bright apparently admitted that he "did not inform the Nisga'a people of his activities on behalf of the Kitwancool community" and concluded his remarks with "an assurance that, as one who had originally come from Kitwancool, he would have no difficulty in counselling the people there to abandon their claim of land in the Nass River Valley."[111] Bright was born, and died, a member of the Gitksan nation, village of Gitanyow. He was first and foremost a member of the House of 'Wiix̱a. His responsibility was to record for posterity his ancestral lands between Gitanyow, Gitxsits'uuts'xwt, and Meziadin Lake and to convey Gitanyow history to his nephews and nieces. There was no reason for him to inform the Nisga'a about lands that do not concern them. Finally, it is unbelievable that he would counsel the Gitanyow to "abandon their claim": as a Gitanyow hereditary chief by birth and upbringing, Bright could not, and would not, counsel his people to reverse their own history.

It is a tribute to the foresight of Gitanyow chiefs at the village of Gitanyow, and on the Nass River, that they attempted to record their ancestral territory as a single registered trapline in 1926. The subsequent administration of traplines by the provincial government, and conflicting cultures (systems of inheritance, etc.), have resulted in a trapline today that shows the pattern, but is less than the whole, of Gitanyow territory.

Royal Commission on Forestry (1956)

By 1956 tremendous changes had occurred in Gitanyow territory: an economic boom following the Second World War led to an interest in the vast forests in Gitanyow territories on the Nass River, and changes to the Indian Act in 1951 affected the daily lives of the Gitanyow with the removal of the "Potlatch Laws."

It was partly in this context that Peter Williams and Walter Douse, on behalf of the Gitanyow, made a submission to the Royal Commission on Forestry in March 1956 after the provincial government had opened the Nass Valley to clearcut logging. The Gitanyow submission sought to impress on the government that their land claim should be settled and that they should have timber harvesting rights on their ancestral lands between Gitanyow and Meziadin:

> 5. The Kitwancool Natives should be legally given priority to obtain Timber sale limits on the ground that the Kitwancool maintain its own road from ten mile post and Northward. That a Timbersale limit within the Kitwancool boundary may not be sold by publi[c] auction untill [sic] a satisfactory settlement of the Kitwancool LAND controversy between them and the Brit[ish] Columbia Government is established.

6. That the Forest Management already given to the Columbia Cellulose, in the region of Maiziadin [Meziadin] Lake, which is within the Kitwancool boundary, as we consider that they are wasting other Timbers and young trees and will also destroy our trap lines and fur industry, and should be cancelled untill [sic] a satisfactory settlement is established by the Kitwancool and the Government of Bri[t]ish Columbia.

Williams and Douse stressed the basis for their demands:

8. We humbly assure all Governments concerned that the Kitwancool are the rightful owner of the Kitwancool lands from time immemorial and therefore we humbly pray for a satisfactory settlement.

11. The Kitwancool beg to inform the Government that the Maiziadin Lake regions was the price of the Kitwancool blood caused by the people now known as "Stickine People" after they massacre the Kitwancool which resulted in war until the said "Stickine People" surrender the [M]aiziadin Lake region to the Kitwancool people. Did the Government of British Columbia bought the Kitwancool lands from the Kitwancool? Did the British Columbia Government or any Government ever bought the Kitwancool lands or make treaty with the Kitwancool like Sir James Douglas in the early days?[112]

Of this document, Mr. Locke, commission counsel, stated: "It appears to be very much tied up with certain agreements which have been made between the Government of British Columbia and the Kitwancool Band concerning the Meziadin Lake region."[113]

Despite the impact of industry and government on the lives and lands of the Gitanyow, they sustained a single-minded quest for recognition of their ancient claims to the Nass River and Meziadin Lake.

Gitanyow Petitions of 1958 and 1962

As British Columbia celebrated its centennial in 1958, the Gitanyow submitted to the provincial government a request for an honourable and negotiated settlement. The document, which expressed concern about the allocation of a tree farm licence to Columbia Cellulose over Gitanyow traditional territories to and including land around Meziadin Lake, included the following statements: "the forest management already given to the Columbia Cellulose, in the region of Meziadin Lake, which is within the Kitwancool boundary ... The Kitwancool beg to in-form the Governments concerned that Meziadin lake region was and is the price of the Kitwancool blood shed caused by the people now known as the 'Stikine People' after they massacre the Kitwancool which resulted in war until the said 'Stickine People' surrender the Meziadin Lake region to the Kitwancool People."

The latter point was repeated in another request sent to the provincial government in 1962: "The Kitwancool already give both Governments information that the lands at the Maziadin region and along the NASS River was the price of the Kitwancool blood and therefore, Honourable Gentlemen, because the Provincial Government of British Columbia make their Law and enforce their Laws within the Kitwancool territory without first come to any agreement with the Kitwancool, the Kitwancool respectfully pray for a settlement for the benefit of all the Canadian citizens, as well as the Kitwancools, without any longer delay."[114] Here the Gitanyow refer to their adaaw<u>k</u> and to their ownership of territory at Meziadin Lake.

Histories, Territories and Laws of the Kitwancool (1957-9)

In the late 1950s, the Gitanyow took advantage of the interest expressed by Wilson Duff in preserving Gitanyow's totem poles. When Duff and Provincial Archivist Willard Ireland presented their project to the Gitanyow, they agreed, on the condition that Duff write and publish their statements of territorial ownership as evidenced in their adaaw<u>k</u> and on their totem poles.

A committee was organized, and an interpreter (Constance Cox) was hired to assist with translation of the narratives to be related by Gitanyow elders about their histories and territories. This culminated in the publication, by the BC Provincial Museum, of a memoir, with the aforementioned title. Included in the memoir was a map of Gitanyow territories (see Appendix 8). This map was based in part on one loaned by Fred Good.[115]

The memoir provides details about the history of the Gitanyow, including their wars with the Tsetsaut and their acquisition of Tsetsaut territories. It describes Gitanyow territories from near the village of Kitwanga on the Skeena River to the Nass River at Gitxsits'uuts'xwt and beyond Meziadin Lake to Xsigisi'am'maldit (Surveyors Creek) at Bowser Lake:

> There is a piece of territory that starts at Mile 53 and goes on beyond the Nass River, following the mountain ranges. It includes all tributaries flowing easterly into the Nass River and west of Kinskuch River and northwesterly to Meziadin Lake, thence northerly to the headwaters of the Cottonwood River (Surveyor's Creek) near Bowser Lake, thence easterly beyond the Nass to the top of the mountain range, thence southerly to a point 40 miles north of Kispiox on the Kispiox River (the mountain which is the boundary is called Lip-ha-hut-quk), thence southerly to the headwaters of Douglas Creek at the mountain called Gwen-ga-nik, and thence westerly to the point of commencement.

These boundary lines take in all the trapping and hunting territory of the Kitwancool people. The united power and title of all this land belongs to the people of Kitwancool.[116]

This description provides exceptional detail about the Gitanyow border, especially on the Nass River at Gitxsits'uuts'xwt and on the Bell-Irving River at Surveyors Creek, and corroborates the many statements made and the maps produced by the Gitanyow.

The memoir is clear about the Gitanyow claim to territories on the Nass: "The Kitwancool might be said to belong more to the Nass than to the Skeena, for their territories extended far to the north and, in fact, included more of the Nass Valley than was held by the Nass [Nisga'a] tribes themselves."[117]

It is significant, in closing, that Wilson Duff, an acknowledged expert[118] on the peoples of the Northwest Coast, was called to testify by the Nisga'a after he had published the Gitanyow material. The Gitanyow memoir is a concise statement of ownership by the Gitanyow and is consistent with their maps and statements over the years.

Gitanyow Research Submission (1978)

Peter Williams spent nearly his entire life in a dignified and single-minded quest for a just settlement of the Gitanyow land claim. After the federal government initiated its land claims policy in the 1970s, as the president of Gitanyow (and with the assistance of Gitanyow land claims resource persons), he wrote a detailed submission on the Gitanyow land claim to the federal government. This 1978 submission contains information relevant to this study.

The Nass River was the proposed site for a CN rail line. An archeological study was undertaken, and both Aiyansh and Gitanyow informants were consulted:

And as a result, the knowledge of several Kitwancool band members led the archaeological survey to the discovery of several sites near the confluence of the Cranberry and Kiteen Rivers, and along the Nass River.

Site 5 was identified by Aiyansh informants as being the fishing camp named Gitsheoaksit [Gitxsits'uuts'xwt], belonging to Chief Skat'iin of the Wolf Clan. The location of this site is the south bank of the Nass River, 200 yards upstream [sic], opposite the mouth of the Tchitin River. This is outside the Kitwancool boundary and has never been included in their maps.

Site 2 is located at the junction of the Kiteen and Cranberry Rivers on the north side of the Cranberry, well within the Kitwancool boundary. A cabin which belonged to Chief Wi-tax-ha-yetsxw of the Frog Clan once occupied this spot ... The area is now covered by dense bracken and nettle undergrowth and no trace of the cabin could be found.[119]

Nass River Boundary
The boundary which lies between the Kitwancool and Git-lak-damax is at the ancient village of Git-kse-'tsuutsxw, the history of which is recorded in the *Histories, Territories and Laws of the Kitwancool*. This is the village where Fred Good's grandfather stayed, and his mother was raised there until she grown up. Today the site is a grassy plain, high above the Nass Canyon's west bank. It is owned by Chiefs K'am-lax-yeltxw, Sindihl, and Sin-Gi-win of the Frog-Raven clan of Kitwancool.

Running back over the mountain ridge of Lax-wijix[120] thus including the entire valley of Gins-Guux owned by Luu-xhoon and 'Tsii-wa, the boundary line extends back to Win-naa-skan-gymdit,[121] bordering the territory ruled by Gwaas-hlaa'm and 'Wii-xa'a. The line then runs in a north-westerly direction to the glaciated country called 'Kse-s'yun.[122]

On the east side of the Nass opposite Git-kse-'tsuutsxw, a small creek called Ksi-tekw spills over the canyon wall. The Git-lak-damax people own the land on the other [south] side of the creek. Two smokehouses once stood on the other side, belonging to K'yee-xaxw[123] (Wolf clan), and Ksem-xsaan[124] (Frog Clan) of Git-lak-damax. Fred Good recalls that as a young boy, a fifteen foot pole once marked the boundary line. A large rock was placed on the top of the pole, which was called xhlgi-meda-sook,[125] or "robin's egg."

On the Kitwancool side of Ksi Tekw is the place named K'il-hla-lo'op'-bit.[126] Here once stood a [Gitanyow] Frog tribe smoke house, of which no sign remained on exploration in April 1977.

From K'il-hla-lo'op-bit, the boundary line runs along Ksi-tekw and then crosses over Lax-sak-gat,[127] or Jackpine Mountain, towards the Gyehl-'tin or Kiteen River. Wi tax-ha-yetsxw[128] and Sidook[129] rule over the Kiteen Valley. Gib-xasxw[130] is the name of the village where they stay.[131]

The information provided here is consistent with the information contained on Michael Bright's 1926 map, and it does not contradict any information provided by Gitksan and Nisga'a witnesses to the MMRC hearings.

Gitanyow Fieldwork in the 1980s
In addition to the vast body of information set out by Gitanyow elders orally in hearings and in writing in publications initiated by them, the Gitanyow initiated research in the 1980s. In 1983 Glen Williams accompanied other Gitanyow elders and recorded information on their behalf.[132]

Following is a synopsis of the work carried out in Gitanyow territories in the Nass watershed at this time:

Txaslaxwiiyip
Xsigisi'am'maldit (Surveyors Creek)
An'sgeexs
T'am'matsiiadin (Meziadin Lake)
Anlaagahl T'ax'matsiiadin
   (Meziadin River)
Lax'andzok
Xsitxemsem (Nass River)
Hlguhlsga'nist
Sga'nisimhabasxw
Luubaxgagat
Anda'gansgotsinak
Anxmilit
Anxt'imi'it
Gyahlt'in (Kiteen River)
Xsiyagasgiit (middle Cranberry River)
Xsi'anxts'imilixnaagets (Wolverine
   Creek)
Winsgahlgu'l
Nadiloodit (Brown Bear Lake and
   area)
Anlagamsto'oks
Aksnagyalga (Axnegelga Creek)
Gaksbaxsgiit
Gwinsgox (Kinskuch River)
Xsimaaxsxwt (White River)
Sis'yun (Cambria Icefield)
Anlo'obitlogots
Xsimihlhetxwt (Derrick Creek)
Laxwijix
Xsit'ax (Gitanyow-Nisga'a boundary
   on Nass River, UNGM)
G'ilhlalo'obit (Gitanyow-Nisga'a
   boundary area, UNGM)

Laxsagat (Jackpine Mountain)
Gipgasxw
Txasginax
Xsigwa'angamt (Weber Creek)
Xsi'gwin'aaxwit
Gin'milit (Mount Weber)
Wiilax'gelt
Angildipdaw'it
Xsi'anskeexs (upper Cranberry River)
Sga'nismluulak (aka T'saphl'luulak)
Wii'laahabasxw
Xsi'win'saagiihl'matx
Xsigwits'ilaasxwt (Tsugwinselda
   Creek)
Xsidaniigoot (Weegett/Aluk Creek)
T'amansingekw
T'amlilbax (Sideslip Lake)
Xsits'adagat
T'xasts'adagat
Xsi'andilgan
Xsigwinadapxw
Win'luu'axit'os
Xsiwinluu'axit'os (Little Paw Creek)
Xsigiil'a (Paw Creek)
T'amgiil'a (Paw Lake)
Xsi'tselasxwt (lower Moore-Gleason
   Creek; aka Xsi'ansi'biins)
Sga'nismgohl (Lavender Mountain)
T'amgwinsgox (Kinskuch Lake)
Anhahl'yee (east slope of Hanna
   Ridge)
Xsi'anhahl'yee (upper Hanna Creek)
Xsigwinsalda[133]

As well, prior to this research, in 1982, Ts'iiwa, Art Matthews Sr. (c. 1914-91), of Gitanyow, with Gwisgyen, Stanley Williams (c. 1907-89), of Kitsegyukla, travelled to the Kiteen watershed to map Gitksan place names and territories, including those near the Gitwingax/Gitanyow border at Anxt'imi'it:

Xsa'anxt'imi'it (lower Stenstrom
   Creek)
Lo'oba'gilats'o'oxs
Xsi'skahawagat
Ts'imanmakhl

Xsi'anlek'maawks
Xsi'gwits'oo (upper Kiteen River)
Skahawagat (upper Stenstrom
   Creek)
Xsilaxts'ilaasxwt[134]

Gitanyow fieldwork in recent years shows that they have detailed knowledge of their territory, and are able to identify and name geographic features throughout the claim area.

Conclusion

The Aboriginal documentary record in this chapter shows that the Gitanyow have retained a powerful presence on their territory in the Nass watershed up to the present day. This has been demonstrated verbally and cartographically in a consistent manner for more than 100 years. Cartographic evidence, in particular a series of maps of Gitanyow territory produced between 1910 and 1926, provides proof that the Gitanyow claim is unique and encompasses the Nass watershed from Gitxsits'uuts'xwt to beyond Meziadin Lake.

More specifically, the territorial descriptions by Gitanyow chiefs in the MMRC hearings at Aiyansh and Gitlakdamix in 1915 are crucial. First, the descriptions were made in front of Nisga'a chiefs; second, the Nisga'a chiefs did not dispute the Gitanyow descriptions of their territory; third, they were made only two years after circulation of the famous Nisga'a Petition of 1913; fourth, their descriptions are consistent with their adaawk from the ancient times to and including the 1861 settlement with the Tsetsaut at Meziadin Lake; and fifth, their descriptions of their territory right to the boundary with the Nisga'a at Gitxsits'uuts'xwt are consistent with all Gitanyow mapping of their territory and with the Nisga'a chiefs' descriptions of their territory in the same MMRC hearings (see Chapter 5).

Gitanyow chiefs seized the opportunity to have their statements recorded when ethnologists sought to "study" them, beginning early in the twentieth century, statements that have been consistent to the present day.

The record also shows that some Gitanyow chiefs and house members moved into several Nisga'a villages toward the end of the nineteenth century and that they retained their association with their ancestral village, Gitanyow. And although they specifically retained the privilege to utilize Gitanyow territory with Gitanyow-based house members, they did not carry title to the Nisga'a territory.

Because of their presence in some Nisga'a villages, Gitanyow territory was included in the Nisga'a Petitions of 1908 and 1913. But the record is clear: this was a brief alliance on broad principles and came to a head in 1926 when the Gitanyow formally withdrew from the Nisga'a effort, and Gitanyow chiefs, resident at their ancestral village, continued to assert a separate and distinct claim (with maps accurately setting out the whole of Gitanyow territory) from 1910 to the present day.

The evidence shows not only that the Gitanyow have an ancient presence in the Nass River valley from Gitxsits'uuts'xwt on upstream but also that they have publicly asserted their ownership of their territories for as long as Euro-Canadian individuals and governments have attempted to take their lands without treaty.

4
The Gitksan Documentary Record: Kuldo, Kisgaga'as, and Kispiox

Introduction

Statements of ownership concerning specific Gitksan and Nisga'a territories were recorded in various situations as incursions into their territories proceeded. Euro-Canadians seeking resources most in demand at the time were among the first to come to the northwest: they sought fur, gold, arable farmland, and transportation corridors. They were followed by missionaries and ultimately by government agents.

The chronology of these statements often parallels the lines of Euro-Canadian expansion into the region. For this reason, early statements of ownership are more numerous among the Gitanyow than among the Gitksan farther inland. Some Gitksan territories have been affected only recently, beginning in the 1970s, as logging companies pushed into previously inaccessible areas such as Kuldo. Also in this modern period, the forum for protest has moved from government departments to the legal system, and the written record, previously in statements to various commissions and correspondence to government departments, is more recently found in court documents. Since Kisgaga'as and Kuldo use of their territories has been relatively unaffected by development until recently, the written record for the region begins, for the most part, in this later period.

The village of Kisgaga'as is located on the Babine River near its confluence with the Skeena. Kisgaga'as territories extend northeast to beyond Bear Lake and the head of the Skeena, and north to include the Blackwater-Groundhog Mountain area in the Nass watershed. Kuldo, a village located on the Skeena River west of Kisgaga'as, includes territory in the Nass watershed to and including Bowser Lake and the Bell-Irving River. Kispiox territories extend to the Nass watershed at Kwinageese Lake and at the head of the Nass River north of Blackwater Lake. In spite of their remoteness, however, Gitksan chiefs from these villages did address the issue of their territories in a number of forums in the first part of the century. Specific statements concerning territories are also found in ethnographic research by Marius Barbeau, Diamond Jenness, and Wilson Duff and in land claims research initiated by a Gitksan elder, Luus, Chris Harris, of Kispiox.

In 1972 the provincial government finally completed initial construction of the Stewart-Cassiar Highway, a 500-kilometre link between Kitwanga and Dease Lake. The government also promoted the idea of a railway through the Nass River valley to access forest and mineral resources in the northwest. Almost simultaneously, on the heels of the *Calder* v. *Attorney General of British Columbia* decision, the Gitksan began to prepare for a land claims process that they expected to end in negotiations. Instead, in the 1980s, they were compelled by the provincial government's refusal to negotiate to move the process to the courts. The preparations for land claims negotiations, and subsequently for their court case, *Delgamuukw* v. *The Queen*, included the collection of a written and cartographic record of their territories. In this record – for the most part collected by Madeegam Gyamk, Neil J. Sterritt, with the chiefs and elders in the 1970s and 1980s – can be found much of the written information concerning the Kisgaga'as, Kuldo, and Kispiox territories on the upper Nass.

The Gitksan Petition of 1908 and Statements of Ownership to the Stewart-Vowell Commission (1909)

In 1908 the chiefs of Kuldo, Kisgaga'as, and Kispiox participated in the Gitksan Petition submitted to Prime Minister Laurier. Unfortunately, there is no extant copy. The following year, after a series of incidents in Gitksan territory, the government responded by sending the Stewart-Vowell Commission to gather information on Gitksan grievances.[1] Meetings were held at Hazelton on 13 and 14 July 1909. Only newspaper accounts survive. The following describes the relevant part of the meeting:

Each tribe was represented by a spokesman, who presented each tribe's troubles and demands in turn, each spokesman practically repeating what the first one set forth.

Basing their contention on the assumption that all the land belonged to them to be heredity [sic] and that whites had taken it without conquest or remuneration, they practically asked that the whole country be surrendered to them.

This would involve dispensing with the present system of reserves, the establishment of their ancient tribal laws and customs for the government of the territory and the forfeiture of all rights, claims and interests of the whites etc., practically the establishment of the conditions existing before the white man came among them.

While claims were made separately for the surrender of each tribal chief's "lands of his forefathers," collectively it would involve the entire country.[2]

This passage is significant because it demonstrates the persistence of the Gitksan claim to territory, even though its particular location is not specified.

Kuldo, Kisgaga'as, and Kispiox Ownership Statements: McKenna-McBride Commission Hearings (Babine Agency, 1915)

The McKenna-McBride Commission met with the representatives of Gitanmaax, Kispiox, and Glen Vowell in April 1915 and with the upriver villages – Kisgaga'as and Kuldo – in July 1915.

The meetings with the Gitksan from Gitanmaax (Hazelton), Glen Vowell, and Kispiox were brief and marked with impatience and a degree of hostility by the commissioners. The Gitksan did little more than make opening comments before the commissioners ended the meetings. On 21 April 1915, the hearings opened at "Getanamx." After the chairman explained the scope and purpose of the commission, Edward Spouk[3] of Gitanmaax addressed the commission, explaining what the Gitksan wanted: "Seven years ago we sent a petition right down to Ottawa – our petition meant that we were asking from the Government to give us our land back and also our hunting grounds and all our fishing camps, and we want to hold these for our own use – we want to hold it just the same as a white man holds his land ... and we have been asking the Government to get rid of the Indian Act for us." After a brief exchange, Commissioner Carmichael lectured Spouk at some length, from which the following is excerpted: "There is no use in this Commission, which is a very important Commission and travelling all over British Columbia, wasting its time here if you ... won't answer the questions that are being put to you ... If you have made up your mind not to answer the question, that is your funeral and not ours."[4] Spouk asked William Holland to speak on his behalf, but he was equally unsuccessful with the commissioner. The hearing ended at Gitanmaax and the commission continued on to Kispiox (22 April) and Glen Vowell (23 April), where the pattern was much the same as at Gitanmaax: the commissioners were impatient with and somewhat hostile to Gitksan requests to address the question of Aboriginal title.

On 13 July 1915, Commissioner MacDowall met with representatives of the "Kuldoe Band or Tribe of Indians." William Holland[5] spoke on behalf of the chief:[6] "We sent a petition down to Ottawa for all one Skeena River nation and we need our land back again; that is the Kuldoes, Kisgigax and the Kispaiox, Glen Vowell and Hazelton, and all those tribes right down – we just want one thing and that is to get back our land again – the land was here before we were here and we want to get it back – all the land along the Skeena river."[7] MacDowall then lectured Holland, much as Commissioner Carmichael had earlier lectured Spouk, and called upon Chief William Jackson[8] of Kisgaga'as to address their concerns. Jackson said: "Who gave us this land – It was God ... all we know is that you people are taking away our land. This is our land – our own. No one can go into one house and serve as been in another house." MacDowall adjourned the meeting with a terse comment: "We are sorry that you have not seen fit to answer our questions, and all that remains to be done is to wish you Good-Bye."[9]

A Statement to Marius Barbeau concerning the Gitksan Claim: Abel Oakes (1920)

In 1901 the Gitksan reacted to a white man at Hazelton by the name of Swan, who had taken a number of cords of wood cut and piled in the bush by Gitksan individuals and chiefs living at Gitanmaax. According to Dee, Abel Oakes, a member of the House of Xgwooyemtxw of Kisgaga'as, Swan had the support of provincial police at Hazelton. This alleged support caused a stir among the Gitksan, who were by then concerned about resolving the land question. As Oakes said, "Some wanted to take Swan and hang him and start a war after that. Me and Gitgaldo[10] make peace did not want war. We go in jail one month about that trouble. I did not want so many people killed after that. We wanted to settle the land question before that and we started but not quite yet. The Indians did not want all of B.C. but want only from Kcigonget creek[11] (15 miles below Gitwonge') to Bear Lake and Blackwater. That is all we want."[12] Oakes provided a general description of the Gitksan land claim, with three key geographic points: the upper Skeena watershed commencing at Fiddler Creek on the south; the Bear Lake region, which includes the Sustut River watershed to the northeast; and the Blackwater region, which includes the upper Nass drainage to the northwest (see Map 13).

Gitksan Statements Concerning Territory: To Marius Barbeau and William Beynon (1920)

When Barbeau visited Kispiox in 1920, Gitksan chiefs described their territories and those of the Kisgaga'as and Kuldo. Although the descriptions were brief, perhaps reflecting Barbeau's emphasis on other aspects of Gitksan culture and history, most of the territories on the Nass River were accurately documented (see Map 14).

John Brown, Kwiiyeehl of Kispiox, described the territories on the Nass watershed belonging to Hage, Ksemguneekxw, K'yoluget, Wa'a, Luus, 'Niist, Wiiminoosikxx, and Xhliimlaxha. His statements are quoted here

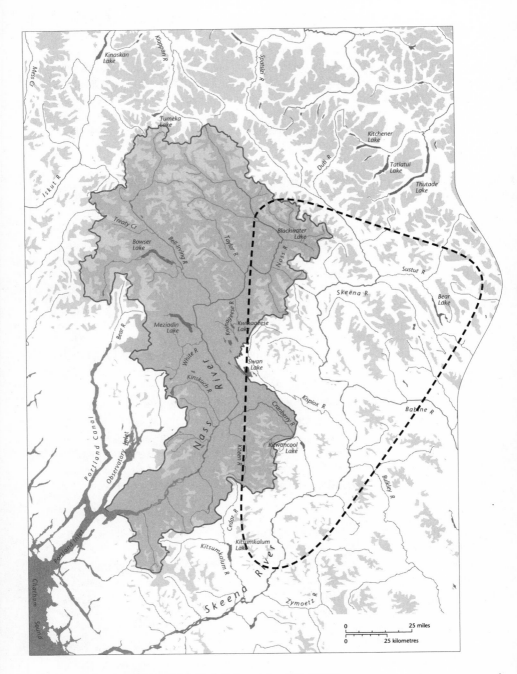

Map 13   Area encompassed by Abel Oakes statement (1920)

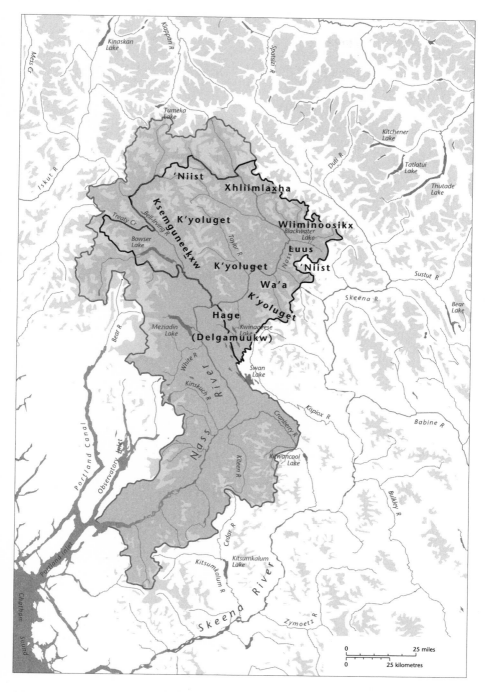

Map 14 Gitksan ownership statements (Kispiox-Kuldo-Kisgaga'as) to Marius Barbeau (c. 1920)

in geographic sequence, beginning at the downriver territories and proceeding to the headwaters of the Nass (see Map 14).

In his description of territories going up the Kispiox River, Brown reached
the uppermost region of the Kispiox and then stated the following:

House of Hage[13]
Hag.e (laxse'el) beaver lake; and from this lake the outlet into the Nass
– not connected the Kispayaks [River].[14]

This refers to the Kwinageese area in the Nass drainage.

House of Ksemguneekxw[15]
Ksemguneq: large hunting ground at headwaters of the Nass: 40 miles
long; 20 miles wide.[16]

This describes the territory of Xskiigemlaxha on the Bell-Irving River,[17] a
tributary of the Nass River. It includes the territory of Dzogoshle on the
lower Bell-Irving River, which Sgawil later gave to him for assistance in
a feast, as described below.

House of K'yoluget Qaldo [Kuldo] hunting grounds. Koluget hunting
ground, about 20 miles in every direction; across Qaldo; only for groundhog and also at the headwaters of the Nass; 10 miles across – for beaver
and groundhog.[18]

The territories of K'yoluget described here are on both sides of the Nass
River near the confluence of the Kwinageese River.

House of Wa'a[19] Between Nass and Skeena above Poison Mountain: about
20 miles square.[20]

This refers to the Wiigoob'l territory on Sallysout Creek, a tributary of
the Nass River.

House of Luus Near Qalanhlgist,[21] above SOB mountain; 20 miles long
and 5 miles wide; along a creek.[22]

This territory is located on a tributary of the Nass River west of the
Slamgeesh River.

House of 'Niist
Near 7th cabin; about 20 miles across; headwaters of the Nass; Beaver.
Another near 4th cabin and Poison Mountain; about 20 miles; creek;
marten.[23]

House of Wiiminoosikx
Wimenozek hunting ground from 5th cabin up to Groundhog mountain, the old trail (Stikine) is in his land.[24]

This describes the Wiiminoosikx territory at Blackwater Lake and River, a tributary of the Nass River.

House of Xhliimlaxha
Xhliemlaxa: ... Other hunting ground at the headwaters of the Nass; at the 6th cabin; 10 miles square.[25]

Jimmy Williams (Giskaast Clan, Kispiox) also spoke of this territory in 1920: "Miinlaxmihl[26] – at the base of/on/level prairie – 'on the prairie at the foot of' was the name of another territory in the neighbourhood of the Nass – it is near to 9th cabin in the groundhog district – very large hunting territory – it is situated in the neighbourhood of Qel's territory – Qel's follows a creek on the Kcan [Skeena] side; while this is on the Nass side."[27]

Gitksan Meetings with the Allied Tribes Concerning the McKenna-McBride Commission Findings (1922)
In 1922 the Allied Tribes of BC, the leading Native political organization, agreed to cooperate in an initiative designed to provide information to help revise the findings of the McKenna-McBride Royal Commission. Tsimshian leaders, Peter Kelly and Ambrose Reid, of the Allied Tribes, met with the Gitksan delegations in the late summer.[28] The Gitksan used the opportunity to state both specific grievances and large territorial claims.[29] Spokespersons for the Gitksan villages made presentations, including that of Abel Oakes of Kisgaga'as, that laid claim to "a huge territorial block and absolute ownership."[30] In summing up their impressions of the Gitksan presentations, Kelly and Reid gave Ditchburn the following warning: "We are under a growing impression that the needs or rather the claims of these people should not be lightly regarded as they are in earnest and may cause a great deal of trouble if not properly cared for. All the people from the Upper Skeena seem to be the same. Maps showing territorial claims attached [not located]."[31]

The Gitksan, the Allied Tribes, and the Skeena Land Committee (1923)
Gitanyow involvement with the Allied Tribes was short-lived. In 1923 W.E. Ditchburn, chief inspector of the Indian agencies of British Columbia, referred Albert Williams to Peter Kelly, chairman of the Allied Tribes. Williams was cool to this suggestion: "I have to state expressly that the Kitwancool is not in a position to allow their way which is directed by 'God' Which is in Heaven above agitated by any man, also that the 'Kitwancool' is far different from the allied Tribes. I therefore cannot

correspond with Mr. P.R. Kelly Chairman of the Allied tribes regarding the Kitwancools."[32] Presumably, the other Gitksan communities concurred with Williams, because they travelled to Prince Rupert in 1924 to act on their own behalf in a meeting with Prime Minister Mackenzie King, and shortly thereafter they formed their own committee.

In October 1924, when Mackenzie King visited Prince Rupert, he was met by a delegation that included "the Kitwancool, Kispiox, Kitwanga and Kitseguecla Tribes." The objective of the delegation was to "discuss land matters."[33] Two documents that were most likely presented by the Gitksan to Mackenzie King have survived.

The first of these documents, dated Kispiox, 9 October 1924, was signed by fifteen Kispiox and Glen Vowell chiefs and endorsed by three other Gitksan chiefs who attended the Prince Rupert meeting: Henry Willitzqu of Kitwanga, Stephen Morgan of Kitsegyukla, and Tom Campbell of Gitanmaax.[34] The statement was headed "Re Indian Land Question," and the preamble points out that the forefathers of the Kispiox and Glen Vowell people were "the occupants and possessors of the land of this country ... before the coming of the white people." For that reason, the chiefs and their people were now "the proper inheritors of this land." Following a reference to the 1908 petition to the federal government, the chiefs stated their claims, which had been reduced to two fundamental demands: first, the abolition of the reserve system; and second, a clear title to a specified territory:

> a strip of land watered by the Kispiox and Skeena rivers; said strip of land to extend from the Kispiox sawmill, midway between Hazelton and Kispiox village to the Brown Bear Lake approximately eighty miles north; said lake bordering on the headwaters of the Kispiox river and draining into the Nass river. And furthermore, we desire that this strip of land shall embrace the territory fifteen miles to the east and fifteen miles to the west of the Kispiox river, thus including the mountain ranges on both sides of the Kispiox Valley.
>
> In short it is desired that a strip of land eighty miles long and thirty miles wide as defined above be granted with full title to the same to the Kispiox peoples of the Kispiox and Glen Vowell villages in place of the present Reserve System.[35]

This statement is significant for three reasons. First, it demonstrates that Kispiox traditional territories include lands in the Nass watershed (see Map 15). Second, the statement was presented to the prime minister of Canada, orally and in writing. And third, Nisga'a leaders witnessed the Gitksan presentation. There is no record that the Nisga'a of the day disputed the Kispiox claim.

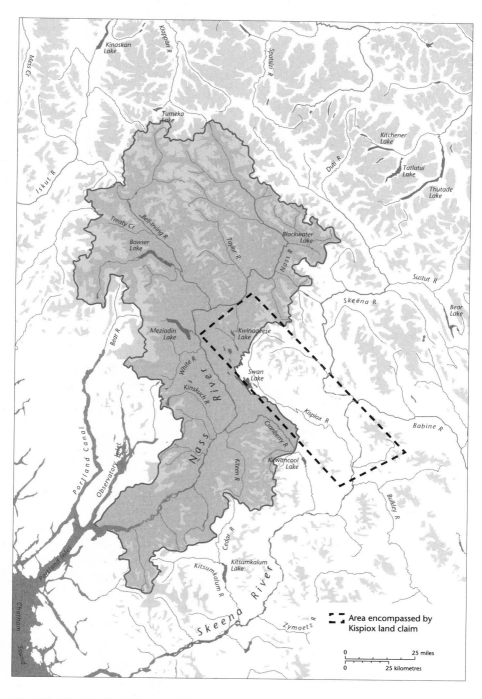

Map 15 Kispiox land claim (1924)

The second document, signed by Albert Williams of Gitanyow, made three essential points:

2. We will control our own lands inside of the Crown, no matter what the colour of our skin.
4. Being the lawful and original Inhabitants and possessors of all lands contained therein from time immemorial ...
5. And whereas, up to the present time our land has not been ceded by us to the Crown nor in any way alienated from us by an agreement or settlement between the representatives of the Crown and ourselves.[36]

In 1925 the Gitksan formed their own organization to deal with territorial issues. Information on this organization, apparently called the Skeena Land Committee, is sparse. Two letters, both signed by Stephen Morgan – a longtime organizer and participant in Gitksan struggles over the land question – gave expression to Gitksan discontent in 1925.[37] In the first, addressed to Mackenzie King, Morgan stated that he was the "Representative of the Country Skeena River" and the president of an unnamed organization. The substance of the letter suggests that the Gitksan were afraid that some kind of settlement might be reached without their participation. Thus, Morgan's first two points were that nothing should be "settled without us knowing" and that, "if any delegation of any tribe from Province of B.C. are there [in Ottawa] ... concerning the Indian Title. Please kindly let us know." Morgan also wished to know if the Gitksan could expect any official visitors and suggested that a Gitksan representative might travel to England in the hope of meeting King George V.[38]

Later in 1925, having been "chosen by the Chiefs of various bands throughout Northern British Columbia," Morgan attempted to secure a meeting with the governor general during the latter's visit to Prince Rupert. This endeavour was not successful, so Morgan wrote a letter "to put our requirement" before the head of state. The requirements amounted to a request for assistance with the projected visit to England: "Therefore our suggestion [is] that you intervene for us that we be permitted to take the matter to Our King as a short road to a final settlement of this burning question." This request, like the earlier one addressed to Mackenzie King, came through the auspices of some unnamed regional organization. Once again Morgan indicated that he was the president and had written "on behalf of the various bands."[39]

Statements Made Concerning Territory to Wilson Duff (1965)
In 1965, after completing work on *Histories, Territories and Laws of the Kitwancool*, Duff turned his attention to the Gitksan of Kispiox, Kuldo, and

Kisgaga'as. He worked with Wii Muugwiluxsxw, Jonathan Johnson (c. 1902-68) of Kispiox, from the House of Xhliimla<u>x</u>ha and son of A<u>x</u>gigii'i, Solomon Johnson (1851-1931), of the House of Delgamuukw. Johnson had knowledge of territories in the Nass watershed, including his father's territory at Gwinhagiistxw.

The Duff interviews took place at Kispiox on 6 and 7 July 1965,[40] where he gathered information about house territories in the Nass and Skeena watersheds. The information appears in his notes, is cross-referenced to a map, and includes reference to an adaaw<u>k</u>. The map covers the area from Kispiox to Damdochax (Blackwater) Lake (see Map 16).[41] The headings below provide house and territory names in the modern orthography and are followed by Duff's notes from his field books.

House of Delgamuukw
T'am Gwinhagiistxw – Wilgidiksit'a<u>x</u> – Xsa'a<u>x</u>goot:
Dam gwanhagi.'stxw – Fred Wright Lake, fathers territory; walgidisda'xw – 3 bodies buried there – 'niaxsqaks,[42] nephew of [Deklamgeiss], deklamges', and a Kitwancool woman; xsa'axgo.t [Saicote] – Creek runs into Kwinageese [River].

Tsetsaut – [illegible?] – there, killed 3 and took one man. He was carrying gun powder, fell in water. Got it wet. He escaped. Jumped Winskatkul [Winsgahlgu'l] – got to Kisgegas – told – nobody from there said anything. Tsetsaut came to Kisgegas later. Wialax [Wii'a'lax] went up – grabbed to scalp – Tsetsaut gave him Kwinageese.[43]

This is a reference to the murder of members of the House of Delgamuukw by the Tsetsaut and to the xsiisxw in which land was forfeited as compensation. Duff also noted the proximity of Gwinhagiistxw to Gitanyow territory:

Gitanyow Territory
Hlguhlsga'nist:
gusgan'isat Mtn – Mtn beyond [Kwinageese territory] to left belongs to Kitwancool.[44]

T<u>x</u>asla<u>x</u>wiiyip is a large area that straddles the Gitksan-Gitanyow border, with Delgamuukw's territory in the Kwinageese drainage.

T<u>x</u>asla<u>x</u>wiiyip:
t'aslaxwiyi'p[45] Mtn
axgigi, Solomon Johnson, JJ's dad, laxse.'l, delgamuq (house), dad was 2nd chief of delgamuq.

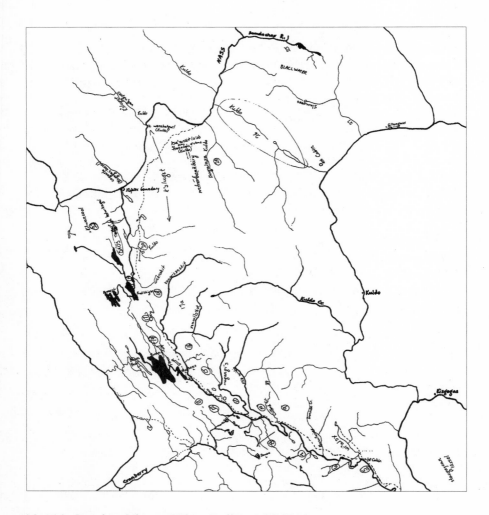

Map 16   Jonathan Johnson-Wilson Duff map (1965)

Txaslaxwiiyip was then managed by Axgigii'i, Solomon Johnson, Jonathan Johnson's father, who was second chief in the House of Delgamuukw.
Johnson then provided other information about the area:

House of Dzogoshle:
cogostle', cabin, laxse'l, Kisgegas, mouth of Kwinageese River, Mtn no. of
Nass[46]

House of K'yoluget
Xsa'axgoot:
xsa'axgo't Creek.[47]

This creek flows west out of Andapmatx (Kologet Mountain) and is also known as Xsi'andapmatx to the Gitksan. Part of the creek is an internal boundary between Gitksan chiefs.[48] Jonathan Johnson also referred to Yanukws, a chief in the House of K'yoluget, who sometimes looked after this territory, as follows:

Yanukws:

yenkws   Wolf (Kuldo).

The lower part of Xsigalixawit (Sallysout Creek on government maps) is a shared boundary between Baskyalaxha and Wii Goobil of Kuldo.[49] Jonathan Johnson referred to this territory and to others north of it:

House of Baskyalaxha
Xsigalixawit:
xsagalisa'wat   Creek
Basgyalaxa'   Kuldo Wolf[50]

House of 'Niist
Xsinihltsenden:
xsinilzendin[51]

House of Wiiminoosikx
T'amt'uutsxwhl'aks:
D'am d'oc'aks   Blackwater L., wimanosak, chief, Kisgegas.[52]

Duff's notes are brief, but along with the map that he and Johnson produced, they provide an important record of Gitksan ownership in the Nass watershed from Kwinageese to Blackwater.

Statements about Place Names and House Territories by Luus, Chris Harris (1972 and 1973)

Luus, Chris Harris (1903-76), of Kispiox, was long concerned about land claims. He conducted his own research and strongly encouraged younger Gitksan persons to do likewise. As a result, he was often approached by anthropologists and linguists who were interested in what he knew about Gitksan history, culture, language, and territory. In 1973 Marie-Françoise Guédon of the National Museum interviewed Luus.[53] During these interviews, he identified the

House of Delgamuukw
Gwinhagiistxw:
Gwinagiisxw – Delgemuukw (Kispiox frog) – gwin hagiisdxw (where\ little shells)

It was given to them [House of Delgamuukw] when a couple was killed by the Tahltan people. They killed the couple there from here. Later the guy [Wii'a'lax] went up and seen the guy when he come to Kisgiga'as. He cut the guy ... and the guy said "no use," and he gave the land. You know, every blood stain has got to be settled, so they have to come back.

Chris was a descendant of Dakhlemges:

My grandmother owns the Ironside Creek.[54] And she takes the name of the one who got killed at Gwinhagiistxw, Deklemgeiss.

House of Xsgiigmlaxha at Awiijii:
The same [type of murder happened at] ... the Bell Irving with Sgawil. The Stikine people they figure it was Kitwancool people, they kill a couple of guys there. But when they [the Tsetsaut] find out they make a mistake they gave them [Sgawil and Naagan] the land. Thats what they did.

This excerpt refers to Gitksan territory on the Bell-Irving River at Awiijii and to the adaawk connected with it.

House of K'yologet
Xsihlgugan:
'Ksa-hl Guu-Gan, young hemlock [trees] creek; Yankws

Luus also mentioned the major creeks in the 'Niist territories at Canyon Lake and Kotsinta Creek.

House of 'Niist
Xsinihlts'enden:
T'sihl-danden – Canyon Creek – Gibeem-Giat [Gibee'imget] and Baasx-ya-Laxa [Baskyalaxha]

Tsinihl Denden – Xsi Tsinihl Denden, goes right to the Nass. Gibee'imget [House of 'Niist] is its head.

Xsiluuwitwiidit:
Xsiluu Witwiidit ("water ouzel"), Kotsinta Creek.

He listed his territory and others north of it:

House of Luus
Xsilax'uu Ando'o:
'Ksa-Lax-oks – Swamp Creek – Luus

House of Wiiminoosikx
T'amt'uutsxwhl'aks:
'Tam-'tuu'tsxw-hl-Aks – blackwater lake
Wii-minoosi'kx

House of Xhliimla<u>x</u>ha
Miinla<u>x</u>mihl:
Miinhl-La<u>x</u>-Mihl – foot of the burn – Kxw-hliiyeemlaxa.

In conclusion, Chris Harris identified Gitksan place names and territories in the Nass watershed and corroborated much of the information provided by Jonathan Johnson in 1965. He also referred to two events that figure prominently in the adaaw<u>k</u> of the Gitksan, confirming Johnson's earlier reference to the murder at Gwinhagiistxw and mentioning a similar event at Awiijii on the Bell-Irving River.

Ownership Statements by Gitksan Chiefs for Land Claims and Court Purposes (after 1973)

Another important source of information concerning Gitksan territories in the Nass watershed north and east of Gitanyow territory is the extensive body of recorded interviews made in preparation for land claims negotiations and litigation since 1973. The Gitksan chose to conduct detailed research to demonstrate the chiefs' intimate knowledge of their territory. The information below is part of that record – proof that the Gitksan legacy endures – and part of an immense documentary record of Gitksan chiefs who told what they knew to Gitksan researchers working at the Gitksan land claims office (see Map 17).

Niik'yap: David Gunanoot (1976)

David Gunanoot (1907-87) had an encyclopedic knowledge of Gitksan culture and history. He had intimate knowledge of Gitksan geography from east of Bear Lake, north to the head of the Skeena and Nass Rivers, and west to the Meziadin-Bowser Lakes area. Since his mother was from Kisgaga'as, his father was Simon Gunanoot, Geel, of Kispiox, and his grandfather was Naagan of Kuldo, David lived much of his life throughout this vast territory. He was raised by his father and great uncle Sgawil at Awiijii in the Nass watershed, and he spent much of the rest of his life there. Daniel Skawil and Simon Gunanoot described the extent of the Awiijii territory to David. They said the boundary line "goes up [the Bell-Irving River] to Owl Creek,[55] and then up to Ninth Cabin mountain, and follow line [height of land] at Awiijii mountain to Thompson [Nass] River ... Bowser Lake[56] is in Skawil's territory too."[57]

On 12 December 1976, a number of chiefs met in Kispiox to identify

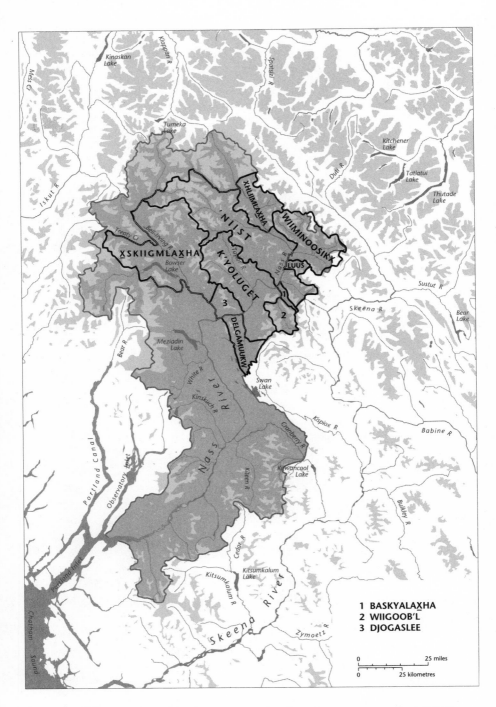

Map 17   Gitksan territories (Kispiox-Kuldo-Kisgaga'as) in the Nass watershed (1995)

the Gitksan boundary. Niik'yap said of X̱sgiigmlax̱ha's boundary: "Old Daniel Skawill's boundary crosses the Bowser River west of Bowser Lake [then] up past and around [the] headwaters of Treaty Creek, down ... Teigen Creek to ... Snowbank Creek to Bell Irving River, across the Bell Irving River then North along the east shore of the Bell Irving to a point opposite the mouth of Owl Creek, then East up the mountain."[58] A few days later, Gunanoot related in detail how and why the Tsetsaut "stepped back" from Awiijii.[59] In the ensuing years, he retold the history that he had learned from his father and Daniel Skawill many times.

David said that his father told him that one of the "Stikines" who gave up Awiijii was "Taashuuts."[60] In 1987 David, Gerald Gunanoot, James Morrison, Horace Wale, and Esther McLean drove to Awiijii with Neil Sterritt, where Gerald showed the exact site of the Tsetsaut cabin.[61] The war party had confronted Taashuuts at this cabin, and the xsiisxw was held nearby. Treaty Creek flows east into the Bell-Irving River near here. David explained that the Indian name for Treaty Creek is X̱oo, meaning "grizzly bear" in the Tsetsaut language, a vestige of their earlier presence.

Niik'yap was taught the place names of the territory, some of which are in "Stikine" (Tsetsaut) and carried forward from their former owners, whom Naagan and Sg̱awil knew well. David provided the following geographic information on Awiijii:

T'ax̱tsimilix (Hidden Lake)
T'amlaaxw (Todedada Lake)
T'ax̱s Sgawil (Oweegee Lake)
T'amganax̱digwanaxw
Sgasgiit T'ax̱
Xsilax̱amaawx (Oweegee Creek)
Xsi'andapmatx̱ (Hodder Creek)
Luu'xsgigeenigit Awiijii (Skowill Creek)
Lax̱amaawx (site of Gitksan-Tsetsaut Treaty c. 1900)
Gwiis Awiijii
Xsigibuu
Xsiluustaalo'obit (Cousins Creek)
T'aabekxwhlt'ax̱ (Hodder [Mehan] Lake)

Anluubiyoosxwt
Xsiluubiyoosxwt (Irving Creek)
Xsiluumaseexit (Spruce Creek)
Max̱hlalax̱uut
Xsi'max̱hlalax̱uut
Lipsga'nist (Bell Irving Mountain)
Xsiluu'alagwit
Xsi'ansalagamdit (Richie Creek)
Xsiwiiluut'aahlts'imilix (Taft Creek)
Xsihis'maawnt (Wildfire Creek)
Xsiluumahaawit (Deltaic Creek)
Anbax̱gitwinx̱ (Mount Skowill-Oweegee Mountain area).[62]

In 1987 David also identified names that originated with the Tsetsaut (now often referred to as the Tahltan) during their ownership of the territory:

Awiijii[63] (Skowill Creek)[64]   Ts'aats'iina (Surveyors Creek)[66]
Suutsii'ada or Thuutsii'ada   Xoo or Kas Xoo (Treaty Creek).
   (Bowser Lake)[65]

David had taught his nephew, Gerald Gunanoot, the boundaries while living, hunting, and trapping at Awiijii.[67]

Recently, enquiries were made of several Tahltan to determine if they were familiar with the xsiisxw at Awiijii and the identity of Taashuuts.

Jack Pete is Tahltan, born c. 1908 and married to a Gitksan from Bear Lake. In 1995 he said: "We follow Creek Ningunsaw down to head of Nass River. We never go to Nass River because they fight before and Tahltan nearly clean them up. They go as far as Bell II[68] and Tahltan quit too, they move away from there. My great-great grandfather Hunter Frank told me that story. He take care of Klappan Mountain, and he keep the Nass off."[69]

Another Tahltan Elder, Benny Frank (c. 1890-1985), son of Hunter Frank, was knowledgeable about the Tahltan who lived and hunted in the upper reaches of the Klappan river system. He said: "Pete Tashoots start that village [Iskut] ... He's the first man put up home there. From there, he go up Klappan trapping; from there, he went over to Nass, boundary line there, come back."[70] Pete Tashoots married Susie Quok, considered to be of the "tlepanoten" (Klappan) group of Tahltans. Pete and Susie were the parents of Jack Pete.

In conclusion, David Gunanoot provided detailed and comprehensive evidence about Gitksan ownership of the Awiijii area when identifying the exact location of the xsiisxw, the family names of those involved, the detailed history of the territory, and the place names (both Gitksan and Tsetsaut) throughout the territory. His evidence was independently corroborated in 1934 when two Gitksan chiefs signed a statutory declaration about their participation in the xsiisxw.

Gla'eeyu: Richard Benson (1976)

Richard Benson (1909-88) was born and raised at Meziadin Lake. His grandfather was 'Wiilitsxw, a Gitanyow chief, and his mother, Anhloo, in the House of K'yoluget, was from Kuldo. He spent nearly forty years on Gitanyow and Kuldo territories in the Nass watershed.

Richard's mother was raised by her aunt, Kwa'amhon, Mary Ann Jack (1879-1959). Mary Ann Jack first took Richard to K'yoluget's territories in 1935, along with her husband, Gwininitxw, Tommy Jack (c. 1891-1970), and his nephews Jasper and David Jack. They travelled to the territory by dog team and toboggan up the Kispiox River, down the Kwinageese to the Nass, and along the ice on the Nass River to their camp at Winsgahlgu'l. Richard spent the next twenty years or so on this and other territory owned by K'yoluget and Luus.[71]

K'yoluget owned territories on both sides of the Nass near the Kwin-ageese River confluence: Xsihlgugan (Taylor River) to the north and Xsanalo'op (Shanalope Creek) to the south. Richard was taught about the former by his aunt when they trapped there in 1935 and thereafter. The territory north of the Nass River includes

Xsitxemsem (Nass River)	Xsik'alidakhl
Xsihlgugan (Taylor River)	Gwiis'xsihlgugan (West Taylor River)
Xsa'anyam (Sanyam Creek)	Xsibana.

Richard said that 'Niist's territory bordered K'yoluget's Xsihlgugan territory to the north in the area of Eighth and Ninth Cabins on Telegraph Trail and to the east at Xsiluuwitwiidit (Kotsinta Creek). He described K'yoluget's territory south of the Nass River:

Xsitxemsem (Nass River)	Xsimasxwtlo'op
Xsa'angyahlts'uuts (Sanskisoot Creek)	Xsa'a<u>x</u>goot (Saicote Creek, aka
Xsigwinhagiistxw (Kwinageese River)	Xsi'andapmatx)
Xsigalixawit (Sallysout Creek)	Xsa'anto'op (Santolle Creek)
Wilsgahlgu'l (unnamed canyon on Nass River)	Xsanalo'op (Shanalope Creek)[72]

He also described territories adjacent to K'yoluget, including that of Wiigoob'l, Albert Brown of Kuldo, where he spent the winter of 1936. He said that an important feature of the territory is Naa'oogil, a 6,644-foot mountain at the head of Xsigallixawit, which is a boundary marker between Wiigoob'l and another territory of K'yoluget – the Xsi'angaxda[73] territory. Another mountain within the territory is Masxwtlo'op, located west of Sallysout Creek and south of Mount Skuyhil.[74] Gla Ee'eyiw said that he and Wiigoob'l had to cross over Masxwtlo'op at Xsimasxwtlo'op[75] in order to get to their main camping site with members of the House of K'yoluget at Wilsgahlgu'l on the Nass River:[76] "The winter trail [from Kuldo] to Naa Oogil is up Xsilaadamus;[77] the summer trail is from Old Kuldo right up the mountain. Naa'oogil is right at the head of Xsilaada-mus. It belongs to K'yoluget. When you stand at the head of Xsigalix-awit, you can look south to see Xsi'angaxda."[78] Place names identified within and on the borders of Wiigoob'l's territory include

Xsigalixawit (Sallysout Creek)	Masxwtlo'op
Xsiluu'alagwit	Naa'oogil.[79]
Xsimasxwtlo'op	

Richard said that the territory originally belonged to Daniel Skawil, who turned it over to his relative Wiigoob'l, Albert Brown: "Dan Skawil himself told me that it was his and he turned it over to Wii Goobil. Jonathan Brown's father[80] helped Skawil out. Dan Skawil got this territory a long time ago. I and my brother looked after this old man [Sgawil]. The first Luus from Kuldo was Dan Skawil's father. We used to take him[81] out on his trap line all the time. I trapped at Wii Goobil's territory with Albert Brown's son, Phillip Brown. Phillip was my brother-in-law. He taught me all about this territory as well."[82]

Richard also spent time on 'Niist's territory at Canyon lake. In addition to identifying some of the landmarks, he described a feat of Gitksan engineering at upper Canyon Creek long ago: "Thomas Brown's great-great-great grandfather and grandmother turned this creek; it used to run into the Nass River, and they switched it around and run [it] into Canyon Lake and Skeena River. They did this because of the fish."[83] He also referred to Dzogoshle's territory north of the Nass River and west of K'yoluget's Xsihlgugan (Taylor River) territory: "Djogaslee used to trap in the mountains northeast of the Nass-Bell Irving junction."[84]

Richard Benson thus provides evidence of a long-standing Gitksan presence in the Nass watershed from the Bell-Irving River to Canyon Lake, and, as will be seen in Chapter 6, it is likely members of the House of 'Niist who found and guided the lost explorer Peter Leech from the Nass River to Kuldo and Kisgaga'as in 1867.

Wiibowax̱: Percy Sterritt (1910-1998)
Wiibowax̱, Percy Sterritt (born 1910), is the grandson of A̱xgigii'i, Solomon Johnson (c. 1854-1931), and the nephew of Jonathan Johnson. He lived, hunted, fished, and trapped at Gwinhagiistxw with his grandfather and uncle as a youth. Later he accompanied his uncles from the House of Xhliimla̱xha to their territories at the head of the Nass River.

Percy has described his grandfather's territory:

House of Delgamuukw – Gwinhagiistxw:
Ṯxasla̱x̱wiiyip is along the mountains running west of Gwinhagiistxw. It means "along the big country."[85]

When I was 16 or 17 years old, Joogaslee told Jonathan (Johnson) about a big log jam on Kwinageese River. Jonathan went to look and then told Roy McDonald (DFO) about it, and he went in and blasted the falls. That winter we set nets through the ice there and we caught lots of steelhead. We caught so many we had to dry them for two weeks. We built a big shed to dry them in – it was 30 feet long.

On the left side of Gwinhagiistxw facing north is the area called Ṯxasla̱x̱wiiyip, a big long mountain. It belongs to Neek't, Solomon

Johnson, from Kispiox. He also owns all along Gwinhagiistxw lake and all along the river down towards the Nass.

There is a lake on the Gwinhagiistxw River called Wilgidiksit'ax̲. Here the river runs, stop and make lake, then go on. It's one hour walk from the outlet of Gwinhagiistxw Lake to Wilgidiksit'ax̲. It's a really good steelhead area just north of Wilgidiksit'ax̲ towards the Nass River.[86]

Percy first travelled to Gwinhagiistxw in 1923 and spent another six or seven winters there. He said that his grandfather's main camp was near Wilgidiksit'ax̲. He was told by his grandfather to run his marten line to "the brow of the hill at Tx̲aslax̲wiiyip, but don't go over the other side – that's Kitwancool on the other side." Percy described the route taken when they returned to Kispiox in the spring: "When we used to walk out in the spring-time on the snow, my grandfather took us an easier way. We walked from T'am Gwinhagiistxw to Naalax̲ts'inaasit, then to Lax̲dit'ax̲ and Mindagan."[87]

As a member of the House of Xhliimlax̲ha, Percy became knowledgeable about the territory at the head of the Nass River. Percy and Wii Mugwilsxw, the late George Wilson (c. 1915-83), spent a number of years at Miinlax̲mihl. This territory had been acquired from the Tsetsaut, and some of the place names still reflected their earlier presence. Their camp was at the confluence of a creek on the Nass River called Agunagana, a Tsetsaut word meaning "the shoulder or spine of a moose";[88] the next creek south, called Atsehlaa, means "[moose] intestines, which they turn inside out and eat."[89] Percy and George said that the territory was acquired by xsiisxw as compensation for a murder committed by the Tsetsaut people.[90]

Percy explained the location of the territory: "Miinlax̲mihl is past sixth cabin (on the Telegraph Trail). Just past sixth cabin is a little bridge on the Nass River, from the East side of the Nass the boundary goes north. Both sides of the Nass River is Miinlax̲mihl right over the summit. Charles Sampson and Alfred Shanoss own between the two Nasses."[91] Percy said that he first went to Miinlax̲mihl with his uncle, Wo'os Sa'lo'op, Phillip Wilson (1876-1940), in 1928. Phillip's brother, Robert, was responsible for the territory, but Phillip used it. Percy described the territory as having lots of moose, goat, and caribou. Percy and George once travelled far up the Nass, but Phillip warned them to be careful because the "Stikines" would go after them. Percy described their trip in 1984:

We used to turn off at the bridge the other side of Sixth Cabin. This was the beginning of our territory. It took us about one day travel to the cabin. [From here] George Wilson and I took about one day travel to the summit. There was a great big balsam blazed on one face, with big long poles (leaning against it). These were for hooking beaver. There was writing like chinese numbers on the tree. They were really old. We turned back here. We could see camp fires in the distance – about three sets. This land was full of beaver. Uncle Phillip was mad at us when we told him because it was someone else's land.[92]

Duubisxw: Arthur Sampson (1982)

Arthur Sampson (c. 1920-85), the son of 'Niist, Charles Sampson (c. 1880-1963), grew up on his father's territories in the Nass watershed. He was familiar with the 100-kilometre area from Canyon Lake to beyond Ninth Cabin: "We used to turn into T'amxsinihlts'enden (Canyon Lake) at Fourth Cabin on the Telegraph Trail. Gwilanamax, Tom Sampson's hunting ground began here at Canyon Lake and went to the Nass River. Tom was a half-brother to Charlie Sampson ('Niist). Walter Laats was a headman too. They owned this land from way back." As Arthur pointed out, this more southerly portion of the 'Niist territory had been held for a very long time and was not obtained by xsiisxw: "There were two lines from the Nass River [commencing at Vile Creek] to Seventh Cabin. Laats used the line on the right and 'Niist on the left. This creek that ran into the Nass was Xsiluuwitwiidit (Kotsinta Creek). Their land went all the way to Seventh Cabin. This land was the property of the Gitksan. There was no bloodshed. The property goes to Shanoss Creek, which runs into Luusilgimbaad Txemsem (Muckaboo Creek) at Seventh Cabin." 'Niist often camped with members of the House of Xhliimlaxha (Phillip Wilson, Percy Sterritt, etc.) at Xadaa Agana (Panorama Creek), which Arthur described: "Phillip Wilson's Trapline begins at Miinlaxmihl. This is where Wilmaxhladokhlagenxwiigwiikw[93] is. This is a mountain 'Niist crosses before he gets to his ground. It's right on the Telegraph Line. In 1942, Thomas Brown, Charlie Sampson and I left Xhliimlaxha's main camp and went one day's travel over 'Niist's land up Luusilgimbaad Txemsem.[94] This belonged to 'Niist from way back. Percy Sterritt knows the area of Xhliimlaxha."[95]

In 1984 Arthur described 'Niist's territories at and near Muckaboo Creek:

Then there is a mountain here that 'Niist crosses before he gets to his other ground. This mountain is right on the Telegraph Line about halfway between Seventh and Eighth Cabin. It was called Wilmaxhladokhlagenxwiigwiikw.[96]

Luusilgimbaad Txemsem belongs to my dad too. A good one day travel is as far as he goes up here, by foot on a good crust of snow. This belonged to 'Niist from way back. He got marten and beaver here. I went too, running on top of the snow with our snowshoes.

Thomas Brown,[97] Charlie Sampson and I left Xliimlaxha's main camp[98] in 1942 and went one day [west]. We were close to Ninth Cabin in really steep country. This was one of Gunanoot's hide-outs. He stood 35 foot poles up all around so no one could see his fire at night ... It used to take a full week from Seventh Cabin to Glen Vowell. This was in May when the days are long.[99]

On another occasion, Arthur discussed what his father had told him about the territory west of 'Niist: "Charles used to talk about Owl Creek and Big Owl Creek, but they didn't own that area ... He said it belonged to the Stikine [Tahltan people]."[100] Owl and Big Owl Creeks flow east into the Bell-Irving River near the confluence of Rochester Creek (Xsiwiig-wanks) and the Bell-Irving.

In summary, Arthur Sampson described his personal experiences and the geographic features in the extensive territories of 'Niist in the upper Nass watershed and corroborated information provided by Niik'yap, David Gunanoot, about the Gitksan-Tahltan border at the Bell-Irving River at Owl Creek.

Delgamuukw: Albert Tait (1982)

Albert Tait (1904-87) was the nephew of Axgigii'i, Solomon Johnson, and heir to the name Delgamuukw. He was knowledgeable about house territories in the Nass watershed, his own at Gwinhagiistxw, and his father's (Luus, Abel Tait, of Kuldo) near Blackwater.

Albert Tait said that Gwinhagiistxw was formerly held by the Stikines[101] and that the area changed hands by blood. His grandfather had told him the history of the Gwinhagiistxw area, in which the Tsetsaut Atsehlaa Taa shot and killed Deklemgeiss and his wife at Wilgidiksit'ax.[102]

In 1986 Tait described some of the features in and around his territory at Gwinhagiistxw: T'amhliloot (Kwinageese Lake). He said that his boundary bisected the arms of this lake, with Malii of Kitwancool on the west and Delgamuukw on the east. He identified other features:

Xsilaalax'uudit	Hlguhlsga'nist
T'amlaalax'uudit (unnamed, locally	Txaslaxwiiyip
called East Bonney Lake)	T'amhliloot.[103]

Albert also referred to Dzogoshle's territory north of Kwinageese and mentioned how it was acquired: "[House of Dzogoshle]: Djogaslee's cabin was at the junction of the Kwinageese River and the Nass River. Djogaslee owns the ground north of the Nass at Kwinageese River because he paid for the funeral of a brother of Daniel Skawil. This happened when I was a young boy about 75 years ago."[104] "Skawil owned it, but Djogaslee paid a lot of money into a funeral feast, so Skawil gave it to Djogaslee."[105]

Albert identified features in the Blackwater area:

Sasmihla   Xsiluu'am'maldid (Slowmaldo
                                           Creek).[106]

He travelled to the Bell-Irving River beyond Ninth Cabin on Telegraph
Trail. He identified a mountain at the centre of 'Niist's territory, Maxhlabil'ustmaaxws, which has a large hanging glacier on it. The creek from
the mountain is called Maxhlabil'uustmaaxws.[107] Walter Blackwater and
Albert Tait said that the name (meaning on or over/ stars / snow or white)
originated with this glacier, which, viewed from their camp, sparkled like
stars in the moonlight.[108]

As mentioned above, Albert knew the upper Nass well and travelled up
and down it as a youth: "Willie [brother] and I walked down Xsitxemsem from Xsilax'uu [his father's territory] to Wilsgahlgu'l in about two
hours on the snow when we were young."[109]

Elders at Kispiox (1983)
The elders of Kispiox called a meeting in preparation for *Delgamuukw* v.
The Queen at the Kispiox band office 8 February 1983 to discuss the territories in the Upper Kispiox and north in the Gwinhagiistxw area. Elders
present at this meeting were Albert Tait, Percy Sterritt, James Angus Sr., Jeff
Harris Sr., David Blackwater, Bobby Stevens, and Pete Muldoe. Also present
were Ken Muldoe, Earl Muldoe, and Lloyd Morrison. Glen Williams, Alex
Morgan, Russell Stevens, and Neil Sterritt were resource persons. Figure 1
shows information recorded in sketch form in Sterritt's field book.

Wiigoob'l: Jessie Sterritt (1983)
Wiigoob'l, Jessie Sterritt (1901-93), was the niece of Naagan and Sgawil.
She travelled by foot to Awiijii a number of times as a young woman and
had the responsibility (after Daniel Skawil died [c. 1871-1938]) of looking after the symbolic feather given by the Tsetsaut at Awiijii. She showed
this feather to provincial and federal counsel while giving commission
evidence under oath in *Delgamuukw* v. *The Queen* in 1985.[110] Jessie also
knew and related the Awiijii adaawk to her family and to other Gitksan
persons. In 1983 she said that the Tahltans had killed a close relative of
Sgawil, that the Gitkuldo (people of Kuldo) had gone to investigate, and
that a feast was held. This "was a xsiisxw, it was permanent, [and] we
own the land."[111]

This territory is one of the most recent acquired by the Gitksan: the
xsiisxw occurred between the Tsetsaut and the Gitksan sometime before
1897. Many Gitksan elders have spoken about it, and there is a clear
record of what occurred (see Chapter 2).

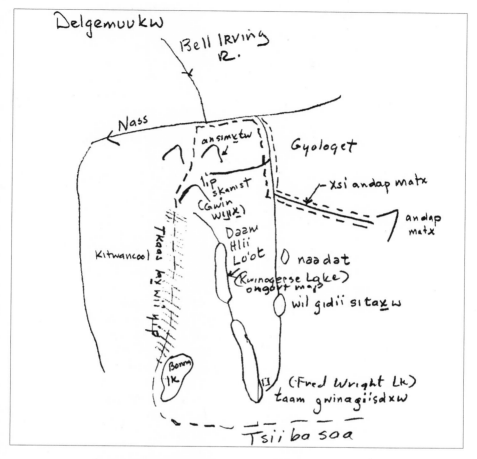

Figure 1   House territories in the Nass watershed (Sterritt field book)

Axhetxwm Hleek: Jeff Wilson (1984)

Jeff Wilson (1919-95) was raised by Phillip Wilson and his wife[112] and travelled to Miinlaxmihl with Phillip. Jeff said: "Miinlaxmihl begins at the bridge camp, where the Telegraph Trail crosses the Nass River. Phillip's main camp, a cabin, was at Panorama Creek on the Nass River. The trail from the bridge followed close to the Nass River all the way to this main camp. Our other cabins were log lean-tos. Phillip told me this territory extends all the way to the source of the Nass. Shanoss owns the territory to Eighth Cabin on the Telegraph Trail."[113]

Xhliimlaxha: Martha Brown (1985)

The House of Xhliimlaxha has a territory at the headwaters of the Nass River called Miinlaxmihl (foot of the burn). According to Martha Brown,

Xhliimlaxha (1900-87), of Kispiox, this territory once belonged to the Stikine (Tsetsaut) people.

A Tsetsaut chief was married to a member of the House of Xhliimlaxha from Kispiox. She and her child were killed by the Tsetsaut, and their bodies were buried in a groundhog hole. Afterward a xsiisxw was held at Xsa'angyahlasxw, north of Kispiox, at which the Tsetsaut gave up this territory (see Chapter 2).

Martha said that there is a post on top of a hill at the corner of her territory called T'imgesha'niidzok,[114] where two rivers separated. It used to take two days to go to each corner of her territory, and there was a place called Wiluusgiihl An'malgwa. She said that it was a Stikine cremation place close to Miinlaxmihl.[115]

Ksemgitgigyeenix: Johnny Moore (1985)

Ksemgitgigyeenix, Johnny Moore (1902-c. 1986), of Kisgaga'as, spent most of his life on Gitksan territories in the upper Nass and Skeena watersheds. His Kuldo relatives owned the territory at Xsigallixawit: "This was my relations' hunting ground: Noxs Skawil and Noxs Diigyet were related.[116] The last time I was there was in 1948. Doug, Steve [Johnny's sons] and I went. This territory was very close to Old Kuldo. The hunting ground goes close to Nass River. There is a mountain – Na'oogil – with snow slides. It's up pretty high on the mountain."[117]

Gwisgyen: Stanley Williams (1986)

Gwisgyen, Stanley Williams, of Kitwanga, travelled throughout Gitanyow territories with Gitanyow hereditary chiefs as a young man and had detailed knowledge of Gitksan territories and boundaries from the Skeena River valley at Legate Creek to the Gitanyow boundary near Bowser Lake. In 1986 he said: "The Kitwancool own all of Nadiiloodit, Swan Lake, less than half of the Gwinhagiistxw area, and own the top of Txaslaxwiiyip, with Malii on the west and Kispiox on the east; then the boundary goes over to Xsigisi'am'maldit (Surveyors Creek)."[118]

Diisxw: Walter Blackwater (1986)

Diisxw, Walter Blackwater (b. 1923), 'Niist, David Blackwater, and Baskyalaxha, William Blackwater, were born and raised at Blackwater by their parents, Wiiminoosikx, Jimmy Blackwater (1888-1966), and Diisxw, Mary Blackwater (1903-74). Walter, David, and Billy are members of Kuldo. Their knowledge of the entire area is extensive, as will be demonstrated in part below.

In 1986 Walter and David Blackwater and Nancy Supernault (raised nearby at K'alaa'nhlgiist – Slamgeese Lake) identified the following geographic features during a helicopter field trip to the area:[119]

T'amt'uutsxwhl'aks (Damdochax Lake)
T'amuumxswit (Wiminasik Lake)
Xsitxemsem (Nass River)
Xsiluu'am'maldit (Slowmaldo Creek)
Naabaad Xsiluu'am'maldit (Yaza Creek)
Xsit'uutsxwhl'aks (Damdochax Creek)
Xsiguuhilin
Xsigenuts'ap (Deadfall Creek)
Xsiluulaxlo'obit
Xsimiin'anhl'gii (upper Barker Creek)
Xsa'ansaksxwmoohl (Sansixmor Creek)
Xsiwilsgayip (Damshilgwit Creek)

Xsigeltsagat
Andamixw
Lo'opguuhanak'
T'imgesha'niidzok (north end of Panorama Mountain)
Ts'aphlgwiikw (Groundhog Mountain)
Miin'anhlgii (unnamed on government maps)
Guuhilin (Slowmaldo Mountain)
Sga'nisim Xsa'ansaksxwmoohl (part of Slowmaldo Mountain)
Sasmihla
Galaxuuhl T'amt'uutsxwhl'aks
Maxhla'anmuuxws
Wilsgayip (Martins Flats).[120]

Walter lived and worked on the territories of 'Niist throughout the Nass watershed. He referred to some of the trips that he made and described geographic features in his brothers' territories below Blackwater. For example, he once travelled to Baskyalaxha's territory with a former holder of the name, Jack Tait (1895-1962): "I went down [from Vile Creek] with Jack Tait[121] to Xsigaliixawit, but not up the creek. We also turned off at Third Cabin and went in [to the Canyon Lake territory] up Xsi'bagayt'-sisagat."[122] The Xsigalixawit territory borders the territory of Wiigoob'l. It extends from the Nass River at the mouth of Xsigalixawit to the Skeena River, and for that reason it is sometimes referred to as the Angawtsaxw (Poison Mountain) territory. Walter identified some of the place names in the Baskyalaxha territory:

Xsigalixawit (lower Sallysout Creek)
Xsiluu'alagwit
Xsitxemsem (Nass River)
Xsinihltsenden Ando'o (Vile Creek)
Xsi'andapmatx (upper Canyon Creek)

Xsi'bagayt'sisagat (Poison Creek)
Xsa'anhlimox (O'Dwyer Creek)
Andapmatx
Angawtsaxw (Poison Mountain)
Bagayt'sisagat
Miinhl Ganu'aloo

Walter also described 'Niist's Canyon Lake territory: "I went in seven or eight times with Tom Sampson,[123] and went up Xsi'andapmatx about fifteen miles. I [also] went up with my mother. She knew this creek. A rock up that creek is called Andapmatx."[124]

As Diisxw, Walter Blackwater, said above, Gibee'imget, Tom Sampson (c. 1870-1960), looked after the Xsinihlts'enden (Canyon Lake) territory.

Gibee'imget and 'Niist[125] had their main camp at an unnamed lake west of Canyon Lake, called Tamangyage'en. Walter identified the key features of 'Niist's territory at Canyon Lake:[126]

T'amsinihlts'enden (Canyon Lake)	Xsiluumasaawit
T'amansa'axws	Xsiluumaaskeexwt
Tamangyage'en	Xsiluulaxlo'obit
Xsitxemsem (Nass River)	Xsigenuts'ap
Xsan (Skeena River)	Xsi'andapmatx (upper Canyon
Xsinihlts'enden (Canyon Creek)	Creek)
Xsinihlts'enden Ando'o (Vile	Xsisk'ama'alt (Shaslomal Creek)
Creek)	Gasalaxlo'obit
Wilsganeekhlm Ho'oxs	Xsa'anluuskeexs
Xsiluulaxleexs	Andapmatx.

The above features were identified during the 6 September 1986 helicopter field trip already mentioned. Walter was familiar with the diversion of Canyon Creek mentioned by Richard Benson (above): "Xsi'andapmatx is by the lake, Canyon Lake, used to flow into Angyage'en,[127] which drained east and west, but somebody altered it so it only flows into Canyon Lake and Skeena."[128]

The House of Luus owns territory at Xsilax'uu Ando'o, a small territory on the Nass River north of 'Niist's territory at Xsinihlts'enden. It encompasses Xsilax'uu Ando'o, which flows west into the Nass River from Blackwater Peak. In 1986 Walter said that the western boundary of the territory is the Nass River and that the territory of 'Niist is to the west at Xsiluuwitwiidit (Kotsinta Creek).

Diisxw said that his father's territory at Tamt'uutsxwhl'aks is large, extending from the mountain range south of Blackwater Lake north to Groundhog and Panorama Mountains. His father was Wiiminoosikx, a chief of Kisgaga'as.

Walter was born fewer than fifteen miles from the southern boundary of Xhliimlaxha at Blackwater Lake. The place names identified by Walter in Xhliimlaxha's territory at Miinlaxmihl include:[129]

Xsitxemsem (Nass River)	T'imgesha'niidzok (Panorama
Luusilgimbaad Txemsem	Mountain)
(Muckaboo Creek)	Lo'opguuhanak'
Xsiwiluusgiihl An'malgwa	Wilmaxhladokhlagenxwiigwiikw
Xsimaxhlab'iluustmaawxs Ando'o	Miinlaxmihl
(Konigus Creek)	Wiluusgiihl An'malgwa.

In 1987 Walter referred to 'Niist's most northerly territory: Luusilgimbaad Txemsem, east of the Bell-Irving River and north of Rochester and

Muckaboo Creeks in the vicinity of Ninth Cabin on the old Telegraph Trail. This territory is adjacent to, but west of, Xhliimlaxha's Miinlaxmihl territory: "Laats owned beyond Ninth Cabin to the mountains, but not to the big river (Bell Irving), and to the mountains past T'amsaabaya'a, then over to the lake called T'amwiits[130] at the head of Xsimaxhlab'iluustmaawxs Ando'o. Taas Aguun was the Stikine who owned this area near Ninth Cabin creek before." He described the northern extent of the territory on the Nass River as well:

> There is a big post with a sign on it. This is the border between Stikine and Gitksan. It's past Miinlaxmihl. A big tree eight feet by eight feet squared off was the boundary. There is a big swamp – at the upper end is a lake that is about three-quarters of a mile long and one-quarter mile wide. This is near this lake. This lake appears to be a widening in the Nass River at the upper end of a swamp. This is the end of Gitksan territory.[131]
>
> There is an area where [there's] a tree at the end of a big swamp, about four miles from the mouth of Xsimaxhlab'iluustmaawxs. [It] had writing like really strange angles, lines. [We] couldn't read it, and Sam and I told Jimmy Blackwater, and he said it was the Stikine boundary.[132]

This description corresponds to the swamp described by Percy Sterritt for the northern extent of the Miinlaxmihl territory of Xhliimlaxha, which borders 'Niist's territory to the east. The Nass River is the boundary between 'Niist and Xhliimlaxha, and their territories end at the tree in the swamp as described by both Percy Sterritt and Walter Blackwater.

The following is a summary of some of the place names on the Luusiligimbaad Txemsem territory:

T'amsaabaya'a
Xsilaxwiiyip
Luusilgimbaad Txemsem
(Muckaboo Creek)
Luudagwigit
Xsiluuwitwiidit (Kotsinta Creek)
Maxhlab'iluustmaawxs
Xsitxemsem (Nass River)
Wilmaxhladokhlagenxwiigwiikw

Sto'ot Xsitxemsem (Bell-Irving
   River)
Lipsga'nist (Lipsconesit Mountain)
Xsiwiigwanks (Rochester Creek)
Lo'opguuhanak'
Xsik'utk'unuuxs (Owl Creek)[133]
Xsimaxhlab'iluustmaaxws
   [Ando'o](Konigus Creek).

In conclusion, Walter Blackwater has detailed knowledge of Gitksan territories belonging to his and other houses in the upper Nass region. His knowledge was acquired through his many years growing up, living, and working throughout the upper Nass region and through the teachings of his parents and grandparents, who had lived there before him.

Gwax̱ Lo'op: Arthur Mowatt (1987)

Arthur Mowatt (c. 1909-92), House of Luutkudziiwus, of Gitanmaax, travelled to K'yoluget's territory at Xsihlgugan (Taylor River) with his mother and stepfather, who was a member of the House of K'yoluget. He described the trip and area as follows: "I went up there with old Sam Green (1881-?)[134] and Wii Naḵ, Bella Green, after my father died. There is a creek there – Xsik'alidakhl. It flows into the Nass River just above the Taylor River, and is about the size of Salmon River.[135] It's about a half-day walk on north side of the Nass River. The Lax̱ Gibuu own this [territory]."[136]

Axti'anjam: Daisy Olson (1987)

Axti'anjam, Daisy (Shanoss) Olson (b. 1911), is a member of the House of Meluulaḵ, of Kisgaga'as, and the daughter of Gwiniiho'osxw, Alfred Shanoss (1881-1963), of the House of 'Niist. She travelled with her parents to 'Niist's territories on Muckaboo Creek in the vicinity of Seventh and Eighth Cabins twice a year, every year, between 1921 and 1939 inclusive. Axti'anjam referred to the territory as follows:

> We went to T'amgwinsaabaya'a, between Seventh and Eighth Cabins. We lived there in a cabin, and fished there in the winter and fall. We go halfway to Eighth Cabin (from Seventh Cabin), then turn left, and the cabin is two miles off the Telegraph Trail. We cross Xsitxemsem to get there.
>
> We go to Luudagwigit. We go two days to get here. We go slow while checking traps. One time we went down one day and visited Willie Wilson [Djogoshle, on his Bell Irving territory]. Alfred used to kill goats at the mountains near Gwinsaabaya'a.
>
> Max̱hlagenxwiigwiikw is the mountains on the right from Gwinsaabaya'a to Luudagwigit.
>
> This area was xsiisxwed to my great grandfather. His Limx Seegit for this territory is called "O Aiyoo."
>
> We had a big cabin at Gwinsaabaya'a. Charlie Derrick was there with Alfred Shanoss long after I went there. He knows where the traps are cached.[137]

Axmanasxw: Charles Derrick (1987)

Axmanasxw, Charles Derrick (born 1920), a member of the House of Guuxsan, and a stepson of Gwiniiho'osxw (House of 'Niist), Alfred Shanoss. He spent eight years (1936-43) with Gwiniiho'osxw on the upper Nass:

> We went by the Telegraph Trail to Seventh Cabin. We took horses. Charlie Sampson, Phillip Wilson, George Wilson, and George Sexsmith

went to their territory [Miinla̲xmihl] at halfway between Sixth and Seventh Cabins. There is a creek that flows from a lake, and it flows into the creek at Eighth Cabin. Halfway between Seventh and Eighth Cabins is where T'amsaabaya'a is.

Peter Shanoss, William Green, and Bob Lawson went past Luudagwigit. It is two days from there to Stewart.

We crossed the Xsitxemsem [Muckaboo Creek] between Seventh and Eighth Cabins on a Ganeexsim Duutsxw (a bridge made of telegraph wire) and go half an hour to our main cabin. There are lots of Dolly Varden in that lake. There are three lakes up there. We took a raft to get to Luudagwigit. Charles Olson (husband of Daisy) and George Wilson were there in 1939. We had two camps from the lake [T'amsaabaya'a] to K'alaanhl Luudagwigit. We had a camp there at the head [of Luudagwigit]. There was twelve feet of snow there.[138]

On another occasion, Charles Derrick provided further detail about the area:

Xsila̲xwiiyip is a creek between Eighth Cabin and Ninth Cabin that belongs to 'Niist. Ninth Cabin is close to the Bell Irving River, and it is two days' walk from Seventh Cabin to Eighth Cabin. Ninth Cabin is in a pass.

Hlagen̲xwiigwiikxw is a mountain above Gwinsaabaya'a. We hunted groundhog on the left (east) of Gwinsaabaya'a. There is another cabin about fifteen miles from the lake, on the left side of the creek. There was only one mountain for Ansin Matx [goat hunting]. Luudagwigit flows out away from T'amsaabaya'a. We used to use a raft at the first lake. 'Niist was upriver from Alfred Shanoss at Eighth Cabin. Peter Shanoss, David Louie, and William Green had their territory down Xsitxemsem [Muckaboo Creek] to below Seventh Cabin.[139]

Delgamuukw: Ken Muldoe (1988)

Ken Muldoe (1937-91) was taught his history and the boundaries and place names of his territory by Albert Tait and other members of his family. He assumed the name Delgamuukw in 1987. He identified some of the geographic features of his Gwinhagiistxw territory as follows:

T'amlaala̲xuudit (locally, East Bonney Lake)
Xsigwinwijix
T'am Gwinhagiistxw (Fred Wright Lake)
Anyuusxw Adam (Adam Creek)

T'amhliiloot (Kwinageese Lake)
Wisinsgiit
Wilgidiksit'a̲x
Gwinwijix
Xsigwinhagiistxw (Kwinageese River)

Txaslaxwiiyip
Xsi'andapmatx (Saicote Creek)
Andapmatx (Mount Kologet)

Xsilaalaxuudit (Bonney Creek)
Xsi'anlagahl'hliloot.[140]

Dzogoshle: Walter Wilson (1988)

Walter Wilson (1927-93), a chief of Gitanmaax, owns the territory that extends north of the Nass River and east of the Bell-Irving River at the Nass-Bell-Irving junction. It was part of the original Awiijii territory acquired by Sgawil before the turn of the century. Walter said that the territory was transferred as follows:

> Oh yes, that's where he (Daniel Skawil) spent most of his time in the early days. He's a real good trapper. And he had to put up a big feast, and he didn't have enough money and the hides and everything, so he talked to my great uncle Willie [Willie Wilson, a former Dzogoshle], if Willie could help put up that big feast. It costs really a lot of money and hides, everything. So Willie did it. That's how Willie got that area. In return to pay Willie back, Daniel gave him that area. So every village, the whole eight villages, was there to witness what was happening, so everybody knows. Every high chief in each village knows the transfer of that land to Willie Wilson, and he knows Daniel Skawil gave them the [territory] – they walked the boundary them days. So that's how we know the boundary, the traditional boundary, not the one DIA give out them days.[141]

Walter described a camp called An Tsok on the south bank of the Nass, which his uncles and other Gitksan chiefs also used. In his affidavit, Walter Wilson also described the main geographical features of his territory as follows:

Xsitxemsem (Nass River)
Xsiluubiyoosxwt (Irving Creek)

Sto'ot Xsitxemsem (Bell-Irving River)
Xsilaadamus (Saladamus Creek).[142]

In 1995 Wogalwil, David Green, of the House of Wiik'aax of Kisgaga'as, said that he had been to Dzogoshle's territory: "I spent over two years up there. I stayed with Willie Wilson (Djogaslee) two winters, and I stayed with David Gunanoot and Skawil on a nice flat by the Bell Irving River [at Awiijii]. It's really nice country for goats and caribou, marten and everything. Willie Wilson helped Skawil out, and he gave him some money, so Skawil gave the land by the Nass River and part way up Bell Irving."[143]

Conclusion

As with other tribal groups throughout British Columbia, the Gitksan objected to Euro-Canadian incursions into their territory from the earliest times. In 1908 Gitksan chiefs with territory in the Nass watershed produced a petition outlining their position and presented it to Prime Minister Laurier. This petition, and other statements even more specific, demonstrate that the Gitksan, in opposition to Euro-Canadian encroachment, have asserted their claim to territory over a vast portion of the Nass watershed prior to the twentieth century.

In a statement to ethnologist Marius Barbeau in 1920, a Gitksan chief set out a broad claim that included the Nass watershed at Blackwater Lake. In the same year, other Gitksan chiefs made statements of ownership to Barbeau that encompass the upper Nass and Bowser Rivers from near Meziadin and Kwinageese Lakes to the Nass headwaters. The ownership statements and geographic detail provided by Gitksan chiefs demonstrate the depth of their knowledge about the upper Nass watershed (see Map 36).

More recently, Gitksan chiefs such as Jonathan Johnson (1965) and Chris Harris (1972-3) added their voices to those of the 1920s and identified Gitksan territory and place names in the upper Nass watershed. In the recent era, since 1973 and the establishment of the federal Comprehensive Claims Policy, many more Gitksan chiefs have described their territory, place names, and day-to-day experiences growing up and living in the upper reaches of the Nass watershed.

5

The Nisga'a Documentary Record

Introduction

Much has been written about the Nisga'a in recent years, most of which deals with efforts to obtain recognition of their land claim, and some of which deals with related public relations. Two extensive ethnographic studies were conducted by Barbeau and Beynon and by Stephen McNeary. The Barbeau and Beynon record is the only study that deals in some depth with Nisga'a territory. The McNeary report and dissertation deal with Nisga'a society and economy and include a discussion on territory and a map of place names.

The Nisga'a struggle has spanned more than a century. In its earliest years, the claim was advanced by Nisga'a men and women who lived within, worked upon, and defended their territory. They knew their house territories (ango'osxw), fishing sites, and berry grounds; they knew the history of their internal and external boundaries; this is the Nisga'a legacy. The documentary record of significance to this study commences with the expedition of Hudson's Bay Company clerk Donald Manson, who travelled by boat part way up the Nass River in 1832 (see Chapter 6). The record includes the writings of missionaries, explorers, and first settlers thereafter, and it acquires a significant Aboriginal voice after the Nisga'a and their neighbours forced government surveyors and commissions to meet with them in the 1880s.

Nisga'a leaders, as did those of the Gitanyow, sought to impress on government representatives the nature of their ownership by describing Nisga'a territoriality. Largely ignored, the Nisga'a redoubled their effort. The minutes and correspondence of commission hearings over a thirty-year period, between 1887 (IRC) and 1915 (MMRC), reflect a pattern: opening comments; description of territories and sites important to the house or village members; reference to Nisga'a law and territoriality; and the caveat that claims are to Nisga'a territory, beyond living and fishing sites.

During this period, the Nisga'a sought to take their issue beyond the provincial government to the Privy Council in London, England. This approach demanded a more concise expression of their claim, along the lines of efforts by provincial Aboriginal organizations such as the Allied Tribes of BC. Thus the Nisga'a Petitions of 1908 and 1913, of which the latter is best known, for the purpose of "overcoming the constitutional difficulties encountered by reason of the refusal of the Government of British Columbia to agree to a reference [to Privy Council] ... asking for a determination of their rights and the protection of his Majesty."[1] The Nisga'a Petition is often quoted but little understood, despite a seemingly precise metes and bounds statement. Thus, the extent of territory claimed by the Nisga'a in the petition of 1913 requires scrutiny. The documentary record is clear on this issue and is reviewed here.

This record shows three periods of political activity for the Nisga'a: first, the thirty-year period ending about 1916; second, the rise of the Nisga'a Tribal Council in the 1950s, which culminated in the *Calder* v. *Attorney General of British Columbia* decision in 1973; and third, the period from 1973 to the present, during which the Nisga'a have attempted to negotiate a treaty with British Columbia and Canada. This study deals with Nisga'a statements of ownership in each period.

To understand Nisga'a statements of ownership, it is important to understand where they lived on the Nass River and how they organized themselves there. Historically, the Nisga'a defined themselves by geography, tribe, and phratric affiliation. The earliest documentary record shows that the Nisga'a lived in several villages over the centuries and established today's villages soon after missionaries arrived in Kincolith, Greenville (Laxgalts'ap), Canyon City (Gitwinksihlxw), Gitlakdamix, and Aiyansh.

Generally, the Nisga'a live in villages along the lower Nass River. The distance from Kincolith at the mouth of the river to the uppermost village at Gitlakdamix is fewer than 100-kilometres.[2] However, it is in the context of their relative location that the Nisga'a refer to themselves as being Gitka'din (of the lower Nass) or Gitwandilix (of the upper Nass). For example, Bathle, Charles Barton, of Kincolith, told Marius Barbeau in 1915: "In the old times the Nass was divided in 2 parts: Lower Naas called Gitxatin – people/live/by/fish trap [and] upper Nass called Git'anwiliks[3] – people/who move at certain place at certain time. Gitxatin: because there were many fish traps in the village. [Gitwandilix] ... because at certain times they moved to the lower Nass ... in the oolachen fishing time, in the spring. That was not their place. It was up the river."[4]

In 1916 the villages and four tribal divisions of the Nisga'a were explained by K'eexkw, Timothy Derrick, a leading Wolf Clan chief of Gitlakdamix:

(1) kitxat'en – "people of the fish traps," [were] located at the mouth of the river. They occupy the two villages of ... Kincolith, and ... Greenville.

(2) kitgige'nix[5] – "people further up stream" (from the point of view of the preceding tribe). Their village is named lax'anla'c[,] "mountain slide." They are considered the main tribe of the Nass River Indians.

(3) kitwankci'lku – "people of the home of lizards" ... They are located at [Canyon City] ...

(4) kit'anwi'likc – "people moving regularly from and back to their home village" ... They occupy the two villages of Gitlakdamix, and ... Aiyansh.[6]

Derrick also described the four clans of the Nisga'a as Wolf, Frog-Raven, Eagle, and Killer Whale.

In their statements to government representatives in various forums, Nisga'a spokespersons have made frequent reference to the "head of the Nass" or the "upper Nass." Clearly, these statements are made relative to their location on the lower Nass. For example, the Nass River as it appears on maps today is about 384 kilometres from mouth to source. But as is evident in the following statement, the Nisga'a consider the "head" of the Nass to be near Gitlakdamix. Chief of Gitwinksihlxw, George Palmer, stated on 7 October 1915: "Another thing which the people here would like ... to have a good road built by the Government from the mouth of the Naas up to Aiyansh and this is to include a telephone line because when the water is low it is very hard to get connection and also when the river is frozen it is very dangerous and so we would like to have this road from the bottom of the Naas to the head of the Naas."[7]

The Gitksan, Tsimshian, and Nisga'a nations have always had the same system of land tenure and recognized each other's property rights. This system of territorial control was understood by all three groups, and all were equally knowledgeable about the history and geography of their respective territories. It is evident from the statements of Nisga'a spokespersons below that they have an intimate knowledge of their hunting, berry, and fishing grounds and that they are able to name the creeks, lakes, mountains, and fishing sites that they own, as well as some of the more well-known names of territory belonging to their neighbours at or near their borders (see Map 27).

The Gitka'din: Nisga'a of the Lower Nass
Although this study is primarily concerned with the territorial boundary of the upper Nass Nisga'a, a search was made for possible evidence that the lower Nass people claimed territories in the vicinity of Gitwinksihlxw, Gitlakdamix, or Aiyansh. It was found that they did not. The eastern limit

of lower Nass territories appears to be about twenty-two kilometres above Greenville near a place known as Haniik'ohl[8] on the Nass River, and the western limit seems to be at the heads of Alice Arm, Hastings Arm, and Portland Canal. For example, in late August or early September 1887, Job Calder, speaking on behalf of the chief, Victoria Nagwa'un, to Indian Reserve Commissioner O'Reilly at Stoney Point on the Nass River, said: "She is my wife, she does not want the people to speak much, but she wants you to do what they wish. Victoria, and all the chiefs from this part of the Naas, wish our reserve to extend from Canaan,[9] on both sides of the river, to Hal i colth, from mountain to mountain."[10] Later, on 17 October 1887, representatives from Kincolith, Greenville, Kittix, and other places presented their statements of ownership to Commissioners Cornwall and Planta of the Royal Commission of Inquiry into the Northwest Coast Indians. Here Mountain, chief at Greenville, stated: "The Hydahs, Stickeens and others all call the land on each side [of Portland Canal] 'Mountain's land,' and the land I want and have been using is at the head of the canal ... It takes three days to reach the head of the canal where I make my dried salmon."[11]

In 1915 similar statements were made by several Nisga'a to the MMRC hearings, Nass Agency, at Kincolith, especially by Cornelius Nelson, S.L. Allan, and Charles Barton, Bathle. Barton was especially clear that the Nisga'a could name features within their territories to the head of Portland Canal and to the head of the Nass River without specifying the location of the latter: "If there was more time we could name every one of these mountains from Kitimax to the head of Portland Canal, and to the head of the Naas River ... Therefore your honours that is why our tribe claim[,] the Nishga tribe[,] and now show you the boundary as now shown on our petition."[12]

Before dealing with ownership statements by the Gitwandilix (upriver Nisga'a), we may draw two conclusions about the Gitka'din based on Barton's statement: first, their claims do not extend north of Haniik'ohl (to the east) nor much beyond the head of Portland Canal (to the west); and second, a high standard existed for the Nisga'a in 1915 – the ability to name "every mountain ... to the head of the Nass River" and therefore, by extension, every geographic feature within the petition boundary as advanced by the Nisga'a of today.

The Gitwandilix: Nisga'a of the "Upper" Nass: Statements to the Indian Reserve Commission (1887)

In the 1880s, with the growth of salmon canneries, non-Native settlement, the establishment of Indian reserves, and the conflicts at Metlakatla, the Tsimshian and the Nisga'a engaged in a variety of protest activities concerning the land question. In February 1887, a number of

Nisga'a and Fort Simpson leaders met with Premier Smithe and other officials at the premier's residence in Victoria. In the published account of the meeting is a discussion of Nisga'a claims to sites above Gitlakdamix:

> Charles Barton: The people at Kit-lak-tam-aks have got their fishery further up than where they are living.
>
> Mr. O'Reilly: With regard to the Kit-lak-tam-aks having a reserve farther up the river, that is not yet a reserve. That part of the work has not been touched. It has yet to be done. It is a long way up the river; and can be more conveniently reached when the reserves at the Forks of the Skeena are being dealt with. That has nothing to do with the reserves we have been talking of [at Observatory Inlet and from Gitlakdamix down the Nass].
>
> B[a]rton: These are on the Nass River.
>
> O'Reilly: The fisheries above Kit-lak-tam-aks, on the Naas River, have not been laid out yet. We have been talking of those below – all the way to Kincoleth.
>
> B[a]rton: You see, the people at Kit-lak-tam-aks are expecting to hear something from you this time.
>
> O'Reilly: Their reserves will be laid out for them, but, probably, not this year.
>
> B[a]rton: That is more like it.
>
> O'Reilly: When I was up there [in 1881] I explained to the Chief Scot-een[13] that I could not go up. He spoke of reserves 50 miles [80 km] further up the river; and I considered it more convenient to locate them when dealing with the reserves on the Skeena River; the reserves we are speaking of, from Kit-lak-tam-aks, extending down the river to Kincoleth, are settled.
>
> Dr. Powell (to B[a]rton): Mr. O'Reilly says that he will attend to these reserves at the head of the Naas another time, when he goes up to the Skeena.
>
> O'Reilly: Reserves will be made for them. I only went to the point on the Naas River, where the Grease Trail begins.[14] The reserves above that point will be made at some future time.[15]

However, when one carefully analyzes the 1881 record of O'Reilly, the most detail appears in his diary entry for 13 October 1881: "Fine day. Did not move camp. Walked to 'Kitlacdamax' – had an interview with the Chief 'Scot-tein.' Indians – went in Canoe to Can[y]on view of fishery reserve, & also reserve from above village to below Iyennis [Aiyansh]."[16]

One may theorize as to what Sgat'iin actually said to O'Reilly. However, Sgat'iin taught his nephew and successor, a later Sgat'iin, about his territories. In 1915 this later Sgat'iin made statements to the MMRC that did not include territory on the Nass River beyond Gitxsits'uuts'xwt. Similarly, in 1916 E.N. Mercer, son-in-law of the latter Sgat'iin, and his emissary to Ottawa produced a map and a verbal description of "Gitwinlkul" and "Aiyansh" hunting grounds that entirely corroborate the statements of Gitanyow chiefs and demonstrate that Nisga'a territory ends at Gitxsits'uuts'xwt.

In this context, one can only assume that the senior Sgat'iin was referring in 1881 to specific fisheries: there is no dispute that, from the time of the xsiisxw in 1861 (and prior to it), the Gitanyow fished at Meziadin. Chief Sgat'iin, who spoke to O'Reilly in 1881, surely would have been knowledgeable about that. In other words, it is a misconception to assume, as McNeary does below, that O'Reilly's reference was that the Nisga'a held substantial territory above Gitxsits'uuts'xwt.

After Barton's meeting with the premier and others in Victoria in February 1887, O'Reilly agreed to make a second visit to the Nass River valley. On this trip, he went up the river to Aiyansh and Gitlakdamix. At a meeting at Aiyansh, on 4 September 1887, O'Reilly recalled his previous visit to the Nass River valley (in 1881) and said: "When I was here before I invited you to accompany me, and every place you pointed out was reserved, therefore it is your own fault if all you wanted is not reserved. I have made a slight mistake, the Chief Scoteen told me at that time of some fisheries above the Can[y]on, about 50 miles [80 km] from here. I told him I could not visit them, but that they would be secured to them later."[17]

The Babine Agency was established in 1888, and Richard Loring was appointed Indian agent and sent to Hazelton in 1889. Although O'Reilly visited the upper Skeena in 1891, neither he nor Sgat'iin, nor his successor (see MMRC hearings, Nass Agency), made further mention of this fishery.

In October 1887, the Royal Commission of Inquiry into the Northwest Coast Indians came to the lower Skeena and Nass Rivers. Chairman J.B. Planta had been instructed by Attorney General Davie to assure the Indians that all they said would be duly "reported to the proper authorities" and "not to give any undertakings or make promises, and in particular you will be careful to discountenance, should it arise, any claim of Indian land title to Provincial lands."[18] Clement Cornwall had been nominated to represent the government of Canada. The commission, which opened at Kincolith on 17 October 1887, provided an opportunity for the Nisga'a to set out their claim.[19] However, apart from the following comment in Cornwall and Planta's report, specific Nisga'a claims beyond Gitlakdamix do not occur: "The Greenville people and some of the chiefs living still further up the Naas River, and Tsimpseans of Port Simpson, hold pronounced views on the question. They also professed to speak for the

Upper Skeena people ... The Greenville and Upper Naas people demand that a treaty be made with them with reference to the land in their neighbourhood, outside of the reserves they desire to appropriate."[20] It is not clear who the "Upper Skeena people" referred to are, perhaps the Gitanyow.

In conclusion, relevant to this study is O'Reilly's reference to an 1881 discussion with Sgat'iin about the fishery and reserves eighty kilometres upriver, beyond Gitlakdamix. On whose behalf was Sgat'iin speaking, however: his or the Gitanyow's? The answer lies with his successor in evidence given to the MMRC in 1915, in which he is explicit about the limits of his territory and fishery at Gitxsits'uuts'xwt (see below).

Priestley and Hickman Incidents (1907-8)

J. Priestley was a white settler who, in 1907, staked and applied to pre-empt a piece of land on the east side of the Nass river near Aiyansh. In January 1908, he attended a meeting with eighteen Aiyansh and Gitlak-damix chiefs. He was told that "they wanted – and would have – NO strangers on the Naas River – an Indian, Chief Joe Capilano, had seen the King, who had promised to restore their rights, and a number of their chiefs were going to Ottawa in May next to say what these rights were – they claimed 40 miles [sixty-four kilometres] up and 40 miles down, the river, and (I believe) 40 miles each side, in which they were resolved to have no white people as settlers."[21] As the crow flies, it is eighty kilo-metres from Aiyansh east to the village of Gitanyow (Kitwancool) and ninety kilometres north to Meziadin Lake. This metes and bounds descrip-tion by the meeting of chiefs at Aiyansh, as reported by Priestley, there-fore includes an area that extends east to Gitanyow village and north nearly to Meziadin Lake.

Later, in 1908, C.P. Hickman, fisheries overseer at Nass Harbour, went on a trip to Meziadin Lake and was confronted with Aboriginal demands. He informed the attorney general: "On my return from Meziadin they [upper Nass people] demanded ten dollars from me for walking over their trail they claiming all the land as their own." Hickman refused to pay and was told that "they did not want me to pay but they did not want the Gov to use the trail as they had not given them any money or axes towards making it and they had this year made a law that they charge every white man 10 dollars who walk it in the future."[22] Given the Gitanyow presence in Nisga'a villages, it may be assumed that the meet-ing with Priestley included Gitanyow chiefs and that the delegation had described both Nisga'a and Gitanyow territories. Nevertheless, the claim reported by Priestley does not include the Nass watershed beyond Meziadin Lake.

There is nothing in the Hickman incident to indicate whom he encountered and where: given the documentary record, and their willingness to confront trespassers, as well as his reference to Meziadin, it was likely the Gitanyow. Nevertheless, by 1910 (see below) the Nisga'a had posted notices of their own and might have protested to Hickman in 1908.

Nisga'a Petition (1908)

At the same time that the Nisga'a and Gitksan chiefs on the Nass River were confronting individual Euro-Canadian settlers such as Priestley and Hickman with their claims, they were taking steps to address more rigorously the land question on a broad political front. The Nisga'a Land Committee, created in 1907,[23] and which included Gitanyow chiefs, set out a more precise articulation of the Nisga'a claim in the Nass watershed. In March 1908, copies of the early Nisga'a Petition had found their way to a Vancouver newspaper and the Department of Indian Affairs. The newspaper included extensive quotations "from the scriptures" and a claim to "land in the Nass Valley, about one hundred and forty miles [224 km] in extent, [which] is all needed by themselves as hunting grounds, timber and fishing grounds."[24] These claims were repeated to IRC Commissioner Vowell when he visited the Nass in May of the same year. As noted above, the Nass River valley is 384 kilometres long, which means that the 1908 petition falls short of the headwaters of the Nass, as known today, by 160 kilometres. On this issue, the second Nisga'a Petition (see below) is consistent with the first.

Nisga'a Protest Notices (1910)

It was about this time that the Nisga'a, like the Gitksan, became involved in wider Native protests over the Aboriginal title issue. As noted earlier, an important step in this wider process was the preparation and submission of the Cowichan Petition of 1909, with its invocation of the Royal Proclamation of 1763. Nisga'a familiarity with these developments is reflected in the notices issued by the Nisga'a Land Committee in 1910. The objective was still to prevent the influx of settlers and the staking of land in the valley, but the language of the notice reflects a new legal awareness. The notice stated:[25]

AGAINST WHITE SETTLERS COMING INTO THE AIYANSH VALLEY, NAAS RIVER, BRITISH COLUMBIA

WHEREAS, We the Indian people of the above mentioned valley, being the lawful possessors of all lands contained therein from time immemorial.[26]

In 1911 the Nisga'a hired A.E. O'Meara, one of the people responsible for preparing the Cowichan Petition, as their legal counsel. This step led to the preparation of a second Nisga'a Petition, that of 1913.

Nisga'a Petition (1913)

The Aboriginal leaders of northwestern British Columbia were familiar with the Cowichan Petition of 1909. It was likely this legal undertaking that helped to spread knowledge of the Royal Proclamation of 1763 and formed a model for the Nisga'a Petition.[27] The Nisga'a Petition was developed following a meeting at Kincolith on 22 January 1913. W.J. Lincoln, chairman of the meeting, issued the following statement: "From time immemorial the Nishga Nation or Tribe of Indians possessed, occupied and used the territory generally known as the Valley of the Naas River, the boundaries of which are well defined."[28] By May the Nisga'a Petition was refined into a lengthy legal document containing fifteen paragraphs over many pages that dealt with constitutional principles that the Nisga'a wished to address politically – principles supported by the Gitksan when A.E. O'Meara visited the upper Skeena in August 1913 and later, in 1924, when Prime Minister Mackenzie King visited Prince Rupert. The nature of Gitksan support was expressed in February 1915 by W.J. Lincoln, chairman of the Nisga'a delegation to Ottawa: "We should explain how the matter of consulting other Tribes now stands ... In August [1913] we met the Haydas [Haidas] and Kitiksheans [Gitksans] who passed resolutions approving our main proposals."[29]

Although the Gitksan again expressed support for the Nisga'a in 1924, the Kispiox statement presented to the prime minister at the same time then included a claim to land in the Nass watershed (see Chapter 4). This demonstrates that the Gitksan were supportive of the "main proposals" in the Nisga'a Petition, not their territorial claim.[30] At issue in this study, however, is the extent of land claimed by the Nisga'a in the petition.

The documentary record shows that the Nisga'a long considered the Nass headwaters to be at or near Gitlakdamix. Other evidence supports this view, including their 1908 petition. Unfortunately, the Nisga'a, unlike the Gitanyow, seem not to have drawn maps that set out the extent of their territory. Two blueprint maps were attached to the Nisga'a Petition of 1913, but they were made by the Department of the Surveyor General in British Columbia, not by the Nisga'a. The maps are still to be found in the Privy Council Office in London, England, and show Crown preemptions in two areas: along the Nass River in the vicinity of Gitlakdamix, and further upstream at Meziadin Lake.[31] The maps contain no information supplementary to the Nisga'a Petition to indicate the extent of Nisga'a claims: the imprecise language in the petition was the fullest description of the territory until the 1916 Mercer map (see Barton-Mercer

Delegation, below). The notation, "Aiyansh hunting ground," on Mercer's map shows that Nisga'a territory ends well below the Nass-Cranberry Rivers confluence. Mercer's map supports the argument that the 1908 and 1913 petitions include the Nass watershed from the Tchitin River to Meziadin Lake because of a one-time alliance between the Nisga'a and the Gitanyow – an alliance that was terminated by 1926.[32]

Two people, one a longtime missionary[33] among the Nisga'a, the other a high chief and respected member of the Nisga'a Land Committee, are more specific, providing direct evidence that Nisga'a leaders and elders considered the "head of the Nass" to be at Meziadin Lake. McCullagh noted in 1918: "Medziadin – a magnificent lake at the head of the Naas. It is pronounced Med-zee-ah-din, with accent on the ah." And James Adams explained in 1930 that "the Allied Tribes had made a claim for the whole province of British Columbia but they (the Nishgas) were more reasonable, and only wanted the Nass River country, from the headwaters of the Nass at Meziadin Lake down to the mouth."[34]

McCullagh played a diverse role as resource person among the Nisga'a for many years. He was present during the development of the Nisga'a Petition and appears to have had a hand in writing it. The late Eli Gosnell[35] said that McCullagh wrote the 1913 petition, although it is more likely that he wrote the 1908 petition and may have assisted O'Meara in the latter one: "This was their story as told by my father. The Reverend J.B. McCullough heard this and accepted it as the truth, and that was how the Land Petition was written when he wrote it. So that no one will make a mistake about it. That was how it was that MET'SIADIN was written down."[36] Significantly, in 1905 McCullagh travelled to Meziadin and met 'Wiilitsxw, the Gitanyow chief, who told him the Gitanyow history and the lament sung by the Tsetsaut when they abandoned the area in 1861 (see Chapter 6).

Many years later, in 1986, the leadership of the Nisga'a Tribal Council tendered, to the Gitksan-Wet'suwet'en leadership, documents that would substantiate their boundary in support of their position during a meeting to discuss tribal boundaries.[37] The documents included a letter from Wilson Duff to Frank Calder, accompanied by an extract of the metes and bounds in the 1913 Nisga'a Petition, two maps (labelled Map #1 and Map #2), and two pages with additional explanatory details about each map (see Appendix 9).

The first map is a photocopy of Exhibit 2 in the *Calder* v. *Attorney General of British Columbia* case (see Map 18), with a total land claim area of 9,516 square kilometres (3,674 square miles). The second, Map #2, is similar to Exhibit 2, except that the boundary line includes Meziadin Lake and encompasses an area of 15,893 square kilometres (5,750 square miles; see Map 19). Two of the four explanatory notes that accompany Map #2

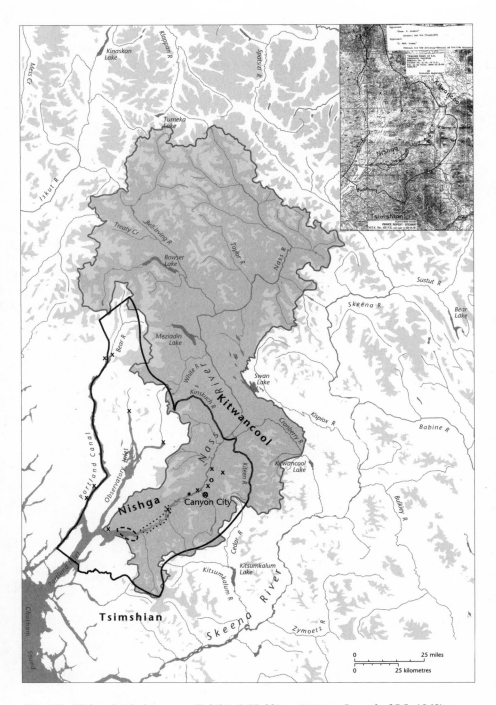

Map 18   Nishga land claim area: Exhibit 2 (*Calder* v. *Attorney General of BC*, 1969)

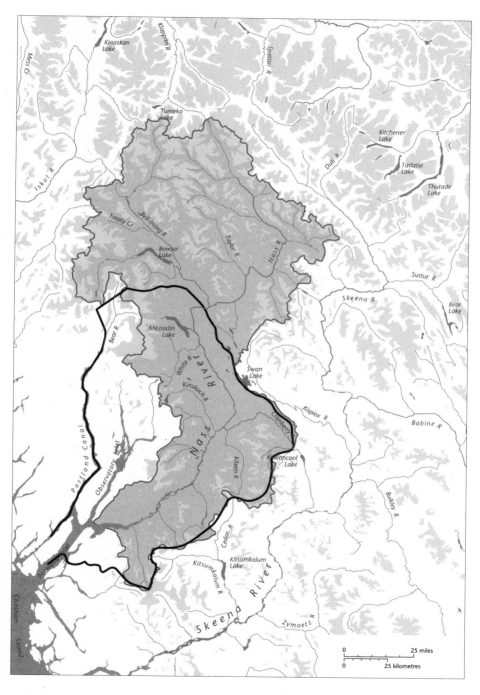

Map 19   Nisga'a Petition of 1913 (as interpreted by NTC, 1986)

explain unequivocally that Map #2 represents the metes and bounds description in the Nisga'a Petition:

RE: Map #2

1. MAP #2 REPRESENTS THE NISHGA LAND CLAIMS BOUNDARY AS DETERMINED AND OUTLINED IN THE NISGA'A PETITION WHICH WAS SUBMITTED TO THE KING'S MOST EXCELLENT MAJESTY IN COUNCIL, LONDON, ENGLAND, IN THE YEAR 1913.
4. MAP #2 AS PER THE NISGA'A PETITION IS THE BASIS OF NISHGA LAND AND RESOURCES EVALUATION RESEARCH. (SEE WILSON DUFF LETTER).[38]

It is clear, then, what the geographic extent of the Nisga'a Petition is: it includes Meziadin Lake in the Nass watershed, as in Map 19.

There is no confusion about the extent of land that the Nisga'a meant to claim in 1913, but given the clear historical record the wording of the metes and bounds description in the petition lacks precision:

Commencing at a stone situate on the south shore of Kinnamox or Quina-mass Bay and marking the boundary line between the territory of the said Nishga Nation or Tribe and that of the Tsimpshean Nation or Tribe of Indians, running thence easterly along said boundary line to the height of land between the Naas River and the Skeena River, *thence in a line following the height of land surrounding the valley of the Naas River and its tributaries to and including the height of land surrounding the northwest end of Mitseah or Meziaden Lake,* thence in a straight line to the northerly end of Portland Canal, thence southerly along the international boundary to the centre line of the passage between Pearse island and Wales Island, thence northeasterly along said centre line to the point at which the same is intersected by the centre line of Kinnamox or Quinamass Bay, thence in a straight line to the point of commencement.[39] (emphasis added)

Because many people, including the Nisga'a, considered Meziadin Lake to be "the head of the Nass" in 1913, it is easy to see why the petition contains this anomaly: that is, that the metes and bounds can be read to include the entire Nass watershed, or to include the Nass watershed up to "the height of land surrounding the northwest end of Mitseah or Meziadin Lake." Based on this map (Map 19), the Nisga'a believe that the 1913 metes and bounds description extended only to include Meziadin Lake, not the entire Nass River.

Another issue needs to be addressed in this discussion. Although the extent of lands claimed by the Nisga'a is clear, less clear is why the petition would include lands near Meziadin Lake if the Nisga'a-Gitanyow boundary is nearly 100 kilometres downstream at Gitxsits'uuts'xwt. Readers are reminded of the discussion of the Gitanyow in Chapter 3, which shows that a number of Gitksan persons from Gitanyow relocated to Nisga'a villages in the late 1800s and that Gitanyow territory was included in the Nisga'a Petition. This is logical, because the common issue for all Aboriginal nations at that time was the complete failure of the provincial government to recognize any of their claims. In 1916 E.N. Mercer, a member of the Nisga'a Land Committee, described the "gitwinlku'n [Kitwancool]" to Barbeau: "The gitwinlku'n tribe (another Nisge' band) occupied territory indicated on map BBB; for the hunting ... Some of the Gitwinlkun live at Ayansh now, all the year around. They began to come to Ayansh 15 years ago."[40]

It is not clear when the Gitanyow became aware that the Nisga'a assumed that they had absorbed the "Gitwinlkun," but by 1926 they had taken steps to deal with the issue, as their actions demonstrate. For example, in 1926 relations were clearly strained when the Gitanyow distanced themselves from the Nisga'a and asked for the return of funds contributed to the Nisga'a effort (see Frank Calder below); also in 1926, Gitanyow hereditary chief Michael Inspring Bright, who lived much of his life in Aiyansh, chose to distinguish Gitanyow place names from those of the Nisga'a on his map of the Nass River between Gitlakdamix and Meziadin Lake (see Maps 10[a] and 10[b]). Not content to leave matters there, about fifteen years later Bright informed Barbeau that he wanted "to make a statement" that his maps also represented the "Gitwinlkul" conquest of the Tsetsaut at Meziadin. These actions by the Gitanyow are consistent with Gitksan and Nisga'a law: people may migrate out of their ancestral village, but they cannot bring territorial title to their adopted nation.

It is evident, then, that Gitksan support for the Nisga'a Petition, expressed at various times after 1914, reflected their agreement with the general principles articulated in that document. In so doing, the Gitksan were simply continuing a policy developed prior to the existence of the Nisga'a Petition; Aboriginal nations in British Columbia followed a policy of solidarity against the government in its denial of any territorial rights.

From 1914, although the Gitksan made statements expressing support for the Nisga'a Petition, they did not prevent the Gitanyow or the Kispiox chiefs, for example, from making clear statements about the extent of their own territories. In addition to the express actions of the Gitanyow, in part these statements rejected the territorial claims of the Nisga'a Petition. For example, the Gitanyow map submitted to the McKenna-McBride Royal Commission clearly contradicts the claim that support for the Nisga'a Petition involved acceptance of the territorial definition contained therein.

Gitanyow territory, as Albert Williams described the Sam Douse map to the MMRC in 1915, bore two features common to Gitanyow maps: the inclusion of territory within a black line, and the lowest point of their territory on the Nass River marked at a creek that is cleary the Tchitin River.

Gitksan support for the Nisga'a Petition concerned the general principles, not a recognition of the validity, of Nisga'a territorial claims. Furthermore, the Nisga'a Petition of 1913 included Gitanyow territory beyond Gitxsits'uuts'xwt. On the latter point, for example, the Nisga'a continue to imply, even today, that the basis for their claim to Meziadin derives from the presence of the descendants of Gitanyow persons living in Nisga'a villages: "Whoever comes to Nisga'a territory we accept that. We accept – it is also in our testimony in [*Calder* v. *Attorney General of British Columbia*] that is finally written. They've got volumes and volumes of people, of Kitwancool people coming into our area, and were accepted, and were accepted into the Nisga'a Nation. We have [the village of Kincolith (?)] and two thirds of them are Kitwancool that are living in Kincolith right now."[41] This statement implies that the Nisga'a believe they absorbed not only the Gitanyow people but, by extension, their territory as well. The significance of the statement for this study is that the Nisga'a, in effect, acknowledge that Gitanyow territory exists, a territory that was well defined at the time in a series of Gitanyow maps.

The Nisga'a Land Committee in Ottawa

The Lincoln Delegation (1915)
In February 1915, a delegation of Nisga'a travelled to Ottawa to meet with representatives of the Canadian government. The delegation consisted of Chairman W.J. Lincoln; Timothy L. Derrick; A.N. Calder; R.S. Woods, secretary and interpreter; and A.E. O'Meara, counsel for the Nisga'a. The delegates appear to have spent one or two months in Ottawa and to have made the following comments during their discussions: "T.L. Derrick (in English): This is the map of the Naas Valley. All the land in the Naas Valley has been taken up by the white friends; not one inch is left for us; just a piece reserved; that is where the trouble is; because the land offered to us before for hunting ground the white friends take them, and we do not trouble them, we do not stop them, but we stop the surveyors because we do not want trouble with them."[42] Derrick's comment suggests that the map shows lands in the Nass River valley that had been taken up by white settlers: it is likely one of the two maps that accompanied the petition to the Privy Council in 1913, seemingly the only maps mentioned by the Nisga'a in the context of their claim.

On 4 February 1915, Nisga'a representative R.S. Woods discussed with Deputy Superintendent General Duncan C. Scott the difficulties of land selection in the Nass River valley, given that settlers had already taken up the more desirable land. Clearly, the lands discussed are in the lower Nass River valley:

> Mr. Woods: You gentlemen can satisfy yourself that there are no lands to be given by the Royal Commission unless they are prepared to give us already disposed of land. There is no transportation up here (looking at the blue prints).
> Mr. Scott: You are out in very young country up there. In 50 years from now it will be quite different.
> Mr. Woods: We thought we would be entitled to have first choice in the land and the whites would go further up.[43]

Although Derrick is not specific about the location of the lands referred to below, the map that he was using shows lands alienated by Euro-Canadians: "We have shown you our grounds on the Naas (the map) and how far the hunting grounds extend. (We get our living from hunting.) We have told you that these have been taken up. We are not asking anyone for these lands, they belong to us, are all our own. Whites have come in and taken up our lands."[44] Derrick refers again to white settlers in the lower valley.

The delegation held further meetings in Ottawa on 25 March, with the following people present: Hon. Dr. Roche; Mr. Duncan C. Scott, deputy superintendent general; Mr. A.E. O'Meara; Mr. W.J. Lincoln; and Mr. R.S. Woods, interpreter. W.J. Lincoln, on behalf of the delegation, made a supplementary statement (no. 3): "We want to be free men, to have free possession of so much of the territory of our forefathers as we require to keep for our own use, to be free to live independent lives and make full use of the fisheries and other resources of our territory, and to work out a future for ourselves."[45] Following is the ensuing discussion:

> Mr. Woods: If it can be shown to us, proven that the Royal Commission [MMRC] is able to give us lands that have already been disposed of and some of those lands that the Indians on the Naas need, why this question of coming to an agreement with the Government would be easy, and our questions, asking the Minister of Justice for information, were based on that.
> Dr. Roche: You would not be satisfied with taking the other lands in lieu of them?
> Mr. Woods: Well no, because, as we explained by that blue print we gave you in February, that there are no lands to be given outside of those that have been disposed of.
> Dr. Roche: You mean in that valley?

Mr. Woods: In that valley, yes.

Dr. Roche: Are there not other lands in the Province?

Mr. Woods: I suppose there are lands in the Province, but we are referring to the Nishga territory at present, and I know there are none in what we call the Nishga territory, unless you go away inland, as we showed you by the blue prints.[46]

Another meeting was held at the office of the deputy superintendent general of Indian Affairs in Ottawa on 6 April: "Mr. Woods: If we suppose that the Judicial Committee will decide that the claims made by the Nishgas are right, we think that the Nishgas are making a big concession because the Nishgas claim that they hold rights to all this Naas River territory; if there is a decision passed that the Nishgas are right, why the Nishgas have a right to pick out what lands they need themselves and to decide on what lands are to be sold."[47]

Apparently, the only maps of this era that have been located are copies of the preemption "blue prints" that accompanied the 1913 petition to the Privy Council (see above). These may be the maps to which Derrick was referring.

The Barton-Mercer Delegation (1916)

In May 1916, a second Nisga'a delegation visited Ottawa to obtain support for the Nisga'a Petition.[48] The delegation included E.N. Mercer, a "Chief of Aiyansh," son-in-law of the leading Gitlakdamix Wolf chief Sgat'iin, and member of the Nisga'a Land Committee. During the visit, Mercer provided important historical and territorial information to Marius Barbeau. Mercer specifically identified Meziadin Lake, the Gitanyow-Nisga'a border on the lower Nass, and produced a map of the areas discussed. He also explained the reason for his participation in the Nisga'a delegation: "I married the Daughter of Sgadi.n. That chief is the one that appoints me to come here [to Ottawa]."[49]

Mercer's map shows the "hunting ground" connected with the Nisga'a village of Aiyansh (Gitlakdamix). It also shows, in particular, Gitanyow territories extending along the Nass and Cranberry Rivers from Meziadin Lake to southwest of Kitwanga Lake and down the Nass River to well below the Cranberry confluence (see Map 20). Mercer's interview with Barbeau is explicit:

Ottawa, 1916, Nass River chiefs
E.N. Mercer, Aya'nsh
Lax̱kibu; Nane'[50]
Tsimshian Nisge'

The Kitwinlku'n [Kitwancool] lived further up but near, camped with us.

Our (Ayansh hunting ground) extended from the Nass to Lava lake. The Gitwinku'n village is near Kitwanga Lake. It is called gitwinlku'n Lake. Village indicated NN on small map; Some of the Gitwinlkun live at Ayansh now, all the year around. They began to come to Ayansh 15 years ago. Their [Gitanyow] hunting ground is from that lake [Meziadin], down to the Nass River, also towards gitwanga.[51]

According to Wilson Duff, who examined Barbeau's notes, Mercer put the history of the people of the area "in a nutshell"[52] when he said: "The Gitwinlkun [Kitwancool] & Nass river people had fight Met'sia.dan Lake. Some other tribe inland lived at Meziadin Lake; the Gitwinlkul fought them, and since they won they have kept that place for hunting; These people were the lax'wiyip; they are of different language. They are the T'set'sa.ot."[53]

Mercer specifically identified the Gitksan and Nisga'a "hunting grounds" of Gitanyow and Aiyansh as Barbeau cross-referenced, alphabetically, his notes to the map: "Gitwinlkun hunting ground indicated on small map KK ... Ayansh hunting ground DD."[54]

During this interview, Mercer identified seventeen Nisga'a fish camps along the Nass from the Tseax River to Gitxsits'uuts'xwt and demonstrated detailed knowledge of the river, much as Nisga'a chiefs Niisyok, Sgat'iin, Minee'eskw, and others had in the MMRC hearings a year earlier:

1. Niisyok camp called: Sii'aks (new stream) camp
2. Camp of Tok called Sgasginist (a pine-like tree[,] camp)
3. Gisgahe' [Gisgaast ?] camp called Ts'imanwihlist (from basket net), and
4. Gwinsmak (looks like a bear[,] camp)
5. And the camp behind Gilaksi (sun bar camp)[,] was by anybody long ago. It was on the trail.
6. Ksdiyaawak camp named Anxsanskw (hauling canoe)
7. Anukskwiyinskw is the name of the 2nd camp (looking down the high canyon)
8. The 3rd camp called Gwinhamook (wild rhubarb camp)
9. Gwinyoo camp, called Xmatkt (climbing hill with heavy pack)
10. Hewa camp, Anukswok (somebody sleeping and waiting there – waiting [for] the canoes coming up the river)
11. Laxts'imilix camp, Wilukst'aas Sgawoo (where Sgawoo mother sit down and looks on the other side of the river ...)
12. Minee'eskw camp called Gitksidaksit (Ksidaksit[,] name of a rock submerging in the river)

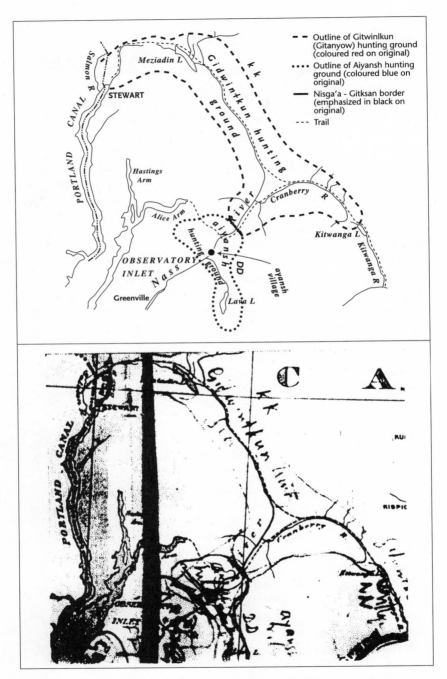

Map 20   Aiyansh and Gitanyow hunting grounds showing Nisga'a-Gitanyow border (E.N. Mercer, 1916)

13. Ksim X̱saan camp called Gitkalt (meaning? old ...)
14. Axdiiwiluugooda camp[,] Gwinsok̲ (many robins there)[55]
15. T̲xa'anlax̲hatxw and
16. K'eex̱kw camp are called Gitangyahlxw (people of spearing salmon)
17. Sgat'iin camp Gitxsits'uuts'xwt (lots of all kinds of little birds on it).[56]

Mercer obviously had intimate knowledge of Nisga'a place names along the Nass River. Clearly, his map of Gitanyow and Aiyansh hunting grounds is supplemented by his detailed list of place names between Aiyansh and Gitxsits'uuts'xwt. There can be little doubt about the location of the Nisga'a border at Gitxsits'uuts'xwt.

Important conclusions may be drawn from the record left by these two Nisga'a delegations to Ottawa. First, the two maps that accompanied the 1913 Nisga'a Petition to London were probably used in discussions in Ottawa in 1915, and these discussions centred primarily on the map of the Aiyansh area. Second, in 1916 it was crucial that an important Nisga'a chief, a member of the Nisga'a Land Committee and the emissary for Sgat'iin, the first Wolf chief of Gitlakdamix, corroborated in every respect, and with a map, the Gitanyow claim, to and including Meziadin Lake, and located the Gitanyow-Nisga'a border well below the Kinskuch River.

Nisga'a Ownership Statements to the
McKenna-McBride Commission (Nass Agency, 1915)

The MMRC arrived on the Nass River in October 1915 and made its way upriver from Kincolith, listening to witnesses village by village. It is not surprising to find that nearly all Nisga'a spokespersons were members of the Nisga'a Land Committee. The Upper Nass Hearing commenced 7 October 1915 at Gitwinksihlxw. Chief Paul Zaloo described territory on the Nass River between Greenville and Aiyansh: "We ask for additional lands from a point known as Haliaulth to a point up the river known as Ikshininik.[57] I am very pleased to be able to tell you that what we require gentlemen, we won't always have the privilege of having you gentlemen in our midst and that is why we sent you our humble petition asking you to stay with us."[58]

Chief George Palmer then addressed the commission:

I am a Chief of a family of this tribe. There are over twelve male members of the family over which I am Chief, not counting the women and children. When Captain Jemmett first came up to survey these parts up here he just went wherever there were anyone camped at the mouth of this Ikshininik Creek ... I know where the posts stand. I remember the point at the mouth of the creek that flows into the Naas but I cannot

say how far down the other post is. John Wesley of Kincolith was working for the surveyor at the time and he knows where the other post is.
From the mouth of this creek right up into the valley was recognized by
all as belonging to my brother, and I now want to explain to the Royal
Commission – I now want the whole of this flat which belongs to our
family to be handed over to the people of this village.[59]

Palmer claimed, on behalf of his brother, all of Ishkeenickh Creek, which
flows north into the Nass River near Greenville. At the same time, he
wanted a road built from the mouth of the Nass to Aiyansh. He empha-
sized this point by repeating it and, in the context of his earlier statement, equated "the head of the Naas"[60] with Aiyansh.

The commissioners took evidence on 8 October at Aiyansh, where the
upper Nass Nisga'a chiefs made their statements of ownership. The testimony of Chiefs Niisyok and Sgat'iin is detailed and of particular interest.
They name a series of sites within Nisga'a territories from the Tseax River,
up the Nass River to Gitxsits'uuts'xwt, and then back down the river,
emphasizing that these sites are connected to the nearby mountains. The
crucial point here is that the evidence of Niisyok and Sgat'iin does not
contradict any information presented by the Gitanyow chiefs at the
MMRC hearings at Aiyansh: William Gogak, Daniel Guno, Richard and
Arthur Derrick, and Walter Dasque.

Peter Nisyok, a knowledgeable Nisga'a elder, born c. 1845, thus addressed
the commission:[61]

I want to tell you a story about our grandfathers and our great grandfathers and all these men that you see here. There are three rivers by
the name of SII'AKS[62] and SGASGINIST[63] and GWINSMAK – from that it
went on right up to the canyon to Gilaxksip, Angwihlgolxen, Anukswok,
Gitskas, Gidiluut, Winatkxw, Gwinbaxwee'esxw,[64] Gwinglank (?), Gwingak,
Gwinsmak, Ts'imanwihlist, Gitangyahlxw, then crossing the river and
coming down on the left[65] bank Gitxsits'uuts'xwt, Dagits'in, Gitsaksgan,
Minluk, Gitgyalk, Gitksidaksit, Gwindip'win, Aksgan, Wilukst'aas [Sgawoo],
Sgarvin [?], Gwindibilx, Gitsigaltkw, Gitksagaugasn and Gwingilkw.[66]

Niisyok listed Nisga'a "salmon fishing camps" and went on to emphasize
(perhaps to demonstrate the basis for his knowledge) his age ("almost
seventy") and the comprehensive nature of his claim:

None of these camps that I have named to you gentlemen were just camps
– they were all connected up by trails and also from these camps we had
trails running up to the tops of the mountains where we used to get the
mountain goat and the whistler. We did not always know how to garden

– the only way we had of gardening was to set a fire to the timber and on this burned over ground all kinds of fruits would grow up which we used for our food ... In my case it is the same thing – my hunting ground is up the Sheax Valley and I had a hunting trail up to this Valley and the Government used this hunting trail of mine for its telegraph line – they built houses all along the trail at different places so that now my hunting is spoilt and I don't go there anymore to hunt.[67]

In a subsequent statement, made on 9 October, Niisyok identified territories claimed by the Gitlakdamix Wolf Clan, up the Tseax River and near Lava Lake, over which he was "boss":

I want to make known to you about my grievance about the land of which I am boss known as the Sheax Valley ... It is four years now since the government took away my hunting-ground from which I got my living starting at a point at Lava Lake from that my hunting trail went up into the mountains and right along this hunting trail of mine this telegraph line runs and I haven't hunted up there for the last four years ... The creek of which I speak – from this creek we get salmon and I don't stop any man from coming there – all the men and Chiefs of this village go there to get their supply of salmon. When we do this we are all happy together because we are able to get salmon from this creek; the same from time immemorial. I have a fish house at the mouth of this creek and just on this side of where the white man is camped I have another fish house and three miles further on from the fish-house I have another hunting lodge and two miles still further on again I still have another one – that is right up to the end of the lake I mentioned, that is Lava Lake. Then right up from Lava Lake following my trail, I have the last hunting trail ... and I also mentioned the number of different camps along the river; these were passed down to me from my great grandfather and as it is I don't think this area would be sufficient for my family, as part of this land is all rock.[68]

The MMRC files contain a map[69] of the Nass River, with the place names described by Niisyok (see Map 21), including Gitxsits'uuts'xwt, Gwinmoots, and Gitangyahlxw, which were the uppermost names given in his 1915 oral presentation (see Map 36). The map shows the Kinskuch River farther upstream without any claim by Niisyok on behalf of the Nisga'a present.

In conclusion, there is little doubt that Peter Niisyok's comprehensive claim is to fishing sites and surrounding territories and sets the Nisga'a boundary twenty-five kilometres (sixteen miles) above Gitlakdamix at Gitxsits'uuts'xwt and Gitangyahlxw.

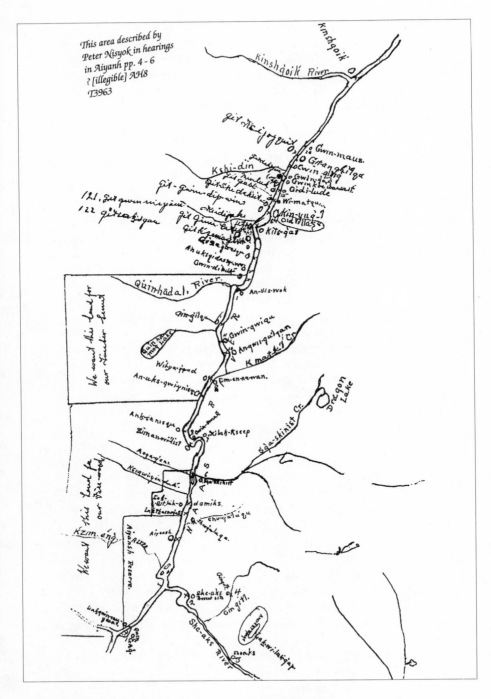

Map 21   Nisga'a Territory: Peter Nisyok map (MMRC, 1915)

Minee'eskw was the leading Eagle chief of Gitlakdamix. He addressed the MMRC hearings at Aiyansh on 9 October:

> The part that I ask you is starting from the river Sheak down as far as the river and back on the top of the mountain as far as Grease Harbour;[70] not for myself only but for the use of all the people in the village. We are the boss of this parcel of land and we, if possible, want this piece of land because we want to start gardening and raising cattle as there is some very good land on the other side. We also have fruits and berries growing on the other side, which we use in the winter time. We will also be able to get our firewood over there as it will be impossible for us to get firewood elsewhere. We would be very happy if the government gave us this piece of land although we think it belongs to us and all we ask is that the Government should endorse this for us.[71]

Minee'eskw laid claim to land from the Nass River, presumably east to the mountains, and from the Tseax River to Grease Harbour, several kilometres above Gitlakdamix. Minee'eskw's territory does not reach the Gitanyow-Nisga'a border at Gitxsits'uuts'xwt.

[?] Gosnell, another prominent Nisga'a leader, addressed the commission on 9 October:

> As you see gentlemen right back at the foot of this mountain behind the village and running up to a place called Gwinhatal.[72] Amongst these trees and all around this land we have worked all our lives getting our food – we were practically born amongst these trees around here. We are not asking for anything we don't know about – as we were born here and this we consider ours down to a creek known by the name of Ks-gamal[73] – all of this land we consider belongs to us and we use this for a working round both to support our children and also our old men so we ask you gentlemen as we look on you to represent our Governments and also our King, we ask you to have mercy on us and do all in your power to help us as this is the place where we know God placed us.[74]

Gosnell's claim to Nisga'a territory between the Nass River and the mountains to the west, and from Shumal Creek to Kwinatahl River, does not reach the Nisga'a-Gitanyow border at Gitxsits'uuts'xwt.

The next witness, Les Bethle, chosen by the Gitwandilix to clarify the nature of their claims, addressed the commission on 9 October:

> On the request of the people of Aiyansh I have been asked to address you and confirm a few words that has been laid before you by the different

speakers. Commencing on the names of the different places yesterday which were laid before you and which was stated there were for salmon fishing camps, I may tell you that it is more than that they are wanted – the people of Gitladamiks used to move up to these places as soon as they would come back from their ooligan [oolichan] fishing and they would live there all summer until later than what it is now before they would move back to the village of Gitladamiks – these are more than camps; they are regular homes of these people and these are laid before you to show that we possessed these lands for many years back up until the present; therefore we are not putting claims before you that is not true to be known as the Gitladamiks and Aiyansh people in this meeting ... Therefore you have seen for yourself from the mouth of the river up to the head and all the information that has been given to you and we are very thankful for your taking down all the information that has been laid before you.[75]

Bethle's statement corroborates that of Niisyok that the Nisga'a claim includes more than fishing sites. His remark about the "head" of the river is clearly in the context of the sites listed by the previous speakers, which end at Gitxsits'uuts'xwt, twenty-five kilometres above Gitlakdamix.

Since 1984, in meetings with the Gitksan and Gitanyow to discuss issues associated with treaty negotiations, Nisga'a leaders have commented that their predecessors neglected to claim the entire Nass watershed and that the historical record on this point is incomplete. The Nisga'a were not silent on this issue in 1915, as the following exchange between Gitlakdamix Wolf chief Andrew Mercer and Commissioner MacDowall shows:

Mercer:
We have heard the words of the Chairman of the Royal Commission and we ask the Chairman if we find out that we have omitted anything will it be alright to hand it to you on your way down the river or to forward it to Victoria.

MacDowall:
That will be quite satisfactory or if you can hand them to Mr. Perry because Mr. Perry is coming up to go over these applications with you so that he can point them out on the map and then he is coming down to Victoria to be examined.[76]

The linear distance from Mill Bay (near Kincolith) to Gitxsits'uuts'xwt by river is fewer than 100 kilometres. It is inconceivable that 284 kilometres (about 75 per cent of the entire river) were overlooked by leaders such as Niisyok, Minee'eskw, Sgat'iin, and others.

K'ee̲xkw, Timothy L. Derrick[77] (born c. 1857), a high-ranking chief of Gitlakdamix, played a prominent role in the Nisga'a land claims struggle.

In 1915 he was appointed by the "Aiyansh tribe" to answer the commissioner's questions. Many of the questions and answers deal with issues other than the land question. Derrick's comments relevant to the topic at hand are excerpted below:

> Commissioner Shaw:
> What is the name of the tribe or band of Indians that we have heard yesterday and today?
> Derrick:
> Gitamwilks [upriver Nisga'a] is the name of the people from Gitwalushtqu [Gitwinksihlxw?] to Gitladamiks.
> Q: ... now I think it was Mr. Derrick himself that stated that you wanted the place called Grease Harbour; are there any Indian improvements at Grease Harbour?
> A: Years ago from Gitanzalqu[78] to Grease Harbour there is a road between from Gitanzalqu for at that time the Indians did not go up any further than that place. They used to pack everything from Grease Harbour up and when coming back they would pack down to this place Gitanzalqu.[79]

Derrick's Gitanzalqu is a fishing station on the left (east) bank of the Nass opposite the mouth of Tchitin River.[80] Derrick states with certainty that the Nisga'a "did not go up any further than that place [Gitanzalqu]."

Later he addressed the question of the position of Daniel Guno and Michael Bright in Nisga'a society. These two men, originally from Gitanyow, were residents of Grease Harbour in 1915 when Derrick stated in response to questioning by the commissioners that "he [Bright] is an Aiyansh man and also Daniel [Guno] is an Aiyansh man. They have been here in this village [Aiyansh] over thirty years and they are citizens of this place."[81] The key point in interpreting this statement is to determine what Derrick meant by "citizen." Fortunately, the Constitution of Aiyansh, a document written in the early 1900s and reprinted in 1917, provides a full explanation. Written when people were being attracted to the village "from various outlying districts" (such as Gitanyow), Article I states: "'The People of Aiyansh' are (a) those individuals of the NISHGA tribe who have been born in any one of the villages on the Upper Nass, and have settled at Aiyansh for the purpose of leading a civilized and Christian life; and (b) those who have come from other villages on the Lower Naas or Skeena River, and who, having joined themselves to the Aiyansh Community, either through marriage or from a desire to lead a new life, have been admitted to membership in the Band by the general assent of all the Members in Council assembled."[82] Article II sets out the conditions and privileges of membership in the Aiyansh Band: "Indians from outside villages thus admitted to membership in the Aiyansh Band

(a) relinquish their title to membership in the Band to which they formerly belonged, together with all rights and privileges attaching thereto, and (b) become entitled to all rights and privileges attaching to membership in the Aiyansh Band, such as proportionate interest or share in all moneys derived from the sale or leasing of lands belonging to the Band, or any other benefits accruing to the same from any source whatsoever."[83] It is apparent that the Aiyansh Constitution is meant to deal with membership under the Indian Act of the day and to deal with community matters, not Aboriginal title.

One of the last witnesses to provide testimony to the MMRC in the Nass Agency was Sgat'iin, a leading chief in Gitlakdamix. His description commenced with Gitxsits'uuts'xwt at the Nisga'a-Gitanyow border and included territory down both sides of the Nass River. Sgat'iin corroborated the Nisga'a evidence of Peter Nisyok and the Gitanyow evidence of Walter Dasque, Richard and Arthur Derrick, and William Gogak: "We already have the length of territory we require from a place called GITSIZUTQU [Gitxsits'uuts'xwt] then it crosses the river to a point known as Gitanzalq [Gitants'alkw], then down the river to a river by the name of SIAKS, crossing the river again to a creek flowing into the river known as KSGAMAL and back again to the point of commencement."[84] Sgat'iin's Gitanzalq, on the east bank of the Nass River opposite Gitxsits'uuts'xwt, is identical to Timothy Derrick's Gitanzalq (Gitants'alkw). Clearly, Gitxsits'uuts'xwt and Gitants'alkw represent the Nisga'a border on the Nass River. Sgat'iin does not mention Meziadin Lake and leaves no doubt that he has described the territory of his predecessor: "This was the territory that my uncle [Chief Sgat'iin of the 1880s; see above] first worked over when the first surveyor visited us and when he left this world he left this [territory] in my hands and I hold it still."[85] It is equally clear that Sgat'iin was describing his ancestral territories to the commissioners: "Another thing my uncle was against the surveyor giving us what is known as 'THE RESERVE' – he did not want this – he was still against it when he died and he kept on saying he did not want this land surveyed and it is the same with me here today – I don't want the reserve – I want the land to the points mentioned."[86] Sgat'iin completed his ownership statements to the MMRC and then provided information on other issues. During this process, Sgat'iin specifically stated that the Gitanyow have territory on the Nass River:

Commissioner MacDowall:
Where do you want this school established?
Sgat'iin:
I would like to inform you that you cannot obtain any good land anywhere on the river outside of the territory occupied by the Gitwanltqu

[Kitwancool], the Aiyansh and the Gitladamiks people. I know in order to make a success of the school it would have to be erected on good ground.[87]

Finally, Commissioner Carmichael offered to be available that evening should the Nisga'a wish to add to their evidence, to which Sgat'iin responded: "We thank you for coming here, and only wish to say that if we had another meeting tonight we would only smash up what we have already said to you."[88]

Sgat'iin's comments are vital. His claim was based on the teachings of his uncle, who had dealt with O'Reilly in the 1880s; it was a claim for territory, not fishing sites; it commenced at Gitxsits'uuts'xwt and encompassed land downriver; he stated that the Kitwancool people had territory on the Nass River; and, finally, he was content that he had said all he intended. In short, Sgat'iin corroborated not only the statements of Nisga'a and Gitanyow witnesses to the MMRC in 1915 (Nass and Babine Agencies) but also, significantly, the map and statements of Mercer to Barbeau in 1916 (see Map 20).

The commission moved on to Grease Harbour to take evidence from Inspring Bright and Daniel Guno on 10 October 1915. In addition to statements made by Bright and Guno (see Chapter 3), Nisga'a chief K'eexkw, Timothy L. Derrick, made the following statement:

> (At Michael Inspring's house)
> We are very glad to be able to be present here and to hear the statements of our brethren and also to hear the kind words that you have given us. The trail started from here and went up to our hunting grounds – the road is called the SKINAK[89] road and this was the way we used to come and go and we would separate and all go in different branches on this trail ... You heard that my uncle [K'eexkw] was one of the first to locate on this piece of land [Grease Harbour] and that is why we ask for this piece of land as it is our base and station and if it is given to white men it won't prevent the trouble. We will always come here to get our wood.[90]

This statement completed the statements of ownership by Nisga'a spokespersons in the Nass Agency. The only other person to provide evidence to the commission was Indian agent for the Nass Agency, C.C. Perry. He travelled to Victoria in December and spent from 16 to 30 December responding to the commissioners' questions. His comments echo in large part those of the Nisga'a and Gitksan who gave evidence in the Nass Agency.

In summary, knowledgeable, respected Nisga'a chiefs, in sworn testimony to the 1915 MMRC, located the Nisga'a-Gitanyow border at

Gitxsits'uuts'xwt on the Nass River. This boundary is consistent with the Nisga'a Petition, the Gitanyow mapping and statements of ownership, and the adaaw<u>k</u>.

Statements Made to Diamond Jenness Concerning the Nisga'a Upriver Boundary (1923)

Further evidence about the location of the boundary of Nisga'a territory on the Nass River comes from Old Dennis, a Wet'suwet'en elder. When interviewed by anthropologist Diamond Jenness in 1923, he related an incident involving the Nisga'a and the Wet'suwet'en. The events probably took place in the mid-1800s when the Nisga'a boundary was marked by a post surmounted by a rock: "The Nass River Indians oft came to Kitsegyukla Valley to the Bulkley to trade oolichan grease for marten and other skins. Once when the Hagwilget people were starving they set out for the Nass River intending to buy oolichan grease. Old Dennis' father went with them."[91] The group had close relations on the Nass and stayed with them while there. After the Wet'suwet'en had acquired the grease they needed, they decided to return home:

> All day they travelled and in the evening came to a big stump which had a huge stone on top, there they camped. In fun they tried to push the stone over, each trying in turn. Finally, they did push it over whereupon they gave a great shout and returned to their camp. Now some Kitwancool [Gitanyow] men heard the shouting and came up and said, "What was that shouting about?" Dennis' father said, "oh, the young men were pushing the stone off the stump," but the Kitwancool men said that was the grave of the late chief of the Nass River.[92]

This is the boundary marker referred to by the Gitanyow as "xhlgi-meda-sook (the robin's egg)," on the east bank of the Nass River opposite Gitxsits'uuts'xwt (see Chapter 3).

Many Wet'suwet'en were still at Gitlakdamix participating in feasts with their Nisga'a hosts. When the Nisga'a learned of the actions of the young Wet'suwet'en, they sounded an alarm in the village and chased after them, with Gitanyow and Kispiox people as allies. They captured a Wet'suwet'en woman, Anhlo'o, who said: "Why take me prisoner, there is Gitdumskanees (Denis' uncle) it was his family that molested the grave, not I or my family. The Nass River [warriors] rushed upon Gitdumskanees and he was disarmed by a Kispiox man."[93] With Gitdumskanees[94] and his brother prisoner, the Nisga'a took them back to the Nass and forced them to run up and down on the ice on the river, while the Nisga'a shot at them, killing them both. According to Old Dennis, "the name of the Nass village was Gitlaxdamax." Here some of the Wet'suwet'en, including Bini (the prophet), remained in hiding in one house. The Nisga'a threatened the Wet'suwet'en all night, but in the morning the chief said: "Come to my House the fight is over, I will give them white eagle down. They blew eagle down from the House where they were congregated to the chief's House. The chief sent a white feather and took the prisoners to Denis' father['s] camp, one days journey ahead."[95]

The Wet'suwet'en returned to the Nass eventually to gather the bones of Gitdumskanees and his brother and return them to Hagwilget, "where they placed them on top of a pole." Trade was restored between the two peoples, because "the Hagwilgets had accepted the white feather and had to keep the peace. The conflict occurred three years before the fight of the Hagwilgets and Tsimsheans at Mission Flats where two more of Denis' uncles were killed."[96]

This incident corroborates frequent references by the Gitanyow about the "robin's egg" pole that marked the Gitanyow-Nisga'a boundary on the Nass River. It demonstrates the symbolic significance of eagle down and a feather in settling the matter, and it shows the Gitanyow presence at, and knowledge of, this border marker opposite Gitxsits'uuts'xwt on the east bank of the Nass in the 1860s, when the Gitanyow, who were within earshot when the Hagwilgets pushed the stone off its perch, expressed their concern about the "grave of the late chief of the Nass River."

Nisga'a Statements Concerning Territory: To Marius Barbeau and William Beynon (Gitlakdamix and Aiyansh, 1927-9)

In the 1920s, the Nisga'a, Gitksan, and Tsimshian were dealing directly with issues of territorial ownership as a result of Euro-Canadian incursions into their territory. When Marius Barbeau and William Beynon visited the Nass in 1927 and 1929 as part of their efforts to make a written record of the important aspects of Northwest Coast society, several Nisga'a chiefs took the opportunity to have descriptions of their territories recorded. Among the Gitlakdamix chiefs were Minee'eskw, Peter Nisyok, Susannah Hlek, Andrew Nass (Ksdiyaawak̲), Peter Adams, and Charles and John Morven (House of Tok̲).

Significantly, the Nisga'a did not include the Kiteen and Kinskuch areas in their statements to the MMRC in 1915, and they produced a map and statement in 1916 that specifically excluded the Nisga'a from these two areas (see E.N. Mercer above). Nisga'a chiefs added to their claim in 1927, and, as has already been noted, 1926 appears to have been a pivotal year in which the Gitanyow people formally distanced themselves from the Nisga'a; Michael Bright drew a map of the Nass River, distinguishing Gitanyow place names from those of the Nisga'a, and the Nisga'a began to register traplines (see note above about Cornelius Nelson "Scodain [Sgat'iin]"), as did other tribal groups.

Nevertheless, in a series of interviews, the territories of the following chiefs of Gitlakdamix were recorded: Hleek, A͟xgigii'i, Ksim X͟saan, Pa'atneexhl, Minee'eskw, Ksdiyaawa͟k, Gwingyoo, K'ee͟xkw, To͟k, Gwandemexs, Sgat'iin, and Niisyok. Approximately fifty-two places – rivers, fishing sites, hunting grounds, villages, and general territories – were described, ten of which are in the Tseax-Lava Lake region and twenty-three between the Shumal-Nass confluence and the Tchitin-Nass confluence.

Between the Tchitin-Nass confluence and the Cranberry-Nass confluence, ten places were described, five of which are on the Tchitin River. The other five are listed below.

Here the statements of Charles and Johnny Morven are quoted in geographic sequence beginning at the downriver sites and proceeding up the east side of the Nass River (see Map 22).[97]

House of K'ee͟xkw and To͟k
Ksaxbiluust (Waters of Stars)
K'ee͟xkw and To͟k.
There are shelters at several other places on the grounds. Following river from: Ksaxbiluust (Waters of Stars) – creek runs from a glacier. Lowest creek on lower frontier. Only trout here. I7 on map.[98]

Ksaxbiluust and Ksana'oot appear to be sites in the Nass River valley below Gitangyahlxw (opposite the Tchitin River confluence).[99]

Ksana'oot (Water of Roasting [Baking])
K'ee͟xkw and To͟k.
On the upper frontier there is a creek named Ksana'oot (Water of Roasting [Baking]), a place where they often gathered Ax fern roots and bake them. Small creek. No salmon. I8 on map.[100]

Gitangyahlk (People of Place of Spearing)
K'ee͟xkw and To͟k.
Gitangyahlk (People/Salmon Spear), fishing station on Nass. I1 on map ... It is the only fishing station. There is another fishing station together with this. It belongs to Ksim X͟saan (C9).[101]

This is the same Gitangyahlk (Gitangyahlxw[102]) referred to a number of times as the location of the Nisga'a-Gitksan border in the Gitanyow adaaw͟k.

In the next two statements of ownership, Minee'eskw described two areas that represent the uppermost limits of territory claimed by Nisga'a in the late 1920s, at and near the Kinskuch River on the west side of the Nass River:

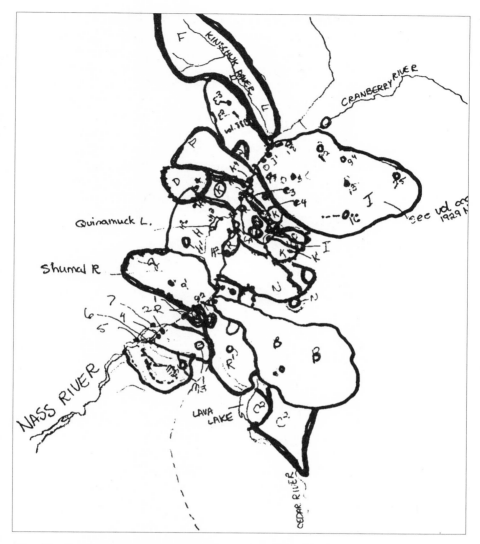

Map 22   Nisga'a statements to Marius Barbeau (from Barbeau Files, 1927-9)

House of Gwandemexs (Extinct)

Kinsgoix (Receptacle To Catch Drips, Going Across by Canoe, Towards Ferry)

Hunting territory of Gwandemexs: the Kinsgoox (Towards Ferry) River – contains the whole valley to the headwaters. Luugalaginsgoix (In/From Mouth of River Up/Towards Ferry) – F on map – is the name of the territory. Fishing station close to E1 adjoins it for salmon. Salmon does not run up Kinsgoix – falls – and is swift. Trails on each side of the river the whole length, they have been told (Adams). Menesk has been up. No houses. General hunting grounds. No groundhogs there. The Gitwinhlkul people are beg[inn]ing to come on it, those belonging to House of Luux-hon. The House of Gwandemes is extinct. No other hunting ground.[103]

In this excerpt, two points should be stressed: first, it is Minee'eskw's evidence that the area was held by a house now extinct – that of Gwan-demexs; second, Gitanyow adaaw<u>k</u> show an ancient presence for the fam-ily of Luuxhon in the Kinskuch watershed, not a recent one as Minee'eskw suggests.

On another occasion, Minee'eskw had more to say about the Kinskuch area:

House of Sgat'iin (Gwandemexs, extinct)
Kinsgoix
When Sgat'iin came over at a later date from Gitenmaks [Gitanmaax], he was received by this group [Gwandemexs] and owing to his being of royal rank he was absorbed into it. Then they had a big valley called Kinsgoix (Toward Ferry). They had many names along there. On the trail they had one of them, Wiluuskihlgenix (Where/In/Lies/Trail). Another was Ts'im'axhlogast (Mouth/Snake). This group of Laxgibuu were very numerous. There was a man of the Laxgibuu who married a woman of Luuxhon, Laxse'el, Gitwinhlku'l, and their child's name was Singewin. He grew up with the Laxgibuu on this territory. And when all the people were gone at the mouth of the Lisems for oolichan, Singewin stayed on the hunting territory of the Laxgibuu. And after that the Gitwinhlku'l claimed it as their territory for the fact that Singewin had stayed while the others had gone away from it. The family of Gwandemexs is now extinct. Menesk is the only one left of his father's house. But the Gitwinhlku'l have absolutely no claim to this territory whatever. That is exclusively.[104]

Clearly, Minee'eskw's evidence was that Luuxhon of Gitanyow had rights to the Kinskuch, that the House of Gwandemexs had become extinct, and that Sgat'iin had assumed the territory. However, there was no evidence brought to light thus far that Sgat'iin himself had claimed the area: it was only Minee'eskw's assertion. In other words, even if one recognizes the Nisga'a position in 1927 as stated by Minee'eskw, there is recognition of Luuxhon's presence, and therefore his adaaw<u>k</u>, as a basis for the Gitanyow claim to the area.

Minee'eskw then described a mountain "towards the Medzeeaden" as belonging to Sgat'iin:

Gadiit (Meaning ?)
Sgat'iin has a territory towards the Medzeeaden, Kaditt (meaning ?), S.W.
of Medzeeaden – E3 on general map C
Nass 1929 – for groundhog. Acquired at the same time as the other
territory.[105]

The Gitanyow know Gadiit as a low (1,317 metre), bald ridge (Kinskuch
Peak) located on the north side of the Kinskuch River, about forty kilometres south of Meziadin Lake. If the Nisga'a ridge, Gadiit, is the same
as the Gitanyow ridge, Gadiit, then it represents a competing claim with
the Gitanyow.
On the Cranberry River watershed, specifically along the Kiteen River,
nine places were described. Charles and Johnny Morven made their statements on behalf of the House of K'ee<u>x</u>kw and To<u>k</u>, as follows:

Gwinstimoon (Like Humpback Salmon)
K'ee<u>x</u>kw and To<u>k</u>.
There is [a] trail following the mountain crests, the continuation of the
Gwinstimoon [Mount Hoadley] Range. The mountain range goes into
the Gyihlt'in [Kiteen] River district. Groundhog and all kinds of animals
in this mountain country. Trout on the upper reaches of river. Mountain
top and trail I6 on map.[106]

This mountain is generally acknowledged to belong to the Nisga'a.

Gyihlt'in (Fish Weir, Look at Trap)
K'ee<u>x</u>kw and To<u>k</u>.
(Laxgibuu). Gyihlt'in (trap – think it applies to a pattern of a trap) is the
name of the hunting ground and that is the name of the river (Kiteen).
Salmon runs up – spring, coho, steelhead (no sockeye, no pinks or chums)
– in no great quantity. They stop a few miles above junction with the
Cranberry. The large river is named Gyihlt'in. The Cranberry River territory is Luuxoon Gitwinhlkul, Ksiyagaskit (Newly/Down From Hills/Lies
[follow the valley]). [Places on this territory are] Wilsgayipt, Ksa'anmaxslo'op, Anmaxslo'op, Ksiwosan, Wilnaku', Gwinstimoon.[107]

Here the Morvens acknowledged Gitanyow ownership of the Cranberry
River, a part of the Nass watershed, which contradicts the current Nisga'a
claim to the entire Nass watershed. To the extent that the Gitanyow
generally consider the Gyahlt'in (Kiteen River) from Wilsgayip upstream
to be their boundary with the Nisga'a, this is not a competing claim.
However, as will be seen below, the Nisga'a claim a berry ground
(Winba<u>x</u>t'aahlgibuu) north of the Kiteen that is in Gitanyow territory.

The next site, T'amginlo'otsen, is considered by the Nisga'a to be a border marker with Luuxhon of Gitanyow:

T'amginlo'otsen (Lake of Elderberries)
K'ee<u>x</u>kw and To<u>k</u>.
Tamginlo'otsen (Lake of Elderberries) is a lake on the frontier of Luuxoon grounds. They come to the edge of it. Beaver lake of the past. I9 on map.[108]

Anmaxlemgan (Over and Across Tree)
K'ee<u>x</u>kw and To<u>k</u>.
A trail goes from Gitangyahlkw to the berry and groundhog area, Anmaxlemgan (Over Across/Tree [owing to precipice-like country of the trail]). The berry ground is called Wilbaxt'aahlgibuu (Where/Up Towards Hill/Sits/Wolf [on the trail there seems to be 2 carvings of wolves in stones]).[109]

Wilba<u>x</u>t'aahlgibuu (Where Up Towards Hill Sits Wolf)
K'ee<u>x</u>kw and To<u>k</u>.
A trail goes from Gitangyahlkw [on the Nass River] to the berry and groundhog area, Anmaxlemgan (Over Across/Tree [owing to precipice-like country of the trail]). The berry ground is called Wilba<u>x</u>t'aahlgibuu, a mountain, (Where/Up Towards Hill/Sits/Wolf [on the trail there seems to be 2 carvings of wolves on stones]). Mountain goat, groundhog, marten, fox, etc. There is a house here at Wilsgayipt (Where/Across/Earth [a sort of delta?]). I2 on map.[110]

Wilsgayipt (Where Across Earth)
K'ee<u>x</u>kw and To<u>k</u>.
A trail goes from Gitangyahlkw to the berry and groundhog area, Anmaxlemgan (Over Across/Tree [owing to precipice-like country of the trail]). The berry ground is called Wilba<u>x</u>t'aahlgibuu (I2 on map), a mountain (Where/Up Towards Hill/Sits/Wolf [on the trail there seems to be 2 carvings of wolves on stones]). Mountain goat, groundhog, marten, fox, etc. There is a house here without name. The site is named Wilsgayipt (Where/Across/Earth [a sort of delta]). The house is on I2 on the map.[111]

As mentioned above, Wilsgayip is located on the Kiteen River and is the exact point at which the Gitanyow describe their boundary – a line running generally west of this point, over Jackpine Mountain, and down to Gitangyahlxw on the Nass River opposite the mouth of the Tchitin River. The Morvens named several other sites farther along the Kiteen River:

Wilnaku' (Where Against Together Shoot)
K'ee<u>x</u>kw and To<u>k</u>.
A trail goes to the upper ground, up the Kiteen, to Ksiwosan (waters of Willow) [from Ksa'anmaxslo'op, the house at its junction]. There is a cabin there at Wilnaku' (Where Against Together Shoot) (I5 on map). Difficult country to get in, waterfalls and rugged.[112]

Ksa'anmaxslo'op (Water Where Stands Stone)
K'ee<u>x</u>kw and To<u>k</u>.
A creek (also called Anmaxslo'op [Where/Stands/Stone] [it seems large stones growing out of the ground]). A mountain at its source, 'Anmaxslo'op (I4 on map). A house at the junction of Ksa'ammaxslo'op (I3 on map). For hunting goat etc. The cabin is for this district. Beaver along this creek. [In between the two sections of information on this creek, there is the comment that] Dennis Wood (Gook) is on the southern frontier. And Luxhoon on the northern frontier. I3 on map.[113]

The comment included in this excerpt recognizes the ownership of Gitanyow chief Luuxhon in this area and the boundary there between the Nisga'a and the Gitanyow.

Ksiwosan (Waters of Willow)
K'ee<u>x</u>kw and To<u>k</u>.
A trail goes to the upper ground, up the Kiteen, to Ksiwosan (Waters of Willow – runs through willow marsh). There is a cabin there, Wilnaku' (Where Against Together Shoot) is the name of the cabin and the site. (I5 on map). Difficult country to get in, waterfalls and rugged.[114]

On the subject of portions of To<u>k</u>'s territory, Charles and John Morven made the following comments:

There is a controversy as to the ownership of portions of Tok ground especially with the Gitwinhlkul Wudaxhayetsxw and T'ooxens. T'ooxens in the former years had married into the Nisga' House. The Nisga' chief then gave as a wedding dowry to the Gitwinhlkul the privilege of using portions of his hunting grounds for the benefit of his children. The rights of the dowry ended on the death of the Gitwinhlkul man. But the Gitwinhlkul still claim the privilege claiming that the right has never been extinguished. The present T'ooxens may not claim it. But the House of Wudaxhayetsxw claim it. They are Tsetsaut people in origin.[115]

Minee'eskw and Niisyok also described territory claimed by the Nisga'a east of the Nass River at Gwinstimoon:

Gwinstimoon (Like Humpback Salmon)
Ksim X̱saan
Owns the mountain Kwunstim'oon (Like Humpback – owing to the appearance – "Like the Hump").[116]

As mentioned above, this is Mount Hoadley, considered to be Nisga'a territory.

In conclusion, the statements of ownership of Nisga'a chiefs in 1927 and 1929 demonstrate that the Nisga'a recognize the Gitanyow presence at the border in the Kinskuch and Kiteen Rivers area; that there are competing claims and a basis for that competing claim (intermarriage); that the Nisga'a do not claim territory north of the historical border, except in the Kinskuch River-Kinskuch Peak area and at Wilbax̱t'aahlgibuu, a berry ground on the north side of the Kiteen River. Apart from these two areas, the evidence of Nisga'a chiefs in the 1920s nowhere includes territory beyond Gitxsits'uuts'xwt. In other words, if a competing claim exists between the Nisga'a and the Gitanyow, it is in two specific and small areas on the Kinskuch and Kiteen Rivers.

The Establishment of Nisga'a Traplines (1930s)
This discussion of Nisga'a traplines is not meant to be exhaustive. Its main purpose is to demonstrate (by their existence today) that the Nisga'a did register traplines and that the pattern of Nisga'a (and Gitksan and Gitanyow) traplines broadly supports other evidence on Nisga'a territory in this study.

An examination of trapline records indicates that the Nisga'a registered their traplines at about the same time (c. 1930) and in much the same way as the Gitksan (other than Gitanyow): in other words, as "company" lines. Nor is it surprising that a similar debate occurred between the Nisga'a and the province (about the imposition of provincial regulations), as with the Gitksan (above). The Nisga'a make a distinction between ango'osxw (house territory) and trapline, just as the Gitksan do, but sometimes use the terminology interchangeably. To illustrate this point, while addressing the subject of how development was "eroding traditional rights," Rod Robinson said: "I wish to elaborate on the subject of traplines. There are 60 registered traplines in existence in the Nass valley, and there are 160 persons trapping on those 60 traplines ... and, as industry moves further into our territory, more traplines will be destroyed."[117]

In 1974, McNeary attributed to the late Eli Gosnell, Wiigadimx̱sgaak, a high-ranking chief in Canyon City and an authority on Nisga'a traditional life, the following: "The most tightly held property was the trap line. A non-relative found trespassing on a trap line was liable to be killed. There is a pictograph by Lava Lake which is supposed to commemorate the killing of a trespasser [EG]."[118] One may infer from Gosnell's comment that, despite their limitations, traplines are considered by the Nisga'a to represent a chief's ancestral territory.

In fact, when traplines were registered, discrepancies did occur partly because accurate maps did not exist at the time and because of the insensitivity of the provincial Game Department (Fish and Wildlife Branch today), which frequently ignored the natural boundaries used by Aboriginal people.[119] They also often ignored Aboriginal custom, especially matrilineal descent, which meant that the trapline was registered to the wrong clan (or house).

Although there are discrepancies in the details of trapline maps today, and though they are not a perfect fit with known Aboriginal boundaries, they do generally reflect the pattern of Aboriginal territories of interest to this study (see Map 23). The traplines reflect that the Gitksan and Gitanyow own territory on the upper Nass and that the Nisga'a own territory on the lower Nass. In this respect, it is vital to note that the outer limit of external Nisga'a traplines corresponds approximately to the Nisga'a territory defined by Exhibit 2 in *Calder* v. *Attorney General of British Columbia* (see Map 18).

The relevance of Nisga'a traplines to this study, in light of Eli Gosnell's strong comment to McNeary, is apparent: the Nisga'a did not go beyond Gitxsits'uuts'xwt when they attempted to protect their Aboriginal territories through trapline registration on the Nass River, and nowhere in the Meziadin, upper Nass, and Bell-Irving River watersheds do the Nisga'a have traplines.

E.G. Newnham, Dominion Constable (1930)

The Department of Fisheries began to issue food fish permits to Aboriginal people throughout British Columbia and on the Nass in 1930. This was handled, or perhaps more correctly mishandled, by Fishery Officer Angus McIvor of the Nass River Fisheries Patrol. Newnham, the dominion constable stationed at Kincolith, seemed to be more sensitive than McIvor to the need for better communication with the Nisga'a in implementing this policy.

On 2 June 1930, Newnham wrote a letter to W.E. Ditchburn, Indian commissioner for British Columbia, in which he outlined his difficulties with McIvor and described a meeting of the Nisga'a Land Committee that he attended at Aiyansh on 22 May:

As a result of my warning the Aiyansh Indians regarding the Fisheries Regulations also a previous warning I had given, in compliance with instructions from the Indian Agent, relating to carrying firearms in launches and other vehicles, I was requested to attend a meeting of the

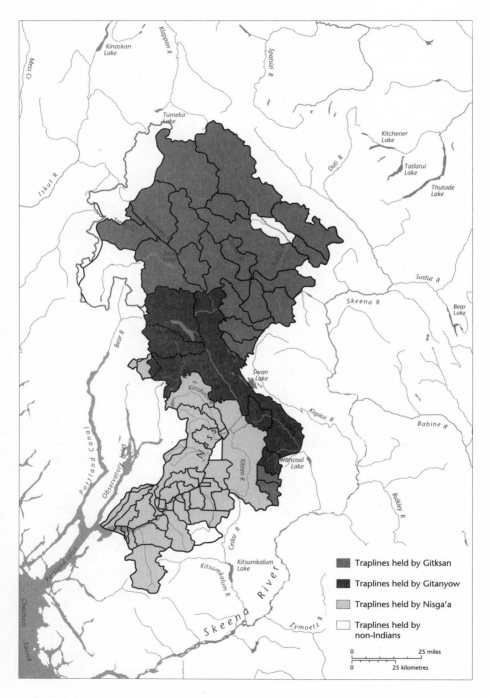

Map 23   Traplines in the Nass watershed (c. 1985)

Nishga land Committee at Gitlakdamix and the attached was handed me with the request that I forward it to the Indian Commissioner with my report. I am glad to do so, because in the event of these Indians being called to account, at some future date, after they have had time to coolly reflect, it is quite likely that they would deny having ever adopted the attitude on which I am now reporting and without reliable witnesses, I could not have my statements corroborated.

I asked them if they realized what the consequences would likely be, if they carried out these threats to disobey the law and Michael Inspring replied that they intended to take a firm stand on the land question. I told them that this was all settled and James Adams replied that the Government had only settled with the Allied Tribes not with the Nishgas whose case was independent. I then asked them exactly what it was they wanted and several of them yelled "We want the whole country." I told them that they could not have the whole country and James Adams explained that the Allied Tribes had made a claim for the whole province of British Columbia but they (the Nishgas) were more reasonable, and only wanted the Nass River country, from the headwaters of the Nass at Meziadin Lake down to the mouth.[120]

This comment by James Adams, Axdii Wiluugooda, a Nisga'a hereditary chief and a prominent member of the Nisga'a Land Committee, deals with the issue of the extent of the territory described in the 1913 Nisga'a Petition. It is clear from the comment that the Nisga'a at this point considered the headwaters of the Nass to be at Meziadin Lake; that Adams spoke in the presence of the Nisga'a Land Committee; and that the committee did not correct him to include the Nass watershed beyond Meziadin Lake. There was no need for the Gitanyow chiefs present to correct Adams because his description included Gitanyow territory.

Wilson Duff (1969-74)

The trial of the landmark *Calder* v. *Attorney General of British Columbia* case, based on the persistence of Native title in Nisga'a territories, was heard in the Supreme Court of British Columbia in 1969. Wilson Duff, professor of anthropology at the University of British Columbia and former curator of ethnology at the BC Provincial Museum, testified on behalf of the Nisga'a. Duff's evidence and expert opinion were based on extensive research among the Nisga'a and Gitksan and were a summary of what chiefs and elders had stated from 1915 to the date of the trial. His work with the Gitanyow was among the first of its kind and contributed to his credibility as an expert on the Tsimshian, Gitksan, and Nisga'a.

Clearly, the Nisga'a considered Duff the expert in his field when they retained him for their case. Their success in the Supreme Court of Canada must be partly shared with Duff. Thomas Berger considered Duff to be a "key witness" in two important Aboriginal rights cases: *R.V. White and Bob* and *Calder* v. *Attorney General of British Columbia:* "I began working with Wilson Duff in 1963. Even then his knowledge of the history of the Indian people of our province was highly regarded, his reputation as a scholar approaching its pinnacle ... His view was based on his profound knowledge of Indian ideas of tribal title, and the fact that those ideas were not moribund, but still informed notions of their own past and present."[121] "Wilson Duff's contribution" said Berger, in closing his tribute, "was unique in Canada."

It is difficult to know what to make of the comments of Nisga'a leader Frank Calder when he stated that the Nisga'a first learned in 1961 about Duff's role in the *Histories, Territories and Laws of the Kitwancool* and the Gitanyow claim: "To the knowledge of the Nisga'a Nation this was the first time, since time immemorial, that its tribal members had ever heard of a neighbour tribe claiming part of the traditional Nisga'a hunting ground."[122] Given the Gitanyow and Nisga'a documentary record, this is a confusing statement. Calder then wrote: "The Nisga'a delegation confronted Mr. Wilson Duff in Victoria and in no uncertain terms condemned the Wilson publication as a farcical incomplete document due to his lack of foresight to interview the Nisga'a Nation for verification of Kitwancool stories."[123] This is faint praise indeed for Duff.

Nevertheless, the *Calder* v. *Attorney General of British Columbia* case did proceed, with Duff as one of its key witnesses. As part of his evidence, he prepared a map, Exhibit 2, showing the extent of Nisga'a territory (see Map 18). In the trial judgment, it is stated: "for the purpose of the litigation that 'their ancient tribal territory' in question consisted of an area in excess of 1,000 square miles [2,590 square kilometres] in and around the Naas River Valley, Observatory Inlet, Portland Inlet, and the Portland Canal, all located in north-western British Columbia, as described on the map Ex. 2 and hereafter sometimes referred to as the 'delineated area.'"[124] In 1973 the Supreme Court of Canada issued its ruling on the case. The dissenting judgment of Mr. Justice Hall contains a segment of the trial transcript in which Duff is asked: "Did you ... prepare for counsel the map that has been marked Exhibit 2 in this case?"; he replies, "Yes, I did."[125] Exhibit 2 shows that Nisga'a territory does not extend beyond the Kinskuch and Kiteen Rivers. In other words, Nisga'a territory as defined in the *Calder* v. *Attorney General of British Columbia* case overlaps only slightly with that of the Gitanyow as set out in the *Histories, Territories and Laws of the Kitwancool* (see Appendix 8).

Correspondence between Wilson Duff and Thomas Berger, counsel for the plaintiff, contributes to our knowledge of Duff's role in *Calder* v. *Attorney General of British Columbia* and of his opinion about the extent of Nisga'a territory that could be defended in the Nisga'a Petition:

17 June 1968

This is a rather late reply to your letter of April 19th, asking for a sketch of the territories claimed by the Nishga, the Kitwancool and the Kispiox. I have tried to sum up the situation on two maps [see Maps 24 and 25].

The plain black map (marked "A") shows my present summary of the valid claims of the Gitksan bands. You will see that the Kitwancool, Kispiox, Kuldo, and Kisgegas claimed parts of the Nass River drainage ... These tribal areas are based on extensive ethnographic information gathered by Marius Barbeau in the 1920's, supplemented by my own investigations at Kitwancool and Kispiox. I would not stake my reputation on them without reworking the basic data, but I think they are substantially correct.

On the other map (marked "B") I have first of all marked in the Nishga claim as I understand it from the Nishga Petition. You will see that the upper Nass and its tributaries from the Kinskuch and the Cranberry up are in dispute with the Gitksan claims. The Kitwancool claim, as published in "The Histories Territories and Laws of the Kitwancool" is shown in (green): I think there is room for debate [by the Kitwancool] with the Nishga over the Kinskuch River, and [by the Kitwancool] with the Kispiox over the Kwinageese River, but generally the [Kitwancool] claim is valid. I have shown the claim of the Kispiox-Kuldo in blue, and it includes the uppermost Nass branches except for one, the Damdochax (Blackwater) which belonged to a Kisgegas chief.

Bowser Lake and the upper Bell-Irving River are within the Nishga claim, but that claim is not supported by any ethnographic evidence known to me. This area was long ago occupied by Athapaskans from the Stikine River system in the north, whose closest surviving relatives are probably the people of the Telegraph Creek area.[126]

Berger certainly knew that Duff considered the Kitwancool claim to be valid, and there is little doubt that he conveyed this information to his Nisga'a clients.

In the aftermath of the Supreme Court judgment, Gitksan and Gitanyow leaders expressed concern when Nisga'a leaders stated that Exhibit 2 (see Map 18) was a symbolic representation of a small part of their claim for court purposes and asserted that their land claim included Meziadin Lake as defined by the Nisga'a Petition of 1913.

To obtain support for their contention, Calder phoned Duff to have him confirm that there was no dispute about Nisga'a territory during the case. The following is Duff's written response to Calder's phone call:

August 8, 1974

This will confirm our telephone conversation of yesterday, during which I confirmed your statement that during the course of the "Nishga Case,"

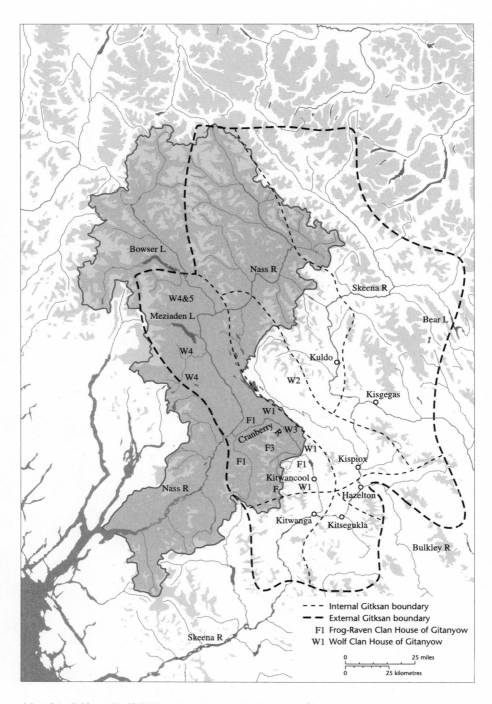

Map 24 Wilson Duff "Map A" to Berger, highlighting Gitksan territories (1968)

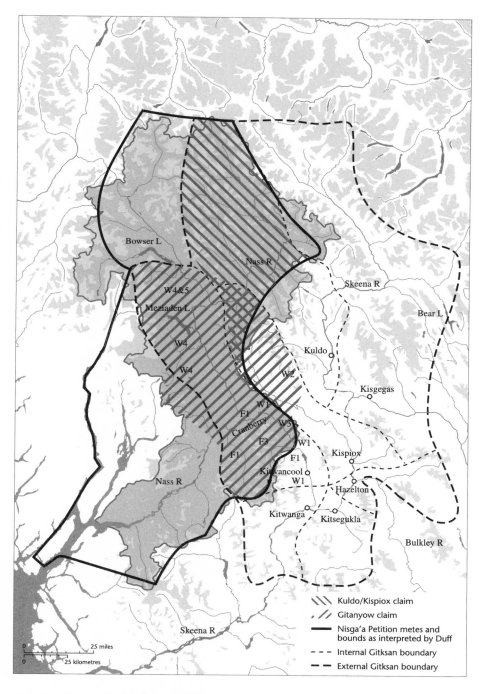

Map 25 Wilson Duff "Map B" to Berger, highlighting Nisga'a/Gitanyow/Kuldo/Kispiox claims (1968)

recently concluded by the Supreme Court of Canada, there was no dispute concerning the boundaries of the Nishga territories. As you will recall, your lawyer Tom Berger asked me, as an expert witness, to prepare a map showing those areas to which the Nishga had undisputed claim, and that map was accepted by both sides as delineating Nishga territory for the purposes of the case.[127]

Significantly, Duff's response was not referred to by Calder in his review of documents made at the request of the Nisga'a Tribal Council in 1993.[128] Moreover, the area of the upper Nass to which the Nisga'a had an undisputed claim did not extend north of the Kinskuch area. As noted above, Duff considered the Gitksan bands, including Kitwancool, to have valid claims in the Nass watershed. Duff's letter shows that the Nisga'a could not prove the territories set out on the basis of a literal reading of the 1913 Nisga'a Petition. In other words, Duff's map was concerned with the principles of Aboriginal title, not with determining the location of specific boundaries (see Map 18). "As I recall," Duff wrote,

it was not the intention to settle the question of tribal boundaries for all time, nor to jeopardize any future settlement of that question, but to establish an agreed-upon area for which to establish the unextinguished existence of Aboriginal title. The necessity for the above-described map arose from the wording of the Statement of Claim, which carried over from the former Nishga Petition a description of Nishga territory that included the entire drainage basin of the Nass and all its tributaries, and would therefore conflict with the claims of other tribes or bands, including those of the Tsimshian and the Gitksan (especially Kitwancool). The Nishga case was therefore a test of the concept of native title, and not of specific boundaries between tribes.[129]

The problem with the Nisga'a Petition is in its language,[130] even though it is apparent that the 9,516 square-kilometre (3,674 square-mile) area defined by Duff in Exhibit 2 was not merely a symbolic portion of Nisga'a territory for the purpose of the case. It is in fact the area containing Nisga'a ango'osxw as described by knowledgeable Nisga'a elders since time immemorial. This is corroborated by the following note by Duff: "Prof. Duff testifies [in *Calder* v. *Attorney General of British Columbia*] – made map [Exhibit 2] to safeguard Kitwancool."[131] Also identified in the Duff collection are four maps pertaining to the "Nishga Case." These maps (presumably those referred to in his 1972 notes) show Gitanyow territories as in the 1959 publication. It is more than coincidence that the boundary line Duff drew on Exhibit 2 is generally consistent with the area defined by Gitanyow and Nisga'a witnesses to the McKenna-McBride Royal Commission and in the Barbeau-Beynon files.

At about the same time, in 1974 (or perhaps in 1973), A.G. McIntyre, CNR construction engineer, made inquiries of Duff regarding Aboriginal title and Native ownership of lands along a rail line to run north of Terrace through the Nass River valley. Duff's response to McIntyre deals with the issue of Nisga'a and Gitksan territorial ownership along the route. Duff described his work on the Barbeau files in Ottawa, and with "the Indians concerned," including the "Nishga Case," as the basis for his opinion about "proof of ownership" in the Nass River valley:

> To go over the route in slightly more detail: Kitsumkalum River and Lake were claimed by the Kitsumkalum tribe (now band) of Tsimshian Indians, who now live at Terrace. Across the divide, Lava Lake, the Tseax River valley, and the Nass Valley itself up to the Kinskuch River are within what is indisputably Nishga territory. The claim might be put forward by the Nishga Tribal Council as a whole, as it was for the Nishga case, or by the Aiyansh (Gitlakdamiks) band itself, whose families specifically claimed these parts of the area. The Nass valley from the Cranberry River up to the Bell Irving River was within the territories of the Kitwancool tribe (now band) in early historic time. They had earlier won the Meziaden Lake section of the area in warfare with a band of Tahltans from the Stikine River area. The uppermost headwaters of the Nass and Skeena, as the map shows, were claimed by other Gitksan tribes: Kispiox, Kuldo, and Kisgegas. The two last named are no longer separate bands. Their old village sites are now deserted. But that does not mean that they are extinct or have lost their reserves and land rights. The Kuldo band has been amalgamated with Kispiox, and the Kisgegas tribe with Hazelton. Hence the above list.[132]

Duff included two maps that showed the information in his letter to McIntyre, one of which is identical to Map 19; the other, containing Duff's handwritten notations, is set out in Map 26.

Before his death in 1976, Duff spent some time preparing a manuscript about the Northwest Coast peoples. The following information on the Nisga'a claim to territories in the Nass watershed is taken from a handwritten draft (undated) in the Duff Papers: "*Up the Nass:* Niska claims again overlap with those of the Kitwancool. Both have claims of some validity on the Kinskuch River, and the Giteen. The Niska do not have clear claims to the Nass above this point, in recent times the upper Nass was under Kitwancool domination. (For a period between about 1890 and – nearly all of the Kitwancool people lived on the Nass – this contributed to the notion that the upper Nass was Niska territory.)"[133]

In conclusion, the evidence of Wilson Duff is that the Gitksan, including the Gitanyow, have a valid claim in the Nass River valley from the Kinskuch River north. This corroborates not only the Gitksan and

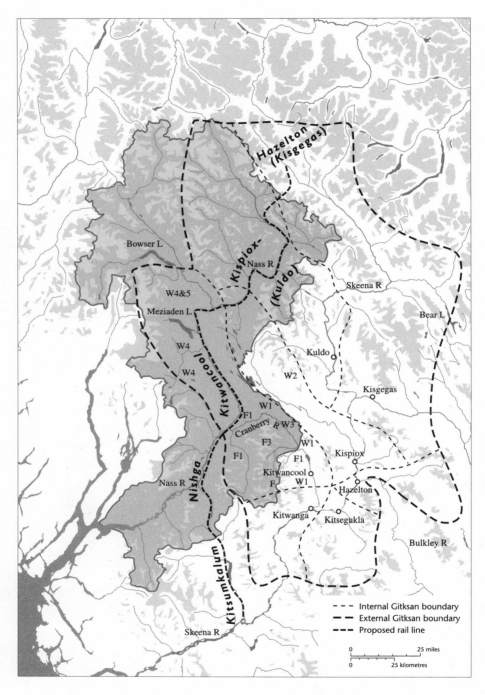

Map 26   Gitksan villages and territories showing proposed rail line: Wilson Duff to
A.G. McIntyre (c. 1974)

Gitanyow documentary record but also the Nisga'a documentary record until the 1973 decision in *Calder* v. *Attorney General of British Columbia*, after which contemporary Nisga'a leadership assert a competing claim to Meziadin Lake and, later still, to the entire Nass River watershed.

Statements of Nisga'a Elders (1973-4)

In the 1970s, Nisga'a elders provided information about place names and other aspects of Nisga'a territoriality during Stephen McNeary's two-year study of the Nisga'a. The results of his work appear in two separate documents, a report and a dissertation. Both studies include a numerically coded map of place names with an accompanying key (see Map 27).[134]

A number of Nisga'a spoke to McNeary, but his "principal sources of information were" the following:

Eli Gosnell, 74 ... a native of Canyon City ... Wigademxskaak,[135] "Great Man of Eagle," a very high-ranking name in the Canyon City Wolf tribe (phratry). He is generally recognized by the upriver Niska as the best authority on traditional life.

Hubert McMillan, 60 ... chief of the Gitwilluyaxw division of the Aiyansh wolf phratry. His Niska name is Kstyawk.

Titus Niisyok, 81, a native of Aiyansh. Mr. Niisyok has taken the name Meneesk, a chief's name in the Aiyansh eagle phratry.

Peter Nyce, 83 ... originally from Kitimat and belongs to the killerwhale phratry. His wife is from Canyon City ... Mr. Nyce is now most at home in the Niska tongue ...

Abraham Williams, 74, holds the name Gwingo and is head chief of the Gitwinagi'l division of the Aiyansh wolf phratry.

Lucy Williams has the Niska name Niis Angwadikskw, the highest woman's name in the house of Gwixmaw, an eagle house of Canyon City. She is the wife of Abraham Williams.[136]

In his opening chapter, McNeary refers to Nisga'a territory as

the valley of the Nass River and adjacent Observatory Inlet and Portland Canal in west-central British Columbia, including a strip of land (the northwest shore of Portland Canal) in Alaska. The heartland of Niska territory, containing all the winter village sites, is the valley of the Nass River from its mouth at Kincolith roughly to the junction of the Cranberry River, about 70 miles inland. The upper Nass and Portland canal areas were occupied in the early nineteenth century by Athapaskan-speaking peoples referred to collectively by the Niska as Ts'ets'awt (T'sets'aut). Tlingit speakers also made claims to Portland Canal, while the upper Nass drainage in the Meziadin area has been disputed between the upper Niska and the people of Kitwancool village ever since its desertion by the Ts'ets'awt.[137]

In his chapter "The Land: Boundaries and Neighbours," McNeary refers to the territory claimed by the Nisga'a as follows: "The Niska winter villages were all located in the Nass Valley between Nass Bay and the mouth of the Cranberry River. Niska today claim to have occupied the land 'from time immemorial,' although the origin legends of particular Houses do describe migrations into the Nass valley from elsewhere. Barbeau recorded a tradition that Niska was once spoken only on the upper river. These up-river people are supposed to have taught their language to the newcomers, some of whom came from the north and spoke Tlingit."[138] As a general statement, this is correct, but McNeary would have been more accurate in situating the Nisga'a villages between Nass Bay and the mouth of the Tchitin River. The early documentary record (see Chapter 6) places the Gitanyow in several villages between the Tchitin and the Cranberry Rivers in 1867 and 1874.

The bulk of McNeary's comments about ownership in the Meziadin area agrees with the Gitanyow version of events: "The Laxwiyip-Tahltan also fought the upper Niska and their neighbours, the Gitksan of Kitwancool, both of whom were interested in the rich trapping grounds of the 'groundhog country' around Meziadin Lake. The Laxwiyip were either exterminated or driven back to the Stikine country well before the end of the last century. Kitwancool histories claim the victory over the Laxwiyip and consequently the Kitwancool assert their rights to the Nass trapping grounds above Cranberry River. Numerous village sites in this vicinity were recalled. The officially registered trap lines in this area now belong to the Kitwancool."[139] According to McNeary, however, a Nisga'a chief said in 1974:[140] "The Laxwiyip granted the territory to the Gitlaxt'amiks Niska to settle a conflict in which some Niska chiefs were killed."[141] This comment is inconsistent with the evidence of Nisga'a chiefs in 1915 and with Mercer's map and interview with Barbeau in 1916. Furthermore, under Gitksan law and probably Nisga'a law, land is never granted to an entire village. It is always compensation to the aggrieved house for a murder or murders committed. And it is the responsibility of the aggrieved house to organize the war party to obtain settlement.

McNeary goes on to say: "In the nineteenth century the Gitlaxt'amiks chief Skat'een claimed reserves '50 miles up the river' – i.e., near Meziadin Lake.[142] Niska claims to the area have always been active, and many older Niska recall trapping expeditions far up the Nass."[143] This is presumably a reference to O'Reilly's 1888 comments about Sgat'iin. As described earlier, there is no quotation in which Sgat'iin "claims reserves 50 miles up the river" in the 1881 O'Reilly diary, nor did O'Reilly say this in 1888.

His only comment was that Sgat'iin "spoke of reserves 50 miles further up the river."

This comment by McNeary must be compared, of course, with the explicit statement and map made by the son-in-law of Sgat'iin, a leading member of the Nisga'a Land Committee, E.N. Mercer, to Barbeau in Ottawa in 1916, when he stated that this was Kitwancool territory. This point was discussed extensively above.

McNeary also refers to the fact that the history, language, and social relationships between upriver Nisga'a and Gitksan peoples were close and that some Gitanyow had moved "to Nass River villages."

In his summary of land and boundaries, McNeary writes:

> The undisputed Niska territory included Observatory inlet and the Nass valley up to Cranberry River. Peripheral areas claimed by the Niska were Portland Canal and the upper reaches of the Nass. The "known World" of Niska travel and mythology extended in a distant radius of about 200 miles from the winter village sites. Distant tribes were more likely to visit the Niska, attracted by the eulachon, than vice versa. Probably, few Niska other than the more adventurous traders, trappers, shamans, and warriors travelled more than sixty miles, as the crow flies, from their home base. Most, if not all, marriage alliances were made within the 60 mile radius.[144]

Here McNeary is generally correct, except for his comments about "peripheral areas claimed by the Niska." Because it is generally accepted that the Nisga'a absorbed the family of twelve Western Tsetsaut of Portland Canal and their territories, the Nisga'a may not agree that this constitutes a "peripheral claim." By contrast, it cannot be said that the Nisga'a have even a "peripheral claim to the upper reaches of the Nass," unless McNeary based his opinion on the comments of early Nisga'a chiefs who considered the head of the Nass to be between Gitlakdamix and Gitxsits'uuts'xwt.

On the topic of place names and hunting territories, McNeary writes: "I have collected the names of major geographical features near the upper Niska villages [see Map 27], but have barely scratched the surface of the detailed names which were given to minor landmarks within each hunting territory."[145] In his dissertation, he notes:

> From an economic point of view, the most significant features of the Nass Valley are the smaller valleys of the many tributary streams. It is much easier to follow one valley than to cross from one to another; the valleys are therefore the basic unit of hunting territory ownership. The upper valleys of some streams give access to mountain goat hunting or marmot

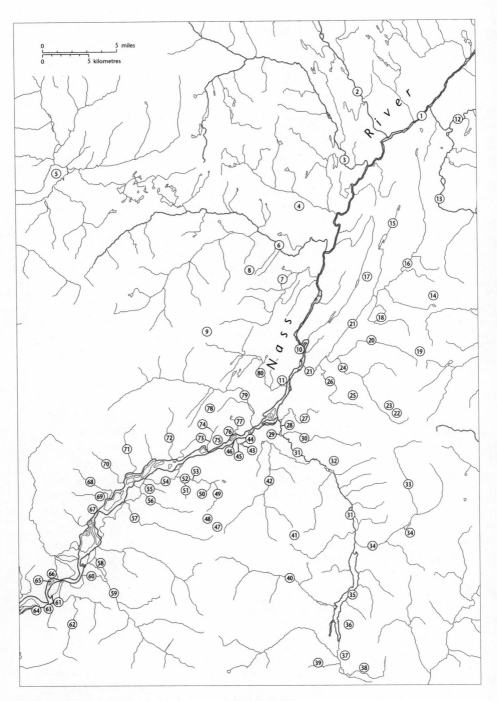

Map 27   Niska place names (Stephen McNeary, 1974)

Key To Map 27

1 Kaliaks niska', "River of the Niska"
2 Ginskuuxw, Kinskuch River
3 Ksit'in, Tchitin River
4 Ansewok'ooks
5 Laxgitsoohl, Alice Arm
6 Gwinadal, Kwinatahl River
7 Gwinamook, Kwinamuck Lake
8 K'alwogn, northeast slope of Number 9
9 Guxagayt, unnamed mountain
10 Ts'im anwilis, camp at Grease Harbour
11 Gitlaxt'amiks
12 Anxoon, Cranberry River
13 Ga'ahl t'een, Kiteen River
14 Gwin stimoon, unnamed mountain
15 T'aam ansekokhl, Hoodoo Lake
16 Gisawillaxoom, valley area
17 Kaslaxanso'ox, a long ridge
18 T'aam ginlaaxw, Dragon Lake
19 Ts'im skiyt, Mount Hoadley
20 Ksi skiyt, creek near Nass Camp
21 Ksa ska skinis, North Seaskinnish Creek
22 Wildegwantkayt, peak of Mount Priestly
23 Ts'im sto'ot, Mount Priestly
24 Ksi ts'im sto'ot, South Seaskinnish
25 Logom staahl, Mount Hoeft
26 Ksi logom staahl, Chigatlque Creek
27 Gingitl', Gingit Creek
28 Ts'im ts'its'it, outlet of Spencer's Lake
29 T'aam andii hat'al, Spencer's Lake
30 Gits'yan, Gitzyon Creek
31 Siiaks, "New water," Tseax River
32 Wilskayip, low ridge east of the Tseax
33 Willuwitgwun masaawut, unnamed peak
34 Wilksibaxmihl, "Where fire ran out"
35 Sii t'ax, Lava Lake
36 Yagahlolo'obit, unnamed mountain
37 Luumin gwinaniis, "Stream of urine"
38 T'aam gitiks yoon, Sand Lake

39 Ksi an gaahl, Poupard Creek
40 Ksiluuyim andoo, unnamed stream
41 Kinuu axwt, unnamed mountain
42 Ksiluuyim angii, Vetter Creek
43 Anjokslekee, "Where Lekee camps"
44 Laxksiwasandit, a small lake
45 Amatal, A small spawning creek
46 Wilhiiskinis, mouth of Number 45
47 Hlawut, Vetter peak
48 Anxeegusk, Vetter Mountain
49 Ts'im hakwhl, valley at #52
50 Noojit, unnamed
51 Antxomiks, at #52
52 Ts'alts'ap, Zolzap Creek
53 Saxwhl Ts'alts'ap, smokehouse site
54 Gisanin anxeegusk, steep cliff
55 Ksits'imelix, an unnamed stream
56 Gwinya'a, Kwinyarh Creek
57 Ansidagan, Ansedagan Creek
58 Anleexga'askw, smokehouse site
59 Ksit'een, Kseaden Creek
60 Gwinhaak, "Place of geese"
61 Ginluulak, "Place of ghost"
62 Ksiginluulak, Ginlulak Creek
63 Laxanhlo', river bank west of #61
64 Loot'up angidaa, a river side channel
65 Wilskiihl jayn, unnamed island
66 Laxando'osk, Curve of river N. of #65
67 Anixuuhl, Indian Reserve 31 (?)
68 Wegilaxdap, Wegiladap Creek
69 Skanasko'odit, site at mouth of #68
70 Wilyaxyaklanohl, Wilyayanooth Creek
71 Giswatsx, Giswatz Creek
72 Gingitl', Gingietl Creek (also # 27)
73 Ksagahlist, creek behind Canyon City
74 Ksk'eelst, tributary of Number 73
75 Gitwinksihlkw, Canyon City
76 Wilsasaak, ridge NE of Canyon City
77 Ts'im giist, Gish Creek
78 K'alixaja, mountain north of Canyon City
79 Skamaal, Shumal Creek
80 Xtsimenk, Chemainuk Creek

[*Sources:* Abraham Williams (2 field trips, above Tseax and in Tseax Valley); Eli Gosnell (using maps, below Canyon City)] trapping areas above the timber line, while the lower parts of the streams serve as spawning grounds for the salmon.

To the Niska, the Nass valley is far from a wilderness. It is a collection of familiar locations, each with its own particular resources. The ownership of each place is known and many old village sites and fish camps dot the valley. There is a richness of historical and supernatural associations which make the landscape virtually a textbook of Niska history and religion.[146]

One might assume from the above extract that the Nisga'a can produce detailed place names for all the territories that they claim in the Nass watershed. The map produced by McNeary with his Gitlakdamix sources demonstrates the "detailed names" of Nisga'a territory below Gitxsits'-uuts'xwt, but not above. Thus, the absence of comparable data for the areas above Gitxsits'uuts'xwt and the Cranberry River is eloquent testimony to the limits of Nisga'a place names and, by extension, territory.

McNeary's Nisga'a sources also told him about hunting and trapping: "Each hunting territory had its trap line or lines and one or more hunting cabins. The time spent on a particular expedition depended in part o[n] the distance of the trap line from the winter village. EG's [Eli Gosnell] territory was directly across from Canyon City. With a good start, he said he might return the same night. AW's [Abraham Williams] territory was farther removed: he might spend several days or a week at a time hunting and trapping. Sometimes people went to Meziadin to trap and stayed away several months."[147] The comment about Meziadin is not sourced, nor is it indicated who went to Meziadin, but it was likely those Gitanyow families who lived among the Nisga'a who were legitimately using Gitanyow territory at Meziadin. For example, in his appendix,[148] McNeary does list a number of Ganada chiefs, including one prominent Gitanyow name (Luxhoon), which may explain the following comment about Meziadin: "In the last century the Niska had to travel far up to Meziadin Lake to get moose, and moose hides were mainly obtained by trade with the Babines of Bulkley Valley. In the last fifty years, however, moose have become common in the flats of the Nass River valley, and have displaced the deer and caribou. They are hunted in the fall and winter, and their meat makes a very large contribution to the winter diet of the present-day Niska."[149] It is common knowledge that, when accompanied by the Gitanyow, the Nisga'a traded at Meziadin.

In his report, McNeary's comments about salmon fishing on the Nass are too general for the territorial issues addressed in this study. About the fur trade, however, McNeary stated: "The demand for furs also fostered competition for the trapping grounds on the upper Nass in the Meziadin region. Tradition records numerous villages in the Nass valley above Cranberry River, including villages of the Tahltan-La<u>x</u>wiyip, the Gitksan, and the Niska." Once again, McNeary must be referring to Gitanyow tradition as he must have heard it from the Gitanyow on the Nass. Perhaps when he relied on Emmons, McNeary also did not appreciate that Emmons was confused by the fact that his Gitanyow source lived at Gitlakdamix (see Chapter 6):

> In the nineteenth century, the struggle between these three groups for control of trapping became so intense that permanent villages in this area were no longer tenable. An old Tahltan told Emmons, "the upper Nass land is ours, and when we find a Nishka hunting there, we kill him." Tahltan presence on the upper Nass was particularly troublesome because they did not usually trade with the Niska, but took their furs to the Stikine where they traded with the Tlingit. The upper Niska (and Gitksan) destroyed the Laxwiyip-Tahltan power in the Nass valley, even extending their depredations to the villages on the Stikine River. Today, as noted in Chapter Three, the area remains in dispute between the Niska and Kitwancool-Gitksan.[150]

This reference to the Tahltans killing trespassers on their territory has been dealt with in Chapter 4: to reiterate, the Tahltan people referred to any tribal group on their southern boundary as "Nathka" or "Nasska" and did not distinguish between the Gitksan and the Nisga'a, who spoke the same language. The confusion may have been compounded by the fact that the Nisga'a sometimes traded inland at Meziadin Lake.

McNeary spent much time studying the relationship between Nisga'a houses or clans and territoriality. In his section on "Ownership and Access," he writes:

> The land was divided into stream drainages which, along with specific fishing sites, were the units owned by house groups. The spawning grounds on the creeks often belonged to the house which owned the rest of the creek, while fish sites along the river were sometimes not contiguous to other property of the owner.[151]
>
> Some chiefs had "hunting names" which referred to particular hunting grounds which they controlled [EG]. All this indicates a close relationship between economic rights and the intangible property of a house or clan. Mr. Gosnell, my principal source, insists that crests are "a sign of right" much like a deed.[152]

McNeary elaborates this topic, and it is worth quoting him at length:

> My own list of Gitlaxt'amiks house chiefs includes a little over thirty names (Appendix 3). McCullagh estimated that there were about forty "large houses or compounds with low-pitched roofs" at Gitlaxt'amiks.

There is not enough land near Gitla<u>x</u>t'amiks to make up thirty or forty separate hunting territories. I know of twelve territories and would estimate there may have been as many as sixteen. This is more than the number of clans, but less than the number of houses. Again using the Gitwinagil as an example, each of the main chiefs within this clan had his own territory; two were contiguous and one was directly across the [Nass] river. I was not able to locate the fourth: possibly it is the subject of a dispute. All four of the fishing camps are located next to each other on the Nass. There is a similar situation in the Vetter Creek and Zolzap drainages across from Canyon City. These were formerly owned by a single wolf phratry house, which later divided into the houses of Wigadem<u>x</u>skaak and Ba<u>x</u>k'ap. EG usually referred to the territory as a whole, belonging to the senior house, but once added that certain areas were designated for each house. The following picture can be inferred: There is no doubt that every clan had rights to hunting territory in the neighbourhood of the village where they were based. Some large clans contained two or more powerful and semi-independent houses which claimed territory of their own. On the symbolic level, they were probably able to claim crests of their own and raise them to the level of major crests, although they also shared crests and maintained close ceremonial cooperation with the rest of the clan. There must also have been a number of junior houses which were not established independently and continued to share the territory of their closest relatives, under the administration of the senior chief.[153]

On the subject of access to resources, McNeary writes: "EG asserted that it was not 'legal' for a chief to deny sources of staple food to those in need. This applies in particular to the larger salmon spawning grounds, such as on the lower Tseax. Menees<u>k</u> had a large smokehouse there, which he opened to all the people of Gitla<u>x</u>t'amiks, regardless of phratry."[154]

McNeary also describes the Nisga'a concept of property ownership: "EG said that owned territories were contiguous with 'no space' in between, but there seem to have been a few areas not claimed by any family, which were open to anyone from a particular village. For example, the hill behind Canyon City is said not to be owned by any one house, but to have been set aside by the Canyon City chiefs as a berrying ground 'for all the people' (EG)."[155]

McNeary comments further about the nature of land ownership at Gitlakdamix:

Useless or inaccessible land was unowned. For example, between Zolzap and Ansedegan Creeks there is a stretch where the mountain rises steeply from the river (No. 54 on Map 5) which is a "no man's land" between the territories of Wigademxskaak[156] and Nawis.[157] It was also said that some of the high mountain areas were unowned, or belonged to all the people of the nearest village. Most of the upper reaches of the Naas seem to have been considered common property of the Gitlaxt'amiks village, although some Houses did make claims, usually hotly disputed, to particular hunting and trapping grounds in the Meziadin area.[158]

In his final sentences above, McNeary – having worked for about twelve months over a period of two years with knowledgeable Nisga'a elders, including Eli Gosnell, whom he considered to be his "principal source" and the person "recognized by the upriver Niska as the best authority on traditional life" – comes to the conclusion that the "upper reaches" of the Nass River are considered the common property of the Gitlakdamix people. McNeary does not provide details to support either this claim or the disputes to which he refers.

His reference to general Nisga'a ownership must be contrasted with those of the Gitanyow and Gitksan, whose chiefs have identified and mapped on numerous occasions and in detail their histories, house territories, and place names from Gitxsits'uuts'xwt on up the Nass to Meziadin, Blackwater, and beyond, and to Awiijii and beyond on the Bell-Irving River, and which the Nisga'a have demonstrated they are equally capable of doing from Gitxsits'uuts'xwt on down the Nass. For example, Chief Mountain stated the Nisga'a concept of territorial ownership clearly in 1883: "We occupied this land before we ever saw a white man; each tribe had its piece of land bounded by some stream or mountain ... Each tribe then subdivided their land among villages and family for fishing, trapping, hunting and berrying so each man occupied his own place and no one would interfere with him."[159]

In conclusion, McNeary's work with the Nisga'a contributes significantly to our appreciation of their "traditional economic and social life." However, his treatment of Nisga'a territoriality is too general for the purposes of this study and perhaps reflects the contemporary political views of the Nisga'a, without exploring the detailed historical record of prominent Nisga'a leaders, who stated their case precisely on numerous occasions early in this century.

Nisga'a Tribal Council Draft Map (1984)

In 1984 the Nisga'a Tribal Council produced a map depicting the Nisga'a claim to territory from tidewater at the mouth of the Nass River north to its headwaters and to Treaty Creek on the Bell-Irving River (see Map 28).

This map bears features that reveal several significant anomalies. The most obvious feature is the extensive house territory detail along the Nass River from Kincolith to the Kinskuch and Kiteen Rivers area, but not

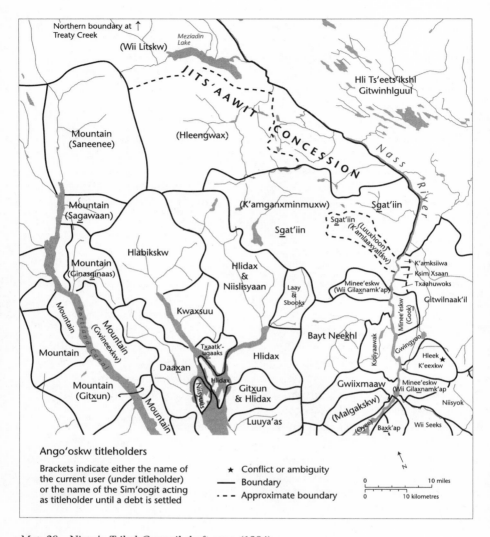

Map 28   Nisga'a Tribal Council draft map (1984)

beyond. The next feature of interest is the portion of the map west of the Nass River and north of the Kinskuch entitled "Jits'aawit [Tsetsaut] Concession." A note on the map indicates that this "concession" extends north beyond Meziadin Lake to Treaty Creek near Bowser Lake. This part of the Nisga'a claim is questionable.

The Nisga'a made their claim to the concession after a 1977 meeting with the Tahltan Tribal Council leadership. The Gitksan and Gitanyow were not invited to this meeting. As a result, any deal between the

Nisga'a and the Tahltan regarding Gitksan or Gitanyow territory could not have been intended to affect the Gitksan and Gitanyow. Prior to that meeting, the Nisga'a located their boundary just north of Meziadin Lake based on the Nisga'a Petition of 1913. On this basis, the "Jits'aawit Concession" seems to be a recent event. However, even if the concession is based on historical events, its depiction on this map does not pass close scrutiny.

Prior to the Meziadin wars (c. 1850-60), Tsetsaut territory did not extend south of the White River near Meziadin Lake. As the adaaw<u>k</u> make clear, the Tsetsaut relinquishment of land at Meziadin Lake (c. 1861) to the Gitanyow included a territory that extended from White River north to Surveyors Creek. And by 1900 the Tsetsaut had relinquished additional territory from Surveyors Creek north to Treaty Creek and the Awiijii area to the Gitksan. In other words, the purported concession involved two separate pieces of land, at two separate periods of time, and with two different groups of people. The historical record is clear that these two settlements of the Tsetsaut were not with the Nisga'a but with the Gitanyow in the first case and other Gitksan in the second case.

On several occasions in public meetings, notably at Gitwinksihlxw in October 1984, the Nisga'a have recounted how the mythical figure Txemsem created the entire Nass River and that this is why they are known as Gitxsitxemsem (people of/water of/Txemsem). They say, "The Nisga'a own the Nass, the Gitksan own the Skeena." Assuming for the moment that this is true, and that the Nisga'a have owned the Nass watershed "since time immemorial," as they also say, this apparent concession by another nation in the last 100 years contradicts any reliance on their version of the Txemsem story. In this regard, the Nisga'a appear to be grasping for any possible basis to claim Gitksan and Gitanyow territory in the Nass watershed, even when the bases contradict each other.

Finally, although the map is entitled "Hlits'eets'ikhl Nisga'a," which translates as "territory owned by the Nisga'a," two further anomalies appear on the map. First, the phrase "Hlits'eeks'ikhl Gitwinhlguul," which translates as "territory owned by the Kitwancool people," appears east of the Nass River, which shows that as recently as 1984 the Nisga'a acknowledged that the territory east of the Nass River belonged to the Gitanyow. Second, the names of several Gitanyow chiefs, "Luuxhoon, K'amlaaxyaltkw, Wii Litskw," appear west of the Nass River, which shows that the Nisga'a are aware that specific Gitanyow chiefs own territory in this area.

This map is obviously the product of extensive work at a time when the Nisga'a were faced with governments that would only acknowledge a claim to territory to which the Nisga'a could prove they had Aboriginal title. They were also faced with the challenge by the provincial government, in its defence in *Delgamuukw* v. *The Queen*, that the Nisga'a establish where their boundary was in relation to the Gitksan. Nowhere north of the Kinskuch and Kiteen Rivers do the Nisga'a provide any house territory detail, as required by indigenous law to prove ownership of territory, but this map reveals that they are capable of doing so south of that area. Furthermore, no evidence has surfaced in the numerous meetings held between the Nisga'a, Gitanyow, and Gitksan since the making of this map. Nor have the Nisga'a at any time between October 1995 and October 1997 responded in substance to the evidence contained in the 1995 report, upon which this book is based.

In conclusion, what this map does portray is a small competing claim between the Nisga'a and the Gitanyow in the Kinskuch and Kiteen Rivers area and between the Nisga'a and the Gitksan in the upper Kiteen watershed. The anomalies on this map, as drafted by the Nisga'a, are evidence that the balance of the claim by the Nisga'a to lands in the so-called "Jits'aawit Concession" area is spurious and, as Dr. Peter Williams so aptly termed it in 1984, "an act of aggression."

Frank Calder (1995)

Frank Calder recently produced from his files a document that he and the Nisga'a purport to be a Gitksan endorsement of Nisga'a boundaries. This one-page document bears the notation "COPY OF ORIGINAL 1927 Skeena River Indian Land Question" and is included in its entirety below:

Prominent Members of the Committee

1. Charles Martin   –   Hazelton
   Charles Wesley   –   Kispiox
   Silas Johnson   –   "
   Richard Morrison   –   "
   Stephen Morgan   –   Kitwanga
   Joseph Williams   –   "
   George Moore   –   "
   Arthur McDames   –   "

2. Of note is the fact that up to 1926 the village of Kitwancool was a member and supporter of the B.C. Allied Tribes in its quest for the settlement of the B.C. Indian Land Question.

3. During one of the campaigns for the Nishga and Gitksan Land Question Funds, Michael Inspring Bright collected from the Kitwancool people the sum of $140.00.

4. In 1926 when the village of Kitwancool decided to withdraw its support to the Land Question, it requested that the $140.00 which it had contributed to the Fund, be returned to Kitwancool.

5. The above request was fulfilled by Anthony Adams, who was the Aiyansh Secretary of the local Land Question Committee.

6. The Skeena River Indian Land Question Committee had full knowledge of the contents of the Nishga Land Petition at the time of its drafting, and it supported the claims and boundaries set forth in the Petition, just as the Nishga Tribes supported the Gitksan claims of all lands embodied by tributaries which flow in the Gitksan territories of the Skeena River.

The following inserted December 1, 1955 by MLA Frank Calder, President, Nishga Tribal Council: 'From the files of the late Chief Arthur Na-Qua-On Calder of Greenville. Chairman, Nishga Land Question Committee."[160]

Some of the "facts" in this document are not consistent with the historical record. The documentary record does not support the contention that "Kitwancool was a member and supporter of the B.C. Allied Tribes." Meetings between representatives of the Allied Tribes and the minister of the interior in July 1922 led, the following year, to an exchange of letters between Albert Williams of Kitwancool and W.E. Ditchburn, chief inspector of Indian agencies of British Columbia. Ditchburn, in response to an enquiry from Williams, suggested that Williams write to the chairman of the Allied Tribes, Peter Kelly, for information about a particular issue. As we have seen, this was a step that Williams refused to take: "I have to state expressly," Williams replied, "that the Kitwancool is not in a position to allow their way which is directed by 'God' Which is in Heaven above agitated by any man, also that the 'Kitwancool' is far different from the allied Tribes. I therefore cannot correspond with Mr. P.R. Kelly Chairman of the Allied tribes regarding the Kitwancools."[161] The Gitanyow, unlike the other Gitksan, did not participate in the meetings with Kelly and Reid in August 1922.

If Calder's document is meant to demonstrate that the Gitksan totally supported the Nisga'a claim to land at Meziadin Lake and beyond, it does not achieve its purpose. Rather, it shows a parting of the ways between the Nisga'a and the Gitanyow in 1926, perhaps because by then it was apparent that the Nisga'a were attempting to absorb Gitanyow territory. It has already been demonstrated that chiefs in Gitanyow and at least one Gitanyow chief in a Nisga'a village – Michael Bright – found it necessary to take extra steps to distinguish the two claims. This may also explain why the Gitanyow requested the return of their $140.

With respect to point 6, there was no "Skeena River Indian Land Question Committee" in 1913, so it could not have had "full knowledge of the contents of the Nishga Land Petition at the time of its drafting" or have "support[ed] the claims and boundaries set forth in the Petition." The position (that the Nisga'a own the Nass, whereas the Gitksan own the upper Skeena) has been stated in the last decade or so by contemporary Nisga'a leaders, but it was not an issue in 1924 when the Gitksan delegation asserted their claim to territory in the Nass watershed before Prime Minister Mackenzie King, and in the presence of Nisga'a leaders in Prince Rupert, and, apart from the Calder document, it has not surfaced in the documentary record anywhere else after 1924.

Conclusion

The statements of prominent Nisga'a chiefs since the late nineteenth century are the best evidence of the extent of the Nisga'a claim on the Nass River. The Gitwandilix (Nisga'a of the upper Nass) record from the 1880s to the mid-1920s shows that they consider the "upper Nass" to be situated in the vicinity of Gitxsits'uuts'xwt, about twenty-five kilometres above Gitlakdamix. In other words, there is no evidence in this crucial period – when witnesses and participants to the hostilities of the 1850s to 1860s were still alive – of a Nisga'a chief claiming territory north of Gitxsits'uuts'xwt.

The Nisga'a claim that the petition of 1913 is proof of their ownership to the entire Nass watershed is not supported by their own record. On the contrary, the Nisga'a record shows that the metes and bounds description in the 1913 petition is imprecise. There is no question that the petition includes Meziadin Lake, but only because it includes Gitanyow territory.

Proof exists that the language of the petition is imprecise and only recently interpreted to mistakenly include the entire Nass watershed. In 1908 the Nisga'a drafted a forerunner to the 1913 petition that claimed 224 kilometres of the Nass River, far short of its 384-kilometre length. In 1913 the uppermost of two maps that accompanied the latter petition covered Crown lands in the Meziadin area. In 1915 Nisga'a statements of ownership to the MMRC ended at Gitxsits'uuts'xwt. In 1916 a prominent Nisga'a chief, son-in-law of leading Gitlakdamix chief Sgat'iin, and his emissary drew a map showing the extent of Nisga'a territory as being slightly above Gitlakdamix, at a point that is clearly Gitxsits'uuts'xwt. In 1918 and 1930, two prominent persons connected with the petition and the Nisga'a claims effort defined Meziadin Lake as being at "the head of the Nass."

The Nisga'a chiefs who described their claim before the MMRC in 1915 made no claim to the Nass watershed above the Tchitin River at Gitxsits'-uuts'xwt. On the basis of their evidence to the MMRC, there is no doubt that the Nisga'a knew their territory and were fighting against the government for its recognition. In 1915 Nisga'a territory went upriver as far as the mouth of the Tchitin River. Nothing has occurred since that date to justify its expansion.

The documentary record of the Nisga'a shows that their claim in the Nass watershed has been fluid: the Nisga'a boundary (exclusive of Gitanyow territory) would find its upriver limit at Gitxsits'uuts'xwt based on the Nisga'a Petitions of 1908 and 1913, the statements of prominent Nisga'a leaders to the MMRC in 1915, and the map and statement of Naana, E.N. Mercer, in 1916.

Thus, with Gitxsits'uuts'xwt as the reference point, in 1929 the Nisga'a asserted a small claim to two specific areas immediately north of the Kinskuch and Kiteen Rivers (see Map 3); in 1973 the Calder boundary was at, but not beyond, the same two rivers (see Map 18); in 1979 the Nisga'a asserted a claim many kilometres beyond the Kiteen and Kinskuch Rivers to the junction of the Nass and Bell-Irving Rivers (see Appendix 2); in 1983 their claim extended to Treaty Creek on the Bell-Irving River (see Appendix 2); in 1986 the Nisga'a retreated south from Treaty Creek to Bell-Irving Mountain, but by 1995 they had restored their claim to Treaty Creek and almost the entire Nass watershed (see Appendix 7).

Other documentary evidence supports the Nisga'a boundary at Gitxsits'-uuts'xwt: the history of the "robin's egg" pole related by Old Dennis in 1923, the testimony and subsequent correspondence of Wilson Duff in *Calder v. Attorney General of British Columbia,* and place name mapping of Nisga'a elders with McNeary in 1973-4.

In summary, the Nisga'a documentary record is explicit. The Nisga'a own territory on the Nass River to Gitxsits'uuts'xwt; from this point east, they own the territory south of the Kiteen River itself, commencing at Wilsgayip; from this point west, they own to the height of land south of the Kinskuch River. The limited claim just north of these two rivers represents a competing claim with the long-established territory of the Gitanyow. Claims by the Nisga'a to territory north beyond the immediate vicinity of the Kinskuch and Kiteen Rivers are unsupported by their own substantial documentary record.

6

Witnesses on the Land: The Euro-Canadian Record, 1832-1930

Introduction

This chapter presents evidence on the ownership of territory on the upper Nass River, as observed and written down by European Canadians in the 100 years from 1832 to 1930. The territories involved are those of the Gitanyow, Kuldo, Kisgaga'as, Kispiox, and Nisga'a. For the most part, these travellers were explorers and surveyors sent by commercial interests seeking to exploit the region's various natural resources and travel routes. This work was essentially commercial intelligence gathering. It required recording any information likely to affect the company's fortunes and getting it in writing to head office. Many of the travellers' journals, letters, and reports have been preserved in archives.

The travellers' principal interaction with Aboriginal people was to employ them as guides and packers, although the early explorers were also interested in establishing fur trading alliances. Travellers often recorded the chiefs' names and villages of origin of the guides whom they employed. Many of the travellers were making long journeys across major watersheds, and their accounts of how far over a specific area a guide was prepared to take them provide an accurate, if inadvertent, record of which territories were linked with specific villages, chiefs, or their extended families. In many records, the boundaries of territories are marked by the point where the guide stated that he did not know the country ahead or said that he was afraid to proceed. Only the records that contribute this kind of evidence are reviewed in this chapter.

The early explorers had fairly limited objectives: easy routes for canoes, telegraph lines, pack trains, cattle drives, and railways and the identification of specific mineral and other resources and, as a result, they travelled more in certain areas of the region and less in others. Their observations therefore tend to predominate along the main river valleys and low passes and do not represent an even sampling of Gitksan and Nisga'a territoriality in the Nass watershed. Nevertheless, their records augment the other, more direct, sources reviewed in this document and are consistent with them.

The travellers had no axe to grind when they set out on their expeditions. They simply wanted to get to their destinations the best way possible, and they naturally relied on those who knew the country to help them get there. On this basis, the travellers provide independent, unbiased corroboration of Aboriginal presence and, by extension, Aboriginal territoriality.

The documentary record by Euro-Canadians in the Nass watershed reviewed here commences in 1832 with Hudson's Bay Company employee Donald Manson's trip up the lower Nass River, and it ends 100 years later with notes about upper Nass place names by provincial land surveyor P. Monkton. In the intervening years, various persons explored and visited the Nass River valley, some only to the lower river and others throughout the entire system.

Some early travellers were intent on finding a route from southern to northern British Columbia through the Skeena and Nass watersheds; a telegraph link from North America to Europe via Siberia in 1865-6 and in 1899-1900 to Dawson City in the Klondike goldfields; and a trail over which to drive cattle to the Cassiar goldfields in 1874-5. Others made brief forays into or through the valley on prospecting expeditions or for other reasons.

The written record shows that all travellers relied heavily on the Aboriginal people who knew the valley best to assist them with the object of their journey. For example, in 1867, Peter Leech was lost and travelling in the wrong direction on the upper Nass River when he was found by a party of Gitksan, who then guided him to Kispiox. Eight years later, A.J. Gardiner relied heavily on Gitanyow persons for information about the Nass country between Cranberry River and Meziadin and Bowser Lakes. His diaries include an invaluable, but little-known, record about the Gitanyow, their territories, and their historical relationship with the Eastern Tsetsaut, who then owned and occupied Bowser Lake.

For the casual reader, some notations in the early travellers' journals will be confusing, particularly the parts that deal with the identification of place names. Although the valley was rich in Aboriginal place names, there were few, if any, European place names to assist Euro-Canadians. In 1867 Peter Leech, with a Tahltan guide, was clearly descending what eventually became known as the Bell-Irving River, but he called it the Nass River. Later on the same journey, he ascended the Nass River as it appears on maps today and was totally confused about the river he was on.[1] In another example, in 1875 William Humphrey walked a mile down the Damdochax River, at Blackwater Lake, and called it the Nass River.

To assist the reader, place names identified in the travellers' journals will be followed by modern spellings in parentheses and in some cases the name that appears on modern government maps.

Donald Manson (1832)

In 1832 Donald Manson, the Hudson's Bay Company clerk stationed at Fort Nass, was sent to gather geographical information on the Nass and Skeena Rivers. On his first trip, he travelled up the Nass to Gitlakdamix. On 14 September 1832, he left the fort by canoe "with ten of the Company's Canadian Servants" and that day made fifteen miles fighting an ebb tide.[2]

The following day, Manson made his way up the Nass proper. He noted signs of habitation along the river, and at the end of the day's journey he came to a large settlement that was likely Laxgaltsap (Greenville), where people could not agree on information about the "upper Country": "Upon making known our friendly intentions we were kindly received and altho still early, I crossed the stream and encamp'd opposite the village in hopes of getting some information regarding the upper Country in this however I was disappointed as no two of them could agree in their statements. This is one of their principal fishing stations and to present appearances an abundant one as they brought me more than I could take."[3]

Manson continued to Gitlakdamix. There he was well received by the chief, with whom he may have been acquainted and who accompanied the expedition farther upriver about as far as the Cranberry River. Manson's comment about the Gitlakdamix chief's lack of knowledge of the interior is significant: "I have repeatedly endeavoured to draw information from the chief respecting the interior but without any success, in fact he is unacquainted with the country himself and the only motive I had in bringing him with me was that he might serve me as an interpreter should I fall in with Indians who are not in the habit of visiting Fort Simpson [Fort Nass]."[4] This comment indicates that the Gitlakdamix were not in the habit of travelling past the Cranberry River and were in fact unacquainted with the area beyond it. Had the Nisga'a owned territory in the upper Nass watershed beyond Gitlakdamix at the time, they should have been able to guide Manson on his journey.

P.J. Leech (1867)

The Western Union Telegraph Company[5] commenced surveys for construction of an overland cable through British Columbia and Alaska to St. Petersburg, Russia, via the Bering Strait. In 1866 Peter Leech, an engineer, was hired by the company to survey the telegraph line north from Quesnel on the Fraser River through the valleys of the Skeena and Nass

Rivers to Telegraph Creek on the Stikine River. In 1899 he published a summary of his daily journal, the source of most of the extracts below. However, his journal contains some details not in the summary, and where relevant they are quoted directly.

Leech reached the Kispiox River in the fall of 1866, at about the same time that another advance survey party, under Burns, reached the Nass River north of the Kispiox River (see Map 29): "[By the] end of September work was stopped for the season ... Burns had explored about fifty miles beyond the termination line[6] and had got to what he considered was the Naas River."[7] Leech then made his way along the Grease Trail to the Nass River, travelled down it by boat, then up the coast to the Stikine River. There he ascended the Stikine to Buck's Bar.

In January 1867, James Schaft and his wife, Lucy, with assistants Miller, Rankin, Kotsinta, and his wife, made an effort to get to the Nass River via a trail that followed "the first south fork [Mess Creek] of the Stikine," to and down the Iskut and Bell-Irving Rivers to the Nass:[8] "They travelled very slowly for Schaft was troubled with rheumatism, and by the time they got within twenty miles of the Naas [Bell-Irving] River their provisions were nearly all used up. Schaft then detached Miller and Rankin, giving them four days' provisions, with instructions to go down the Naas [Bell-Irving] River to try and purchase salmon from the Indians, telling them that he would not move camp until they returned."[9] According to Leech, Miller and Rankin then travelled south to a river that they referred to as "the Naas [Bell-Irving] and down the Naas seven days until they had eaten all their provisions and found no Indians." Given the route that they had taken, they could only have travelled down today's Bell-Irving River, and Miller's destination was possibly Meziadin Lake, where he could obtain food from Aboriginal people. Given their lack of success, Schaft and his party, with Miller and Rankin trying to catch up, returned to Buck's Bar on the Stikine.

Miller and Rankin did not encounter anyone when they travelled through the area in 1867. This is not surprising, however, because the "La̱xwiiyips" likely visited the Bell-Irving-Bowser area during the summer fishery and were probably farther north in the upper Klappan-upper Stikine region at this time.

On 24 March 1867, Leech proposed to Elwyn, who was in charge, that he form a party for the purpose of connecting the points reached by Miller (near Meziadin Lake) and Burns (upper Nass). Elwyn agreed to Leech's proposal: Leech departed Buck's Bar on 28 March and, retracing Miller's route, "reached the Naas [Bell-Irving] River at 9 a.m. on the 12th of April." This route is shown on Map 29.[10] He continued downriver for several days and on 17 April "About 10 a.m. ... we came to a wide stream [Nass River] entering the Naas [Bell-Irving River] on the left bank and at

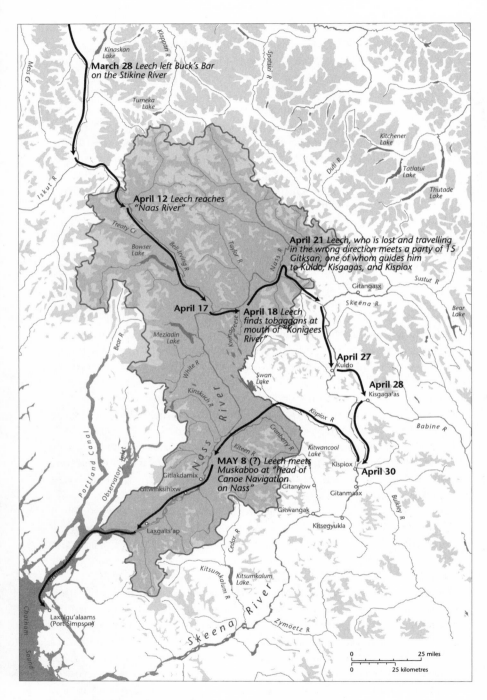

Map 29   P.J. Leech journey (1867)

the mouth of the stream was a tree marked with the letter T."[11] Leech then crossed the Nass proper and made his way upstream along the left bank of the river. The next day, he achieved his objective, although he did not know it at the time:

At 9 a.m. on the 18th we came to a point where the stream forked, one coming from the E.S.E. [Kwinageese River] and the other from the N.E. [Nass River]. At this point we found toboggans, which Bonner identified as belonging to McNeil's party.[12] We were therefore in high spirits as we were certain we were on McNeil's tracks, but decided on continuing in a N.E. direction, as I did not consider I had gone quite far enough to intersect Burn's line of route, which was a mistake, as I afterwards learned that the point where we found toboggans was the mouth of the Konigees [Kwinageese] River (the fork coming from the E.S.E.), and the actual point where Burns said he struck the Naas.[13]

Leech's journey up this portion of the Nass River was difficult until 21 April, when he

got into an open country, the hills on each side of the river being low and gentle of ascent. We made ten miles before stopping for breakfast, at 9 a.m. Just then an Indian came in sight, the first we had met since leaving Buck's Bar. He came up to us but we could not speak to him. He neither understood Chinook or Stikine. We made him understand by signs that we wanted to go to Kyspyox [Kispiox village]. That we had come from the Stikine; had been a long time on the journey and had very little to eat. We learned from him by the same method that if we would return with him to where he had left his party we would meet a woman who understood the Stikine [Tahltan] language.[14] We went back with him about six miles, and found a party consisting of three men, four women and eight children camped. They had been hunting in the mountains; had come down that morning, and seeing our tracks had followed us.[15]

Leech and his guide (who spoke only "Stikine") were lost on the upper Nass when they were overtaken by an Aboriginal person, one of fifteen people on a spring hunting trip in the nearby mountains. Leech found the members of the hunting party knowledgeable of the country:

Apr 21: ... One of the women spoke the Stekin [Athapaskan] language and she told us that we were turning our backs to Kispyox, that we would have to return down stream about 8 miles and go up a small creek [Vile Creek: Xsi Tsinihldenden Ando'o] that comes from a lake [T'am

Angyage'en] cross the lake and strike another [Canyon Lake: T'amtsinihl-denden] whose waters [Canyon Creek: Xsi Tsinihldenden] flowed east-ward by following which we would reach Kuldo on the Skeena in two or three days. Then for the first time I knew that I must be above Byrne's [Burns'] line to the Nasse. The whole party including Men Women and Children returned to the camp we left this morning.[16]

Leech was in territory belonging to the Gitksan House of 'Niist, and, as will be seen below, these were Gitksan people. The ability of one of the women to speak the "Stikine" language suggests intermarriage in the northern territories between the Gitksan and the Athapaskan-speaking peoples (Tsetsaut) in the Stikine watershed. This corroborates the long-standing presence for the Gitksan in the headwaters region. The Gitksan people knew the route to Kispiox. On 22 April, Leech

succeeded in engaging the indian who followed our tracks to act as a guide for me to Kispyox. He said he would go for three four point Blankets a shirt some powder and shot provided I would wait over a day at his camp as he wanted to fewt [fetch?] some Carriboo Meat he had cached in the hills. Although I have very little provisions I agreed to his terms on his telling me that he would give me some meat and that we would fall in with indians as soon as we would strike the Skeena. Gave the woman who gave me information an order on the Company for five Dollars worth of goods at Kispyox.[17]

Leech and his Gitksan guide set out for Kispiox, via Kuldo and Kis-gaga'as: "We started the following day [23 April] and arrived at Kuldo[18] on the 27th. At 11 a.m. the following day we reached the Kiskukause village,[19] to which our guide belonged, and here all the [200] inhabitants turned out and insisted on my stopping for the day."[20] This confirms that Leech was guided by Gitksan from the upper Nass.

The next day, Leech set out to walk the forty miles from Kisgaga'as to Kispiox. At Kispiox, Leech met with Decker and other COT members stationed there. He rested for a few days, then set out for Fort Simpson. During this leg of his journey, Leech crossed from Gitanyow territory below the Cranberry River into Nisga'a territory on the lower Nass, where he met prominent Nisga'a chief Maas Gibuu, probably on 8 May:

On the advice of Decker[21] I resolved to go by what was called the grease trail, across the mountains to the Hudson's Bay company's post on the Naas River a distance of about 120 miles and then by canoe to Fort Simpson. Accordingly, after remaining Saturday and Sunday at Kispyox I took Big Bill and Frank, with seven days' provisions and started on Monday morning at 6 o'clock, and the following Saturday at 10 a.m. I reached the head of canoe navigation on the Naas, where I found Muskaboo,[22] a chief of the Naas Indians, trading for furs with a lot of Indians from the interior. Muskaboo asked me where I was going, and when I told him I was going to Mr. Cunningham's at the Hudson's Bay Company post, he immediately offered me and my party a passage in his canoe, provided I would wait until noon, when he would be finished trading. In the meantime he gave me a couple of tots of very good rum and some tobacco, which were very acceptable, as we had not had a smoke for a week. We passed two large villages on our way down the river, the first called Kit-la-toms [Gitlakdamix] and the second Kit-whim-chis [Gitwinksihlxw]. At the latter I met Mr. Cunningham coming up with goods to trade with the interior Indians.[23]

It is evident from this passage that the Nass people traded up the Nass "to the head of canoe navigation,"[24] and that the Nisga'a villages commence from near that point and on down the Nass River.

According to his own trip summary, Leech and his "Stikine" guide considered the Bell-Irving River to be the Nass River and the Nass, as we know it today, to be the Northeast Fork of the Nass: "My route from the Stikine to the Konigus [Kwinageese] River was: Up the first South Fork to the divide between it and the Skoote [Iskut River], thence down the Skoote to its junction with the Ninqunsau [Ningunsaw], up the Ninqunsau to the divide between it and the Naas [Bell-Irving River], down the Naas [as before] to the Forks [Bell-Irving-Nass confluence], up the N.E. Fork [Nass River] to the mouth of the Konigus River."[25] Leech, who travelled nearly the length of the Nass River, encountered Gitksan from Kisgaga'as and Kuldo in the upper reaches and Nisga'a in the lower reaches. His account of the trip corroborates other evidence of a close relationship between the Gitksan and the "Tsetsaut" in the "headwaters region."

R. Scott (1867)

In a report on the newly purchased territory of Alaska, Scott (of the US army) included information on the Native population of adjacent areas. Robert Cunningham operated a post for the Hudson's Bay Company at the mouth of the Nass River and provided information to Scott on the peoples of the Nass. This information included the following statement: "There is a tribe of about 200 souls now living on a westerly branch [Bell-Irving River, near Bowser Lake at Awiijii] of the Naas near Stikeen River; they are called 'Lackweips' [Eastern Tsetsaut], and formerly lived on Portland Channel; they moved away in consequence of an unsuccessful war with the Naas [Gitanyow], and now trade exclusively with the Stikeens [Tahltan]."[26] This Eastern Tsetsaut group, led by Saniik, had acquired access to Portland Canal probably during the fur trade period, where Saniik was killed by the Nisga'a. The hostilities arising from this act resulted in war at Meziadin for a period of time, the eventual defeat of the Tsetsaut by the Gitanyow in 1861, and the immediate retreat of the Tsetsaut north to Awiijii in the upper Bell-Irving area. The Eastern Tsetsaut continued to live on the Bell-Irving River near Bowser Lake, with the Gitanyow as their southern neighbours, until the Gitksan of Kuldo received the region as compensation for a murder committed by them c. 1890-1900 (see Chapter 2). Scott's report on this group of Eastern Tsetsaut is consistent with the Gitanyow and Kuldo adaaw<u>k</u> of the region.

George Chismore (1870)

Chismore was a veteran of the Collins Overland Telegraph. In 1870, with a gold rush to Omineca under way, he wished to return to the Skeena region, through which he had travelled several years earlier. Arthur Wellington Clah, a Tsimshian from Fort Simpson, accompanied Chismore on his expedition to the mining region and guided him up the lower Nass and across to the Kispiox River.

The party left Kincolith and were joined at Gitlakdamix by Clah's Nisga'a brother-in-law Maas Gibuu, the same person referred to by Leech as "Muskaboo." Chismore's account of the trip demonstrates three important points: first, that the territories of each "tribe" were respected by the other "tribes"; second, that the Nisga'a territory extended part way along the Nass; and third, that Aboriginal people "from the interior" met the Nisga'a at the limits of their territory (see Map 30).

After leaving Gitlakdamix on 5 July, Chismore met "a number of Nass-car families preparing to take the trail with loads of grease ... Those who have brought the grease up the river transport it a certain distance on the trail, where they are met by Indians from the interior, who buy it from them to trade it in turn to others at the confines of their territory. Each tribe is exceedingly jealous of its privileges, and it is only on rare occasions that a member of one is allowed to pass through the territory of another."[27]

During the trip, Chismore referred to the main trail, other trails, graves, sweat houses, trading huts, bridges (including a description of one crossing the Cranberry River), and the antiquity of the trail beyond: "Bridges span the wider streams; one, a suspension crossing the Har-keen [Anxhon], built long ago, replacing a still older one, has a clear span of ninety-two feet ... In one place the trail leads over the top of a hill denuded of soil, and is worn deeply into the solid granite by the feet of succeeding generations."[28] Chismore's descriptions confirm the antiquity of the trading route and the relationship between the coastal and the inland peoples.

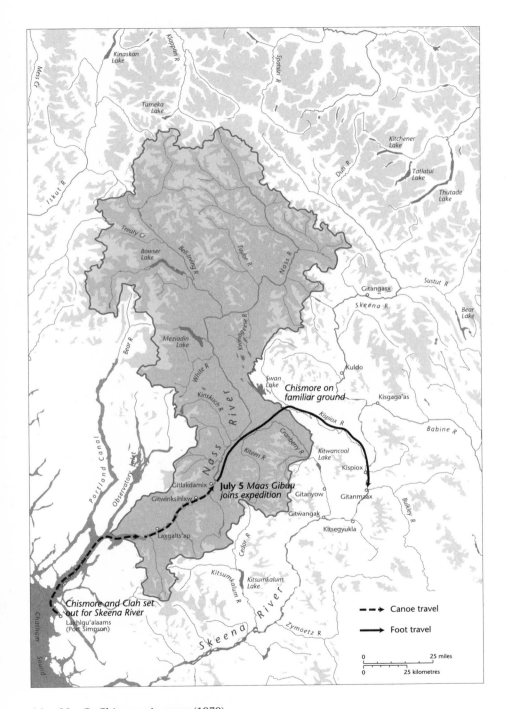

Map 30   G. Chismore journey (1870)

Chismore was on familiar ground: "Soon after crossing the divide between the Harkan [Anxhon, Cranberry River] and Kis-py-aux [Kispiox], we struck the end of the completed portion of the Russian-American extension of the Western Union Telegraph. I had the honor of being medical officer of the American division of that expedition, and accompanied the party that built the line; hence from this point the ground was familiar to me."[29]

Just before reaching Kispiox, Chismore noted of Maas Gibuu: "He knew every point of the country, and had some story to tell of them all. He had journeyed here in peace; fought for his life there; thrown the strongest man of that village, and distanced the fleetest one of this; in one place, killed an enemy in battle, and in another, got a grievous wound."[30] Maas Gibuu no doubt participated in battles against the Gitksan in earlier times. Nevertheless, Chismore's earlier comment confirms that access to Gitksan or Nisga'a territory was regulated according to Aboriginal law.

William Humphrey (1874)

In 1873 gold was discovered in the Cassiar region, and the ensuing rush brought a sudden influx of non-Native miners to the Dease Lake area. Supplying this population brought considerable logistical problems and the need for a land route to agricultural portions of the province. As a result, the provincial government supported an expedition to seek such a route. William Humphrey, a member of the expedition, kept a diary and wrote a report on his activities.

Humphrey went up the Nass River and along the Grease Trail to Kispiox and Hazelton, then up the old COT trail to Kispiox, where it ended in 1867. From there he followed Gitksan trails to the Skeena River at Kuldo, thence north to the Slamgeesh River. There, on 6 April, Humphrey noted three separate encampments of Gitksan people between Slamgeesh Lake and the Nass River (see Map 31):

> Came to a camp of Kitsagas Indians. This valley heads N.W. Our Indians [Gitksan] are getting afraid of the Stikeens. We follow up 6 Miles more pass two lakes. 5 miles more Tum to Clax [T'amt'uutsxwhl'aks] lake entering into the Naas. Cross this lake 2 Miles and find a Kitsagas Chief Camped. The Indian trail crosses the Valley on the summit and is now on our right, follow down the Naas [Damdochax River] 1 Mile and Camp with Kaale the Kispyoox Chief making 17 Miles here a large Stream Comes in from N 40 E. Sun Sik Mass [Xsa'ansaksxwmoohl].[31]

During this one-day trip, Humphrey walked from the Skeena to the Nass watershed, where he met a Kisgaga'as chief and later met and camped with Geel, a Gitksan chief, in the Gitksan territory of Wiiminoosikx. Humphrey, in a letter to his superior, comments on Geel's familiarity with the area: "Followed down this stream 7 miles [inlet and outlet of Damdochax Lake], and found Kale a Kyshpyox Chief; he appears to know the country better than any other Indian. I engaged him to go with me to the Skeena."[32]

Humphrey continued north past Groundhog Mountain to the Skeena River with Geel as his guide. From this point, "Kale says this Valley continues to the head of the Skeena about 25 miles from here."[33] Here the party ran out of supplies and returned to Hazelton. Humphrey later returned with Geel and the construction party to the Blackwater region to continue their work: "Tuesday June 17th: Two men went ahead Chopping and 3 finished grading. Hamilton and Kale stopped with the Cargo whilst the train was moving Camp, moved 4 Miles";[34] "Friday July 3rd: Cut 4 miles ahead struck the water of the Nass in 2 Miles from Camp."[35] By the end of the month, the work party had commenced construction up the "Shil Awa Mile Dit [Slowmaldo Creek],"[36] while Humphrey and Geel explored beyond the headwaters of the Skeena: "Wednesday July 29: Followed up the west branch of the Stikene to its source 6 Miles. Crossed a low divide and found the waters of the Klapada [Klappan River]. Camped Making 10 Miles this is as far as Kale knows the Country. And no sign of any Stikene Indians being here this summer."[37] Humphrey spent the entire summer of 1874 in the upper Nass and Skeena watersheds in Gitksan territory: the people whom he met throughout the entire period were Gitksan from Kisgaga'as and Chief Geel from Kispiox, who guided him north into "Stikine" country.

Humphrey's 1874 record of his trips on the upper Nass and Skeena confirms not only Gitksan presence on the upper Nass watershed but also Nisga'a absence at a season when Aboriginal people would be on their territory to preserve fish and berries for the winter. It also demonstrates detailed Gitksan knowledge of the territory, knowledge that could only have been acquired by a long presence on the territory.

James A. Gardiner (1875)

Dissatisfied with the results of the 1874 Humphrey expedition, the provincial government supported another survey by A.J. Gardiner in 1875. Like his predecessor, Gardiner kept a diary and wrote a report of his experiences.

Starting from the Stikine River, Gardiner and Vital Laforce[38] headed south via the Klappan, Nass, Skeena, and Kispiox valleys to Hazelton, then continued to Gitanyow, Bowser Lake, Gitlakdamix, and the lower Nass. Gardiner's diary provides an account of the people using the upper and lower Nass and upper Kispiox area. Gardiner also recorded a number of

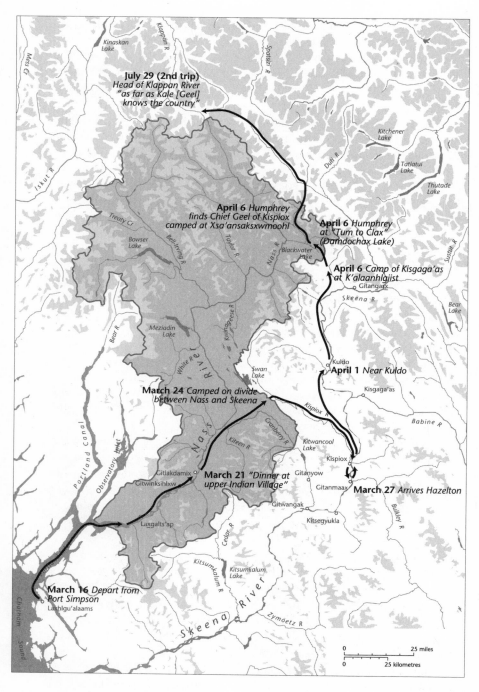

Map 31   W. Humphrey journey (1874)

place names and an account of the Gitanyow wars with the Eastern Tsetsaut.

Gardiner set out from Telegraph Creek on 27 May 1875 and reached the headwaters of the Klappan and Nass Rivers by 16 June (see Map 32):

> Wed – June 16: Left Camp for the Lake this is the lake that some says is the Head of the "'Klapada [Klappan River]" But the Indians say it is the Head of the Nass went up through a swamp a Mile wide and 3 miles long to the Head of the lake [Nass Lake]. The water runs to the 'Klapada till you get within 300 yards of the Lake and then there [is] a gentle Slope to the lake there is no Timber on the Swamp But grass and willows from a foot to three feet high We went around the shore of the Lake it is in the form of a Crescent 3 miles long and half a mile wide.[39]

This excerpt demonstrates Aboriginal knowledge of the headwaters of the Nass, but it is not clear who provided the information.

On 25 June, still on the upper Nass, Gardiner arrived at the Blackwater River. Farther downriver on 27 June, Laforce recognized the terrain and described it, using Gitksan reference points, as follows:

> Friday [June] 25: Left Camp and went 2 miles through an Aspen Opening here we saw Black Pines the first on the Nass 2 miles farther we Came to a large river Coming from the North East we suppose it to be the waters of the ground Hog and "Tamtoos [Damdochax River]" forks made a raft and went down the Nass 6 miles ... dis – made to day ten miles killed Nothing don't even see a squirrel to shoot and we have no Indian Trail I don't think they Come here[,] only in the winter to Trap Marten.
> Sunday [June] 27: ... just above the green Timber a large stream[40] comes in from the East it makes a large pass in the Mountains Vittal thinks it the pass [that] goes to "Kul Do."[41]

Laforce, obviously familiar with the area, described the route to Kuldo taken by Leech and his Gitksan guide in 1867. One of the outstanding features on the upper Nass River is a very narrow canyon called Winsgahlgu'l by the Gitksan.[42] On 30 June, Gardiner wrote about the site: "Just where the Canyon ends there was an Indian Bridge[,] the Canyon is only 15 feet wide and when Vittal went at low water it is only nine feet."[43] The canyon, within the territory of K'yoluget (see Map 17), and Gardiner's reference to "an Indian Bridge," demonstrate use and ownership (trails and travel) of the area by Aboriginal people at the time.

On 8 July, Gardiner found a trail and decided to follow it, but he took a wrong turn. His continued use of Gitksan place names demonstrates

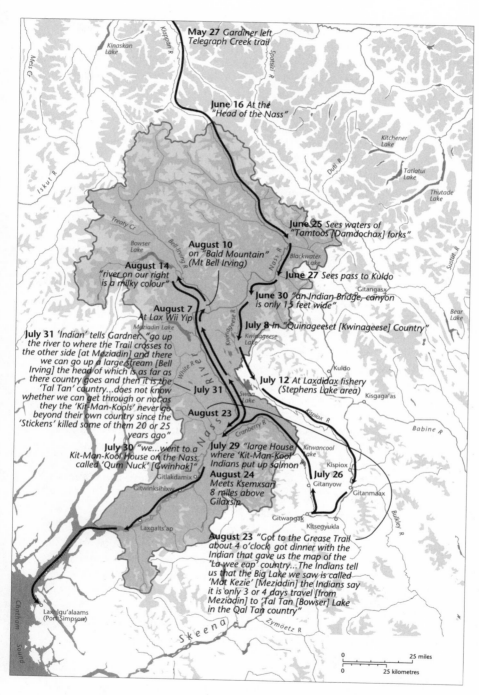

Map 32   A.J. Gardiner journey (1875)

Gitksan presence over a large portion of the upper Nass: "The Trail just run up into a 'Horse shoes' so we will have to return tomorrow ... The Indians call this Mountain and the Country around here at this Lake 'Quinageeset. The range of Mountains to the South West of us is the 'Lea,we,ape.'"[44]

Gardiner and Laforce left the Nass watershed and travelled south through the upper Kispiox valley, where they saw Swan Lake, Stephens Lake, and the general area around Stephens Lake:

> Monday [July] 12: ... killed nothing to day 2 miles back we saw a large Lake to our right name[d] "Mat-sa'-rane" [T'ammatsiigogat, Swan Lake] ... Tuesday July 13: Left camp and came 3 miles to the end of a long lake found a raft and went down to the outlet where we found a lodge of Indians. The lake lies East and West "Mun dan" [Mindagan, Stevens Lake] is the name of this lake it is 6 miles long and a mile wide the Tyhees name "Sum-mil-yan" and the name of this place is "Laugh-Ne-Taugh" [La<u>x</u>dit'a<u>x</u>, area around Stevens Lake] the waters run into the "Kyespox" ... The Indians has done all they can for us gave us plenty of "grub" such as they had and one of them will go with us to Skema [Skeena].[45]

This was a well-settled area, as Gardiner noted: "Wednesday [July] 14: Laugh-Na-Taugh is a very pretty place on the south side of the Kyspyox river it is a nice dry meadow of about 40 acres with the Indian Houses in the middle of it the Indians have their fishery on the stream that runs out of lake 'Mandan.'"[46]

Gardiner and Laforce made their way from La<u>x</u>dit'a<u>x</u> to Hazelton. After a brief rest, they set out for the Nass River via Gitwanga<u>k</u>: on 26 July, they reached Gitanyow; on 28 July, they reached the Cranberry River-Kispiox Grease Trail intersection; and on 29 July, near the Nass River, they "Came to a large House where the 'kit-man-kool' Indians put up Salmon they are just beginning to run up this far. Saw a nice patch of Potatoes here ... I think we will strike the Nass tomorrow noon."[47] This territory, with its fishery and vegetable garden, was actively occupied and used by the Gitanyow. Given its proximity to the Nisga'a boundary, the Gitanyow could not have settled here without Nisga'a knowledge. Why would the Nisga'a acquiesce to a Gitanyow house and garden if it was their territory? The only explanation is that this territory was owned by Gitanyow and that the Nisga'a knew it was owned by Gitanyow.

Gardiner and Laforce reached the Nass River at the confluence of the Cranberry River on 30 July: "Came on to our river [Cranberry River] again which now runs west for a mile and runs into the Nass we Crossed [Cranberry River] on an Indian Bridge and went to a kit-man-kool House on the Nass called "Qum Nuck [Gwinha<u>k</u>]" here we found there was no Trail on the other side of the Nass and that our best way was to go back to the kit-man-kool House that we passed yesterday."[48]

It is evident in Gardiner's record that Gitanyow territory extended from "Kitwancool" in the Skeena watershed, down the Cranberry River, to the Nass River, and that the Gitanyow people lived within this territory and exercised control of the resources there. Gardiner assessed the situation and decided not to go to the "head of canoe navigation"; instead, he would retrace his steps a few kilometres and set out for the headwaters of the upper Nass. On 31 July, he and Laforce

> turned to the North west and went over a low divide to the Nass the first six miles the Timber is all burnt off and nothing but a few logs and bushes ... then six miles more to this place which is an Indian House and Salmon fishery this is a good camp. We saw an Indian this afternoon who told us to go up the [Nass] river to [Meziadin River] where the Trail crosses to the other side and there we can go up a large stream [Bell-Irving River] the head of which [Bowser Lake] is as far as their ["Kitwancool"] country goes and then it is the "Tal Tan [Eastern Tsetsaut]"[49] country.[50]

Gardiner's statement is relevant to this study as independent, unbiased, corroborating evidence. His source was a Gitanyow person, with a detailed grasp of the geography and history of the area, including the exact location of the boundary between the Gitanyow and the Eastern Tsetsaut: "the head of a large stream" (the Bell-Irving River up to Bowser River) at Bowser Lake.[51] Gardiner continued: "The Indian does not know whether we can get through ... as they the 'kit-Man-kools' never go beyond their own Country since the 'Stickeens [Eastern Tsetsaut]' killed some of them 20 or 25 years ago. I think it is up in where we are going [Meziadin area] that ... the Kit-Man-Kools were killed."[52]

The northern border of the territory of Gitanyow Wolf chiefs 'Wiilitsxw and T<u>x</u>awo<u>k</u> is Xsigisi'am'maldid (Surveyors Creek), a tributary of the Bowser River at Bowser Lake. This boundary was established, as Gardiner's Gitanyow source states, after their final battle with the Eastern Tsetsaut "20 or 25 years ago" (1861 or 1862).[53]

On 7 August, Gardiner arrived in the Meziadin Lake area:

> Crossed the creek and had the trail plain for a short distance when it got so blind that we could not follow it. Kept along in the open country for two miles when we saw the mouth of the "La wee epe [La<u>x</u>wiiyip, Meziadin River]." Went down to the Nass and found a canoe badly split, pitched it up and crossed over to an Indian House on the point between the two rivers. There is no Indians here at present the "La-wee-eap" is a

pretty river, the water is clear and of blue colour it is one hundred yards wide. Where it comes into the Nass is very rapid and a quarter of a mile up there is two falls where the Indians catch salmon. 1/2 mile up it is smooth as a lake but how far it is like that I do not know.[54]

Gardiner missed the Meziadin-Bowser trail, which ran west of Mount Bell-Irving, and tried to walk up the west bank of the Nass and Bell-Irving Rivers. Lost, he and Laforce climbed Mount Bell-Irving on 10 August to try to get their bearings:

Left camp and kept up the divide got on to the *Bald* Mountain [Mount Bell-Irving] about noon. Saw a large lake [Bowser] down to our left, the lake is eight miles long and a mile wide, it runs up to the foot of the coast range right in among the glaciers. I think this is the upper lake that the Indian marked for us [see Map 32] as I was up on the Mountain this afternoon and could see another Lake [Meziadin] far down the [Nass] river we came nearly parallel with the lake [Meziadin Lake, several days earlier] there is no show for a pass on the "La wee eap" so the Indians has told the truth once more if we had went [followed the trail] the way they told us it would have been much easier for us than the way we have come. The "La wee eap" Valley [from Meziadin to Bowser] is from three to five miles [sic] wide and full of large meadows ... I do not know what waters we are on all the Indians knew was that it was the "Tal.Tan [Eastern Tsetsaut]" Country there is a low range of hills running along the other side of the valley that is where the Indians go to kill marmots but they don't go far as they are afraid of the Stickeens [Eastern Tsetsaut].[55]

Gardiner believed the "upper Lake" to be one of the lakes on his "Indian" map (see below); it is, no doubt, Bowser Lake.

The next day, Gardiner reached the Bowser River: "Saturday August 14: ... we kept on our course over a low ridge and just below we camped we could hear a river [Bowser] running on our right the river is of an inky colour and very cold it comes out of the snow."[56] Frustrated with their progress, Gardiner and Laforce decided to retrace their route downstream to the Nass, down the Nass to Fort Simpson, and thence by boat to the Stikine. Over a week later, on 23 August, they arrived on the Cranberry River and

got to the Grease Trail about 4 o'clock got dinner with the Indian[57] that gave us the map[58] of the "La wee eap" country got a salmon and started down went 3 miles and Camped for the night. The Indians tell us that the Big Lake we saw is called Lake "Mat Kezie [Meziadin]" and the large river putting out is the same name they the Indians say it is only 3 or 4

days travel to "Tal Tan [Bowser]" Lake in the "Qal Tan [Tahltan]" country but what lake that is I have no idea for there is so many over there.
The Indians all say there is a show [?] to take a road through to "Tal Tan
[Tahltan Village]" but I cannot tell to what place they go. But it must be
over on the third South fork for they all say it is not far from "Kla Pah
[Klappan]" valley. The lake they talk about may be the one where Vittal
went to this spring dis- made to day 17 miles. Killed nothing to day. I
see that the frost has nipped the potatoes here.[59]

This too is an important excerpt. Here it is explicit that an Indian, clearly
from Gitanyow, drew a map to guide Gardiner on his journey north in
late July – a map of the "La wee eap country" (see Map 33). Finally, lest
there be doubt about the identity of "Tahltan Lake," with certainty it is
Bowser, given Gardiner's source, who said that it is "only 3 or 4 days
travel" from Meziadin Lake, and given the juxtaposition of the two large
lakes on the map drawn by a Gitanyow person in Gardiner's diary.

Gardiner and Laforce set off down the Nass on 24 August and spent
the night near the Gitanyow-Nisga'a border in Nisga'a territory with the
Nisga'a chief Ksim X̲saan:

Started and intended to make kill "laugh, Cheep [Gila̲xksip]." But it rained
hard all forenoon. Some [so we?] only got to "Samsom [Ksim X̲saan,
Nisga'a chief, Frog-Raven Clan]" house 8 miles from "kill Laugh Cheeap
[Gila̲xksip]" here we was well used by Sim, mill. Sam [Ksim X̲saan] who
gave us flour tea sugar and salmon so we had a square meal. He S.m.S
has just got back from McDames Creek[60] at all the Indian ranches that
we passed to day there is none of there potatoes touched with the frost.
Course South East dis made 25 miles. Killed nothing.[61]

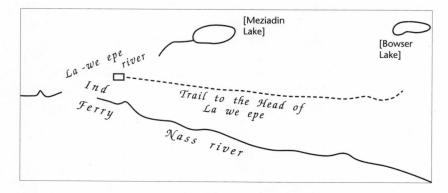

Map 33 Gitanyow elder's map of La̲xwiiyip country (from A.J. Gardiner
Journal, 1875)

Gardiner's layover with Ksim X̱saan is significant. He had finally arrived in Nisga'a territory, "eight miles" above Gilax̱ksip, at the Gitanyow-Nisga'a border. As mentioned in Chapter 3, Nisga'a chief Ksim X̱saan owned a fish camp on the east bank of the Nass River opposite Gitxsits'uuts'xwt – the site of the "robin's egg" monument referred to by Jenness. Gardiner completed his journey a few days later.

In conclusion, Gardiner's daily journal, written 120 years ago in 1875, provides powerful independent, unbiased, corroborative evidence of Gitanyow and Gitksan presence, history, use, and ownership of their territory on the Nass River. Moreover, with a "kit'man-kool House on the Nass" at Gwinhak and "Ksim X̱saan's house eight miles from Gilaxksip," his journal provides strong evidence for the location of the Gitanyow-Nisga'a border in between.

A.W. Clah (1877 and 1880)

Clah, as noted earlier, was a Tsimshian from Fort Simpson. He was married, however, to a Nisga'a woman and visited the Nass valley with some regularity. In the 1860s and 1870s, he made a series of trading trips to Gitksan territory via the Nass and the Skeena. He was, in other words, familiar with the grease trails and trading protocols of the region.

In 1877 and again in 1880, he went on prospecting expeditions up the Nass River above Gitlakdamix to the vicinity of Meziadin Lake. On the first occasion, he was accompanied by "Lucharn [Luuxhon]" of Gitanyow; on the second occasion, he met Luuxhon at the latter's fishing camp. Clah's party was subsequently accompanied by five of Luuxhon's men.

The following excerpts are from the diaries kept by Clah.

1877

Sep 27 head for Nass prospect i left Seax on the 27 of Septr 1877. Lucharn [Luuxhon] and Jim or Caink and Arthur Wellington Clah 3 of us. Calling Killaghtamax in about 1/2 in hour. again start up. gain in Canyon all day got up were good place to cache Canoe. the night was cleared and cold.[62]

Clah probably cached his canoe and camped at Grease Harbour, the head of canoe navigation on the Nass. He did not mention any sites above Gitlakdamix until, after a good day's walk, he got to the Cranberry River.

Sep 28 start walk this morning. and all day get up where the fishing house, staying one night

Sep 29 start walk. Get up anahghon[63] staying one night

...

> Oct 1 start walk left Anahgharn ... to walk heade nass river walk 30 miles camp fore dark
>
> Oct 2 start up to day encampped evening woforming creek 20 miles walk.[64]

Wolverine Creek,[65] which flows west into the Nass River about forty miles above the Nass-Cranberry junction, belongs to the Gitksan House of Gamlaxyeltxw, Frog-Raven Clan of Gitanyow.

With a walk of two more days, Clah and Luuxhon arrived at Meziadin Lake, where they found "old man Hatchen [Hayts'imsxw]," a chief from Gitanyow.

> Oct 3 walk way. get up lauch-wilhaup [Laxwilo'op] 25 miles walk
>
> Oct 4 last night 2 men kindly for food fresh salmon an Beaver mead. Some mountain sheep. this morning old man Hatchen feed us Salmon fresh Beaver mea[t]. Grizzley mea[t] start all day head nass river get up the lake October 4, 1877 6 days walk.[66]

"Hatchen's" hospitality is important and signifies Gitanyow ownership of the territory and resources within it. Clah canoed to the upper end of Meziadin Lake, where he prospected for several days before deciding to end his expedition. It took Clah and his party four days to reach the Cranberry River at Anxhon and a long day's travel by foot and canoe to reach the Tseax River.

A few years later, Clah launched another expedition to the Meziadin Lake area. The following entries are taken from his 1880 journal.

> 1880
>
> Aug 19 at Seax ready to start prospecting trip up Nass
>
> Aug 20 left Seax 10 oclock. this morning 3 Canoes come up from Kitwenselco[67] My [?] hom pulling old house down. moved. low place calling John mantsons[68] place at 12 oclock had dinner in his house. arthur wellington an Robertson. left one oclock get up laghsipe [Gilaxksip][69] an walking up by grease trail encampped 6 oclock. walk 4 miles methodies [Methodist] teacher. Robertson he wished loos is work he likes gone up prospecting with me.[70]

As Clah made his way upriver, he passed several Nisga'a sites before camping about a half day's travel above Grease Harbour. However, after another half day's walk, Clah, ever respectful of Gitksan territorial protocol, camped and sought out Gitksan chief Luuxhon, whom he wished to have accompany him to Meziadin Lake:

Aug 21 ... get up fishing house about noon. walk down Deep Canion. go Crost laghones [Luuxhon] place. prayer fore gone a sleep. thank great god for all is Bless

...

Aug 23 start walk up this morning. encampped evening acrost Bridge Canyon [over the Cranberry River] is Very Deep

Aug 24 get up anahome at 11 oclock fore noon. fishing Village 6 men 4 women some children they Very Happy when i came I walk round Shake them hand one of them was Blind and one give us food. Lochone [Luuxhon] calling all his friends to go up with us. 5 men were promise to go with us.[71]

Luuxhon, who appealed to his friends at Anxhon to join the Clah prospecting expedition, was clearly the leader of the group.

In his journal, Clah frequently refers to the source, or "head," of the Nass River in the context of Meziadin Lake. As has been discussed extensively, this assumption was prevalent then and for more than fifty years thereafter.

Aug 26 ... left grease trail yesterday 2 1/2 days walk an walk again trabing [trapping] trail go[e]s of head Nass River

Clah party We all 6 Company Loochore[72] is good for mines ...

Aug 27 walk way. encampped evening

Aug 28 start of walk cleared at 7 oclock this morning the trail is very rough full of leaps [?] we cannot travel fast encamped 10 miles Below laghwehip.

Aug 29 Sunday ... we all travel get up lagh-weip at 5 oclock 4 men crost the River 2 come Back with 4 fresh Salmon 2 watching all night for trying to shot large Brown Bear.[73]

At Meziadin (Laxwiiyip), Clah was aware that some members of his party, Luuxhon's "friends," were concerned about the Eastern Tsetsaut ("stickeen siwash"), and he refers to the Gitanyow-Tsetsaut war of 1861: "Aug 30 morning to crost lagh-wip place hooking 40 salmon in 5 minuts ... some Boys were fraiden for stick[ine] siwash [Eastern Tsetsaut]. they use the fight some years ago stickeen swashs."[74] Shortly after his arrival at Meziadin Lake, Clah, convinced by some members of the expedition to turn back, set out for the lower Nass on 1 September and arrived at the Tseax River, near Gitlakdamix, "at 12 oclock noon" on 6 September, "6 days from [the] head [of the] Nass river."[75] Once again, the journal entry indicates that Clah considered Meziadin Lake to be the "head [of the] Nass river."

The record of his trip shows that, after leaving the head of canoe navigation in Nisga'a territory, only Gitanyow people were encountered along the Nass River (Chiefs Luuxhon and Hayts'imsxw); only they used the territory and its resources, and they were singled out as Clah observed Gitanyow protocol.

Helen Woods (1880)

Helen Woods was the sister-in-law of Anglican missionary Robert Tomlinson. He had established a mission at Kincolith in 1867 and then in 1879 had established a new mission among the Gitksan at Ankitlas[76] near Kispiox. The following year, Woods journeyed to join Tomlinson at Ankitlas. Her account indicates Gitksan use of the area along the grease trail to Kispiox.

Leaving Kincolith in April, Woods was accompanied by a Nisga'a as far as Gitlakdamix. There, she noted, "We were fortunate in finding a Skeena [Gitksan] Indian to take his place, named Yack-o-Dades [Wiiyagadeets]."[77] The party left Gitlakdamix on 13 April and proceeded along the winter trail to the Nass River. There they met some "Indian women" at a hunting camp, continued along the Nass, and passed the mouth of an unnamed (Cranberry) river. On 18 or 19 April, they came to a "salmon house" and a graveyard. Woods met a man there who was fishing, continued on, and met two families travelling from the east. On 23 April, she met a man with two dogs who had just come from Kispiox: "He was on his way to the lake we had just passed to set his trap for trout."

The route along the Kispiox Grease Trail took Woods across a Gitanyow-Kispiox boundary into Kispiox territory, where she encountered a man with his dogs, indicating Gitksan use and ownership of the area.

G.M. Dawson (1887)

G.M. Dawson, of the Geological Survey of Canada, spent the field season of 1887 in northern British Columbia and Yukon District. His subsequent report contained information on the Native peoples of the Stikine watershed. The following account of the feud between the Tahltan and the "Nass Indians" was based on information provided by J.C. Callbreath, a merchant and resident of the region since at least 1881.[78] It is more general than the account recorded by Reverend McCullagh with Gitanyow chief 'Wiilitsxw on the shore of Meziadin Lake in 1905, and the major variation worth noting reflects Dawson's lack of familiarity with the geography of the area and the identity of the Aboriginal people there.

Knowledge of local history, geography, tribal affiliation, and Aboriginal law help the reader to understand better the Meziadin wars and Dawson's version. To reiterate: Gitksan, Nisga'a, and Tsetsaut law for murder requires compensation through forfeit of land or another life; the Eastern Tsetsaut had rights on Western Tsetsaut territory at the head of Portland Canal before the Meziadin wars commenced about 1850; Dawson (and most writers of the day) used "Tahltan" and "Nass Men" generically, without distinguishing the Western from the Eastern Tsetsaut, or the Gitksan from the Nisga'a;[79] the Eastern Tsetsaut probably amalgamated with, and became known as, Tahltan soon after their defeat by the Gitanyow c. 1861.

Dawson's account of the events is better understood when read with these points in mind (see McCullagh below): "Between the Tahltan [Eastern Tsetsaut] and the [Gitanyow] Indians inhabiting the Upper Nass there has been a feud of long duration, which is even yet outstanding ... For a long period preceding 1856 there had been peace between the Tahltan and the Nass Indians,[80] but in or about that year the latter, following up one of the branches of the Nass River into Tahltan [Tsetsaut] territory, killed two individuals of that tribe, who happened to be men of importance."[81]

Gitksan, Nisga'a, and Tsetsaut sources are clear on this point: Dawson's "men of importance," Saniik, Wolf chief and leader of the Eastern Tsetsaut, and his nephew Aminta, were killed by Nisga'a Wolf chief Hlidax at the head of Portland Canal c. 1850. Unless the Nisga'a immediately made peace and forfeited land or one of their children, revenge could be exacted in kind by the Eastern Tsetsaut. Hlidax did not inform his Nisga'a brethren of his act, which left no peaceful recourse for Saniik's kin: "Two or three years later, the Tahltan [Eastern Tsetsaut] found an opportunity of killing in retaliation four of the Nass."[82] The Eastern Tsetsaut, on good terms with the Gitksan of Gitanyow, sought only to retaliate against Hlidax's relatives, who were camped with the Gitanyow on a trade mission at Meziadin Lake. Although the Gitanyow were warned in advance, Gitksan were killed with the Nisga'a in ambush on the trail to the lower Nass River. The Tsetsaut had avenged the murder of Saniik and Aminta, but now they found themselves forfeit for life, land, or both to the Gitksan of Gitanyow.

In the ensuing hostilities, the Gitanyow defeated the Eastern Tsetsaut. As McCullagh noted, and prominent Nisga'a chief E.N. Mercer corroborated (see Chapter 5), the Gitanyow obtained the lands of the Eastern Tsetsaut in 1861 in a Gawaganii[83] held on the shore of Meziadin Lake: "The year preceding the first gold excitement on the Stikine,[84] a peace having been meanwhile concluded, the Nass [Gitanyow] Indians induced some of the Tahltan [Tsetsaut] to visit them in their own country, a short distance from the recognized boundary, at a place called Yak-whik [Laxwiiyip], which is the furthest up fishery of the Nass Indians, and at which they have a large house."[85]

This event, obviously of major significance, appears in the journals and reports of Euro-Canadian visitors to the Nass and Stikine Rivers for more than a century. Dawson, whose report was based on a Tahltan perspective in 1888, used "Nass" in a general sense; by contrast, Gardiner, like others, obtained directions and sought guidance from those who best knew the terrain into which he was heading, namely, the Gitanyow, and he recorded their comments and had a map drawn by one of them. Although Dawson obviously heard a version of the adaaw<u>k</u>, his lack of distinction between Gitksan and Nisga'a makes it difficult to use his account as a reliable source.

Kamalmuk and Skeena Expeditions (1888)

In 1888, with a growing non-Native presence in the Skeena-Nass region, a complex train of events was set in motion, culminating in the murder of a Gitanyow man by a policeman of the Skeena River Expedition. The following discussion focuses on those aspects of the events that concern the use of the upper Nass region.

Beginning with a dispute over the inheritance of a name at Kitsegyukla, the affair escalated into a feud in which "Kamalmuk [<u>G</u>amgaxmilmuxw]" of Gitanyow killed "Neatsqua [Niitsxw]" of Kitsegukla. Subsequently, whites became involved, and the provincial government despatched a party of five special constables to the upper Skeena region to apprehend Kamalmuk.

Indian Agent Todd, who was responsible for this vast region, was instructed to assist with the capture. Todd was reluctant to join the expedition from the beginning because he thought that the specials were too inexperienced to handle the situation. Indian Superintendent I.M. Powell, in a letter to his superiors, wrote that Todd had "proceeded to the Upper Skeena and found that the Indian for whom they had been looking had gone (they assumed) to evade pursuit, to the headwaters of the Nass."[86] The party of specials reached Hazelton on 23 May, having stopped at Kitsegyukla en route.[87] At the latter village, Todd sent a message to Kamalmuk before parting company with the specials and returning to the coast.

The message, however, achieved its objective. By the middle of June, Kamalmuk was in Gitwanga<u>k</u>, in the house of "Legenetta [Liginihla]," a chief of that village. He was in possession of Todd's letter and, according to his wife, intended to surrender. Three specials, Holmes, Parker, and Green, despatched from Hazelton to carry out the arrest ran into difficulty: on 16 June, after two unsuccessful attempts to arrest him, Kamalmuk, while fleeing from "Legenetta's" house, was shot and killed by Constable Green.

When Marius Barbeau was doing fieldwork among the Gitksan in the 1920s, he collected a good deal of information on the Kamalmuk affair, sufficient information, in fact, to write a book about it: *The Downfall of Temlaham*. The following comments, taken from the accounts collected by Barbeau, reflect the Gitksan view of the event.

When the detachment of police arrived on the Skeena in May 1888,

Kamalmuk, of course, had disappeared. Some informants attributed this disappearance to a "flight" from the police; others pointed to the breakdown of Gitksan compensation procedures due to police presence; still others implied that Kamalmuk was following the normal annual round of activities. There may be some truth in all these explanations, but there is general agreement that Kamalmuk spent the spring months in the territory to the northwest of Gitanyow on the Nass watershed.

Significantly, all but one of the narratives that identify a destination for Kamalmuk during this period refer to locations on the upper Nass River. The exception, Semedik (Simediik), refers to the Tsetsaut country, which is a difference in the form of the identification rather than the location,[88] as follows:

1. A fishing station – Gitanx[h]on, on the Nass; Hilin, on the Nass, and about 68 miles from Kitwanga.[89]
2. A village station – Gwuntaax, on the headwaters of the Nass.[90]
3. Hunting territory – Lamingittin [Luumin Gyahlt'in], hunting territory of Kamalmuk's father near Grease Harbour and a little above Kitladamax; presumably the same as Hilin.[91]

Gitanxhon, Hilin, and Gwindaax are Gitanyow fishing sites on the Nass River near the Cranberry confluence; Luumin Gyahlt'in refers to Kamalmuk's father's territory on the Kiteen River. Kamalmuk, a chief in the House of 'Wiixa of Gitanyow, had the right to be at these sites through his father (privilege of amnigwootxw), a member of the House of Wudaxhayetsxw, Gitanyow. Thus, Kamalmuk was in Gitanyow territory near, and at, the Gitanyow-Nisga'a boundary.

George Derrick, of Gitanyow, one of Barbeau's sources, said that Gamgaxmilmuxw "took to the mountains and there fleeing people. After this murder he came to the Nass ... He was on his father's hunting grounds."[92]

Police correspondence and ethnological research related to the Kamalmuk incident of 1888 demonstrate that the Gitanyow held territory on the "upper Nass" near Gitlakdamix, where Kamalmuk himself sought refuge in his fishing camps along the Nass River at the Cranberry confluence and on his father's land up the Kiteen River. There is no evidence that the Nisga'a disputed the presence of Kamalmuk and the Gitanyow in the territories that he used at the time.

J. McEvoy (1893)

McEvoy was an employee of the Geological Survey of Canada. He spent part of the 1893 field season conducting surveys in the Nass River valley. After hiring a canoe and crew of "Nasse Indians" at the mouth of the river, he went upstream past "Kit-wan-chilt." He did not mention Gitlakdamix or Aiyansh but continued on the "Grease Trail." Travelling along the trail, in Gitanyow territory, he crossed an old "Indian bridge" over the "Au-kon [Anxhon] River," noting some "Fish Houses at the mouth of Gin-mielt-kun [Gwinmihlgan] Creek."[93] Leaving the main trail, he followed "an old indistinct trail" to "Tam-a-tsi-a'ten Lake." Of the area around Meziadin Lake, he reported: "The ownership of this place has long been a disputed point between the Tahltan [Eastern Tsetsaut] and the Kit-wan-cool peoples, and here many battles and massacres have taken place."[94]

McEvoy clearly understood that the Gitanyow were central to the dispute at Meziadin. He makes no mention of any involvement of the Nisga'a in claims to Meziadin.

Franz Boas (1894)

Boas (1858-1942), an anthropologist who made significant contributions to linguistics and ethnology, was attracted to study the Tsetsaut of Portland Canal on the northwest coast of British Columbia in 1894. He wrote one of the few published accounts of the Western Tsetsaut, who, reduced to a population of twelve persons, were taken in and had become absorbed by the Nisga'a at Kincolith by 1890.

By 1861 the Eastern Tsetsaut had established their village at Awiijii on the Bell-Irving River near Bowser Lake; by 1894, at the time of Boas's visit to Kincolith, they had established "their principal villages on the head waters of the Stikeen River." This location is consistent with Gitksan history on the upper Nass. The accidental killing of Kuldo chief X̱skiigmlax̱ha meant that the Eastern Tsetsaut had to forfeit a large portion of territory to the dead chief's nephews, Naagan and Sg̱awil (see Chapters 2 and 4). This incident is memorialized by the name Treaty Creek, near Awiijii.

The Nisga'a "speak one of the three main dialects of the Tsimshian language," said Boas; "the other dialects are the Tsimshian and the Gyitkshan [Gitksan]. They [Nisga'a] inhabit the Nass River, except its upper course."[95]

Boas appears to have relied on Chief Mountain in particular as his source of information: "These [referring to further details on the phratric and 'totemic' subdivisions of the Nisga'a] are the old recognized subdivisions of the Niska which were given to me by 'Chief Mountain,'and corroborated in part by other members of the tribe."[96] Mountain seemed knowledgeable about the Gitksan, as Boas noted: "Turning towards Skeena River we find the Gyitwuntlku'l, who are considered a separate tribe, and whose dialect is intermediate between the Niska and the Gyitkshan. They have two clans: the Kanhada [Ganada] and the Laqkyebo [Lax̱gibuu] ... Chief Mountain gave me the following subdivisions of the Gyitkshan: the list, however, is incomplete ... Gyitwunga ... Gyitsigyuktla ... Gyispayokc ... Gyitanma'kys."[97]

Boas worked with Nisga'a and Tsetsaut peoples at a crucial time, because in 1894 many of his sources were participants, directly or indirectly, in the earlier hostilities.

It was clear to Boas, based on his work among the Tsetsaut and the Nisga'a at Kincolith, that the Nisga'a did not "inhabit" the upper Nass. His work, acknowledged as the only original work on the Tsetsaut of the day, demonstrates that the Nisga'a did not occupy the upper Nass and that two distinct Tsetsaut groups were important to the history of Portland Canal and the upper Nass, who are identified in this study as Western (Portland Canal) and Eastern (La̱xwiiyip-Meziadin area) Tsetsaut.

J.B. McCullagh (1897-1918)
McCullagh was an Anglican missionary stationed at Aiyansh and Kincolith between 1883 and 1921. As Raunet pointed out, "when he arrived at Aiyansh, his first goal was to build a house and start learning the Nishga language."[98] McCullagh eventually became fluent in the language, conducted services in Nisga'a and English, and wrote "several textbooks in Nishga and translated part of the Gospel."[99] McCullagh seems to have performed a variety of functions – in addition to his missionary duties – during his many years on the Nass: translator, magistrate, editor-publisher of Hagaga, writer, poet, advocate, mapmaker, and general resource person to the Nisga'a.

In 1915 prominent Nisga'a leader Timothy L. Derrick referred to McCullagh and his daughter at the MMRC hearings in Aiyansh and conveyed the regard in which they were apparently held by the Nisga'a:

Commissioner Shaw:
And that[100] would account then for the great reduction in the population?
Derrick:
Yes, when I got big, there was a gold excitement at Stikine and I went there too and there was quite a lot of our people went there and it was the same; a lot of diseases started among the people there.
Q Did you not have a resident doctor here until a short time ago?
A We never saw a Doctor yet among us in this place but I will tell you about a man who helped us for a short time. When Mr. McCulloch [sic] came among us he cured a great many people in giving them medicine.[101]
...
Q Did you ever make application to the Government for a school?
A ... many times Rev. McCulloch would act as a School Master himself as he had no help. When his daughter got back why she taught the children. They learned the children very well.[102]

And, as Stephen McNeary wrote in 1976, "James B. McCullagh devoted his whole life to mission work on the Nass. He learned to speak Niska fluently, developed an alphabet, and translated a good deal of scripture. He wrote valuable descriptions of Niska life in his reports to the Church Missionary Society."[103]

In 1897, as magistrate for the District of Cassiar, McCullagh was involved to a degree in a border dispute between two Gitksan chiefs, 'Wiilitsxw of Gitanyow and Naagan of Kuldo, at the Gitanyow-Kuldo border near Bowser Lake. Since 1861 'Wiilitsxw had contended with the Eastern Tsetsaut on his northern border. However, as we have seen, in the early 1890s,[104] Naagan and his brother Sgawil, Gitksan Frog-Raven Clan chiefs from Kuldo, received a large portion of Tsetsaut territory at Bowser Lake in compensation for the murder of their uncle Xskiigmlaxha. 'Wiilitsxw now had to contend with new chiefs on his northern border, Naagan and Sgawil, and to resolve the exact boundary between them. McCullagh found himself in the middle of this situation and chose (by letter) to have Indian Agent Loring deal with the matter at Hazelton, because it affected the Gitksan, not the Nisga'a with whom he was concerned:

Dear Sir,

The bearer hereof, Peter Wilizqu of Gitwinlgol, has appeared before me to lay information against one Nagan of Hazelton for that he Nagan unlawfully took up, and now unlawfully detains three beaver traps, the property of Complainant, and set for beaver in his (Complainant's) hunting grounds in the upper Naas district.

Complainant states that an agreement was entered into some time back before you by both Nagan and himself in which each agreed to respect the rights of the other on the hunting grounds in question. Nagan it appears has now violated this agreement by crossing the boundary,[105] said to have been decided upon by you, and taking up and away the three traps above mentioned.

I send the Complainant on to you at once as I think it more practicable to settle this matter at Hazelton than at Aiyansh. I would merely add that these hunting ground disputes are a growing evil, and seem to call for serious consideration.[106]

McCullagh's letter confirms Gitksan control of the upper Nass. By 1897 McCullagh had lived among the Nisga'a for fifteen years, was fluent in the Nisga'a language, and recognized that 'Wiilitsxw and Naagan were Gitksan, with territory on the upper Nass, and that Loring would have to deal with the issue there. In other words, the boundary dispute was a Gitksan concern.

In 1905 McCullagh was hired by the Dominion Fisheries Department to inspect salmon spawning grounds on the upper Nass and in particular an obstruction at Meziadin Lake. For the month-long trip, McCullagh engaged four Gitanyow men at Aiyansh to assist him: William Gogag (Guugaak), Edwin Haizimsqu (Hayts'imsxw), Arthur Gwisilla, and James Nakmanz. It is apparent from McCullagh's record of the trip that Gitanyow chief Gogag was not only knowledgeable about the country between Aiyansh and Meziadin Lake but was also senior guide in the group and necessary to allow McCullagh access to Gitanyow territory.

The details of this trip, the relevant sections of which are set out below, are taken from McCullagh's journal, published several years later. The party set out from Aiyansh on 19 September, with McCullagh and Gogag walking up the right (west) side of the Nass River (see Map 34): "William Gogag and I proceeded on foot over the Gitlakdamiks trail to Gitlaksipqu [Gilaxksip], a distance of 7 miles. The other men ... started at the same time in a small canoe with the packs ... When the canoe arrived we embarked and crossed over to the other side where the trail begins, and there we hauled the canoe up the bank and stowed it safely among the bushes."[107] The group then hiked a short distance up the Nass and camped for the night. The next day, the party travelled until about 5 p.m. and camped at a site opposite and somewhat above the confluence of the Kwinatahl River, "at a place between Ksiwiaks and Zikgan's Spring."[108]

Still well within Nisga'a territory on 21 September, the party travelled until 2 p.m., then stopped for lunch at "Wilkbiwau's Spring [Wilxbiwo'os]" in Nisga'a territory. Afterward the party continued to an abandoned Indian village, which McCullagh described in detail: "I should very much like to excavate on the site of this old town; the places (square pits) where the houses stood are as plain as if dug yesterday. Judging from appearances the vicinity was at one time the habitat of a very large Indian population. On every hand are to be found traces of habitation – salmon pits without number, and footpaths stereotyped in the stony hillside running in various directions, evidently to where houses once stood ... The name of the place is Gitangialqu [Gitangyaahlxw], and we have made our camp here in a sheltered hollow."[109] This site is significant because it is located on the east bank of the Nass River, opposite Gitxsits'uuts'xwt, in the vicinity of the "robin's egg" monument of Ksim Xsaan referred to above. Here a small stream (Xsit'ax) flows across a large flat rock (G'ilhlalo'obit) and cascades into the Nass at the precise location of the Gitanyow-Nisga'a border. As the reader may recall, it was the upper termination point for Nisga'a chiefs Niisyok, Sgat'iin, and Timothy Derrick, in particular, and the point of commencement for Gitanyow chiefs (see Chapter 3). From this point north, the party would be in Gitanyow territory.

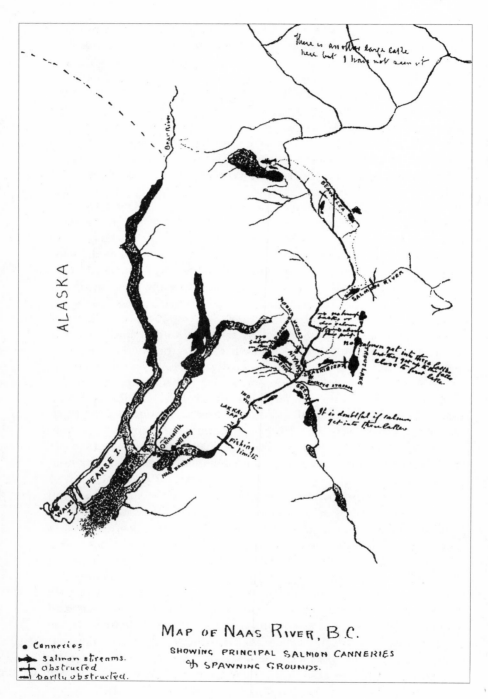

Map 34 Map of Naas River, BC (J.B. McCullagh, 1905)

Due to heavy rains the next day, McCullagh and his companions, with a late start, travelled about five miles when they "passed through a deserted hamlet of six or seven houses. I remember many years ago visiting this place and finding it lively enough then with Indians – old men and grannies, young men and maidens, mothers and children. But where are they now? The many tombs around the houses, even up to the very doors, answer, 'Here.' And there in those tombs, which are like miniature bathing machines open at one side, hang fluttering in the wind the garments – tattered remnants, rags, and pathetic little bits of finery – once worn by the deceased."[110] McCullagh must have visited the village shortly before its demise, and Gogag clearly witnessed the event, which probably occurred in 1888 or 1889: "I remember the time well," Gogag said. "The medicine men did their patients to death by spurting ice cold water over their naked bodies, and otherwise exposing them. The name of the place is Gwinlaqu [Gwinhlakw]."[111] Gwinhlakw, a Gitanyow fishing site on the east bank of the Nass River, belonged to Yal, a member of the Fireweed Clan, then resident in the village of Gitanyow. Clearly, the party was well into Gitanyow territory: they camped at "Wil-lu-ama-gaud – the happy place [Gwinamagoot]"[112] that night.

McCullagh got an early start on 23 September: "At 12 noon we reached the crossing at Salmon River where the old Indian suspension bridge used to hang."[113] The Gitanyow name for this part of the river is Anxhon, literally "where/eat/salmon." This bridge was located on the Cranberry River near its Nass confluence. By 5 p.m. that day, McCullagh had arrived within sight of a house that he referred to as follows: "When we stood on a ridge overlooking an extensive valley to the north, where ... about three miles away, we could discern the roof of a house, but as no smoke was seen to be issuing therefrom we concluded that Laknitsk [Laganitsxw] was not at home."[114] Laganitsxw was a Gitwangak Frog-Raven Clan chief with close ties to Luuxhon.

The following day, Sunday, the group rested. On Monday, 25 September, they travelled another eight miles up the Cranberry River,[115] at which point they "halted for a rest in a charming little grove where, not many years ago, a party of Gitwinlgols was surprised and massacred by some Tenne [Eastern Tsetsaut] Indians, who took away some children as captives, one of whom is still alive at Tahl Tan, the Tenne Village on the Stickine river."[116] The party's respite was near Xsigigyeenit, at the site of another incident during the hostilities between the Eastern Tsetsaut and the Gitanyow. That evening McCullagh arrived at his destination, the "Falls of Salmon River," which were blocked by logs, preventing salmon from ascending farther. They spent the night at Xsigigyeenit, a Gitanyow village, in "Arthur [Gw]isilla's hunting lodge." The next day, the party set out for the Nass to continue their journey to Meziadin Lake. McCullagh expected to strike the Nass some twenty kilometres[117] above where he had left it at the Cranberry confluence on 23 September.

On 27 September, McCullagh followed the left (east) bank of the Nass and referred to himself in jest and to the terrain as follows: "You all say I belong to the Lak-Gibu [Wolf Clan] ... and this being my ancestor's country, I ought, I suppose, to know it pretty well! We kindled up at a place called Wil-sga-lgol (where-across-small, ie., the Narrows) [Wilsgahlgu'l], so called because it is the narrowest place on the Naas."[118] This site, in Gitanyow territory, is an extremely narrow canyon on the Nass River about eight miles above the mouth of the Cranberry River. That evening the group camped at "Ksi-an-k-gasq (out of/where/eat/lily-root) [Xsi'angasx], ie. Lilyroot stream."[119]

The next day, travel was difficult until noon, when "for the first time since we started we found the river navigable. Finding a number of cotton-wood canoes bushed at this place, we helped ourselves to one, and ... continued our journey by water for about 15 miles."[120] Located within Gitanyow territory, the canoes indicate frequent use of the area by the Gitanyow.

At about noon the next day, the party arrived at "Diwens' [Hewin/ Tigewin] hunting lodge,"[121] where they surprised the old man, who was dreaming and singing and thought McCullagh part of the dream. McCullagh did not give the location of this lodge, but he described their campsite that evening as follows: "We must have made good progress during the remainder of the day, for we reached a place called the DAMIKS in time for camping, which Diwens thought we would not reach before noon tomorrow ... We have made a very good camp here by the swamp, for that is what DAMIKS means."[122] "Damiks" was not far from Wolverine Creek, because by noon the next day, on 30 September, they had arrived at an area that McCullagh also referred to as "Beaverlea" (see Map 36): "WIL-K-ZIMELK'L-NAUSIK (Where-eat-beaver-wolverine). It consists of a succession of lakes, muskegs and water meadows ten miles long or more. A stream runs throughout the entire length, flowing down to the Naas from both extremities."[123]

By now the party was approaching Meziadin, La͟xwiiyip country, as McCullagh described it: "Immediately after leaving Beaverlea ... it ascended again for a few miles, and then after that it kept low all the way through the woods of LAK-WI-YIP (On-the-great-land)."[124] Travel was difficult on 2 October, and the party camped early in the day. With continued bad weather and a late start the next day, they arrived at a site of historic significance to the Gitanyow people, on the east bank of the Nass River, below Meziadin Lake. Here the Eastern Tsetsaut had ambushed the Nisga'a to avenge the death of Saniik and Aminta and killed, by mistake, two leading Gitanyow chiefs. On this spot, McCullagh heard firsthand the story of what had transpired, who had been involved, and how the Eastern Tsetsaut had eventually compensated the Gitanyow.

McCullagh and his companions spent a week at Meziadin inspecting spawning streams for obstructions. He finally met 'Wiilitsxw, whom he already knew, on 6 October: "It [a black object that got into a canoe some distance off] turned out to be WI-Lizqu, his wife and boy who were out trying to trace a bear which had walked away with one of their traps ... WI-LIZQU did not know me at all [at first] ... About a quarter of a mile above the rapids [Meziadin Falls] the lake begins to open out, and there on the shore, on a sloping grassy mead, stood the WI-LIZQU cabin, two in fact, one for living in, and the other for dressing furs in."[125] 'Wiilitsxw and his family lived at Meziadin Lake and used its resources because it belonged to him and his Gitanyow kin. McCullagh noted the meaning of Meziadin: "Meziadin – pearly water – is so called, in the language of the Tenne Indians, because of its peculiar colour, a bluish mother of pearl, which charms the eye which ever way the sun shines. The name is pronounced Med-zee-ah-din."[126] McCullagh also commented on 'Wiilitsxw's family: "Wi-Lizqu's little girl, (Maksqum Lags) Ivory Nails ... and ... There were four of them, – two big boys, Ivory and a little chap to whom the men gave the name of Barney Barnato ... the boys, one of whom is about 14 and the other 12 years of age."[127] One of these children, probably one of the bigger boys, was Fred Johnson, who, as a member of Gitwangak, later assumed the title of Lelt. During *Delgamuukw* v. *The Queen*, Lelt provided evidence about the Tsetsaut-Gitanyow wars and sang the "Tenne [Tsestaut] song of expiation,"[128] as taught to him by his father (see Chapter 2).

His objective achieved, on 12 October McCullagh, Gogag, and the others set out on their return journey to Aiyansh. When they got to where they had cached food, rifles, and other supplies, they discovered that a fire had burned the cache and contents. McCullagh's journal entry for that day makes it clear that Hewin and others whom they had met along the trail on the way to Meziadin were from Gitanyow. Diwens had left a tree blazed with Indian notations that indicated "five days gone of the week: on the fifth day Diwens and his two partners turned off from the trail at this point, and proceeded eastward in the direction of Gitwinlgol. Thus, as we surmised, they had gone back to their village for provisions and blankets [which had also burned in the fire]."[129]

On 13 October, McCullagh camped at a lake on the trail between the Nass River and the Cranberry at "LAK-GWIN-HA – the airy place [Laxgwinha]"; rested (on the 14th) at: "Ksi-gigient – the locality mentioned under date 25th September – a lovely place."[130] The party camped at the Gitanyow-Nisga'a border, at "Gitangialqu [Gitangyaahlxw]," on 16 October and were back in Aiyansh by 17 October (see Map 36).

In summary, McCullagh was skilled in the Nisga'a-Gitksan language and was completely immersed in Nisga'a social and political life for nearly half a century. These facts distinguish his writing from that of those who just travelled through the area. If any Euro-Canadian knew the extent of the Nisga'a claim at that time, it was McCullagh. As an advocate for the Nisga'a, he would have commented on any dispute raised by the Gitanyow chiefs establishing lodges on Nisga'a territory. Instead, McCullagh wrote a letter on behalf of Gitanyow chief Peter 'Wiilitsxw in 1897 recognizing that a dispute on the upper Nass involved Gitanyow and Gitksan, not Nisga'a. He made a trip to Meziadin Lake with several Gitanyow persons, including William Gogag, the Gitanyow chief who accompanied him in 1905. The conclusion to be drawn from McCullagh's records is that the Gitanyow claim from Gitxsits'uuts'xwt on the lower Nass River to and including Meziadin Lake was recognized and at that time undisputed by the Nisga'a.

The Gunanoot Saga (1906-33)

When two men were murdered near Hazelton in 1906, Simon Gunanoot of Kispiox was the leading suspect. He was G̲eel, a Kispiox chief. His father was Naagan of the House of X̲skiigmlax̲ha. Gunanoot's thirteen years as a fugitive were spent in the headwaters region, especially in the territory of his father, Naagan, at Bowser Lake and in his own territory on the Skeena River north of Groundhog. He successfully avoided all police attempts to locate him before surrendering in 1919.

There are numerous references to Gunanoot's presence throughout the Gitksan territory between 1906 and 1919. This study is only concerned with his presence in the Nass watershed and the headwaters region, as reported by Constance Cox, Pinkerton detectives, and Fred Gunanoot.

According to Hazelton pioneer Constance Cox (c. 1881-1960),[131] Simon had an older brother, 'Din, who had shot another boy of his own age by accident. 'Din subsequently ran off to hide in the woods near Hazelton and was eventually found dead: he had hung himself. In grief Naagan and Noxs 'Din[132] moved away, first to Kisgaga'as for a couple of years and then to the upper Nass area, where Naagan taught the young Simon how to hunt and trap and survive in the bush: "This time they went to Muzadden lake where they put in five or six years of trapping and hunting, where Simon's father taught Simon the law of the woods. He taught him how to be shrewd and cautious."[133] It was common knowledge among the Euro-Canadian community in Hazelton that Naagan, a Gitksan from Kuldo, owned territory in the Meziadin Lake area at Bowser, where Simon grew up and later hid. This was consistent with the Gitksan law of amnigwootxw, which allows children to use the resources on their father's territories, even though their father is of a different house and clan.

In 1909 two Pinkerton agents, hired by the provincial police to capture Gunanoot, obtained information on Gunanoot's use of two hunting grounds: one on the upper Skeena and the other on the upper Nass. The first territory below refers to Simon's own hunting grounds at the head of the Skeena at Groundhog Mountain and beyond: "The hunting grounds of which Burns[134] drew on the map he gave us, of Simon's winter hunting grounds,[135] is some 90 or more miles North of the No. 5 [Yukon] telegraph cabin."[136] This refers to the territory of Kispiox chief Geel, a name later held by Simon, and, as the reader may recall, the territory on which Chief "Kale" was found in the vicinity of Blackwater by William Humphrey in 1874.

The Pinkertons did not understand Gitksan culture and assumed that Simon owned the Nass River territory of his father, Naagan, and uncle, Daniel Sgawil: "Burns also told us Simon had hunting grounds about due West of this place, on the Nass river, where he got Moose in February and March. He gave us details of the Indians never hunting on each other's hunting grounds."[137]

For much of this period, Gunanoot was accompanied by his entire family. In 1947 Fred, one of his older sons, wrote of his experiences in *The Native Voice*.[138] This letter confirms Simon's family's presence on his father's territory and their intimate knowledge of the entire area. Fred was born on 1 July 1904 in the Nass River valley, probably at Awiijii, in his grandfather's territory,

80 mile away from Stewart, B.C. Here is Fred six years old. I remember my father told me to put of experience and use snow-shoes like a man, and I did use snow-shoes like a Big Bear quality. After three years time I can travel day and night. One time in 1911 we went into telegraph Creek – at winter time it sure cold, it was 52 below zero – we keep the fires going from night until next morning. We got all what we want in Telegraph Creek, and back down to Hazelton again. We do that many times. (Gun-a-Noot secured supplies from his many sympathizers.)

Back to Naas River – First we arrive in Bowser Lake at Fall time 1913. We take a good chance and cross the high mountain behind Stewart, B.C. [via American Creek]. The open place. It was 41 mile long to the green timber on the other side. We cross, that day rain and snow half all the time – it sure take time. We arrive in Stewart, B.C. late at night, and we cross the line and we got all what we want (supplies) in Hyder, Alaska, U.S.A. We arrive back in B.C. before day light. Here we cross the mountain again. I have four hundred pound on my dog team, we arrive back in Bowser Lake before daylight. We make it without anybody found it out.

... Dan Skewill [Sgawil] told the police (it was big river not very far from here) "you are in danger now." Police knows what going to happen so police said "O.K. will go home, we all safe from trouble." The policeman was safe too.[139]

The information provided by Constance Cox demonstrates that the Gitksan Naagan, who taught Simon "the way of the woods" at Awiijii when he was a child, was present at Awiijii some ten years prior to 1890. This is consistent with David Gunanoot's explanation that Xskiigmlaxha, Naagan, and Sgawil were present and on good terms with the Eastern Tsetsaut before the accidental killing of Xskiigmlaxha.

Pinkerton evidence demonstrates that Simon exercised both his ownership rights at his "hunting grounds" ninety miles north of Fifth Cabin at Groundhog Mountain and the Gitksan privilege of amnigwootxw "due west of this place [Fifth Cabin]" on his father's territory at Awiijii during his fugitive years.

Simon's son, Fred, described the Gunanoots' intimate knowledge of the entire region from long use of the territory.

Richard Loring (1908)

Loring was the Indian agent, upper Skeena and Babine Agency at Hazelton, between 1889 and 1920[140] and the person whom McCullagh referred 'Wiilitsxw to in 1897. In 1908 he wrote a declaration that dealt with a Gitksan territory on the Nass River south of the Blackwater area. This document deals with the territories of 'Niist, a Gitksan hereditary chief in the Wolf Clan:

– To Whom it may concern –

This is to state that the Lake Dam Dilch Sandon [T'amxsinihlts'enden (Canyon Lake)] and the little Lake Anghegain [T'amangyage'en] and the Sandon Creek [Vile Creek], coming from the former lake and empties into the Naas river, and the mountain going up on the left side of the trail, called Neest ['Niist] mountain – opposite the Chlaa [Baskyalaxha] – is the hunting ground of Adam and Neest, and families, of Kuldoe, and comprises the beaver grounds there.

The aforesaid Chlaa mountain is the hunting ground of the Chlaa family represented by John Tait, of Kispi[o]x, and consists solely of hunting as far down as the foot of that mountain, but does not include any of the beaver grounds on the aforesaid two lakes and the creek (Sandon creek) emptying into the Naas river.

The aforementioned decision was mainly derived on the statements of Chief Paul Chliem-la-ha [Xhliimlaxha], of Kispiax and Mrs Mo-loo-loch [Melulek] of Kisgegas, who formerly was a connection of the Chlaa family by marriage.

Given under my hand and seal   R.E. Loring,
at Hazelton, B.C. this 7th day   Indian Agent
of January, 1908.[141]

The contents of this declaration refer to the area where P.J. Leech, forty-one years earlier in 1867, met with fifteen Gitksan people as he ascended the Nass River. The Gitksan guide, hired on the spot by Leech, took Leech up Vile Creek, past the two lakes mentioned in the declaration, to Kuldo and Kisgaga'as. Loring's declaration places Kuldo chiefs 'Niist and Baskyala<u>x</u>ha with their Kisgaga'as spouse(s) in the same valley thirty-one years after the Gitksan rescued Leech from the territory described. This 1908 declaration confirms Gitksan ownership on the upper Nass. In light of McCullagh's recognition that the 'Wiilitsxw dispute downriver near Meziadin was a Gitksan dispute, this petition confirms that, as of 1908, there was no Nisga'a claim this far up the Nass River.

G.T. Emmons (1907-9)

Emmons, an ethnographer, studied the Tahltan and Tsimshian peoples of northwest British Columbia and visited the Nass-Skeena area between 1907 and 1909. The results of his work among the Tahltan were published in 1911. His manuscript on the Gitksan and Nisga'a was never published. In general his work is marred by confusion about the identity of the Gitanyow, who are clearly Gitksan, but whose territories encompass the entire middle Nass system. His manuscript is in draft form and perhaps at a stage before it was necessary to identify his primary sources.

Emmons never did resolve some of the distinctions between the Gitanyow and the Nisga'a that arose when some Gitanyow relocated to the Nass. His manuscript demonstrates that he sometimes considers the Gitanyow to be Gitksan, at other times Nisga'a. This is apparent in the next two excerpts: "[Gitanyow territory] includes the Kitwancool lake and they hunt and trap well in towards the head waters of the Nass and Skeena in what might be called 'no man's country' as it is claimed by both the upper Niska and Kitiksahn as well as the Tahltan."[142] At other times, he indicates an understanding of the identity of the Gitanyow and their territory on the upper Nass River: "Kit win kool (people [in/of] the narrows) from the narrow valley in which they live. Their country includes the valley of the Kitwin kool river some twenty two miles in from the Skeena River, the Kitwankool lake and well in towards the Nass, and some of these people hunt on the head waters of the Nass. In 1907 i met an old Kitwancool man at Aiyansh who hunted well in towards the head waters of the Stickeen and had in war with the Tahltans (Eastern Tsetsaut] killed two of the latter family when a young man."[143] According to this excerpt, Emmons's aged Gitanyow source had participated in the hostilities at Meziadin and had the "right to trap" in the upper Nass. Emmons connected this elder's "right" with the "war with the Tahltans." He wrote elsewhere, of the same Gitanyow elder, that "in maintenance of [his] claim ... he had killed two Tahltan [Eastern Tsetsaut] whom he found there."[144]

It seems, however, that Emmons did not realize that the Gitanyow were Gitksan. The "Kit-win-kole, People on the narrows," Emmons wrote, "are the most distant village of the Nishka some ninety miles distant from Aiyansh on the South bank of the Kit-wan-gar river."[145] He may have based this comment on the migration of some Gitanyow to Nisga'a villages before the turn of the century. This is no doubt why he wrote that "the hunting grounds of the Nishka"[146] extend to the headwaters of the Stikine and concluded that Nisga'a country "comprises the mouth of the Nass and the river and its tributaries. Their living places have always been on the river banks from the mouth to Kit-winl-kole about one hundred miles inland, but their hunting grounds have embraced the whole river basin and the contiguous country meeting the 'Tahltans' on the north and the 'Kit-ich-shans [Gitksan]' on the [south? (illegible)]."[147]

Emmons published the results of his work on the Tahltans of the Stikine watershed in 1911. His understanding of who were Nisga'a and who were Gitanyow seems to have been further confused by the Tahltans' use of the term "Nathka."

> Their hunting grounds, however, cover an extended area, including the drainage basin of the Stikine and its tributaries as far down as the mouth of the Iskoot, the interlocking sources of the Nass ... The Nass region as a hunting ground was always in dispute with the Nishka, and was the cause of bitter feuds and disastrous wars that ever kept these two peoples apart. As an old Tahltan expressed the situation, "the upper Nass land is ours, and when we find a Nishka hunting there, we kill him" ... The right of might was the principal factor in determining the boundary at different periods.[148]

As has been shown, the "Nishka" or "Nathka" are, to the Tahltans, any tribal group to the south of Tahltan territories.

Emmons's work on the Western Tsetsaut of Portland Canal deals mainly with their Athapaskan origin (as Kaska), rather than with the issue of territoriality.[149] Thus, this work is not directly relevant to this study. He comments later, however, on Tahltan war customs: "From the fragmentary stories of their fighting and wars it would appear that in the early days the Tahltan were embroiled with their neighbours most of the time ... With the Nishka of upper Nass river they were constantly in conflict

... Their last hostility was with the Nishka in 1862, since which period peace has prevailed, although they speak of occasional trouble with the latter people."[150] Emmons refers here, in fact, to the Gitanyow-Eastern Tsetsaut war at Meziadin and assumes the Gitanyow to be Nisga'a.

The conclusions to be drawn from Emmons's work are that the Gitanyow have territory on the upper Nass and that they won the territory in battle and exercised their rights thereafter. Unfortunately, Emmons assumed that the Gitanyow are Nisga'a, perhaps because some Gitanyow were based in Aiyansh when he was doing his research. In any event, his assumption that the Gitanyow were Nisga'a is no basis under Nisga'a or Gitksan law to justify a Nisga'a claim to Gitanyow territory.

Ronald Campbell-Johnston (1908-16)

Ronald Campbell-Johnston came to British Columbia with his family in 1890. Later, as a mining engineer, he travelled to many remote parts of the province; his travels included a survey of the Groundhog coalfields in 1908, 1909, 1910, and 1912 for the Groundhog Anthracite Coal Company of Quebec.[151] His report on the Groundhog coalfields, completed in 1913, contains numerous pictures of Gitksan persons who guided and packed him into the area, including pictures of Wiiminoosikx and his family, who were living near Groundhog Mountain at Blackwater, as his ancestors had for generations.

Campbell-Johnston's wife, Amy Campbell-Johnston, accompanied him on several of his trips to the upper Skeena area. She remained at Blackwater with the Wiiminoosikx family while her husband conducted his fieldwork north of Groundhog Mountain and in the Klappan area. She sought recognition from the Department of Indian Affairs for an act of kindness by her host:

Two years ago I made the trip up North with my husband Mr. R.C. Campbell-Johnston to the "[G]round-hog" coal fields, I stopped on the hunting grounds with Chief Wememnassac [Wiiminoosikx] of Black Water, alone for some weeks whilst my husband went further north prospecting for coal. During my stay with the Indians I heard the account of how the Old Chief had saved a white man's life whom he had found roaming about nearly two hundred miles from civilization and raving mad.

Chief Weymennassac took care of and nursed and fed him till it was possible to get him back with great difficulty to Hazelton.

I had this account confirmed on returning to old Hazelton where I was told that the Old Chief struggled with this powerful lunatic for days and nights and saved his life at the risk of his own ... Weymannassac has a great idea of the white man's justice.[152]

This event happened toward the end of the Klondike gold rush.

Amy Campbell-Johnston wrote a second letter to the Department of Indian Affairs with details about the location of Blackwater and of the people resident there: "Yours No. 434838, of 17th inst. came duly to hand re Chief Weymannassac [Wiiminoosikx] of Blackwater. The Blackwater Lake he lives at is between the 5th and 6th cabins of the Yukon Telegraph line, subsidiary to Kispio[x] not to Fort Fraser. May I suggest also if possible that this Chief Weymannassac, wife, sister 'Witch Mabel,' daughter Mary Anne and husband, Mabel's son Jim, be all protected with a reserve at Blackwater Lake."[153]

Ronald Campbell-Johnston later appeared before the McKenna-McBride Commission in an effort to help set aside reserves at New Kuldo and at Blackwater. He was mistaken, however, about the nature of Wiiminoosikx's intentions. As noted above, the process began with the letter from his wife to the Department of Indian Affairs recommending that Wiiminoosikx and his family be "protected with a reserve at Blackwater Lake." As a result, Indian Agent Loring was directed to make enquiries. His report stated that Wiiminoosikx disclaimed that the reference was to a small piece of land, "but that it was meant that he get title to an hunting ground extending in range to the Stikine" (see Map 35).[154] In other words, Wiiminoosikx, of the Frog-Raven Clan of Kisgaga'as, just as many other Gitksan chiefs did at the MMRC hearings (see Chapter 4), laid claim to his ancestral territories at the headwaters of the Nass.[155]

Amy Campbell-Johnston later wrote an account of her trip and experiences at Blackwater while awaiting her husband's return from the Groundhog coalfields. She referred to Blackwater thus:

"BLACKWATER LAKE" tributary to Nass River. Cassiar District, B.C. 3 miles long, 1 mile wide ... stretching far beyond Chief Wemannassac's hunting ground, this wide area lay close to one of the tributaries of the Nass River. Here we unpacked our spent and half-starved horses to pitch our mud-soaked tents close to the Chief's log cabin situated near a sinister and sullen looking lake.[156]

At Blackwater Lake, near Chief Weymannassac's hunting grounds ...[157]

Chief Weymannassac had a daughter of whom he was justly proud. Her not too romantic name was "Mary-Ann," though, like all true Indians, she also possessed an Indian name ... We first made her acquaintance on the trail going to Blackwater Lake. She was just returning to the hunting ground after her wedding ... The happy bridegroom was a Nass River Indian [Gitanyow], and, according to the Indian custom, he had come to live with and belong to his wife's tribe ... Mary Ann's husband was adopted into her tribe of "Kishnagast [Kisgaga'as] Indians."[158]

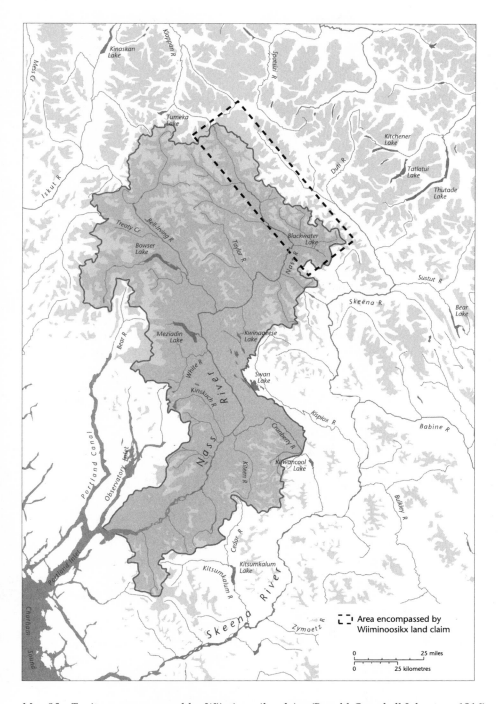

Map 35   Territory encompassed by Wiiminoosikx claim (Ronald Campbell-Johnston, 1916)

The evidence of Ronald and Amy Campbell-Johnston corroborates the long-standing presence of the Gitksan in the upper Nass watershed and in particular that of Wiiminoosikx at T'amt'uutsxwhl'aks (Blackwater region).

Geological Survey Reports (1912)

In 1911 and 1912, G.S. Malloch of the Geological Survey of Canada visited the "Groundhog Coalfield" of the upper Skeena region. His report for the latter year contains some comments on the Aboriginal peoples of the area:

> At one time the region about the Groundhog field was a meeting place for the Skeena [Gitksan] and Stikine [Eastern Tsetsaut] Indians. Many of the former at one time caught salmon below Blackwater Lake, and other families hunted in the coal field[,] as is abundantly proved by sharp stakes set up over groundhog holes, either to guide the Indians in stalking them or for the suspension of traps. On the other hand, the Stikine Indians have long been accustomed to make trips from Telegraph Creek to Bear lake and pass up the east fork of the Klappan and the Kluyetz [Kluayetza Creek] fork of the Stikine, down Moss creek for some distance across to the Duti [River], and thence east by a pass through the mountains. These Indians still travel very generally on foot, but many of the Skeena Indians now use horses.[159]

Malloch corroborates that the Gitksan harvested salmon in the upper Nass at Blackwater and refers to their long-standing interaction with the "Stikine [Tsetsaut]" in the headwaters region.

This report of Gitksan in the upper Nass is contemporaneous with the Nisga'a Petition. It shows that, while the Nisga'a were drafting their petition, the Gitksan were hunting and fishing in their territories on the upper Nass.

C.C. Perry (1912)

In 1912 a mining boom was under way at the head of Portland Inlet, in the vicinity of Stewart. The influx of miners and prospectors to the adjacent territory generated conflicts with Native inhabitants. Perry, the Indian agent for the Nass Agency, stationed at Metlakatla, reported one such incident involving "Ambrose Derrick and son and a man named Frederick and his son, all Indians of the Gitwanga and Gitwanthcool tribes." In a letter to the secretary of the Department of Indian Affairs, dated 12 July, Perry continued: "Mr. Martin ... of Stewart, told me that whilst engaged in beaver trapping in the Nass Valley he had been accosted by Derrick and his son and told to get out of the country as it belonged to the Indians. The Indians he alleged left him to examine traps which he had place[d] to catch beaver and as they were returning towards him he noticed the Indians unsheathing their rifles as though to shoot him ... Mr. Martin states that he ordered the Indians to return to the trail and make for their camp near Aiyansh."[160] Ambrose Derrick was chief Luuxhon of Gitanyow. The man named Frederick could well have been Frederick 'Wiilitsxw, or Freddy Benson, who was born at Meziadin and was a member of the Gitwangak̲ band.

The location of Mr. Martin's trapping area was most likely in Gitanyow territory. This reaction by Gitanyow chiefs was consistent with their other statements of ownership and with the location of Gitanyow territory on the Nass River.

H.A. Collison (c. 1912)

H.A. Collison, the son of a missionary, was stationed at Kincolith, grew up among the Aboriginal people of the Northwest Coast, and was fluent in the Nisga'a language. His brother, Max Collison, was the translator for the Nisga'a during the 1915 McKenna-McBride hearings in the Nass Agency.

About 1940 Collison wrote about the Nass River valley in a manuscript entitled "Teeming Waters." Included were some ethnographic commentary and an account of a trip that he made to Meziadin Lake shortly before the First World War. Significantly, the party included "Edwin Hi jamusk [Hayts'imsxw]," from Gitanyow, as a guide. Hayts'imsxw indicated to Collison the location of his ancestral hunting grounds along the upper Nass. Moreover, Collison recorded an account of the wars between the Gitksan and the Eastern Tsetsaut – probably based on information from Hayts'imsxw. Collison wrote of the Nass River country and the peoples who inhabited it: "The Native races of this area are the Nishgahs on the lower river, Kitkhateen, or the people of the Valley, as they call themselves and chiefly the Kitiksheans (originally from the Upper Skeena River) on the upper, the former having been in possession for thousands of years."[161]

Collison described his guide, Hayts'imksxw: "Besides being a first rate hunter, canoeman and woodsman, he knew the country thoroughly. He had lived in these parts all his life, and this was perhaps, his chief qualification. It is always wise when about to undertake a long journey in a country to which the Indians have exclusive right, to have as a guide one who not only knows the country, but who also has the right to hunt and fish there. This helps to disarm suspicion."[162] There can be little doubt that Collison relied on Gitanyow persons to assist him and that he wanted Hayts'imsxw, a Gitanyow person, as guide and protector on this expedition: "Not only was the country through which we journeyed thoroughly familiar to him, but he knew its history, both actual and legendary."[163] As they travelled, it must have become increasingly apparent to Collison that Hayts'imsxw was making him a witness to Gitanyow ownership of the territory:

> Edwin Hi jamusk, as we plodded along the trail, informed me that the country through which we were journeying was privately owned. This tract in particular was the ancestral hunting and fishing preserve of the Eagle Clan. He pointed to some hills in the dim distance which marked the dividing line between the Eagle and Wolf Crests; then in a lighter vein, with a twinkle in his eye, knowing that I was a member of the Wolf Crest, warned me to respect the hunting rights of the Eagle Crest. But later on when we passed the boundary line and found ourselves in country which had been in the possession of the Wolf Crest for centuries, he said I could make myself quite at home and hunt and trap and fish to my heart's content, the lodges, canoes, and hunting and fishing equipment were at my disposal. He was himself a member of the Wolf Clan and this had a great deal to do with the cordiality which characterized his behaviour towards me throughout the trip.
>
> Hunting rights amongst these Indians have always been most closely guarded and strictly enforced, and any infraction of them severely dealt with, in extreme cases the penalty was death.[164]

Hayts'imsxw knew the internal Gitanyow boundaries, described them, and had the authority to provide Collison access to the territory that they were in and to use its resources.

They arrived at Meziadin Lake on their tenth day from Grease Harbour. At Meziadin, like McCullagh before him, Collison recorded what he was told by Hayts'imsxw:

> On the triangle formed by the Nass and Meziadin Rivers, we found ourselves standing on historic ground. It was here that the Taltan [Eastern Tsetsaut] Indians, otherwise known as the Nahanais, from the Upper Stickene country, and the Kitiksheans [Gitksan] from Kitwancool Lake, met annually in the late summer for purposes of barter; the Taltans bringing furs and the Kitiksheans food in the shape of dried salmon, [oolichan] grease, and probably sea foods obtained from their intercourse with the Tsimsheans of the Coast.
>
> The Taltans were essentially a race of hunters, led a roving, hand to mouth existence, never having much to spare, so this annual meeting with the Kitiksheans was the only way to obtain sufficient food to tide them through the long winter. How long these peoples had been meeting in this way we have no means of finding out. We only know that

they came to an abrupt end between sixty and seventy years ago when Edwin Hi jamusk, my guide, was a child.[165]

Thus, Hayts'imsxw was a child (c. 1850-5) when peaceful relations between the Gitanyow and the Eastern Tsetsaut ceased with the accidental killing of the two Gitanyow chiefs.

Collison had lived on the Nass River much of his life, was familiar with Nisga'a history, and was fluent in the Nisga'a and Gitksan languages. On their return trip, Hayts'imsxw pointed out the site where the Eastern Tsetsaut, "armed to the teeth," set upon the Gitanyow. The Nisga'a are not mentioned in this account, but this surely is the site where the Tsetsaut avenged the deaths of Saniik and Aminta by killing some Gitlakdamix chiefs. The Meziadin war impacted directly on his life, for he

was a child at the time, and his father was one of the victims. He remembered having been taken to Meziadin on several successive years to undergo a savage and severe discipline to whet his desire for revenge against the people who had murdered his father. He was shown the very tree which concealed the Taltans [Eastern Tsetsaut] and was taken along the trail on which his father and his fellow tribesmen were journeying when so severely attacked.

Edwin said this went on for many years, until they were recalled by a messenger who had come to their village to bring them the gospel of love and forgiveness. The Taltans never returned and have not been seen in the Meziadin country from that day to this. They did not come back, for they knew what would be in store for them. They have been forgiven, but their dastardly and cowardly act has left an ugly stain upon their history.[166]

Unaware of the events that had led to the Meziadin war, Collison speculated on its causes. Hayts'imsxw did not comment on the causes, nor did any of the other members of the expedition; Collison pursued the issue, however: "I have since been told by an intimate and faithful friend of ours, a comrade on many a hunting trip and the last of the Zitzaows [Western Tsetsaut, at Kincolith] (close kinsmen of the Taltans) that the Meziadin country long ago belonged to the Taltans [Eastern Tsetsaut]. Probably to this fact may be traced the treachery of the Taltans. This desirable territory, so rich in game and fish, must have been forcibly taken from the Taltans by the stronger Gitksan."[167]

As the party continued downriver, Collison noted one evening that his companions disappeared and spent the night with Simon Gunanoot, who, they said, had an "intimate knowledge of the country" and was the nephew of 'Wiilitsxw of Meziadin.

The evidence of Collison clearly corroborates Gitksan adaawk, Gitanyow history and statements of ownership, Nisga'a statements of ownership, especially that of E.N. Mercer, and the evidence of G.M. Dawson and J.B. McCullagh, among others. An obvious conclusion must be drawn from the record of this important expedition, which took place at a time when the Nisga'a claim was being asserted and between the drafting of the petitions of 1908 and 1913: the Gitanyow own the territory along the upper Nass beyond Gitxsits'uuts'xwt to Meziadin Lake. That the Gitanyow held the rights to this territory was clearly understood by knowledgeable white persons close to the Nisga'a (McCullagh and Collison).

P. Monkton (c. 1930)

In the 1930s, P. Monkton, a registered BC land surveyor, spent time in the upper Nass and Bell-Irving area. He noted the Gitksan presence by virtue of place names such as "Mount Skowill" and "Skowill Creek" at Awiijii. In regard to Treaty Creek, he said: "The name refers to a treaty or convention between the Skeena and Stikine Indians – neither group is supposed to trap or occupy this area; a sort of no man's land and breeding ground for beaver between the two tribes."[168] The presence in the area of Naagan's younger brother, Daniel Sgawil, is further corroborated by Monkton's notes: "Mount Skowill [Sgawil] and Skowill Creek; flows SW into Bell-Irving River, S of Oweegee Lake Adopted 24 July 1945 on 104/SE. Named for Skowill, a very old Indian trapper from Hazelton, whose winter camp was at Oweegee [Awiijii] Smokehouse, near this creek."[169]

The evidence of Monkton shows that Sgawil, a leading chief in the Gitksan House of Xskiigmlaxha, brother of Naagan, held the territory at Awiijii. Treaty Creek nearby is so named because of a peace ceremony held c. 1900 between the Eastern Tsetsaut and the Gitksan. Monkton's evidence corroborates Gitksan adaawk and the ownership statements of Gitksan chiefs.

Conclusion

The arrival of Euro-Canadians in the Nass River valley early in the nineteenth century brought a new dimension to the lives of its original inhabitants. Until then, the exercise of Aboriginal ownership and jurisdiction was not in question. The chiefs and tribal groups with territories in the Nass watershed recognized each other's authority and knew its scope: trespass had severe consequences, and death or war was not uncommon.

The documentary record shows that early visitors to the Nass watershed depended on the Nisga'a, Gitksan, and Gitanyow as guides and interpreters. Their intimate knowledge of their own tribal territories was invaluable to the newcomers. The journals kept by Euro-Canadians provide evidence that they were assisted by Nisga'a, Gitanyow, and Gitksan leaders in their respective territories and that strict protocol required the observance of this practice. As early as 1832, a Hudson's Bay Company clerk on an expedition to the Skeena via the Nass was allowed through Nisga'a territory but could not be taken farther by the Nisga'a chief at Gitlakdamix because he was "unacquainted with the country" beyond.

Over thirty years later, a number of expeditions through the Nass watershed further demonstrate the point, of which two will serve as examples. In 1867 Peter Leech, travelling opposite to his Kispiox destination, was found by a Gitksan hunting party on the upper Nass and guided to his objective. Only later, when some distance below the Gitanyow-Nisga'a boundary at Gitxsits'uuts'xwt, did he encounter a Nisga'a, Chief Maas Gibuu of Gitlakdamix. And in 1875, James Gardiner, in an expedition up the Stikine and down the Nass, met Gitksan, Gitanyow, and Nisga'a chiefs. This journey corroborates in a powerful way the adaaw<u>k</u> and documentary record set out in Chapters 2 and 3. Gardiner identified place names, and his assistant showed a familiarity with the terrain from the upper Nass to the Kwinageese Lake area that could only have been obtained from Gitksan sources. The record of his travels from Gitksan territory to and throughout much of Gitanyow territory provides evidence of Gitanyow knowledge of their territory and historic events. It also provides evidence of the transition from the territories of the Gitksan to those of the Gitanyow on the upper Nass and from those of the Gitanyow to those of the Nisga'a well below the Cranberry confluence. His host, a Nisga'a chief, some fifteen kilometres above Gitlakdamix, is eloquent testimony to Nisga'a presence in Nisga'a territory and Gitanyow presence in Gitanyow territory.

In 1894 another visitor, Franz Boas, worked with the Nisga'a and Western Tsetsaut, who were witnesses to the events (if not directly involved) in which a territory surrounding Meziadin Lake was turned over to the Gitanyow. He wrote that the Nisga'a own territory on the Nass River but not "its upper course."

The record reveals that some visitors were confused about the tribal origin of the Gitanyow, who, for various reasons, had several chiefs and their families resident in Nisga'a villages at the time. Their presence, along with the indisputable fact that they owned a vast portion of the Nass River valley, contributed to the mistaken notion among some visitors (especially Emmons) that the Gitanyow were Nisga'a. Historical errors of fact must be corrected, not perpetuated.

Other persons, some long resident in Nisga'a communities, others from the Skeena area and beyond, provide direct and indirect evidence of the historic events described in Gitksan, Gitanyow, and Nisga'a adaaw<u>k</u>.

The correspondence and writings of Loring, McCullagh, and Collison, for example, provide explicit documentary evidence of Gitksan, Gitanyow, and Nisga'a ownership, jurisdiction, and history in their respective territories.

Finally, other Euro-Canadian documentary evidence corroborates that an important boundary exists between the Gitksan and the Gitanyow north of Meziadin Lake (see McCullagh letter to Loring), that Treaty Creek was so named because of a "treaty" that occurred between the "Skeena and Stikine Indians" nearby (see Monkton), that Sgawil, a participant in the treaty, continued to live in the area, and that he too was heralded by Euro-Canadians when they named a mountain and creek after him. The Euro-Canadian documentary record provides powerful, corroborative evidence that the Kispiox, Kuldo, and Kisgaga'as own the entire upper Nass to their boundary with the Tahltan; that the Gitanyow own the entire Nass valley from Gitxsits'uuts'xwt to their boundary with the Kispiox and Kuldo; and that the Nisga'a own the Nass valley to their ancient boundary with the Gitanyow at Gitxsits'uuts'xwt.

7
Conclusion

The requirements of indigenous law have shaped this book and provided the criteria to validate evidence of territorial ownership. In Chapter 2, carefully documented evidence from the adaawk established the existence of ancient settlements in the upper Nass River watershed inhabited by ancestors of the Gitksan and Gitanyow, who still own the surrounding territories; it established the early migrations of the ancestors of the Gitanyow into the Nass River territories that are still owned by the Gitanyow; and it laid out the periods of war in which generations of Gitanyow, Kisgaga'as, Kispiox, and Kuldo successfully defended their territories. The Gitksan have thus presented the adaawk concerning the acquisition and defence of their territories. These adaawk, and the associated songs, poles, and crests, continue to this day, thereby proving the generations of feasts in which they have been perpetuated and witnessed.

In Chapters 3 to 5, the documentary record of the Gitanyow, Gitksan, and Nisga'a proves the knowledge of the territories and the names of their sites (see Map 36 and the Glossary of Place Names). This evidence of ownership has been passed down in an unbroken line and continues in the minds of contemporary Gitksan and Nisga'a.

In Chapter 6, the documentary record of explorers and travellers provided witness to the presence on their territories of the Gitksan, Gitanyow, and Nisga'a. This evidence strengthens the proof of ownership by the Gitksan of their territories.

The wealth of information in this book provides abundant evidence for the location of tribal boundaries in the Nass watershed, as set out below.

Kuldo, Kispiox, and Kisgaga'as Boundaries on the Upper Nass
First, the Kuldo-Gitanyow boundary is situated at Xsigisi'am'maldid on the Bell-Irving River; the Kispiox-Gitanyow boundary is situated at Luubaxgagat on the Nass River.

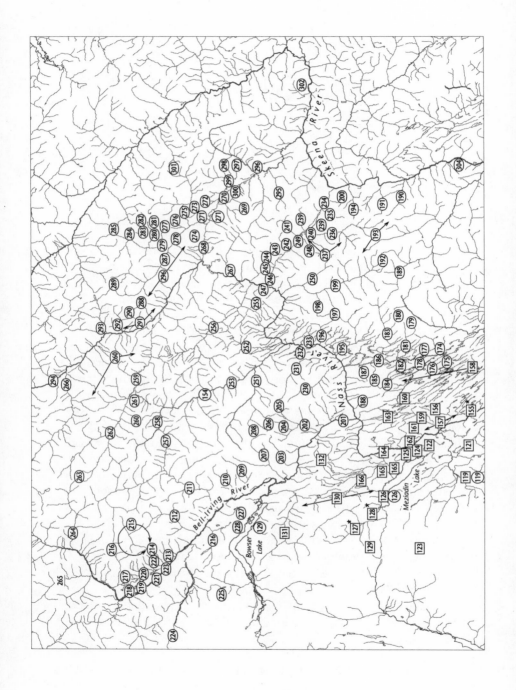

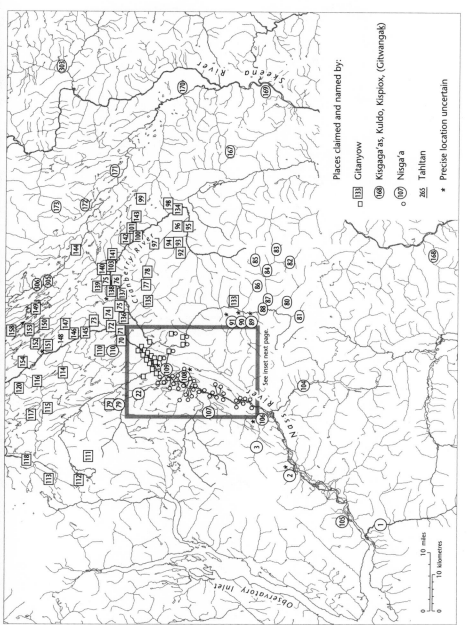

Places claimed and named by:

□ 133 Gitanyow

◎ 168 Kisgaga'as, Kuldo, Kispiox, (Gitwangak)

○ 107 Nisga'a

265 Tahltan

* Precise location uncertain

See inset next page.

10 miles

10 kilometres

Map 36 Aboriginal place names in the Nass watershed (1995)

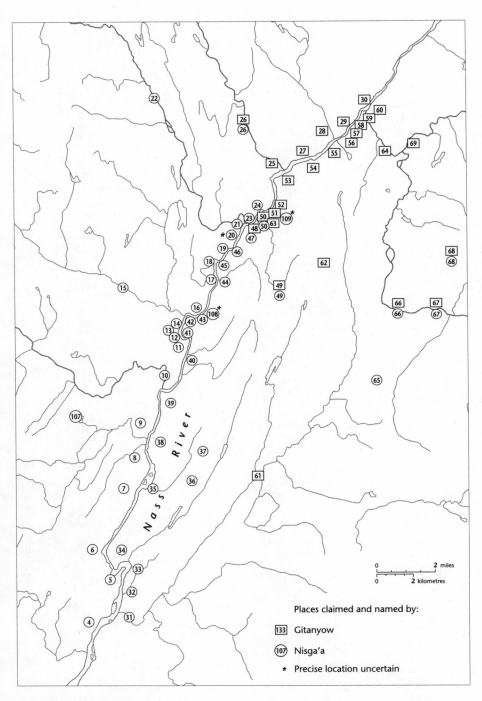

Map 36 (continued)

Key to Map 36

* indicates that precise location is uncertain

1 Hlginx̲ (Ishkeenickh Creek)
2 Haniik'ohl
3 Sgamaalt
4 Gitlakdamix
5 Ts'imanwihlist
6 Anxsa'anskw (Anxsanskw)
7 Anukskwiyinskw
8 Gwin'mal
9 Gwinhamook
10 Winhat'al
11 Gwindibilx
12 Wilukst'aas Sgawoo
13 Aksgan*
14 Gwin'miyeen
15 Ksidipk's
16 Gwindip'win
17 Gitksidaksit
18 Gitgyalk (Gitkalt)
19 Minluk
20 Gitsaksgan*
21 Dagits'in
22 Ksit'in
23 Gitxsits'uuts'xwt
24 Anbax̲hlhon
25 Gwinaxhlantxw
26 Gwinsgox
27 Wu'nisginist
28 Ansiwiik'il
29 Wu'nidagantxw
30 Anxtus
31 Sgasginist
32 Ksigiselt*
33 G̲ada'l*
34 Gilax̲ksip (Gilaksi)
35 Gwinsmak
36 X̲matxhl
37 Angwihlgolxwn
38 Gwingwiikw
39 Anukswok̲
40 Wuts'idaax
41 Gitsk̲as
42 Gidiluut
43 Xsiwii'aks
44 Wilx̲biwo'os

45 Ksigakws
47 Gitangyahlxw
48 G'ilhlalo'obit (Geltsalo'obit)
49 Xsit'ax
50 Wiluukstxawaa
51 Wilukstkiwan
52 Gwinmoots
53 Gwinhlakw
54 Gwinamagoot
55 G̲aldimdak̲
56 T'amhilin
57 Hilin
58 Anlaxgya'asxw
59 Gwinhak
60 Anxhon
61 T'amginlaax̲w
62 Lax̲sagat
63 Gwinbax̲wee'esxw
64 Xsi'anxhon
65 Gwinstimoon
66 Wilsgayip
67 Gyahlt'in
68 Winbax̲t'aahlgibuu
69 Gipgasxw
70 Xsiwii'aks
71 Gangwats
72 Winsgahlgu'l
73 T'amlilbax̲
74 T'amansingekw
75 Xsimihlhetxwt
76 Xsiyagasgiit
77 Sga'nisimluulak
78 Gwin'milit
79 Laxwijix
80 Xsi'gwits'oo
81 Xsilax̲ts'ilaasxwt
82 Xsi'anlek'maawks
83 Ts'imanmakhl
84 S̲kahawagat
85 Xsi's̲kahawagat
86 Anx̲t'imi'it
87 Xsa'anx̲t'imi'it
88 Lo'oba'gilatso'oxs
89 Wilnak*
90 Ksiwosan*

91 Anmaxslo'op
92 Angildipdawit
93 Xsi'gwin'aax̲wit
94 Wiilax̲gelt
95 Xsi'anskee x̲s
96 Xsigwa'angamt
97 Tx̲asginax̲
98 Xsigwits'ilaasxwt
99 Wilahabasxw
100 Anlo'obitlogots
101 Xsigwinsalda
102 Xsidaniigoot
103 Gak̲sbax̲sgiit
104 Sii'aks
105 Lax̲galtsap (Greenville)
106 Gitwilax̲gyap*
107 T'amgwinhamook
108 Zikgan's Spring*
109 Gitants'alkw*
110 Gadiit (Lax̲gadiit)
111 Sga'nisimgohl
112 T'amgwinsgox
113 Wu'nisk'angyamdit
114 Xsigwinadapxw
115 T'amwinluu'ax̲it'os
116 Xsiwinluu'ax̲it'os
117 Winluu'ax̲it'os
118 Xsimaaxwsxwt
119 Ksi Maaksgwit
120 Xsigiil'a
121 T'amgiil'a
122 Wiluugwalgan
123 Xsis'yun
124 Lax̲'andzok̲
125 Anlaagahl Tax̲'matsiiadin
126 T'am'matsiiadin
127 Xsik'alaa'nhlt'ax̲*
128 Xsik'alaa'n*
129 Anda'gansgotsinak̲
130 Anhahl'yee
131 Xsigisi'am'maldit (Ts'aats'iina)
132 Lipsga'nist
133 Luu'min Gyahlt'in

Key to Map 36 (continued)

134 Wilp'am't'uutsxw	178 Xsi'anlagahl'hliloot	221 T'ax̲s Sgawil
135 Gwinmihlgan	179 Wisinsgiit	222 Xsigibuu
136 Xsigigyeenit	180 Andapmatx	223 Lax̲amaawx
137 Genusmax	181 Xsa'ax̲goot	(treaty site, c. 1900)
138 K̲awilihl*	(Xsi'andapmatx)	224 X̲oo (Kas X̲oo)
139 Xsihlgugan	182 T'amhliloot	225 T'amlaaxw
140 Nask'angaledit	183 Xsanalo'op	226 Xsihis'maawnt
141 Gwilax̲anyuusxwt	184 Gwinwijix	227 T'ax̲ts'imilix
142 Xsi'wahl'yans	185 Xsigwinwijix	228 T'amsuutsii'ada
143 Xsigwits'ilaasxwt	186 Xsigwinhagiistxw	229 Bowser Lake
144 Gitangwalkw	187 Anyuusxw Adam	230 Xsilaadamus
145 Winsgahlo'	188 Luubax̲gagat	231 Xsa'anyam
146 Lax̲gwinha	189 Xsi'angaxda	232 Xsibana
147 Tx̲as'tsadagat	190 Xsilaadamus	233 Wilsgahlgu'l
148 Xsits'adagat	191 Xsi'bagayt'sisagat	234 Xsinihlts'enden
149 Tam'matsiigogat	192 Naa'ogil	235 Gasalax̲lo'obit
150 Anlagamsto'oks	193 Bagayt'sisagat	236 Xsi'andapmatx
151 Xsi'angasx*	194 Xsa'anhlamox̲	237 Andapmatx
152 Aksnagyalga	195 Xsa'angyahlts'uuts	238 T'amxsinihlts'enden
153 Nadiiloodit	196 Xsa'anto'op	239 Xsigenuts'ap
154 Xsi'andilgan	197 Masxwtlo'op	240 T'amangyage'en
155 Damiks*	198 Ximasxwtlo'op	241 Xsiluumaskeexwt
156 Xsi'anx̲ts'imilix-	199 Xsigalixawit	242 Xsiluulax̲lo'obit
naagets	200 Miinhl Ganu'aloo	243 Xsiluumasaawit
157 Anx̲ts'imilixnaagets	201 Sto'ot Xsitxemsem	244 Xsiluulax̲leexs
158 Tx̲aslax̲wiiyip	202 Xsiluubiiyoosxwt	245 Wilsganeek̲hlm
159 Xsits'elasxwt	203 Xsiluu'alagwit	Ho'oxs
160 Hlguhlsga'nist	204 Xsimax̲hlalax̲'uut	246 Xsinihlts'enden
161 Anx̲milit	205 Anluubiiyoosxwt	Ando'o
162 An'sgeex̲s	206 Max̲hlalax̲'uut	247 Andzoks 'Niist
163 Sga'nisimhabasxw	207 Xsiluumaseexit	248 Xsanluuskeex̲s
164 Xsitxemsem	208 Sa'gyoo'wilpx̲an	249 T'amansa'axws
165 Xsi'andilgan	209 Xsiluustaalo'obit	250 Xsiluu'alagwit
166 Xsi'anhaahl'yee	210 Xsi'ansalagamdit	251 Gwiis'xsihlgugan
167 Gwingani̲k	211 Xsiwiiluut'aahlts'im-	252 Xsik'alidakhl
168 Xsigwink̲'aat	ilix	253 Xsihlgugan
169 Temlaxam	212 Xsiluumahaawit	254 Xsi Maas Gibuu
170 Xsa'angyahlasxw	213 Gwiis Awiijii	255 Lipsga'nist
(Ankitlas)	214 Luu'xsgiigeeniget	256 Xsiluuwitwiidit
171 Xsiwiluu'wax̲	Awiijii (Awiijii)	257 K'alaanhl
172 Gitsk̲ansnat	215 Anbax̲gitwinx̲	Luudagwigit
173 Liphetxwt	216 Xsi'andapmatx	258 Xsiwiiluudagwigit
174 T'am	217 T'abeekxwhlt'ax̲	259 Luusilgimbaad
Gwinhagiistxw	218 T'amganax̲dig-	Txemsem
175 Xsilaalax̲uudit	wanaxw	260 Wilmax̲hladok̲hla-
176 T'amlaalax̲uudit	219 Sgasgiit T'ax̲	genxwiigwiikw
177 Wilgidiksit'ax̲	220 Xsilax̲amaawx	261 T'amsaabaya'a

262 Xsila̱xwiiyip
263 Ma̱xhlabil'uust-
    maaxws
264 Xsiwiigwanks
265 Xsik'utk'unuuxs
    (Tahltan)
266 Xsima̱xhlab'iluust-
    maawxs
267 Xsila̱x'uu Ando'o
268 Xsit'uutsxwhl'aks
269 Andami̱xw
270 T'amuumxswit
271 T'amt'uutsxwhl'aks
272 Gala̱xuuhl
    T'amt'uutsxwhl'aks
273 Xsa'ansaksxwmoohl
274 Sasmihla
275 Sga'nisim
    Xsa'ansaksxwmoohl

276 Ma̱xhla'anmuuxws
277 Xsiguuhilin
278 Xsiluu'am'maldit
279 Xsigenuts'ap
280 Guuhilin
281 Miin'anhlgii
282 Ximiin'anhlgii
283 Luula̱xlo'obit
284 Xsiluula̱xlo'obit
285 Ts'aphlgwiikw
286 Lo'opguuhanak'
287 Naabaad Xsilu-
    u'am'maldit
288 Wiluusgiihl
    An'malgwa
289 T'imgesha'niidzok
290 Xsiwiluusgiihl
    An'malgwa
291 Miinhl La̱xmihl

292 Athedla
293 X̱adaa Agana
294 Gitksan-Tahltan
    Boundary Area
295 Xsisḵ'ama'alt
296 K'alaanhlgiist
297 Xsigeltsagat
298 Geltsagat
299 Xsiwilsgayip
300 Wilsgayip
301 Wiluuskee̱xwt
302 Gitangasx
    (La̱xgitangasx)
303 Kisgaga'as
304 G̱aldoo'o
305 La̱xdit'a̱x
306 Mindagan

Second, the Gitksan (Kuldo and Kisgaga'as)-Tsetsaut (Tahltan) boundary is situated at Treaty Creek on the Bell-Irving River and at Konigus Creek on the upper Nass. The xsiisxw that established the boundary at Treaty Creek is described in the adaaw̱k and in the documentary record. Other records describe how northern Gitksan chiefs defended their territories in the Nass watershed.

Gitanyow Boundary on the Nass River

First, the boundary between the Nisga'a and the Gitksan of Gitanyow is situated at Gitxsits'uuts'xwt on the north side of the Nass River at the Tchitin River confluence. The precise location of this boundary is a matter for discussion between the Nisga'a and the Gitanyow, but adaaw̱k evidence establishes that Gitanyow chiefs G̱amla̱xyeltxw and Luuxhon migrated to "empty" territory on the Nass River near the mouth of the Kinskuch River centuries before contact. When they arrived there, they found Aboriginal people downriver on the Nass, presumably the ancestors of the Nisga'a. In accordance with their laws, they invited these neighbours and feasted them. In that feasting, they confirmed their rights to the territory at the Kinskuch River in accordance with their laws. From this early time until after the first half of the twentieth century, there is no record of any significant dispute between the Gitanyow and the Nisga'a: as with their territories, they literally lived side by side for centuries.

Second, the Gitanyow, as a result of a relatively recent settlement of their war with the Eastern Tsetsaut, acquired the former Tsetsaut territory at Meziadin Lake in 1861. The adaaw̱k establish that this occurred in the presence of their Nisga'a neighbours, who had travelled with the Gitanyow to Meziadin to trade. This xsiisxw established the Gitanyow in the area north of White River.

Third, confusion about the extent of Nisga'a territory as described in the early years of this century occurred because of the relocation of several Gitanyow chiefs to Nisga'a communities, particularly Gitlakdamix and Aiyansh. Gitanyow chiefs hold vast territories on the middle Nass system. When some of the Gitanyow relocated to the Nass, they allowed their territory to be included in the Nisga'a Petitions of 1908 and 1913. With Gitanyow chiefs in their ancestral village making the same claim, confusion was bound to occur. By 1926 the Gitanyow, including leading chiefs still resident in Nisga'a villages, formally withdrew from the Nisga'a effort.

Fourth, the Nisga'a Petition of 1913 contains an anomaly in its metes and bounds description, which further contributes to the confusion about its extent. Bearing in mind that Gitanyow territory was included in both Nisga'a petitions, the petition of 1908 is the clearer of the two: the uppermost limit of 230 kilometres (142 miles) falls as it should at the Gitanyow-Kuldo boundary at Xsigisi'am'maldid (Surveyors Creek); the 1913 petition may be read to include the entire Nass or to end in the Nass watershed at "the northwest end of Mitseah or Meziadin Lake." But the documentary evidence is unequivocal: the 1913 petition is meant to end at Surveyors Creek, and it includes Gitanyow territory.

The evidence presented in this book can provide the basis for an objective assessment of the Gitksan-Gitanyow and Nisga'a boundary. It can also be the basis for government consideration of the serious implications in treaty negotiations of ignoring any historical basis for Aboriginal claims to territories and for further consideration of competing claims that do have a historical foundation.

8
Epilogue

In November 1995, as part of a Gitksan–Nisga'a protocol under the BC treaty process, representatives of Gitksan houses with territories in the Nass watershed presented their report, *Tribal Boundaries in the Nass Watershed*, to Joe Gosnell, president of the Nisga'a Tribal Council. Copies were also presented to the provincial minister of Aboriginal affairs, John Cashore, and to the federal minister of Indian affairs, Ron Irwin. Although the Nisga'a undertook to respond to the report in 1996 and again in 1997, no response has been received to date, nor have the federal and provincial governments responded to it.

On 15 February 1996, the Nisga'a Agreement-in-Principle (AIP) was signed by representatives of the Nisga'a Tribal Council, British Columbia, and Canada. The AIP designated as "Nisga'a Lands" a territory of 1,930 square kilometres that extended up to, but not beyond, the Kinskuch River, which is slightly north of the tribal boundary between the Gitanyow and the Nisga'a territories as described in this book. This parcel of land represents 20 per cent of the lands to which the Nisga'a can prove Aboriginal title on the basis of available evidence, not less than 10 per cent as claimed.

Most significantly for the Gitksan and the Gitanyow, the AIP intends to allow the Nisga'a to manage wildlife with the game harvest quotas in the Nass watershed extending nearly to the Blackwater area, more than 100 kilometres north of the Nisga'a boundary at the Tchitin River, and to manage fisheries in the entire Nass watershed. In addition, the AIP intends to provide the Nisga'a with six "fee simple" allotments well within Gitanyow and Gitksan territories.

In 1996 representatives of the Gitanyow and Gitksan houses presented their concerns about the above provisions to British Columbia's Select Standing Committee on Aboriginal Affairs and stressed a concern about the precedent for treaty negotiations that would be set by a Nisga'a treaty based on the AIP. In its final report, July 1997, the standing committee recommended that "unsuccessful" attempts to resolve overlaps between First Nations should be referred to the BC Treaty Commission, with the further recommendation that the commission include mediation and arbitration in the resolution process.

On several occasions, representatives of the Gitanyow and Gitksan houses have formally requested that the Nisga'a and the provincial and/or federal governments appoint a mediator for the purpose of resolving this issue. To date the Nisga'a leadership have declined to participate in mediation.

On 11 December 1996, the Supreme Court of Canada handed down its unanimous decision in *Delgamuukw* v. *The Queen*. In that decision, the court overturned all aspects of the 1991 BC Supreme Court decision by Judge Allan McEachern and set out guidelines for the treaty process, including principles that the governments must observe in negotiations when considering development in Aboriginal territory and in the resolution of competing claims between First Nations. The court has acknowledged the process of validating Aboriginal title, which, as this book indicates, Gitksan and Gitanyow hereditary chiefs have pursued since contact and during the land claims process in the 1970s, the *Delgamuukw* v. *The Queen* litigation process in the 1980s, and the treaty process in the 1990s.

The Supreme Court of Canada further stated that "aboriginal title encompasses an *exclusive* right to the use and occupation of the land ... to the *exclusion* of both non-aboriginals and members of other aboriginal nations." The court went on to say: "It may, therefore, be advisable if [neighbouring] aboriginal nations intervened in any new litigation." Because the province has never acknowledged the existence of Aboriginal title, it has never established a process whereby a First Nation has to prove the extent of lands that it is claiming, making it possible for the Nisga'a to claim lands that are not their own. Thus, the federal and provincial governments may have failed to exercise due diligence or to fulfil their fiduciary duty to the Gitanyow and the Gitksan by agreeing to allot lands and resource management regimes to the Nisga'a in Gitanyow and Gitksan territories.

Gitanyow and Gitksan hereditary chiefs hope that the broad publication of the evidence in this book will encourage the federal and provincial governments to be accountable for the treaties that they negotiate and to recognize the serious need to acknowledge First Nations tribal boundaries when negotiating treaties.

Appendices

Action No. 0843/1984
SMITHERS REGISTRY

IN THE SUPREME COURT OF BRITISH COLUMBIA

BETWEEN:

DELGAM UUKW, also known as ALBERT TAIT,
suing on his own behalf and on behalf
of all the members of the
HOUSE OF DELGAM UUKW and OTHERS

PLAINTIFFS

AND:

HER MAJESTY THE QUEEN IN RIGHT OF
THE PROVINCE OF BRITISH COLUMBIA and
THE ATTORNEY GENERAL OF CANADA

DEFENDANTS

STATEMENT OF VERNON MARION, PRESIDENT
TAHLTAN TRIBAL COUNCIL

---

1. I am the President of the Tahltan Tribal Council and as such, pursuant to our tribal constitution, I am authorized to speak on behalf of all people of Tahltan ancestry who are members of our Tribe.

2. The Tahltan people claim Aboriginal rights to traditional tribal territory which is situated for the most part in northern British Columbia and being north of the traditional tribal territory of the Plaintiffs.

3. I am somewhat familiar with the Plaintiffs' court action herein and have read the Further Amended Statement of Claim filed by the Plaintiffs on September 10, 1986.

4. I am aware of the boundaries of the territory claimed by the Plaintiffs in their said court action and set out in Schedule "B" to the said Further Amended Statement of Claim.

5. I have no knowledge of the Plaintiffs" territorial boundary other than that which purports to form a common boundary with the Tahltan people.

6. With respect to the said map as set out in said Schedule "B" I cannot agree that it accurately reflects our respective traditional tribal common boundary.

7. I believe that the following is an accurate description from East to West of the Tahltan southern boundary, which can be viewed as a common tribal boundary with the Plaintiffs, and where this description is inconsistent with the said description outlined in Schedule "B" to the Plaintiffs' said Amended Statement of Claim, I believe that this description portrays the more accurate rendering of historical fact:

Commencing at the northeast end of Thutade Lake; thence in a southwesterly direction along the western shore of Thutade Lake to Thutade Creek; thence in a westerly direction along the southern shore of Thutade Creek to the headwaters of said creek, said headwaters situated northeast of Alma Peak; thence from headwaters to the height of land; thence in a northerly direction along the height of land due east of the Duti River watershed, said height of land going east of Chipmunk Peak, and through Melanistic Peak, Mt. Trygue, Mt. Oakes, Kubicek Pass, Kubicek Peak and Stalk Peak; thence in a northerly and westerly direction along the height of land situated at the most northerly end of the Duti River; thence in a southerly direction along the height of land due west of the Duti River, said height of land going through Gil Peak and along the height of land due east of Tzahny Mtn., and down to a point on Tzahny Creek, said point being approximately 3½ miles upstream from the confluence of Tzahny Creek and Duti River; crossing the said creek at this point to the southern bank; thence in a westerly direction along Tzahny Creek to the confluence of said creek with Tzahny Lake; thence in a southerly and westerly direction along the southern shore of Tzahny Lake to the approximate middle point of Tzahny Lake; thence in a southwesterly direction to the eastern shore of Kluatantan Lake; thence in a westerly direction along the southern shore of said lake to the confluence of Tantan Creek with said lake; thence in a southwesterly direction along the southern bank of said creek to the confluence of Tantan Creek with Kluatantan River; thence in a southerly direction along the eastern bank of said river to the confluence of said river with the Skeena River; crossing the river at this point to the opposite bank; thence in a northwesterly direction along the bank of said river to the confluence of Beirnes Creek with said river; thence in a southwesterly and northwesterly direction along the southern bank of Beirnes Creek to the headwaters of said creek, headwaters situated southwest of Mt. Beirnes; thence in a northwesterly direction to the height of land; thence in a westerly direction along the height of land to the headwaters of an unnamed creek; said unnamed creek situated approximately South 45 degrees West of Mt. Beirnes; thence in a southwesterly direction along the southern bank of said unnamed creek to the confluence of the Nass River; thence in a southeasterly direction along the east bank of said river to the confluence of Konigus Creek, crossing the Nass River at this point; thence in a northwesterly direction along the southern bank of Konigus Creek to a confluence, said confluence being approximately 27 miles from the confluence of Konigus Creek with the Nass River; thence in a northwesterly direction to the height of land, said height of land being the height of land between the Bell Irving River and Konigus Creek; thence in a southerly direction along this height of land to the height of land situated north of Rochester Creek; thence in a generally westerly direction along this height of land to a point on Rochester Creek, said point being approximately 5 miles upstream from the confluence of said creek with the Bell Irving River, crossing the creek at this point; thence in a westerly direction along the southern bank of said creek to the confluence with the Bell Irving River; thence in a southeasterly direction along the eastern bank of said river to the confluence of Treaty Creek; crossing the river at this point; thence in a generally westerly direction along the southern bank of Treaty Creek to the headwaters of said creek.

8.   I attach hereto as Schedule "A" a map depicting the metes and bounds description set out in paragraph 7 above.

9.   Even though the Plaintiffs and/or the Defendants might express informal agreement with respect to the description of the Tahltan southern tribal boundary as set out in paragraph 7 hereof the Tahltan Tribe would not be prepared to sign a "waiver" with respect to same in this court action and we would not be content to have our said common tribal boundary with the Plaintiffs decided by the Court in this action in our tribal absence.

10.   However, the Tahltan Tribal Council would be prepared to sign a "waiver" in this action concerning our said southern tribal boundary if both the Plaintiffs and the Defendants would enter into a binding agreement with our tribe acknowledging their respective formal acceptance of our tribal boundary as set out above and would also file their said acceptance with the Court so that the principles of contract law and the doctrine of estoppel would apply should either or both of them attempt to change their positions at a later date.

Signed at Terrace, British Columbia this 7th day of April, 1987.

Witness:)[originally signed]
[originally witnessed]   )Vernon Marion, President
)Tahltan Tribal Council

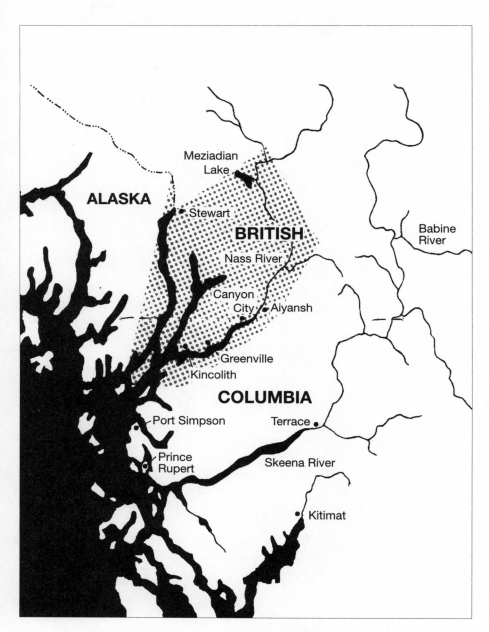

Source: NTC, *Citizens Plus: The Nishga People of the Nass River Valley in Northwestern British Columbia,* 1979

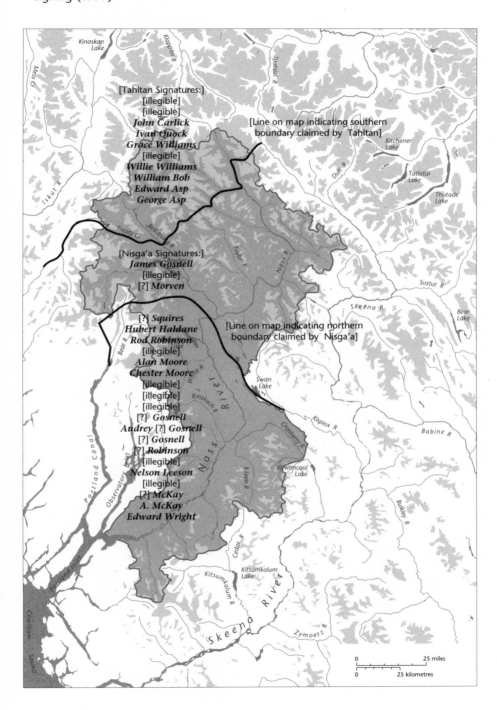

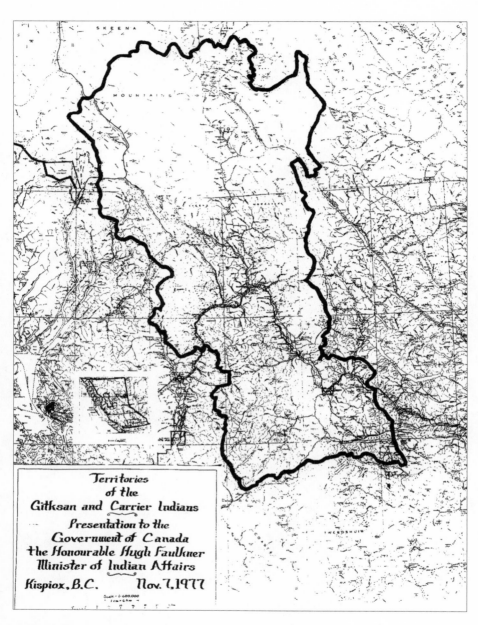

Source: Gitksan-Carrier Tribal Council, 1977

November 5, 1986

Mr. James Gosnell, President
Nishga Tribal Council
Aiyansh, B.C.

Dear James:

This letter is our response to the presentations made by the Ayuukhl Nisga'a Committee at Aiyansh Friday, October 31, 1986. I wish to thank you and your people for the
fine lunch and hospitality extended to our delegation. We also wish to thank you for
the spirit in which we were invited.

With regard to your presentation we now have had an opportunity to provide a report
to the Hereditary Chiefs and families affected, and to receive direction from them.

Our report to the Chiefs included the main points presented by your delegation as
follows:

1. Nishga Petition of 1913.
2. Four areas of concern
   a. Blackwater area
   b. Bowser area
   c. Kiteen area
   d. Sand Lake area

I will deal with each of these in turn.

Nishga Petition of 1913
We are pleased to see that the Nishga Petition of 1913 as now defined by you and as
shown on your maps at Aiyansh October 31, 1986 is consistent with our analysis of the
limits of the Petition. We appreciate very much your willingness to recognize this fact.

However, it is important for you to know that it is also our opinion that the Nishga
Petition of 1913 includes most of the territories (reference: Nishga maps, October 31,
1986, Aiyansh, B.C.) claimed by the Kitwancool Chiefs. It is not for us to resolve the
conflicting claims of the Nishga and Kitwancool. That is an issue between yourselves
and the Kitwancool Hereditary Chiefs. Suffice it to say, we are concerned at this time
with our western boundary.

Furthermore, it is important to raise the questions of how the Nishga can justify any
claim today that extends beyond the limits of the 1913 Petition. We don't believe that
any claim beyond the boundaries of the petition can be sustained. Our comments on
Blackwater, Bowser, and Sand Lake must be seen in this light.

We will now move to consideration of the four areas discussed at Aiyansh.

Blackwater Area (Wil Duutsxwhl Ax)
Alvin McKay and Rod Robinson said the Nishga are prepared not to consider this an
area of over-lap provided the families of Wiiminoosik and Xsim Xsan can continue
discussions.

There are several problems with this position (including the question I raise above
about the boundary identified in the 1913 Petition).

There is nothing to prevent the separate families of Wiiminoosik and Xsim Xsan from
talking, on condition that the criteria set forth by Wiiminoosik in their last meeting are
met.

Finally, you must bear in mind that regardless of what is discussed, Wiiminoosik only
owns a small portion of the area around dam duutsxwhl ax. Other Gitksan houses own
the balance of the territory.

Bowser Lake Area (Awiija)
After Hubert Doolan's presentation on Friday, Alvin McKay, the chairman of your Ayuukhl Nisga'a Committee described the boundaries of the area being claimed by the Gitlaxdaamixs wolves (the height of land from Mt. Madely north to head-waters of Deltaic Creek and westerly up Treaty Creek, then south again). Alvin McKay also asked us to withdraw from this area.

With respect, we cannot comply with this request. The family who owns this area is from the house of Skiik'm laxhaa. Head Chiefs in this lax seel family include Skiik'm laxhaa, Skawill, Naagan, and Biinixs. Their story was told to your delegation in Gitwangak at our first feast in the Spring of 1983. The lady who told that story, Jessie Sterritt, is very ill now. She has told the adawk and her family knows it well. They are prepared to tell it to you again. As well, we have extensive supportive evidence that this territory belongs to the Gitksan lax seel.

We are quite familiar with the story told by Hubert Doolan. It does not include this area. Also, with respect to the "Tahltan Concession," it is our position that the Tahltan cannot give to the Nishga lands which are Gitksan.

Kiteen Area (Gyehl 'Din)
You identified two separate houses as owning land in this area. They are the houses of Hleek (James Gosnell) and Gyeek (Herb Morven). You asked us to withdraw from this territory and to begin a process of family discussions.

As you will recall, we strongly recommended at our last two meetings in Terrace that we get out on the ground and determine, with knowledgeable elders, the exact boundaries in this area, and that this field trip be followed by discussions.

We confirmed our boundary by going onto the territory with the Hereditary Chiefs. We urge, if weather allows for access to the area by helicopter or vehicle that we conduct a field trip as soon as possible to the Gyehl 'Din area. This field trip should include Gitksan and Nishga elders knowledgeable about the area. But it should also include yourself and myself. We should follow that trip with family discussions to see what steps are necessary from there.

Sand Lake (D'aam Gitax ol)
You recommended that we enter three-way discussions about this area. We do not perceive an "over-lap" between ourselves and the Nishga in this area.

We will soon be having a meeting between the Kitsumkalum families and Gitksan families affected here. At that time, they should discuss the need, if any, for tri-partite discussions on this area. If necessary, we shall contact you about the need for meetings.

On behalf of the Gitksan Chiefs, I wish to thank you and the Nishga Chiefs for working with us in a positive way to resolve any question of our boundaries.

We are optimistic that this shall assist the Gitksan and Wet'suwet'en Chiefs to succeed in our case. Such success, will advance not only the Gitksan and Wet'suwet'en Aboriginal rights but also that of all the Indian nations of B.C.

Yours truly,
GITKSAN-WET'SUWET'EN TRIBAL COUNCIL

[originally signed by Neil J. Sterritt]
Neil J. Sterritt
President

NJS/wd

REAFFIRMATION OF TAHLTAN-NISGA'A BOUNDARY

While Treaty Creek land is now being claimed by the Kitwancool, there is irrefutable evidence that the land belongs to the Nisga'a. This boundary was agreed to between the Nisga'a and Tahltan in 1898 and reaffirmed on two later occasions. In the fall of 1898 the Tahltan Nation and the Nisga'a Nation mutually agreed to the boundary at Treaty Rock at Treaty Creek, to avoid bloodshed. The above-mentioned treaty was reaffirmed in an official meeting between the same two nations in Terrace, B.C., on February 12, 1977, by a motion: Moved by Edward Asp – seconded by Rod Robinson – That a resolution be drafted reaffirming the traditional Tahltan/Nisga'a boundary and agreement at Treaty Rock in 1898. The motion was carried unanimously and maps were then signed. The said resolution as follows was drafted officially at a meeting held in Terrace, B.C., on February 2, 1993:

   "We reaffirm the traditional Tahltan-Nisga'a boundary at Treaty Creek, as determined by our forefathers in 1898 and drawn on the map hereto attached, and signed in duplicate by our respective tribal councillors on February 10, 1977, as confirmation thereof." The 1993 resolution was signed by Alvin McKay and Joseph Gosnell Sr. of the Nisga'a Tribal Council and Pat Edzertza and Yvonne Moon of the Tahltan Tribal Council.

Source: NTC: *Lock, Stock and Barrel: Nisga'a Ownership Statement,* 1995

TRADITIONAL NISGA'A TERRITORY

LAND QUESTION BOUNDARY MAP

Source: NTC, *Lock, Stock and Barrel: Nisga'a Ownership Statement,* 1995

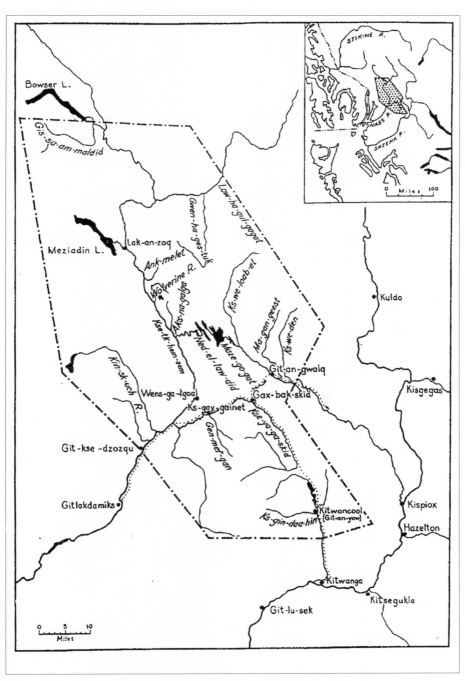

Source: Wilson Duff, ed., *Histories, Territories and Laws of the Kitwancool,* 1959

MEETING BETWEEN THE EXECUTIVE OF THE NISGA'A TRIBAL COUNCIL AND GITKSAN WET'SUWET'EN TRIBAL COUNCIL
AUGUST 8, 1986 – TERRACE, B.C.

PROPOSED AGENDA
1. Call to Order, Opening Prayer
2. Introduction of Executive Members – Nisga'a
   Introduction of Executive Members – Gitksan
3. Appointment of Chairperson(s)
4. Adoption of Agenda
5. Opening Remarks – James Gosnell
                   – Neil Sterritt
6. NTC letter to Gitksan Wet'suwet'en, June 27, 1986
   re their use of information related to Nisga'a
   Canada Fisheries Negotiations.
7. Clarify ultimate objectives of this meeting:
   – explore ways to avoid being dragged into court.
   – establish a clearly defined process for
     resolving the matter of the territorial overlap.
8. Examine process currently being used:
   a) quality of adaawaks
   b) relevance of adaawaks
   c) dates of adaawaks
9. Agreement-in-Principle – establishing the procedures
   for the eventual resolution of the overlap.
10. Wilson Duff's letter to Frank Calder dated August 8, 1974.
11. Other business:
    a)_____
    b)_____

The University of British Columbia
2075 Wesbrook Place
Vancouver, B.C., Canada
V6T 1W5

CONFIDENTIAL
[originally stamped]

Department of
Anthropology and Sociology

August 8, 1974

Frank Calder, M.L.A.,
Parliament Buildings,
Victoria, B.C.

With the Compliments of
Frank Calder, M.L.A.
(originally stamped)

Dear Mr. Calder,

This will confirm our telephone conversation of yesterday, during which I confirmed your statement that during the course of the "Nishga Case," recently concluded by the Supreme Court of Canada, there was no dispute concerning the boundaries of Nishga territories. As you will recall, your lawyer Tom Berger asked me, as an expert witness, to prepare a map showing those areas to which the Nishga had undisputed claim, and that map was accepted by both sides as delineating Nishga territory for the purposes of the case. Mr. Justice Gould labelled it Exhibit 2. The testimony to which both you and I contributed was accepted by Mr. Justice Hall and his two colleagues as establishing the Aboriginal title of the Nishga to those delineated areas. As I recall, it was not the intention to settle the question of tribal boundaries for all time, nor to jeopardize any future settlement of that question, but to establish an agreed-upon area for which to establish the unextinguished existence of Aboriginal title. The necessity for the above-described map arose from the wording of the Statement of Claim, which carried over from the former Nishga Petition a description of Nishga territory that included the entire drainage basin of the Nass and all its tributaries, and would therefore conflict with the claims of other tribes or bands, including those of the Tsimshian and the Gitksan (especially Kitwancool). The Nishga case was therefore a test of the concept of native title, and not of specific boundaries between tribes.

I hope this confirmation of the principles involved in the case will be of assistance to you.

Yours sincerely,

[originally signed by Wilson Duff]
Wilson Duff
Professor of Anthropology

WD/ymc

AUG 9 1974
[originally stamped]

Land Claim Outlined in Original Nishga Petition
[originally hand-written note]

FRANK CALDER
P.O. BOX 243 – PRINCE RUPERT

NISHGA TRIBAL COUNCIL

IN THE MATTER OF THE TERRITORY OF THE NISHGA
NATION OR TRIBE OF INDIANS.

TO THE KING'S MOST EXCELLENT MAJESTY IN COUNCIL.

THE HUMBLE PETITION of The Nishga Nation or Tribe of Indians

SHEWETH AS FOLLOWS: –

1. From time immemorial the said Nation or Tribe of Indians exclusively possessed, occupied and used and exercised sovereignty over that portion of the territory now forming the Province of British Columbia which is included within the following limits, that is to say: – Commencing at a stone situate on the south shore of Kinnamox or Quinamass Bay and marking the boundary line between the territory of the said Nishga Nation or Tribe and that of the Tsimpshean Nation or Tribe of Indians, running thence easterly along said boundary line to the height of land lying between the Naas River and the Skeena River, thence in a line following the height of land surrounding the valley of the Naas River and its tributaries to and including the height of land surrounding the north-west end of Mitseah or Meziadan Lake, thence in a straight line to the northerly end of Portland Canal, thence southerly along the international boundary to the centre line of the passage between Pearse Island and Wales Island, thence south-easterly along said centre line to the centre line of Portland Inlet, thence north-easterly along said centre line to the point at which the same is intersected by the centre line of Kinnamox or Quinamass Bay, thence in a straight line to the point of commencement.

2. Your Petitioners believe the fact to be that, when sovereignty over the territory included within the aforesaid limits (hereinafter referred to as "the said territory") was assumed by Great Britain, such sovereignty was accepted by the said Nation or Tribe, and the right of the said Nation or Tribe to possess, occupy and use the said territory was recognised by Great Britain.

V. & S., Ltd. – [illegible numbers]

RE : MAP # 1.

SUPREME COURT OF BRITISH COLUMBIA

VANCOUVER REGISTRY

EXHIBIT NO. #2.

CALDER VS. ATTORNEY-GENERAL OF BRITISH COLUMBIA

SUBMITTED BY PLAINTIFFS   DATED MARCH 31, 1969

3456/67   U.S.   DISTRICT REGISTRAR.

APPROVED – " THOMAS R. BERGER "
            COUNSEL FOR THE PLAINTIFFS.

APPROVED – " D. McK. BROWN "
            COUNSEL FOR THE ATTORNEY-GENERAL OF
            BRITISH COLUMBIA.

AREA OF NISHGA LAND CLAIM –   3,674 SQUARE MILES
                                            OR
                                     2,351,500 ACRES

RE : MAP #2

1. MAP #2 REPRESENTS THE NISHGA LAND CLAIMS BOUNDARY AS DETERMINED
   AND OUTLINED IN THE NISHGA PETITION WHICH WAS SUBMITTED TO THE
   KING'S MOST-EXCELLENT MAJESTY IN COUNCIL, LONDON, ENGLAND, IN THE
   YEAR 1913.

2. AREA OF NISHGA LAND CLAIM:

                                 5,750 SQUARE MILES
                                        OR
                                 3,680,000 ACRES

3. PLANIMETER SYSTEM WAS USED TO DETERMINE THE AREA OF THE NISHGA
   LAND CLAIM IN MAP #1.

   THE MORE ACCURATE DOT COUNTER SYSTEM WAS USED TO DETERMINE THE
   AREA OF THE NISHGA LAND CLAIM IN MAP #2.

4. MAP #2 AS PER THE NISHGA PETITION IS THE BASIS OF NISHGA LAND AND
   RESOURCES EVALUATION RESEARCH.
   (SEE WILSON DUFF LETTER)

Map #1

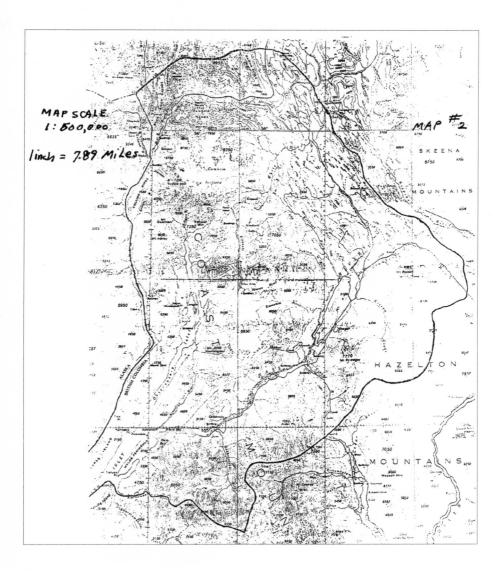

Map #2

Notes

Chapter 1: Introduction

1 *Calder* v. *Attorney General of British Columbia, Delgamuukw* v. *The Queen*, and numerous specific legal cases concerning fisheries, traplines, and hunting grounds.

2 See, e.g., the introduction in Wilson Duff, ed., *Histories, Territories and Laws of the Kitwancool*, Anthropology in BC Memoir No. 4 (Victoria: BCPM 1959).

3 Northwest Coast law included a number of measures by which boundary disputes were resolved. Houses tended to form marriage alliances with houses whose territories were adjacent to each other, thereby creating a chain of territories linked by intermarriage. The leading house chief of the village often married into the leading house of the neighbouring village, thereby linking villages and sometimes nations. Disruption of these centuries-old alliances sometimes resulted in a dispute over ownership of the territory at the boundaries of the villages and nations. These disputes were resolved in battle and a subsequent peace ceremony or by the renewal of the marriage alliance. Boundary disputes also occurred where, in ancient times, clan groups divided and became two distinct houses, one in each of two neighbouring villages. It is quite common for the boundaries between villages to run through what was, in ancient times, a single clan territory. Disputes between two branches of a clan group are most often resolved by shared use, as it is against Northwest Coast law to go to war against members of one's own clan.

4 See Chapter 5.

5 A house or house group is a matrilineal kin group and the fundamental landowning and political unit in Gitksan society. The house always bears the name of its chief. Each house is part of a larger clan group that cuts across national boundaries, the Raven (Frog), Fireweed (Killer Whale), Wolf, or Eagle clan.

6 Access to a territory other than that of one's own house requires the permission of the chief of the other house. The chief allocates rights to specific areas to those related by marriage to members of his house. These rights are formalized at the wedding feast or at subsequent feasts and are only legal during the lifetime of the spouse. The same is the case with rights to use one's father's territory. The chief may also allow temporary access to resources in his house's territory to close clan relatives from other houses. Travel through the territory of a house other than one's own, even on well-established trails, also requires the permission of the chief of that territory and does not include the right to resources. Anyone travelling in a territory other than one's own was accompanied by a member of the house owning the territory. The violation of these strict laws of ownership and rights of access and use was considered trespass, and the killing of the intruder was sanctioned by Gitksan law.

7 All the members of the house are responsible for defending their territory. The punishment of intruders is sanctioned by Gitksan law, and any house member had the right to kill a trespasser in his territory. This extreme measure usually followed several

warnings if the intruder was from a neighbouring territory. Strangers, however, were most often killed on sight. Every generation of chiefs is also expected to defend the house territories. The adaaw<u>k</u> record the Gitksan defence of their territories according to their own laws throughout their history and well into the period of European immigration. When it became clear in the late nineteenth century that the new immigrants intended to stay among the Gitksan while refusing to learn the legal system or acknowledge the territorial rights of the Gitksan, and to use force to impose their own legal system on the Gitksan, the Gitksan responded by learning the European legal system and defending their territory in the political and legal arenas of the immigrants.

8 The songs retain the ancient language in which they were composed, unlike the adaaw<u>k</u>, which are retold in new languages as they evolve or are adopted over time.

9 Xwtsaan, or totem poles.

Chapter 2: The Adaaw<u>k</u> Record

1 In preparation for the Gitksan legal action *Delgamuukw* v. *The Queen,* the Gitksan Wet'suwet'en Tribal Council (GWTC) undertook an extensive project to organize and date the extensive body of recorded adaaw<u>k</u>. Evidence concerning the chronology inherent in adaaw<u>k</u> was given throughout the trial in the testimony of chiefs and elders. The evidence for dating was given by several expert witnesses and in several exhibits. The summary of this evidence can be found in *Delgamuukw* v. *The Queen,* Proceedings at Trial, vol. 232-7, ex. 1051-3, and the Legal Argument.

  Recent archaeological research has added weight to arguments concerning the potential for dating key events related in the adaaw<u>k</u>. See David Archer, "Results of the Prince Rupert Dating Project" (Victoria: BC Heritage Trust 1992); Susan Marsden, "Defending the Mouth of the Skeena: Perspectives on Tsimshian Tlingit Relations," paper presented at the 29th Annual Meeting of the Canadian Archaeological Association, Halifax, 1996; Madonna Moss and Jon M. Erlandson, "Forts, Refuge Rocks, and Defensive Sites: The Antiquity of Warfare along the North Pacific Coast of North America," *Arctic Anthropology* 29,2 (1992): 73-90; and Daryl Fedje, "Millennial Tides and Shifting Shores: A Gwaii Haanas Story and Its Implications for Coastal Archaeology," unpublished manuscript on file at Parks Canada, Victoria, 1998. For the dating of events in the adaaw<u>k</u> that took place during the fur trade period, see Susan Marsden and Robert Galois, "The Tsimshian, the Hudson's Bay Company, and the Geopolitics of the Northwest Coast Fur Trade, 1787-1840," *Canadian Geographer* 39,2 (1995): 169-83.

2 The spellings of Gitksan and Nisga'a words in the quotations in this chapter have been standardized in the modern orthography to assist the reader.

3 Wilson Duff, Files, n.d., Kisgaga'as, UBCMAA.

4 Lt. George Emmons was an ethnographer who studied the Tahltan and Tsimshian peoples and visited the Nass-Skeena area between 1907 and 1909.

5 G.T. Emmons, Fieldnotes, n.d., in Newcombe Family Papers, BCA, add. mss. 1077, vol. 62, file 56, p. 179.

6 Temlaxam, at the confluence of the Bulkley and the Skeena Rivers, and Xsigwinlikstaa't, at the confluence of Wilson Creek and the Skeena River.

7 Duff Files, n.d., Kisgaga'as and Qaldo', UBCMAA.

8 George Derrick, Luuxhon, Ganeda, Gitwinhlkul, 1924, nos. 56 and 57 in M. Barbeau and W. Beynon, "Raven Clan Outlaws of the North Pacific Coast" (Ottawa: Folklore Division, CMC, c. 1950).

9 The last two names are in the Tsetsaut language.

10 Duff Files, n.d., Gitwinhlkul and Qaldo', UBCMAA.

11 <u>G</u>amts'iwa', Gyabask, Hlewa'nst, and Hlamii are closely related houses to those of Luuxhon and <u>G</u>amla<u>x</u>yeltxw.

12 Levi (Dangeli), of the Western Tsetsaut, told Franz Boas that "before our times the country was inhabited first by the ts'ak'e, who wore marmot skins; later on by the futvud'ie, who wore bear skins." Franz Boas, "Traditions of the Ts'ets'a'ut," *Journal of American Folk-Lore* 9,35 (1897): 48. Both were said to have spoken the Tsetsaut language. He also told Boas that the Western Tsetsaut had "no fixed villages but make a camp wherever they intend to hunt. Their staple food is porcupine, marmot, mountain goat and bear.

The skins of these animals provide the material for clothing. In summer they go down to the rivers of Portland Inlet to catch salmon which they dry for winter use." Franz Boas, "Report on the Northwestern Tribes of Canada," *British Association for the Advancement of Science, 65th Report,* 10 (1895): 39.

13 The Tahltan are also called the Stikine.

14 These two songs were recorded in the 1920s, sung by Tsigwe, George Derrick, of the Lax Se'el Clan of Gitanyow, and they continue to be sung by chiefs descended from this group at feasts. They are contained in the CMC collection.

15 Derrick, 1924, Barbeau and Beynon, "Raven Clan Outlaws of the North Pacific Coast."

16 These ayuuks continue to be re-created on the poles at Gitanyow, where they display the history of this wilnat'aahl and validate their territory.

17 Derrick, 1924, Barbeau and Beynon, "Raven Clan Outlaws of the North Pacific Coast."

18 Wilson Duff, ed., *Histories, Territories and Laws of the Kitwancool,* Anthropology in BC Memoir No. 4 (Victoria: BCPM 1959), 23-4.

19 Derrick, 1924, Barbeau and Beynon, "Raven Clan Outlaws of the North Pacific Coast."

20 Duff, *Histories,* 28.

21 Archaeological evidence suggests dates from 2000 to 1300 BP for this period of migration and resettlement. See Archer, "Results of the Prince Rupert Dating Project" and Marsden, "Defending the Mouth of the Skeena."

22 K'eexkw is the Nisga'a spelling. Those who remained among the Gitksan also retained the name spelled as Kyeexw.

23 Matthew Gurney and Emma Wright, Eagle Clan, Gitlakdamix, 1956, no. 8 in M. Barbeau and W. Beynon, "Wolf Clan Invaders from the Northern Plateaux among the Tsimsyans" (Ottawa: Folklore Division, CMC, c. 1950).

24 James Adams, 'Axtiwiluugoodii, Gitlaxdamks, 1956, no. 11b in Barbeau and Beynon, "Wolf Clan Invaders from the Northern Plateaux."

25 Matthew Gurney and Emma Wright, Eagle Clan, Gitlakdamix, 1954, no. 61 in Barbeau and Beynon, "Raven Clan Outlaws of the North Pacific Coast."

26 Ibid.

27 Charles Martin to M. Barbeau, n.d., Duff Files, Gitlakdamix, UBCMAA.

28 Edwin Haits'imsxw to M. Barbeau, 1927, Duff Files, Gitwinhlkul, UBCMAA. Gwinuu's ancestry is complex. Here Gwinuu is said to have preceded others from Temlaxam. Elsewhere Gwinuu's move into the Gitanyow region is said to have been considerably earlier and to have included a period on the coast. These adaawk therefore indicate both inland and coastal ancestry for this house. See Duff, *Histories,* 18-23.

29 It was from Gitsk'ansnat that Sgat'iin migrated to the lower Nass River and joined the Nisga'a.

30 Duff, *Histories,* 26.

31 House of K'yoluget, Lax Gibuu, Galdo'o.

32 Derrick, 1924, Barbeau and Beynon, "Raven Clan Outlaws of the North Pacific Coast."

33 This song was recorded in the 1920s, sung by Ts'igwe, George Derrick, Laxse'el, Gitanyow, and is held in the CMC collection.

34 Ibid. It is a limx'nitguukt, a song of sorrow over and rebuke of the destruction of the village of Gitanyow.

35 Derrick, 1924, Barbeau and Beynon, "Raven Clan Outlaws of the North Pacific Coast."

36 Ibid.

37 The events are said to have occurred before the Gitksan and their northern neighbours had guns but prior to the abandonment of the village of Gitangasx. David Gunanoot dated these events: "About three or four of those, my grandfathers, that's all." *Delgamuukw v. The Queen,* commission evidence of David Gunanoot, 1986, vol. 1, 68.

38 Also called the Luuts'abmts'imyipit, Gitlaxwiiyip, but not the same as the Laxwiiyip.

39 Stikine is a designation that the Gitksan sometimes use to refer to the Tahltan but also, more rarely, to the Tsetsaut.

40 Simon Gunanoot, 1923, no. 66 in Barbeau and Beynon, "Wolf Clan Invaders from the Northern Plateaux." Simon Gunanoot's son, David Gunanoot, told the same adaawk in *Delgamuukw v. The Queen,* commission evidence of David Gunanoot, 1986, vol. 1, 58-66.

41 Isaac Tens to William Beynon, 1920, Duff Files, Qaldo'o, UBCMAA. Tens heard this history from K'yoluget.

42 Arthur Sampson (Smax) to Martha Brown, in Neil J. Sterritt, personal files, 1972.

43 Gunanoot, 1923, in Barbeau and Beynon, "Wolf Clan Invaders from the Northern Plateaux."

44 Ganootsenex (Shadows) and 'Niits'ap'mla<u>x</u>gan (or Tree-Dweller).

45 Gunanoot, 1923, in Barbeau and Beynon, "Wolf Clan Invaders from the Northern Plateaux."

46 John Brown, Kwiiyeehl, Giskaast, Kispiox, 1923, no. 75 in Barbeau and Beynon, "Wolf Clan Invaders from the Northern Plateaux."

47 This book deals only with the Tsetsaut attacks during the fur trade period because they relate to Gitksan territories on the Nass River. The Nisga'a also attacked the Gitksan of Kisgaga'as, Galdo'o, and Kispiox in an effort to eliminate Gitksan control over trade through Gitksan territories. The Nisga'a were ultimately defeated, and Gitksan control over trade through their territories remained unchanged.

48 Boas, "Report on the Northwestern Tribes of Canada," 34.

49 The Stikine (Eastern Tsetsaut) name Taas Aguun was later held by Peter Shanoss (deceased), House of 'Niist, Wolf Clan, <u>G</u>aldo'o.

50 'Niist, David Blackwater, and Diisxw, Walter Blackwater, Sterritt files, 1986.

51 Gitksan who held the name Saniik: Walter Laats (c. 1870-c. 1950), Wallace Johnson (1963-c. 1970), Murphy Green (c. 1970-95), and Lorraine Green.

52 Walter Laats told Mary Johnson about this xsiisxw. Mary Johnson, Antgulilibiksxw, Giskaast, Kispiox, Sterritt files, 1995.

53 C. 1840. Martha Brown, Xhliimla<u>x</u>ha, personal communication, 1985.

54 Ibid.

55 Robert Stewart, Txalaxhatk, Kincolith, 1948-9, no. 122 in M. Barbeau and W. Beynon, "The Gwenhoot of Alaska in Search of a Bounteous Land" (Ottawa: Folklore Division, CMC, c. 1950).

56 Levi (Dangeli) to Boas, in Boas, "Report on the Northwestern Tribes of Canada," 38.

57 Robert Pearl, Bila'a, House of 'Wii<u>x</u>a, La<u>x</u> Gibuu, Gitwinhlgu'l, 1927, no. 80 in Barbeau and Beynon, "Wolf Clan Invaders from the Northern Plateaux."

58 Wi-lizqu and J.B. McCullagh, "An Indian Feud," *North British Columbia News* July 1925: 174.

59 The Nisga'a always travelled with a party of Gitksan when they passed through their territory. As the Nisga'a chief Robert Stewart related, "In olden times, only those who had trading privileges could go to the various tribes to trade. The Nisga'a had no one to trade with, excepting themselves and the Haida, when these came to the Nass. But the Nisga'a could not go to the other foreign tribes. Sometimes the Gitksan came overland from the Skeena and got their supply of oolichans and oolichan grease and other seacoast foods and these they carried over what was called the Gitwinhlgu'l trail, which came from a point above Gitlaxdamiks and ended at Gitwinhlgu'l. Knowing this trail existed and being married to a Gitksan woman, Hlidax, a Laxgibuu Nisga'a, together with other Wolf chiefs and young men, planned to trade by going over this trail ... This was a large party. Their guides were several young Gitksan who had wintered with the Nisga'a." Stewart to Barbeau, 1948-9.

60 Pearl, 1927, in Barbeau and Beynon, "Wolf Clan Invaders from the Northern Plateaux."

61 Gyalge was Ganuxeex's father-in-law, House of Sgat'iin, La<u>x</u> Gibuu, Gitlakdamix.

62 Stephen Morgan, Ganeda, Gitwinhlkul, 1923, no. 63 in Barbeau and Beynon, "Wolf Clan Invaders from the Northern Plateaux." In the account of this war in Duff, *Histories*, 27-30, Saniik is named as one of the Tsetsaut.

63 Pearl, 1927, in Barbeau and Beynon, "Wolf Clan Invaders from the Northern Plateaux."

64 Pearl belonged to the House of Wiixa and was recorded singing the limx seegit, or "song of victory of Wii<u>x</u>a's clan over the Tsetsaut of La<u>x</u>wiiyip." Because this adaaw<u>k</u> was recorded when Pearl lived on the Nass and was translated, as he spoke, by Charles Barton, a Nisga'a, Pearl's effort to accommodate both sides is understandable.

65 Wi-lizqu and McCullagh, "Indian Feud."

66 Ibid.

67 Ibid.
68 Richard Benson, Sterritt files, 1987.
69 Although Fred Johnson does not mention Saniik in this excerpt, he refers elsewhere to Aminta's involvement in these events. The name Gela is a name now used in Iskut and links the present Tahltan to the Laxwiiyip led by Saniik.
70 *Delgamuukw* v. *The Queen,* ex. 69A, 1986, 57-9.
71 Ibid., 61.
72 Ibid., 65-7.
73 Albert Tait, Delgamuukw, Lax Ganeda, Kispiox, Sterritt files, 1985.
74 Stanley Williams, Gwisgyen, Giskaast, Gitsegyukla, Sterritt files, 1986.
75 Percy Sterritt, Sterritt files, 1995.
76 Diamond Jenness, Preface, *The Sekani Indians of British Columbia,* Anthropological Series 20, National Museum of Canada Bulletin 84 (Ottawa: CMC 1937), v.
77 Ibid.
78 Constance Cox, "Simon Gun-a-Noot: The Authentic Story," *Native Voice,* Special Edition (1958): 34-7.
79 Luuskayok's husband, Gayee'is, was also known as Pierre John, the brother of Louie John and Chilly John of the Tahltan. Chilly John owned the head of the Klappan. Sterritt files, 1986.
80 Annie Louie (1912-93), whose mother was Noxs Aax, Mary Dennis (1870-1941), had seventeen children, and nearly all of them had Gitksan names. Alec Dennis (b. 1912 at Telegraph Creek) is an Iskut elder. Peter Himadim was the uncle of Alec and called Alec's father – Gilaa, Paul Dennis – his brother. Peter Dennis was born in 1913 at Fort Graham. Peter's grandmother was Simgal Taata, Mary Madeline, who was Gitksan of the Wolf Clan. Sterritt files, 1986.
81 David Gunanoot's paternal grandfather was Naagan from the House of Xsgiigmlaxha (Ganeda, Galdo'o). His grandfather's brother was Daniel Skawil. *Delgamuukw* v. *The Queen,* commission evidence of David Gunanoot, 1986, vol. 1, 140.
82 David Gunanoot, Sterritt files, 1985.
83 Ibid.
84 NAC, RG 10, Babine Agency Correspondence, 1937, Statutory Declaration of Walter Latz and John Simpson (aka Tom Sampson), 1934.

Chapter 3: The Gitanyow Documentary Record

1 Wilson Duff, ed., *Histories, Territories and Laws of the Kitwancool,* Anthropology in BC Memoir No. 4 (Victoria: BCPM 1959), 3.
2 Ibid., 4.
3 See NAC, RG 10, MMRC, vol. 11023, file 600, "Analysis of File no. 367525." The final instructions were issued to Green on 20 July. The full text of a letter from the secretary of the DIA to Prime Minister Laurier, explaining the context of the Douse telegram, is found in McLean to Laurier, 7 July 1910, NAC, RG 10, vol. 1128, 416-17.
4 Green to McLean, 6 Sept. 1910, NAC, RG 10, vol. 7780, file 27150-3-1.
5 The only information on this point is contained in a letter from Clark to the minister of the interior, 9 Nov. 1909, NAC, RG 10, vol. 7780, file 27150-3-1. Clark stated that he had received some telegrams from Simadeeks indicating that a letter had also been sent. This letter had not arrived, but Clark surmised that it "indicated that the Indians of the Skeena River were preparing to join a number of other tribes of B.C. in associating themselves with the petition of the Cowichan Indians which is now under the consideration of your Government." See also DuVernet to McLean, 4 July 1910, ibid; and Robert Galois, "The Indian Rights Association, Native Protest Activity and the Land Question in British Columbia, 1913-1916," *Native Studies Review* 8,2 (1992): 1-34.
6 Samuel Douse, Biiyoosxw, modern spelling. All genealogical information in this chapter is from Sterritt files, 1995-7.
7 Same person as matriarch on cover, Gamlaxyeltxw.
8 A chief in the House of Gamlaxyeltxw.
9 Presumably a reference to Vowell's visit as the Indian reserve commissioner in 1898. DIA *Annual Report* (Ottawa: Queen's Printer 1898), 248-9.

10 Gwashlaa'm, modern spelling – brother of Samuel Douse.
11 Niiyees Yala<u>x</u>t, modern spelling of Williams's Gitksan name.
12 Presumably Wiigyet, Steven Morgan, of Kitsegyukla.
13 Presumably a reference to J.M. Clark, the Cowichan Petition, the formation of the Indian Rights Association, and the quest for a judicial test of Aboriginal title. See note 5 above.
14 See McLean to McDougall, 26 May 1910, NAC, RG 10, vol. 4020, file 280470-2. McLean had been instructed by the DSGIA (Deputy Superintendent General of Indian Affairs), Frank Pedley, to write to McDougall on the same date (ibid.). McDougall had worked for the DIA on a number of occasions extending back to 1905. His work in 1910 was an extension of that undertaken in 1909 in areas south of the Skeena watershed.
15 The minutes (incomplete) of the Kispiox meeting are located in NAC, RG 10, vol. 7786, file 27151-1; those of the Hazelton/Hagwilget meeting in vol. 4052, file 385968; and those of the Old Kitseguecla meeting in vol. 4055, file 385898. See also Green to McLean, 6 Sept. 1910.
16 See McDougall to secretary of the DIA, 21 Sept. 1910, NAC, RG 10, 971/30-5-1A, vol. 1.
17 See A.J. Gardiner's comment in Chapter 6 about a map given to him by an "Indian." There is little doubt, given the context, that this "Indian" was from Kitwancool. This occurred in the summer of 1875 and is probably the first recorded mention of a map in relation to Gitanyow territory. It deals in part with the "La wee eap [La<u>x</u>wiiyip] country" on the Upper Nass and at Meziadin Lake. See Chapter 6 for the reference to "the Indian that gave us the map of the 'La wee eap' country"; James A. Gardiner, Diaries, 23 Aug. 1875, add. mss. 440, BCA.
18 NAC, RG 10, vol. 11041, file 1-3-1.
19 McDougall to Oliver, 22 Sept. 1910, NAC, RG 10, vol. 4020, file 280470-2.
20 Although this map has not been located, it is likely similar to the 1910 Samuel Douse map and is probably the map that Shotridge photographed in 1918 and/or the map that Ditchburn used to draft the 1920 DIA blueprint labelled "Kitwancool." All the Gitanyow maps that have been located have the same information.
21 MMRC, Babine Agency Hearings, with Kitwancool chiefs, 1915, 16-24.
22 Ibid.
23 *Delgamuukw v. The Queen,* Proceedings at Trial, 10 May 1988, vol. 95, 5897-8.
24 Louis Shotridge, "A Visit to the Tsimshian Indians: The Skeena River (Continued)," *University of Pennsylvania Museum Journal* 10,3 (1919): 140.
25 CMC, photo #71-8444 (copy); original at University of Pennsylvania, photo #14952.
26 NAC, RG 10, vol. 11041, box 1, file 1-3-1.
27 Ibid.
28 Marius C. Barbeau and William Beynon, Northwest Coast Files, CMC, BF 62.5, 1939, 40; Bright's map is in BF 106.16, 1926.
29 Ibid., BF 106.16, 1926.
30 Ibid.
31 Wilson Duff, Papers, GA, c. 1959, Niska B, Bdc Art 35, v. 10.
32 Duff, *Histories,* 13.
33 Ibid., 11.
34 Kitwancool chiefs, "Kitwancool Research Submission to Minister of Indian Affairs," 1978; supervised (if not written) by Williams.
35 Barbeau-Beynon Northwest Coast Files, BF 658.4., c. 1920.
36 Gedimgaldo'o, modern spelling.
37 The Gitksan village of Gitanmaax.
38 Marius C. Barbeau, "Tsimshian Songs," *Publications of the American Ethnological Society* 18 (1951): 106.
39 K'ee<u>x</u>kw, of Gitlakdamix; name later held by Timothy L. Derrick.
40 MMRC, Nass Agency Hearings, 1915, 181-2.
41 "Constitution of the Indian Settlement of Aiyansh," *Trail Cruiser: Aiyansh Mission Magazine* 2 (1917): 15-18.
42 Barbeau-Beynon Northwest Coast Files, BF 106.22, n.d.
43 Duff Papers, GA, c. 1958, CAR-W-002, BDC Art. 35, v. 15, 43-4.
44 Barbeau-Beynon Northwest Coast Files, BF 62.5, 1939, 40.

45 Ibid.
46 Kitwancool chiefs, "Kitwancool Research Submission," 13.
47 Ibid., 13-15.
48 House of Gwinuu, Gitanyow.
49 Gitangyahlxw and Gitxsits'uuts'xwt are about twenty-five kilometres above the village of Aiyansh (see Map 36).
50 MMRC, Nass Agency Hearings, 1915, 138.
51 Anlo'obitlogots, modern spelling, located on the Cranberry River (see Map 36).
52 Gwinhak, modern spelling, a fishing station located on the Nass River below the Cranberry confluence (see Map 36).
53 MMRC, Nass Agency Hearings, 1915, 150-1.
54 There was a younger Richard Derrick as well; he belonged to the Gitksan village of Kitsegyukla.
55 Gitanyow fishing stations (property of Ts'iiwa and Luuxhon) on the west, or right, bank of the Nass River, nearly opposite the mouth of the Cranberry River (see Map 36).
56 These sites are in the vicinity of the Cranberry River-Derrick Creek area. Gitankam, Gwinsak, and Gwilgol appear in the glossary as above. Xsigigyeenit, modern spelling for Ksgigienit; Xsimihletxwit (Derrick Creek), modern spelling for Ksimilatgut.
57 Winsgahlgu'l, modern spelling. According to Gwinuu (Godfrey Good), Sindihl (Robert Good), and Gawagyanni (Edgar Good), Winsgahlgu'l is located about ten kilometres above the mouth of the Cranberry River on the Nass River and is owned by Gamlaxyeltxw, Gitanyow. Personal communication, 8 Apr. 1995.
58 MMRC, Nass Agency Hearings, 1915, 149.
59 Gaksbaxsgiit, modern spelling for Gaksbaksit, a territory and former Gitanyow village site on the Cranberry River near Douse Lake.
60 MMRC, Nass Agency Hearings, 1915, 149.
61 Ibid., 150.
62 Txaslaxwiiyip, modern spelling.
63 Lipahe'etxwt, modern spelling.
64 Gaksbaxsgiit, modern spelling.
65 Dam'magangiist, modern spelling.
66 Nadiiloodit, modern spelling.
67 Anlagamsto'oks, modern spelling.
68 Xsidaniigoot, modern spelling.
69 Barbeau-Beynon Northwest Coast Files, BF 62.10.
70 Gyahlt'in, modern spelling (Kiteen River).
71 Gwinstimoon, modern spelling.
72 Gipgasxw, modern spelling.
73 Xsi'yagasgiit, modern spelling.
74 Gitksan chief, Yaxyak.
75 Luuxhoon, modern spelling.
76 Gamlaxyeltxw, modern spelling.
77 Anxts'imilixnaagets, modern spelling.
78 Barbeau-Beynon Northwest Coast Files, BF 62.16.
79 Laxgadiit, modern spelling.
80 Winbaxt'aahlgibuu, modern spelling.
81 Anmaxslo'op, modern spelling.
82 Ts'imanmakhl, modern spelling.
83 Xsa'anxt'imi'it, modern spelling.
84 Gwingibuu, modern spelling.
85 Barbeau-Beynon Northwest Coast Files, BF 62.15 and 62.9.
86 NAC, RG 10, vol. 11041, box 1, file 1-3-1.
87 Ibid.
88 "Joint Report on Kitwancool Indian Situation"; see note 89.
89 NAC, RG 10, vol. 11041, box 1, file 1-3-1, Collison to Ditchburn, 31 May 1920, transmitting a copy of "Joint Report on Kitwancool Indian Situation," by W.E. Collison and J. Clark.
90 NAC, RG 10, vol. 11041, box 1, file 1-3-1.

91 *Province*, 13 Sept. 1924.
92 NAC, RG 10, vol. 11041, box 1, file 1-3-1.
93 Ibid.
94 PABC, RG 10, vol. 7786, file 27151-1.
95 NAC, RG 10, vol. 11041, box 8.
96 Kitwancool chiefs, "Kitwancool Research Submission," 41.
97 Ibid.
98 BCA, Dept. of Lands, file 026076, #2.
99 Ibid.
100 NAC, RG 10, file 367525.
101 Chief Wee-Litsque ('Wiilitsxw), age forty years, of Kitwanga Village, Hazelton District, registered at Stewart, BC, "the shorelines of Meziadin Lake, Cottonwood Creek [Surveyors Creek] and short creeks running into Meziadin Lake," 26 Dec. 1926; Application for Registration of a Trapline, BCA, GR 1085, vol. 7, file 1, 1925-6.
102 In 1924 Indian Commissioner (BC) Ditchburn wrote to the chairman and members of the provincial game board (Victoria) to suggest options for Aboriginal traplines: (1) offer a "Block System," under which blocks of land would be set aside; (2) register each "individual line"; (3) issue "permits" through Indian agents for each individual line. It seems that the game board adopted the first two options. Gitanyow pursued the first option, whereas most Aboriginal people adopted the second option. W.E. Ditchburn, Kamloops, BC, 21 Aug. 1924, NAC, RG 10, vol. 10872, file 901/20-10.
103 GTO, files, 1979.
104 Delegates included James Gosnell, Hubert Doolan, Chester Moore, Frank Calder, Rod Robinson, William McKay, and Roy Azak. NTC, *Lock Stock and Barrel: Nisga'a Ownership Statement* (New Aiyansh, BC: NTC 1995), 112.
105 Ibid.
106 Ibid., 113.
107 See Duff, *Histories;* and Wilson Duff with Fred Good, in Duff Papers, GA, c. 1958, CAR-W-002, BDC Art. 35, v. 15.
108 NTC, *Lock*, 113.
109 Ibid.
110 Cornelius Nelson Scodain, Kincolith, BC, 7 Jan. 1926, registered his trapline from twelve miles below Aiyansh to Gitwinksihlxw and from the "mountains at a point opposite [the] Lava Plain"; Application for Registration of a Trapline, BCA, GR 1085, vol. 7, file 1, 1925-6.
111 NTC, *Lock*, 113.
112 BC, Royal Commission on Forestry, 1955, *Proceedings*, BCA, GR 668, Exhibit 348, 17231; letter and two-page submission by Peter Williams, president of the Kitwancool, and Walter Douse, vice-president, 10 Mar. 1956, BCA, GR 668, box 15, Exhibit 348.
113 Ibid.
114 NAC, RG 10, file 367525.
115 Duff, *Histories*, 3-4.
116 Ibid., 35.
117 Ibid., 11.
118 E.g., Duff was the editor of *Histories, Territories and Laws of the Kitwancool* (1959) and an expert witness in *Calder v. Attorney General of British Columbia* (1968). For an appreciation, see D. Abbott, ed., *The World Is as Sharp as a Knife: An Anthology in Honour of Wilson Duff* (Victoria: BCPM 1981).
119 Kitwancool chiefs, "Kitwancool Research Submission," 13.
120 La̲xwijix, modern spelling: height of land between the Kinskuch and Tchitin Rivers.
121 Wu'nisḵ'angyamdit, modern spelling: north of Kinskuch Lake.
122 Xsis'yun, modern spelling: Cambria Icefield on government maps.
123 K'ee̲xkw, modern spelling.
124 Ksim X̲saan, modern spelling.
125 Hlgimedasooḵ, modern spelling.
126 G'ilhlalo'obit, modern spelling.
127 La̲xsagat, modern spelling.

128 Wudaxhayetsxw, modern spelling.
129 Sedookxw, modern spelling.
130 Gipgasxw, modern spelling.
131 Kitwancool chiefs, "Kitwancool Research Submission," 15.
132 See Duff, *Histories;* Mae Derrick, ed., *Adaawhl Gitanyaaw* (Kitwancool, BC: Kitwancool Indian Band 1978); and numerous maps that have found their way into the public record since 1875.
133 Luu'logom'skook – Gordon Robinson; Ts'iiwa – Art Matthews Sr.; Wudaxhayetsxw – Barney Good; Gwinuu – Godfrey Good; and Sindihl – Robert Good to Glen Williams and Alex Morgan, meetings and field trip, 1983; all place names retain modern spellings.
134 Sterritt files, 23 Nov. 1982.

Chapter 4: The Gitksan Documentary Record
1 Both Stewart and Vowell were DIA officials. A brief description of the steps in the process of establishing the Stewart-Vowell Commission is contained in NAC, RG 10, vol. 11023, file 600, "Analysis of File no. 292113."
2 See NAC, RG 10, vol. 1589, Loring to Vowell, 14 Oct. 1909 and 30 Oct. 1909; *Province*, 19 June 1909; and *Omineca Herald*, 4 Sept. 1909.
3 Edward Clark, Chief Spookxw (modern spelling), Gitanmaax Wolf Clan.
4 MMRC, Babine Agency Hearings, 1915, 39-43.
5 Holland (1871-1932), Haalus, Kitwanga Frog Clan, husband of Esther Green (1883-1963), Mediik, Kuldo Wolf Clan.
6 Kuldo, House of K'yoluget.
7 MMRC, Babine Agency Hearings, 1915, 44-7.
8 Wiiseeks, of Kisgaga'as.
9 MMRC, Babine Agency Hearings, 1915, 73-7.
10 Gedimgaldo'o, the leading chief of Gitanmaax.
11 Xsigwink'aat, modern spelling, as above; Gitwonge' is the Gitwangak (modern spelling) – also Kitwanga.
12 Marius C. Barbeau and William Beynon, Northwest Coast Files, CMC, BF 94.1, 1920, 2.
13 Hage and Delgamuukw of Kispiox/Kisgaga'as are of the same group, sharing origins, names, and crests. They are effectively the same house today. In the name list for this house is the name Dakhlemges, associated with this territory and the xsiisxw for it described below. Wilson Duff, Files, Kispayaks Laxse'el, 1965.
14 Barbeau-Beynon Northwest Coast Files, BF 76.7.
15 Ksemguneekxw (Ksimganeex) (Frog-Raven Clan, Kuldo) is the same Wilnat'aahl as Sgawil, Xskiigmlaxha, and Naagan. See Barbeau-Beynon Northwest Coast Files, BF 85.5 and BF 85.6.
16 Ibid., BF 79.2.
17 Also known as the West Nass.
18 Barbeau-Beynon Northwest Coast Files, BF 79.2.
19 Wa'a is of the same group at Kuldo as Wiigoob'l.
20 Barbeau-Beynon Northwest Coast Files, BF 79.2.
21 K'alaanhlgiist, modern spelling.
22 Barbeau-Beynon Northwest Coast Files, BF 79.2.
23 Ibid.
24 Barbeau-Beynon Northwest Coast Files, BF 79.1.
25 Ibid., BF 76.7.
26 'Miinlaxmihl, modern spelling.
27 Barbeau-Beynon Northwest Coast Files, BF 78.4.
28 Canada, Houses of Parliament, Senate, Special Joint Committee, p. 154, evidence of P. Kelly: NAC, RG 10, vol. 11041, Ditchburn to Scott, 3 Aug. 1922, and Kelly to Ditchburn, 16 Oct. 1922.
29 The Gitksan representatives were Kispiox – Robert Wilson and Silas Johnston; Gitanmaax – Thomas Campbell and Austin Matthews; Kitwanga – Mathias Bright and David L. Wells; Kitsegyukla – Stephen Morgan and Moses Jones; and Kisgaga'as – Abel Oakes. NAC, RG 10, vol. 11041, Kelly to Ditchburn, 16 Oct. 1922.

30 Ibid.

31 Ibid.

32 NAC, RG 10, vol. 11041, box 1, file 1-3-1, Williams to Ditchburn, 23 Mar. and 2 Apr. 1923, and Ditchburn to Williams, 28 Mar. and 11 Apr. 1923. Kitwancool, unlike the other Gitksan villages, did not participate in the meetings with Allied Tribes representatives Kelly and Reid in Aug. 1922.

33 See *Prince Rupert Daily News*, 14 Oct. 1924. The Gitksan representatives were Kitwancool [Gitanyow] – Chief Weka ['Wiixa], Albert Williams (president of the Kitwancool Land Committee), and G. Williams; Kispiox – J.G. Brown; Hazelton – Tom Campbell; Kitwanga – Henry Willitzqu; and Kitseguecla – Stephen Morgan.

34 See NAC, RG 10, vol. 3820, file 59335, pt. 3A, Walter Gale et al. to Mackenzie King, 9 Oct. 1924. The presence of the endorsers at Prince Rupert was reported in *Prince Rupert Daily News*, 14 Oct. 1924.

35 W. Gale et al. to Mackenzie King, 9 Oct. 1924.

36 NAC, RG 10, vol. 3820, file 59335, pt. 3A, A. Williams to Mackenzie King, 13 Oct. 1924.

37 Morgan had been involved since at least 1908 and was arrested during a police raid on Kispiox in 1909. At that time, he was described by the police as the "worst agitator on the Skeena"; BCA, Provincial Police Correspondence, GR 55, box 52, Maitland-Dougall to Hussey, 18 Nov. 1909.

38 The letter was cosigned by "Secretary J.S. Morgan" and written at Skeena Crossing; NAC, RG 10, vol. 7780, file 27140-3-1B, Morgan and Morgan to Mackenzie King, 15 Mar. 1925. The reference to a projected trip to England was probably a response to the visit by some interior chiefs during the summer of 1925. This trip was opposed by the DIA, and the chiefs did not achieve their objective of meeting George V; NAC, RG 10, vol. 7780, file 27150-3-1B, McLean to Collison, 30 July 1925; see also an unidentified newspaper clipping datelined London, 29 July, in the same file.

39 This letter was cosigned by Secretary Henry Benson and written at Kitwanga; NAC, RG 10, vol. 7780, file 27150-3-1B, Morgan and Benson to governor general, 27 June 1925.

40 Duff was conducting ethnological research for the BC Provincial Museum.

41 Duff Papers, TSI-W-004, BDC Art. 35, v. 8, c. 3, Jonathan Johnson on Kispiox territories, 7 July 1965, at Kispiox. Duff made a tape of this interview, which contains additional detail provided by Johnson as they worked.

42 Niisgaks, modern spelling.

43 Duff Papers, TSI-W-004, BDC Art. 35, v. 8, c. 3, Johnson to Duff, Kispiox, BC, 7 July 1965.

44 Ibid.

45 The term Txaslaxwiiyip (t'aslaxwiyi'p) means "on the big land" or "along the big land." It is used to describe a long, low, timbered mountain or high hill. In this case, it is a forty-mile ridge east of the Nass River, between Swan Lake (Kispiox River drainage) and Mount Madely (Nass River drainage) (Percy Sterritt, personal communication, 1995). This term should not be confused with the terms Lax Wii Yip, Tsim Lax Yip, Git Luu Tsabim Tsim Yip, and Luu Tsabim Tsim Yip, which refer to various Athapaskan-speaking peoples, known collectively as the Tsetsaut.

46 Duff Papers, TSI-W-004, BDC Art. 35, v. 8, c. 3, Johnson to Duff, Kispiox, BC, 7 July 1965.

47 Ibid.

48 Neil J. Sterritt, personal files, 1983.

49 Ibid., 1986

50 Ibid.

51 Ibid. Xsinihltsenden (Canyon Creek on Skeena side) and Xsinihltsenden Andoo'o (Vile Creek on Nass side) belong to the House of 'Niist, Kuldo Wolf.

52 Ibid.

53 Marie-Françoise Guédon Tapes, VII-C-58T and VII-C-60T, recorded in collaboration with Chris Harris and Polly Sargent, 1973, CMC collection, Ottawa.

54 Xsiwiiluu'wax, a tributary of the Kispiox River.

55 Gitksan name, Xsik'utk'unuuxs.

56 Gitksan name, T'amsuutsii'ada, derivation of Tsetsaut name.

57 Sterritt files, 2 May 1986.
58 Land Claims meeting at Kispiox, 12 Dec. 1976: David Gunanoot, Steve Robinson, Peter C. Wilson, Thomas Danes, Martha Brown, Sophia Mowatt, Henry Wright, Joshua McLean, Arthur Sampson (Smax), Bill Blackwater Sr., Gary Patsey, and Neil J. Sterritt.
59 Sterritt files, 21 Dec. 1976.
60 Sterritt files, 2 May 1986.
61 At the time, David was too ill to walk from the road through the bush to the site.
62 Sterritt files, 23 Dec. 1987: David Gunanoot at Awiijii with James Morrison, Gerry Gunanoot, Horace Wale, and Esther McLean. This was David Gunanoot's last trip to Awiijii. He died 3 Nov. 1988 in Hazelton.
63 David Gunanoot said that Awiijii is a Stikine word meaning "whistle" (May 1986).
64 Called Xsi'ambaxgitwinx by the Gitksan, meaning "water/comes from (mountain)/whistles."
65 A Stikine word, according to David, meaning "milky lake."
66 The Gitksan call it Cottonwood Creek, Xsigisi'am'maldit, but its Stikine name is Tsaatsiina, meaning "beaver boil."
67 In 1986 George Asp, Hugh Taylor, and Vernon Marion (president) for the Tahltan Tribal Council and Neil Sterritt (president) and Steve Robinson for the Gitksan Wet'suwet'en Tribal Council engaged in a series of discussions about the common Tahltan-Gitksan boundary. Information about the xsiisxw in the 1890s was provided to the Tahltan representatives. As a result, the Tahltans adjusted their southern boundary, and the Gitksan adjusted their northern boundary. The Gitksan then amended Schedule B to the Further Amended Statement of Claim, and Marion later signed a witnessed affidavit on behalf of the Tahltan Nation that corresponds to the amended Gitksan boundary (see Appendix 1).
68 Bell II is the second bridge crossing of the Bell-Irving River on the Stewart-Cassiar Highway in the Awiijii area. It is the area referred to as part of the boundary between the Gitksan and the Tahltan, as agreed by Taashuuts and Naagan/Sgawil.
69 Sterritt files, 16 Mar. 1995: Jack Pete (with daughter Charlotte Tashoots, son-in-law Wayne Flegg, and Margaret [Etzerza] Klepachek), Terrace, BC.
70 Robert G. Adlam, "The Structural Basis of Tahltan Society" (PhD diss., University of Toronto 1985), 77.
71 *Delgamuukw* v. *The Queen*, commission evidence of Richard Benson, 1987, vol. 1, 19-40.
72 Unnamed mountain on government maps.
73 Kuldo Creek.
74 Mount Skuyhil (from Kuldo chief Sgawil) is the name on government maps; Wiigoob'l and Sgawil are members of the same house and family.
75 Unnamed mountain and creek on government maps, near Sallysout Creek.
76 *Delgamuukw* v. *The Queen*, commission evidence of Richard Benson, 1987, vol. 1, 28-9; Sterritt files, 29 Oct. 1987.
77 Sheladamus Creek, flows east into Skeena River.
78 Sterritt files, 29 Oct. 1987.
79 Modern spelling of names listed: Xsigallixawit, Xsiluu'alagwit, Xsimasxwtlo'op, Masxwt-lo'op, Naa'oogil.
80 Wiigoob'l, Albert Brown.
81 Referring to Daniel Skawil.
82 Sterritt files, 29 Oct. 1987.
83 Ibid.
84 Sterritt files, 1976.
85 Sterritt files, 3 Jan. 1977.
86 Sterritt files, 4 June 1979.
87 Sterritt files, 20 Feb. 1995.
88 Panorama Creek on government maps, flows west into Nass River; Percy Sterritt and George Brown's Agunagana is pronounced Xadaa Agana in Tahltan and means "moose backbone." Willie and Grace Williams, Dease Lake, personal communication, 1995.
89 Unnamed creek on government maps; Percy and George's Atsehlaa is pronounced Athedla in Tahltan, means the intestines of moose or caribou, and is commonly called "bum guts." Ibid.

90 Sterritt files, 5 Feb. 1976; see also Chapter 2 and Martha Brown below.
91 Sterritt files, 4 June 1979.
92 Sterritt files, 1984.
93 Mountain area, unnamed on government maps.
94 Muckaboo Creek.
95 Sterritt files, 1984.
96 Unnamed mountain range near Muckaboo Creek.
97 Dimdiigibuu, House of Gutgwinuxs, Kispiox Fireweed Clan, married to Charlie Sampson's daughter, Elsie.
98 At Miinlaxmihl on the upper Nass River-Panorama Creek confluence.
99 Sterritt files, 30 Nov. 1984.
100 Sterritt files, 20 Dec. 1982.
101 The Gitksan often use the designations "Tahltan" and "Stikine" in place of "Tsetsaut" to refer to their northern neighbours.
102 A portion of Kwinageese River that widens into a small lake, the main camp of Delgamuukw; according to Jonathan Johnson (1965), a third person, the nephew of Dakhlemges, was buried at Wilgidiksit'ax as well.
103 Sterritt files, 7 Aug. 1986.
104 Albert Tait at a Kispiox Elders meeting, Kispiox, Sterritt files, 8 Feb. 1983.
105 Tait and Pete Muldoe, Sterritt files, 17 Oct. 1984.
106 Tait and Muldoe, Sterritt files, 17 Nov. 1982.
107 Muckaboo Creek on government maps.
108 Possible source of the name Muckaboo: to the non-Indian ear, it sounds like Maxhlabil'uust.
109 Sterritt files, 22 Feb. 1985.
110 David Gunanoot, on behalf of Jessie Sterritt, told the adaawk and showed the feather and the pistol to the Nisga'a at a feast in Gitwangak in the mid-1980s.
111 Sterritt files, 8 Jan. 1983.
112 Jeff Wilson was adopted by Phillip Wilson and his wife, Emily (Duubisxw – House of Nikateen).
113 Sterritt files, 1984.
114 Unnamed on government maps.
115 Martha Brown with Steve Robinson, Sterritt files, 1984.
116 Noxs means "the mother of (someone)." Therefore, the mothers of Sgawil and Johnny Moore were closely related.
117 Sterritt files, 27 Nov. 1985.
118 Sterritt files, 5 Sept. 1986.
119 Walter and David Blackwater and Nancy Supernault, Sterritt files, 6 Sept. 1986; the features listed belong to several Gitksan houses (see Map 36).
120 According to Walter and David Blackwater, Martins Flats is wrongly located on government maps and should be located near Fifth Cabin on the south side of Damshilgwit Lake.
121 A former Baskyalaxha.
122 Poison Creek.
123 Gibee'imget, House of 'Niist.
124 Sterritt files, 6 Nov. 1987.
125 Charles Sampson (1880-1963).
126 "Ando'o" is a relative term. Often when two creeks flow from the same source or near it they will have the same name and can be distinguished by this term, which means "on the other side." Thus, when located on the Skeena, Vile Creek is referred to as Xsinihlts'enden Ando'o and Canyon Creek as Xsinihlts'enden. Similarly, when located on the Nass side, one might refer to Canyon Creek as Xsinihlts'enden Ando'o and Vile Creek as Xsinihlts'enden.
127 Nass Drainage.
128 Sterritt files, 6 Nov. 1987.
129 Affidavit of Walter Blackwater, *Delgamuukw* v. *The Queen*, 1988.
130 Unnamed lake at the head of Konigus Creek.

131 Sterritt files, 21 Apr. 1987.
132 Here Walter was referring to Sam Hope and to his own father, Jimmy Blackwater; Sterritt files, 27 Jan. 1988.
133 Often used as a reference point by Gitksan hereditary chiefs; it belongs to the Tahltan (or Tsetsaut) people.
134 A member of the House of K'yoluget.
135 Shegunia River on government maps, flows west into the Skeena River at Kispiox.
136 Sterritt files, 9 Dec. 1987.
137 Daisy Olson with Martha Ridsdale, Sterritt files, 14 Jan. 1987.
138 Sterritt files, 15 Jan. 1987.
139 Charles Derrick and James Morrison, Sterritt files, 18 Jan. 1988.
140 Affidavit of Ken Muldoe, *Delgamuukw* v. *The Queen,* 1988.
141 Affidavit of Walter Wilson, *Delgamuukw* v. *The Queen,* 1988.
142 Ibid.
143 Sterritt files, 24 Apr. 1995.

Chapter 5: The Nisga'a Documentary Record

1 FIBC, *The Nishga Petition to His Majesty's Privy Council: A Record of Interviews with the Government of Canada together with Related Documents,* conference of FIBC (n.p.: FIBC 1915); copy at BCA.
2 The Nass River, as indicated on today's maps, runs 384 km (240 mi) from source to mouth.
3 Gitka'din and Gitwandilix, modern spellings.
4 Marius C. Barbeau and William Beynon, Northwest Coast Files, CMC, BF 104.33, c. 1915, 1.
5 Gitgiigeenix, modern spelling.
6 Edward Sapir, "A Sketch of the Social Organization of the Nass River Indians," *Geological Survey of Canada, Museum Bulletin 19 (Anthropological Series 7)* (1915): 1-30.
7 MMRC, Nass Agency Hearings, 1915, 119.
8 Modern spelling.
9 Canaan is eight kilometres below Greenville on the Nass River; "Hal i colth" is Haniik'ohl.
10 British Columbia, *Papers Relating to the Commission Appointed to Enquire into the State and Condition of the Indians of the North-West Coast of British Columbia* (Victoria: Government Printer 1888), 429.
11 Ibid., 415-62.
12 MMRC, Nass Agency Hearings, 1915, 71.
13 Sgat'iin, modern spelling.
14 This was on O'Reilly's initial visit to the Nass River in 1881. The Grease Trail begins at Grease Harbour, near Gitlakdamix.
15 British Columbia, *Papers,* 271. O'Reilly's report on his 1881 visit to the Nass contains no mention of this claim; see NAC, RG 10, vol. 1275, O'Reilly to SGIA, 25 Mar. 1882.
16 BCA, O'Reilly, 13 Oct. 1881.
17 NAC, RG 10, vol. 3699, file 16682.
18 D. Raunet, *Without Surrender, without Consent: A History of the Nishga Land Claims* (Vancouver: Douglas and McIntyre 1984), 86.
19 British Columbia, *Papers,* 1888, 425.
20 Ibid., 422.
21 BCA, GR 441, box 31, file 1, Priestley to [premier], 15 Jan. 1908.
22 BCA, GR 429, box 15, #3949, Hickman to attorney general, 7 Oct. 1908.
23 Charles Barton, after a trip to Ontario, and Arthur Calder were responsible for the formation of the Land Committee in 1907; Paul Tennant, *Aboriginal Peoples and Politics: The Indian Land Question in British Columbia, 1849-1989* (Vancouver: UBC Press 1990), 86.
24 The full text of the petition was not included; *Province* 28 Mar. 1908. See also NAC, RG 10, vol. 7780, file 27150-3-1.
25 Robert Galois, "The Indian Rights Association, Native Protest Activity and the Land Question in British Columbia, 1913-1916," *Native Studies Review* 8,2 (1992): 1-34.

26 NAC, RG 10, vol. 11020, file 518.

27 The first two clauses of the Cowichan Petition read:
> 1. THAT from time immemorial the Cowichan Tribe of Indians have been possessors and occupants of the territory including the Cowichan Valley containing a large area and situate within the territorial limits of the said Province of British Columbia.
>
> 2. The Indian title to the said territory was always recognized by His Majesty's predecessor King George III on the 7th Oct. 1763. This proclamation ordained among other things as follows ...
>
> There follows a long quotation from the proclamation; the same quotation, with a slight addition, is found in Clause 3 of the Nisga'a Petition.

28 FIBC, *Nishga Petition,* 1.

29 Ibid., 32.

30 Several years after 1913, one tribal group, the Tsimshian, became aware that the metes and bounds description in the 1913 petition included lands claimed by them. O'Meara promised to deal with the situation, but there is no evidence that he did.

31 Public Records Office (London), Privy Council Office, original correspondence (1913), PC 8/1240, file 111,098.

32 Ibid. File 111,098 contains correspondence that refers to the deposition by Messrs. Fox & Preece (solicitors) of ten copies of the printed Nisga'a Petition and two blueprint maps. The first blueprint map covers the area from the north end of Kitsumkalum Lake to the "North Fork" of the Cranberry River. It is approximately 100 by 150 cm and is stamped on the back, "Privy Council Office, Reg[istere]d. 21 May, 1913, No. 111,098." The second map covers an area extending from the headwaters of the Flat and White Rivers in the south to the north end of Meziadin Lake and somewhat beyond. This map is approximately 50 by 50 cm and is stamped in the same manner as the first.

33 Reverend McCullagh. Eli Gosnell stated that McCullagh was the author (see below), but likely he was the author of the 1908 petition and a coauthor of the 1913 petition with O'Meara, the Nisga'a lawyer who also worked on the Cowichan Petition.

34 James B. McCullagh, "Ignis. A Parable of the Great Lava Plain in the Valley of Eternal Bloom," Aiyansh, BC, 1918 (copy at BCA); NAC, RG 10, vol. 11298, Newnham to Ditchburn, 2 June 1930, 2.

35 Father of the late James Gosnell, past president of the NTC, and of the current president, Joe Gosnell.

36 Transcript of taped interview with Eli Gosnell, n.d., p. 3, in John Corsiglia, "The Nisga'a and Their Neighbours." Ayuukhl Nishga Land Ownership and Occupancy Study, c. 1987, NTC, Aiyansh, BC.

37 Present for the NTC were the late James Gosnell (president), Rod Robinson, Alvin MacKay, Herbert Morven, Ed Wright, Harry Nyce, Larry Guno, and others. Present for the GWTC were Neil Sterritt (president), Victor Jim, Stanley Williams, Albert Tait, Vincent Jackson, Art Wilson, and others. Meeting at Terrace, BC, 8 Aug. 1986.

38 As in Appendix 9.

39 NAC, RG 10, vol. 3822, file 58335-2; also included in FIBC, *Nishga Petition,* 4-10.

40 Barbeau-Beynon Northwest Coast Files, BF 106.58.

41 Joint Gitksan-Nisga'a meeting at Terrace, 8 Aug. 1986.

42 FIBC, *Nishga Petition,* 34.

43 Ibid.

44 Ibid., 45-6.

45 Ibid., 72-3.

46 Ibid., 76.

47 Ibid., 85.

48 Apparently this was a joint delegation of Interior Tribes and the Nisga'a. The Interior Tribes were represented by Thomas Adolph, Paul David, and James Teit (interpreter), the Nisga'a by Charles Barton, E.N. Mercer, and possibly others. From "Statement of Nishga Tribe and Interior Tribes," 26 May 1916, NAC, RG 10, vol. 7781, file 27150-3-3.

49 Barbeau-Beynon Northwest Coast Files, BF 106.58.

50 Naana, modern spelling.

51 Barbeau-Beynon Northwest Coast Files, BF 106.58.

52 Ibid.

53 Ibid.
54 Ibid.
55 Not mapped, location uncertain.
56 Barbeau-Beynon Northwest Coast Files, BF 106.58.
57 Haniik'ohl, modern spelling, and Ishkeenickh, as on today's government maps.
58 MMRC, Nass Agency Hearings, 1915, 117.
59 Ibid., 119-20.
60 Ibid., 120.
61 Because Niisyok's detail is complex, modern spelling will be used in this quote.
62 Tseaxs River.
63 Seaskinnish Creek.
64 See Indian Reserve 54, Gwinkbawaueast, on government maps.
65 Here Niisyok likely means the right, or west, bank of the Nass.
66 MMRC, Nass Agency Hearings, 1915, 136-7.
67 Ibid., 138.
68 Ibid., 144-6.
69 See MMRC, Nass Agency Hearings, 1914, Peter Niisyok at Aiyansh, 4-6, BCA, microfilm reel T-3963.
70 Located about four miles above Gitlakdamix at Indian Reserve 2, Tsimmanweenclist.
71 MMRC, Nass Agency Hearings, 1915, 148.
72 Gwinhatal, modern spelling; the Kwinatahl River flows east into the Nass River about eleven kilometres above Gitlakdamix.
73 Sgamaalt, modern spelling; Shumal Creek flows east into the Nass River between Canyon City and Gitlakdamix.
74 MMRC, Nass Agency Hearings, 1915, 148.
75 Ibid., 151.
76 Ibid., 153.
77 Apparently not related to the Gitanyow Derricks.
78 Gitants'alkw, modern spelling.
79 MMRC, Nass Agency Hearings, 1915, 160.
80 Chief Sgat'iin, below, identifies Gitsizutqu and Gitanzalq as being near each other on the Nass River.
81 MMRC, Nass Agency Hearings, 1915, 160-1.
82 "Constitution of the Indian Settlement of Aiyansh," *Trail Cruiser: Aiyansh Mission Magazine* 1,2 (1917): 15-18.
83 Ibid.
84 MMRC, Nass Agency Hearings, 1915, 163.
85 Ibid.
86 Ibid.
87 Ibid., 171.
88 Ibid., 175.
89 Unknown location, possibly Chemainuk Creek.
90 MMRC, Nass Agency Hearings, 1915, 185-6.
91 Barbeau-Beynon Northwest Coast Files, BF 198.11, 13.
92 Ibid., 13-14.
93 Ibid.
94 Wet'suwet'en spelling – Gitdumskanees; Gitksan spelling – Getim'skaniist ("man/of/ mountains").
95 Barbeau-Beynon Northwest Coast Files, BF 198.11, 16.
96 Ibid.
97 While recording their statements, Barbeau also produced a sketch map showing the approximate location of the territories and some of the place names identified by the Nisga'a. Barbeau's notes are alphanumerically cross-referenced to his map (see C9, I5, etc.).
98 Barbeau-Beynon Northwest Coast Files, 1929, BF 106.46.
99 Locations uncertain, not mapped.
100 Barbeau-Beynon Northwest Coast Files, 1929, BF 106.46.

101 Ibid.
102 See Map 36.
103 Barbeau-Beynon Northwest Coast Files, 1927, BF 106.53.
104 Ibid., BF 106.56.
105 Ibid., BF 106.19.
106 Barbeau-Beynon Northwest Coast Files, 1929, BF 106.46.
107 Ibid.
108 Ibid.
109 Ibid.
110 Ibid.
111 Ibid.
112 Ibid.
113 Ibid.
114 Ibid.
115 Ibid.
116 Barbeau-Beynon Northwest Coast Files, 1927, BF 106.50.
117 Joint Committee of the Senate and House of Commons Committee on Indian Affairs, "Minutes of Proceedings and Evidence," Ottawa, 26 May 1960, 582, 585 (after Raunet, *Without Surrender*, 146-7).
118 Stephen McNeary, "The Traditional Economic and Social Life of the Niska of British Columbia," report submitted to CMC, 1974, 128.
119 The DIA maintained duplicate copies of provincial "Indian" trapline maps and files. Sometimes Aboriginal people advised their local Indian agent of errors and changes in status (due to marriage, death, etc.), who then informed the provincial Game Department. The early (c. 1930-60) trapline maps for the Babine Agency illustrate how crude they were, with errors in geography and rectangular territories that ignore heights of land, rivers, etc. They also show that local conservation officers were ignorant of Gitksan custom and territoriality. Unfortunately for the Gitksan and the Nisga'a, some of the errors in the early maps have carried over and are reflected on today's maps, which are not correct historically.
120 NAC, RG 10, vol. 11298, Newnham to Ditchburn, 2 June 1930, 2. Attached to Newnham's letter is a brief letter from "The Gitlakdamix Land Committee" to Ditchburn, Indian commissioner for BC, dated 20 May 1930, signed by fourteen "chiefs." They refuse to accept any "permits or regulations until the Land question be settled." Signatories include eleven Nisga'a chiefs: A.L. Skadeen, Andrew Nash, Gideon Minesqu, Peter Nisyok, Isaac J. Wright, John(?) Davies, Jonathan Mercer(?), Brian Peal, Andrew Mercer, and George Rober(t?)son; and three Gitanyow chiefs: James Smythe, Arthur Derrick, and M.I. Bright. Both letters are stamped "Commissioner's Office, Victoria, B.C., Jun[e] 6 1930."
121 D. Abbott, ed., *The World Is as Sharp as a Knife: An Anthology in Honour of Wilson Duff* (Victoria: BCPM 1981), 49-64.
122 NTC, *Lock Stock and Barrel: Nisga'a Ownership Statement* (New Aiyansh, BC: NTC 1995), 112.
123 Ibid.
124 *Calder* v. *Attorney General of British Columbia*, Proceedings at Trial, 71 WWR, 82.
125 *Calder* v. *Attorney General of British Columbia*, Supreme Court of Canada, Judgement, 31 Jan. 1973, 15.
126 Wilson Duff, Papers, BCA, GR 2809, Duff to Berger, 17 June 1968.
127 Wilson Duff, Files, UBCMAA, 1974.
128 NTC, *Lock*, Appendix 6, 111-21; "President Joseph Gosnell advised me to totally research my personal files with respect to the traditional Nisga'a hunting grounds as outlined in the Nisga'a Petition ..."
129 Duff Files, 1974, marked "confidential."
130 For a full discussion of the imprecise language in the metes and bounds description in the Nisga'a Petition of 1913, see discussion on Nisga'a Petition (1913) in this chapter.
131 Duff Files, 1972, box E, Land Question.

132 Duff Papers, GR 2809, file 110, 1973, Duff to McIntyre, location and construction engineer, CNR, Edmonton, AB, 4, with two maps.
133 Duff Papers, n.d., file 141, 27.
134 McNeary, "Traditional Economic and Social Life," Map 3 with list of place names, 123-8; Stephen McNeary, "Where Fire Came Down: Social and Economic Life of the Niska" (Ph.D. diss., Bryn Mawr College 1976), Map 5 with list, 226-31.
135 Modern spelling for Gosnell's name and each of the other chiefs' names listed thereafter in this quote: Wiigadimxsgaak, Ksdiyaawak, Minee'eskw, Gwinyoo, Niisangwadiksxw, and Gwiixmaaw.
136 McNeary, "Traditional Economic and Social Life," 5-6.
137 McNeary, "Where Fire Came Down," 9.
138 Ibid., 41, after Marius Barbeau, *Totem Poles: Volume 1, According to Crests and Topics,* National Museum of Canada, Bulletin 119, Anthropological Series 30 (Ottawa: National Museum of Canada 1950), 29.
139 McNeary, "Where Fire Came Down," 43, after William H. Collison, *In the Wake of the War Canoe* (London: Seeley, Service 1915), 309; Wilson Duff, ed., *Histories, Territories and Laws of the Kitwancool,* Anthropology in BC Memoir No. 4 (Victoria: BCPM 1959), 27-34.
140 Presumably, Abraham Williams; see McNeary, "Traditional Economic and Social Life," 20: "AW, for example, asserted that the Tse'ts'awut granted these lands to the Niska Gitlaxdamiks as settlement for the murder of some Niska chiefs."
141 McNeary, "Where Fire Came Down," 43.
142 Ibid., 44, after British Columbia, 271
143 McNeary, "Where Fire Came Down," 44.
144 Ibid., 46.
145 McNeary, "Traditional Economic and Social Life," 27.
146 McNeary, "Where Fire Came Down," 60-1.
147 McNeary, "Traditional Economic and Social Life," 46.
148 Ibid., 119 ("Appendix 3: Houses of the Upriver Niska").
149 Ibid., 48.
150 McNeary, "Where Fire Came Down," 123, after George T. Emmons, "The Tahltan Indians," *University of Pennsylvania Musuem, Anthropological Publication* 4,1 (1911): 6, 32-3.
151 McNeary, "Traditional Economic and Social Life," 80; McNeary, "Where Fire Came Down," 143.
152 McNeary, "Traditional Economic and Social Life," 81.
153 Ibid., 81-3.
154 Ibid., 84.
155 Ibid.
156 Wiigadimxsgaak, modern spelling.
157 Naaws, modern spelling.
158 McNeary, "Where Fire Came Down," 144.
159 NTC, *Nisga'a: People of the Mighty River* (New Aiyansh, BC: NTC 1992).
160 From a document hand-delivered to Gitksan representatives by NTC, Terrace, BC, 1994; Sterritt files.
161 NAC, RG 10, vol. 11041, box 1, file 1-3-1, Williams to Ditchburn, 28 Mar. and 11 Apr. 1923.

Chapter 6: Witnesses on the Land

1 According to Edward Asp of Dease Lake, the Tahltan call these rivers the West Nass (Bell-Irving River) and the East Nass (Nass River); Neil J. Sterritt, personal files, 1995.
2 Donald Manson, "Journal of a Trip up the Naas River," HBCA, B 201/a/1, 6.
3 Ibid., 8-9.
4 Ibid., 22-3.
5 More commonly known as the Collins Overland Telegraph (COT).
6 About fifty miles west-northwest of the village of Kispiox.
7 Peter J. Leech, "The Pioneer Telegraph Survey of British Columbia," *BC Mining Record* (Aug. 1899): 18.

8 The current names of rivers and creeks, largely unknown then, will be shown in brackets: thus "Naas [Bell Irving] River," etc.

9 Leech, "Pioneer Telegraph Survey," 20.

10 Thompson's diary is more specific than Leech's published account. Thompson's entry for 10 Apr. 1867 reads: "Struck [camp] at 6 AM. Crossed the highest point of the divide between the Ningunsaw [River] and the Nasse about 8 AM." The "divide" is between today's Beaverpond Creek (Ningunsaw drainage) and Snowbank Creek (Bell-Irving drainage), about eight kilometres from the Bell-Irving River. Thompson Report, GR 1069, file I 143, BCA).

11 Leech, "Pioneer Telegraph Survey," 22.

12 The McNeil party, which left Buck's Bar in January, headed east following a different route to the Nass River: probably up the Klappan River to its head, then to Nass Lake and down the Nass River to Kwinageese River, thence south to Kispiox village.

13 Leech, "Pioneer Telegraph Survey," 22.

14 Leech's guide must only have spoken the Athapaskan (Tahltan) language.

15 Leech, "Pioneer Telegraph Survey," 22-3.

16 Thompson Report, GR 1069, file I 143, BCA.

17 Ibid.

18 Gitksan village on the Skeena River.

19 Kisgaga'as village.

20 Leech, "Pioneer Telegraph Survey," 23.

21 A COT employee, stationed at Kispiox, along with several other men.

22 Maas Gibuu (white wolf), modern spelling.

23 Leech, "Pioneer Telegraph Survey," 25.

24 Likely at Grease Harbour, near Gitlakdamix. At times of the year, canoes can navigate farther up the Nass River. Explorers of the day, however, considered the head of navigation to be near Gitlakdamix, about thirty-five kilometres below the confluence of the Cranberry and Nass Rivers. See James A. Gardiner, Diaries, 1875, BCA, add. mss. 440, 24.

25 Leech, "Pioneer Telegraph Survey," 25.

26 Robert N. Scott, "Indians Living on and Near the Boundary between British Columbia and the Russian-American Territory Recently Ceded to the United States," *Annual Report of the United States Commissioner of Indian Affairs for the Year 1869* (Washington, DC: Government Printing Office 1870), 563.

27 G. Chismore, "From the Nass to the Skeena," *Overland Monthly* 6 (1885): 455-6.

28 Ibid., 456-7.

29 Ibid., 457.

30 Ibid.

31 William Humphrey, Diary, 11 Mar.-26 Aug. 1874, BCA, E/C/H881, 5.

32 Humphrey to Beaven, 21 Apr. 1874, GR 868, Dept. of Lands, Correspondence.

33 Humphrey Diary, 7.

34 Ibid., 16.

35 Ibid., 19.

36 Xsiluu'am'maldit, modern spelling.

37 Humphrey Diary, 23.

38 "Vital Laforce ... one of the Collin's Overland Telegraph Company's explorers. From 1865 to 1867 he explored with parties around the headwaters of the Skeena, Nass and Stikine Rivers (Geological Survey, 1887) ... discovered gold on Vital Creek (Omineca)." See Ralph Hall, *Pioneer Goldseekers of the Omineca* (Victoria: Morriss Publishing 1994), 89.

39 Gardiner Diaries, 6-7. "Gardiner was the returning officer of Omineca in [the] election of 1872 (*Sentinel*, July 6, 1872) ... [He] accompanied Vital Laforce on the relocation trip over the cattle trail from Telegraph Creek to Hazelton in 1875 ... In Cassiar he was often called David Gardiner." Hall, *Pioneer Goldseekers*, 89.

40 Probably Vile Creek.

41 Gardiner Diaries, 11-12.

42 Not to be confused with another site of the same name in Gitanyow territory on the lower Nass River above the Cranberry confluence.

43 Gardiner Diaries, 13-14.

44 Ibid., 17.
45 Ibid., 18.
46 Ibid., 19.
47 Ibid., 23.
48 Ibid., 24.
49 It is not clear just when the Eastern Tsetsaut who occupied the upper Nass-Klappan-Stikine region were grouped with the Tahltan of the lower Stikine-Tahltan River area. Gardiner was familiar with the Tahltan people, whose language, Athapaskan, was similar to that of the Eastern Tsetsaut. In 1875 it would have been more accurate to consider the Athapaskan people at Bowser-Awiijii as Eastern Tsetsaut or Laxwiiyip, not Tahltan.
50 Gardiner Diaries, 24-5.
51 Bowser River (along with Lake) is a major tributary of the Bell-Irving River.
52 Gardiner Diaries, 24-5.
53 For further, independent, corroborating evidence about this boundary, see McCullagh to Loring (1897) below.
54 Gardiner Diaries, 28-9.
55 Ibid., 30-1.
56 Ibid., 33.
57 Probably the "kit-man-kool Indians" whom Gardiner stopped with on 29 July, just before reaching the Nass River. This sketch map is included in Gardiner's journal.
58 See hand-drawn map, last page of Gardiner's second diary.
59 Gardiner Diaries, second diary, 2.
60 In the Cassiar District: probably pursuing Cassiar gold excitement of the day.
61 Gardiner Diaries, second diary, 2-3.
62 Arthur Wellington Clah, Diaries and Papers, 70 vols., Wellcome Institute, London, Eng., WMS, Amer 140 (microfilm at NAC), 1877.
63 A Gitanyow fishing village at the Nass-Cranberry confluence.
64 Clah Diaries, 1877.
65 Wolverine Creek on government maps: Anxts'imilixnaagets, modern spelling.
66 Clah Diaries, 1877.
67 Canyon City.
68 Euro-Canadian settler, John Mathieson, who preempted land near Gitlakdamix.
69 Fishing site near but opposite Gitlakdamix on the Nass River.
70 Clah Diaries, 1880.
71 Ibid.
72 Same as Luuxhon.
73 Clah Diaries, 1880.
74 Ibid.
75 Ibid.
76 At the Kispiox River.
77 Helen Woods, Diary, 1880, BCA, add. mss. 773; Wiiyagadeets, a Gitksan chief, Fireweed Clan, village of Kitsegukla.
78 Callbreath appears on Census, 1881.
79 Not to deny that the Nisga'a are "Nass Men," for they are, but, as the evidence in this book shows, they are not the "Nass Men" of the upper Nass.
80 Here "Nass Indians" refers to both Gitanyow and Nisga'a as referred to above.
81 George M. Dawson, "Report on an Exploration of the Yukon District, N.W.T. and Adjacent Northern Part of British Columbia," *Geological Survey of Canada, Annual Report, 1887-1888* (Montreal: GSC 1889), 194-5b.
82 Ibid.
83 Gitksan/Nisga'a word for a major peace ceremony.
84 The difference in dates for this event is insignificant: Dawson (1861) and Gitanyow (1862). Although this study uses the Gitanyow date, Dawson's date, linked as it is to "the first gold excitement on the Stikine," is probably correct.
85 Dawson, "Report," 194-5b; elsewhere, a date of 1862 is used as the year that the final peace took place at Meziadin.
86 BCA, RG 10, vol. 3802, file 49774, Powell to DSGIA, 14 July 1888.

87 Information on the killing of Kamalmuk is taken from the report of the trial of Constable Green, published in the *Nanaimo Free Press*, 7 Nov. 1888, and from the official report of I.W. Powell, superintendent of Indian Affairs in British Columbia; Powell to DSGIA, 14 July 1888.

88 Marius C. Barbeau and William Beynon, Northwest Coast Files, CMC, BF 201.3, 5; Simidiiks, of Gitwangak̲.

89 Barbeau-Beynon Northwest Coast Files, BF 201.6, 2.

90 Ibid., BF 89.2, 2.

91 Ibid., BF 89.3, 1.

92 Ibid., 1-2.

93 Ginmiltkun Creek on government maps.

94 A.R. Selwyn, "Summary Report on the Operations of the Geological Survey for the Year 1893," *Geological Survey of Canada, Annual Report 7* (Ottawa: Queen's Printer 1894), 15A.

95 Franz Boas, "Report on the Northwestern Tribes of Canada," *British Association for the Advancement of Science, 65th Report*, 10 (1895): 48-50.

96 Ibid.

97 Ibid.

98 D. Raunet, *Without Surrender, without Consent: A History of the Nishga Land Claims* (Vancouver: Douglas and McIntyre 1984), 64.

99 Ibid., 71.

100 Small-pox (author's note).

101 MMRC, Nass Agency Hearings, 1915, 155.

102 Ibid., 158.

103 Stephen McNeary, "Where Fire Came Down: Social and Economic Life of the Niska" (Ph.D. diss., Bryn Mawr College 1976), 7.

104 One gets the impression from Boas that the Tsetsaut had left Awiijii by 1894; see note 95.

105 Xsigisi'am'maldit (Surveyors Creek), which flows east into Bowser River between Bowser Lake and the Bell Irving River.

106 McCullagh to Loring, Magistrate's Court, Nass River, 14 June 1897, in Barbeau-Beynon Northwest Coast Files, BF 202.12.

107 James B. McCullagh, "Autumn Leaves," *Aiyansh Notes* (1907-8), continued as *North British Columbia News* (1909-10), chap. 1. (1908): xv, xvi.

108 Ibid., xvi.

109 Ibid., xvi, xvii.

110 Ibid., xvii.

111 Ibid.

112 Ibid.

113 Ibid.

114 Ibid.

115 To Xsigigyeenit, at the mouth of the Ginmilkun Creek; see entries for 15 and 16 Oct.

116 McCullagh, "Autumn Leaves," *Aiyansh Notes*, chap. 2 (1908): xxiv. This incident is described in Wilson Duff, ed., *Histories, Territories and Laws of the Kitwancool*, Anthropology in BC Memoir No. 4 (Victoria: BCPM 1959), 33-4.

117 The river distance is about eight kilometres; the distance by trail, however, is closer to twenty-three kilometres.

118 McCullagh, "Autumn Leaves," *North British Columbia News*, chap. 3 (1909): xxxii.

119 Ibid.

120 Ibid., xxxiii.

121 Hewin, a Gitanyow chief of the Frog-Raven Clan.

122 McCullagh, "Autumn Leaves," *North British Columbia News*, chap. 4 (1909): xl.

123 Ibid.

124 Ibid., xli.

125 McCullagh, "Autumn Leaves," *North British Columbia News* 1,1 (1909): ii.

126 Ibid., iv.

127 Ibid.

128 Ibid., chap. 7, xlvi.

129 McCullagh, "Autumn Leaves," *North British Columbia News*, chap. 8 (1909): 63.

130 Ibid., 63-4.

131 Constance (Hankin) Cox was the first white child born in Hazelton, to Thomas Hankin, a fur trader, and Margaret McLaughlin (later the wife of Loring); Cox spoke fluent Gitksan.
132 Noxs Din, meaning "mother of Din." It is common among the Gitksan to name the mother after her eldest son.
133 Constance Cox, "Simon Gun-a-Noot: The Authentic Story," *Native Voice* Special Edition (1958): 35.
134 George Biernes, a guide/outfitter resident in the Kispiox Valley. He was familiar with much of the upper Skeena-Nass territory and eventually played a role in convincing Gunanoot to come out of hiding.
135 As Geel, a chief of Kispiox, Simon had his hereditary hunting territory on the Skeena just beyond Groundhog Mountain and contiguous with the territory of Wiiminoosikx.
136 British Columbia, Provincial Police, Correspondence, BCA, GR 55, 4639/09.
137 Ibid.
138 Fred Gunanoot, "The Story of Simon P. Gunanoot," *Native Voice* (1947): 15.
139 Ibid.
140 Richard Loring to R.E. Gosnell, librarian, Provincial Assembly, Victoria, 1896, BCA.
141 Loring Declaration, 1908, copy in Sterritt files.
142 G.T. Emmons, Papers, c. 1908, in Newcombe Family Papers, BCA, add. mss. 1077, vol. 62, file 56, 38, 332.
143 Emmons Papers, 101.
144 Ibid., 38.
145 Ibid., 571.
146 Ibid., 294.
147 Ibid., 570.
148 George T. Emmons, "The Tahltan Indians," *University of Pennsylvania Musuem, Anthropological Publication* 4,1 (1911): 6.
149 For a discussion on this, see Boas, "Indians," 34-48, 66-71; Emmons, "Tahltan Indians," 22-3; and James Tharp, "The Position of the Tsetsaut among Northern Athapaskans," *International Journal of American Linguistics* 38,1 (1972): 15-16, 24.
150 Emmons, "Tahltan Indians," 115-16.
151 Maisie Hurley, "Biography of Ronald Campbell-Johnstone," *Native Voice* (1953): 3.
152 Campbell-Johnston to deputy superintendent general, DIA, 6 Apr. 1913, NAC, RG 10, NNRC, vol. 11022, file 560A.
153 Ibid., 29 Apr. 1913.
154 Loring to secretary, Royal Commission on Indian Affairs, 11 Feb. 1916, NAC, RG 10, vol. 11022, file 560A.
155 See also references to Wiiminoosikx territory in Chapter 2.
156 Campbell-Johnston, 1908-12, 7.
157 Ibid., 24.
158 Ibid., 34.
159 G.S. Malloch, "Reconnaissance on the Upper Skeena River, between Hazelton and the Groundhog Coal-Field, British Columbia," Canada, Sessional Paper 26 (1912), 75.
160 NAC, RG 10, vol. 7780, file 27150-3-1A.
161 H.A. Collison, "Teeming Waters," c. 1940, BCA, F/3/C 49, 5.
162 Ibid., 10-11.
163 Ibid., 11.
164 Ibid., 16. Collison remembered that it was Wolf territory presumably because he was a member of the Wolf Clan and remembered his discussion with Hayts'imsxw regarding his rights there. However, because this was written about thirty years later in 1940, it seems that he did not accurately recollect the identity of the territory through which they passed, because they were in Raven territory, not Eagle territory.
165 Ibid., 16.
166 Ibid., 32.
167 Ibid., 33.
168 Janet Mason, BC Geographical Names Office, Survey and Resources Mapping Branch, BC Department of Lands, Victoria, personal communication, 8 Feb. 1995.
169 Ibid.

Glossary of Terms

House

A house or house group is a matrilineal kin group and the fundamental landowning and sociopolitical unit in Gitksan society. The house always bears the name of its chief. Each house is part of a larger clan group – Raven (Frog), Fireweed (Killer Whale), Wolf, or Eagle – that cuts across national boundaries. Houses are related to other houses if they share the same ancient origins and are closely related if they share a common history until relatively recent times.

Adaaw̲k

The adaaw̲k describe the ancient migrations of a house, its acquisition and defence of its territory, and major events in the life of the house, such as natural disasters, epidemics, and war, as well as the arrival of new peoples and events surrounding the establishment of trade alliances and major shifts in power. The adaaw̲k also contain limx'oy, ancient songs that refer to events in which the people endured great hardship or loss. The ayuuks, or crests, depicted on poles and on ceremonial regalia also arise out of events in the history of the house as described in the adaaw̲k. The adaaw̲k are perpetuated by the memory training of heirs to chiefly positions and are repeated and witnessed by each generation of chiefs at important feasts, or yukw.

Limx'oy

Limx'oy means "song of ancient times." These powerful songs are both historical and highly emotional, and they often express sadness at the loss of members of a house in a great natural disaster or war or the loss or abandonment of a territory or village. The limx'oy of a house frequently forms part of its adaaw̲k referring specifically to places and events related there. These songs also differ from adaaw̲k in that they often retain the original language in which they were created.

Ayuuks

Ayuuks, or crests, are images that refer to specific events in the history of the house. For Northwest Coast peoples, the interpenetration of the material and the spiritual worlds can be seen in historical events of great importance and is manifested in a spirit being that can be perceived and re-created through art. These images, as represented on poles and ceremonial regalia, encapsulate the events detailed in the adaaw̲k.

Yukw

The yukw, or feast, is a complex institution through which the Northwest Coast peoples formalize much of their sociopolitical and legal affairs. All acquisition and inheritance of territory, the declaration of formal rights of access, and the formation of marriage and trade alliances are validated and witnessed in the feast. The yukw is hosted by a house, assisted by related houses of the same clan, and attended by houses of different clans in the village and nation.

Xsiisxw

Xsiisxw is the Gitksan term that describes the system of compensation in which one house relinquishes wealth, names, crests, or territory to repay a crime committed by its members against those of another house. Compensation for the accidental death of an individual might involve a gift of material wealth; for the murder of an important chief, it might involve the transfer of territory for the lifetime of the immediate family of the deceased; and for a series of unprovoked attacks on a neighbouring nation, it might involve the permanent transfer of territory to the innocent party. As with all other legal transactions within Gitksan society, these transfers of territory are formally presented and acknowledged in the feast.

Glossary of Place Names

Order: Gitanyow, Gitksan, Nisga'a, mainly based on their appearing in that order in Chapters 3, 4, and 5; asterisk indicates that exact location is uncertain; numbers are from Map 36 (Aboriginal place names in the Nass watershed); meaning of name is in parentheses if known; nation is given as [G]: Gitksan, [Gy]: Gitanyow, [N]: Nisga'a, [T]: Tsetsaut/Tahltan, [Ts]: Tsimshian, with common boundary or competing claim indicated as [G/Gy], [Gy/N], etc.; italics refer to the name written, or unwritten (*UNGM*), on government maps (generally using maps at 1:250,000 scale); aka: also known as; var.: variant spellings.

Gitanyow Place Names

Aksnagyalga 152 (water/Gyalga) *Axnegrelga*

Anahgharn see Anxhon

anahghon see Anxhon

anahome see Anxhon

Anda'gansgotsinak 129 (where [like]/anthill; aka Sga'nisim'duults: mountain like/clitoris) *near Yvonne Peak UNGM*

Angildipdawit 92 (where/?) *mountain UNGM*

Anhahl'yee 130 (where [Grizzly]/go along) *Hanna Ridge*

Anlaagahl T'ax'matsiiadin 125 (where/out of/lake/Meziadin) *Meziadin River:* var. La wee epe

Anlaagahlt'ax (where out of/lake) *former village site at outlet of Kitwanga Lake UNGM*

Anlag.amsto'ks see Anlagamsto'oks

Anlagamsto'oks 150 (place/to one side) *part of Brown Bear Lake system UNGM:* var. Anlag.amsto'ks

Anlaubiglozatz see Anlo'obitlogots

Anlaxgya'asxw 58 (where/look?) *UNGM*

Anlo'obitlogots 100 (where/[cook with] rocks/wild celery) *meadow area UNGM:* var. Anlaubiglozatz

An'sgeexs 162 (where/cross river) *on Nass River at Meziadin UNGM*

An'uksgimiluxw (where/dance) *UNGM*

Anxhon 60 (where eat/salmon) *former village UNGM:* var. Gitanxhon, Har-keen, anahghon, Anahgharn, anahome, Au-kon

Anxmilit 161 (where/eat/steelhead) *site of Tsetsaut attack on Nisga'a/Gitanyow UNGM*

Anxt'imi'it 86 (where/eat/Kinnikinnik berries) *height of land north of Stenstrom Creek UNGM*

Anxtus 30 (where/wild lily?) *UNGM:* var. Aukdaus

Au-kon see Anxhon

Anxtsimelixnagets see Anxts'imilixnaagets

Anxts'imilixnaagets 157 (where eaten/beaver/wolverine) *UNGM:* see Xsi'anxts'imilixnaagets, var. Anxtsimelixnagets, Woforming creek

Aukdaus see Anxtus
Damiks* 155 (lake or swamp area) *UNGM*
Dam'magangiist (lake/among/fresh water mussels) *UNGM:* var. T'am.ag.angi.s
Gadiit 110 Kinskuch Peak: var. Laxgadiit, Laxg.adihl(t?)
Gahahlahlmatx see Gehlmatx
Gahl'o (?) *former Tsetsaut village on Nass River UNGM*
Galdimdak 55 (vessel [for]/skimming grease) *UNGM*
Gaksbaksit see Gaksbaxsgiit
Gaksbaxsgiit 103 (just newly/upwards/lies the trail) *UNGM:* var. Gaksbaksit, Qakspaxskit
Gangwats 71 (excrement) *UNGM*
Gehlmatx (chest of/mountain goat) *UNGM*
Geltsalo'obit see G'ilhlalo'obit
Genusmax 137 (trap for/bear) *UNGM*
G.epg.isu see Gipgasxw
Gib-xasxw see Gipgasxw
Gihlmihlgen see Gwinmihlgan
Gihlmihlg.en see Gwinmihlgan
Gihltin see Gyahlt'in
Gihlt'in see Gyahlt'in
G'ilhlalo'obit 48 (hill/flat rocks) *UNGM:* var. Geltsalo'obit
Gilt'in see Gyahlt'in
Gin-Guux River see Gwinsgox
Ginhaq see Gwinhak
Gin-mielt-kun see Gwinmihlgan
Gin'milit see Gwin'milit
Ginmiltkun Creek see Gwinmihlgan
Ginsgok see Gwinsgox
Gins-Guux see Gwinsgox
Gipgasxw 69 (fish weir) [Gy/N] *former village at junction of Cranberry and Kiteen Rivers:* var. G.epg.isu, Gib-xasxw
Gisi'am'maldit see Xsigis'am'maldit
Gitangwalk see Gitangwalkw
Gitangwalkw 144 (people/where/dry) [Gy/G] *former village UNGM:* var. Gitangwalk
Gitankam* (people/where/?) *UNGM*
Gitanxhon/Gitanxon see Anxhon
Gitanyow 307 (people/where/reduced in number) *Kitwancool*
Git-inyewo see Gitanyow
Git-kse-'tsuutsxw see Gitxsits'uuts'xwt
Gitksizuzqu/Gitksedzo'otsk' see Gitxsits'uuts'xwt
Gitsheoaksit see Gitxsits'uuts'xwt
Gitwingol see Gitwinhlgu'l
Gitwinhlgu'l (people/where/small in numbers) *Kitwancool* (commonly called Gitanyow): var. Gitwingol, Gitwinlkul, Gitwinkul, kit-man-cool, Gyitwuntlku'l, Gitwinlgol, Kitwin-kool
Gitwinlgol see Gitwinhlgu'l
Gitwinlku'n Lake see T'am Gitwinhlgu'l
Gitwinkul see Gitwinhlgu'l
Gitwinlkul see Gitwinhlgu'l
Gitxsits'uuts'xwt 23 (people/creek/[of many] birds) *ancient village and camp on Nass River UNGM:* var. Gitksizuzqu, gitksedzo'otsk', Kitsizozquiot, Gitsheoaksit, Git-kse-'tsuutsxw, Gitsizutqu
Gunsguk see Gwinsgox
Gusgan'isat Mountain see Hlguhlsga'nist
Gwen-ga-nik see Gwinganik
Gwilaxanyuusxwt 141 (where/cache) *UNGM*
Gwilgol* (where/comes toward you) *UNGM*

Gwinamagoot 54 (where/happy/heart) *UNGM:* var. Wil-lu-ama-gaud
Gwinagiisxw see Gwinhagiistxw
Gwinaxhlantxw 25 (toward where/never/moves) *UNGM*
Gwingibuu (where boils [swift water]) *fishing station on Nass River UNGM:* var. Kwungibu
Gwinhagiistxw (where/little shells) [G] *see Kwinageese Lake and River area:* var. T'am
   Gwinhagiistxw, Xsigwinhagiistxw, Gwinagiisxw, Gwin Hagiisdxw
Gwinhak 59 (where/geese) *UNGM:* var. Ginhaq, Kwunhaqx, Qum Nuck
Gwinhlakw 53 (where/splash) *fishing site UNGM:* var. Gwinlaqu
Gwinganik 167 (where/jackpine pitch) *mountain UNGM:* var. Gwen-ga-nik
Gwinlaqu see Gwinhlakw
Gwinmihlgan 135 (toward/half-burnt trees or forest) *Ginmiltkun Creek:* var. Xsigwin-
   mihlgan, Gihlmihlg.en, Gihlmihlgen, Gin-mielt-kun
Gwin'milit 78 (where/steelhead) *Mount Weber:* var. Gin'milit
Gwinsak* (where/cold or sharp?) *UNGM*
Gwinsgox 26 (place/where fording) *Kinskuch River:* var. Kinsqoik, Kinsg.o'ix, Gin-Guux
   River, Gunsguk, Kinsg.o.ix, Kinsgoix, Kinsgoox, Gins-Guux, Gwinsgox, Ginsgoix
Gwinstimoon see Nisga'a place names
Gwuntaax *village, camp UNGM*
Gyahlt'in 67 (to spear/fish trap) [Gy/N/G] *Kiteen River:* var. Gilt'in, Gihlt'in, Gihltin,
   Gyehl-'tin, Gyehl-'tin, Gyihlt'in, Giteen
Gyehl-'tin see Gyahlt'in
Gyihlt'in see Gyahlt'in
Gyitwuntlkul see Gitwinhlgu'l
Har-keen see Anxhon
Hilin 57 (lonely) *UNGM*
Hlgimedasook see Nisga'a place names
Hlguhlsga'nist 160 (small/mountain) *UNGM:* var. Gusgan'isat Mountain
Kawilihl* 138 *a hill UNGM*
K'il-hla-lo'op-bit see G'ilhlalo'obit
Kinsg.o.ix see Gwinsgox
Kinsqoik/Kinsg.o'ix see Gwinsgox
Kiteen Valley see Gyahlt'in
Kitanqaouqu see Gitangyahlxw
kit-man-cool/kit-man-kool see Gitwinhlgu'l
Kitsizozquiot see Gitxsits'uuts'xwt
Kit win kool/Kit-winl-kole see Gitwinhlgu'l
Ksa'anaxtemi.t see Xsa'anxt'imi'it
Ksadanig.o.t see Xsidaniigoot
Ksagants'iikw (creek where/young marmot) *UNGM*
'Kse-s'yun see Xsis'yun
Ksi-an-k-gasq see Xsi'angasx
Ks-gi-geenit see Xsigigyeenit
Ksgigienit see Xsigigyeenit
Ksi-gigient see Xsigigyeenit
Ksi-mihl-etxwit see Xsimihlhetxwt
Ksimilatgut see Xsimihlhetxwt
Ksit'akxwt (water/dirty or muddy) *Moonlit Creek:* var. Xsihadakxwt
Ksi-tekw/Ksi Tekw see Xsit'ax
Ksiyag.askit see Xsiyagasgiit
Kunks.'l *fishing station near Cranberry confluence UNGM*
Kwungibu see Gwingibuu
Kwunhaqx see Gwinhak
laghwehip/lagh-weip/lagh-wip see Laxwiiyip
Lak-wi-yip see Laxwiiyip
Lamingittin see Luu'min Gyahlt'in
Laq'uyip see Laxwiiyip

lauch-wilhaup see Laxwilo'op
La Wee Eap see Laxwiiyip
La wee epe/La-wee-eap [river] see Anlaagahl Tax'matsiiadin
Lax'anmihl (on/where/dry plateau) *former village UNGM*
Laxgwinha 146 (on/where/windy) *lake UNGM:* var. Lak-gwin-ha
Lax'nmelgul (on/?) [?] *UNGM*
Lax'andzok 124 (on/where/live) *former village site at confluence of Meziadin River UNGM*
Laxbehlit (on/gentle slope) [Gy/G] *UNGM*
Laxgadiit 110 see Gadiit
Laxsagat 62 (on/pine) [Gy/N] *Jackpine Mountain:* var. Lax-sak-gat
Lax-sak-gat see Laxsagat
Laxwiiyip (on/big/land or earth) [Gy/G] *former Tsetsaut territory in the vicinity of Meziadin Lake to headwaters of Stikine River UNGM:* var. Laq'uyip, Lak-wi-yip, La Wee Eap, laghwehip, lagh-weip, Yak-whik
Laxwijix 79 (on/cariboo) [Gy/N] *height of land south of Kinskuch River UNGM:* var. Lax-wijix, Laxwijix
Lax-wijix see Laxwijix
Laxwilo'op *UNGM:* var. lauch-wilhaup
Lipe.'itxut see Liphetxwt
Lip-ha-hut-quk see Liphetxwt
Liphetxwt 173 (by itself/standing [the mountain]) [Gy/G] *locally called Baldy Mountain UNGM:* var. Lipe.'itxut
Lipsga'nist (only/mountain) [Gy/G] *Mount Madely*
Lipsga'nist 132 (only/mountain or standing alone/mountain: aka Wiilaahabasxw "big/grassy" mountain) *Mount Bell-Irving*
Luubaxgagat (properly Luuhak'uuhlgaagat) 188 (sharp grass/crows) *mountain area at headwaters of Kwinageese River UNGM*
Luu'min Gyahlt'in 133 (inside or along/up/Gyahlt'in) [Gy/G/N] *Kiteen River:* also see Gyahlt'in
Mag.angis see Xsimagangiist
Magoonhl Gwinsgox (headwaters of Gwinsgox) see Gwinsgox
Magoonhl Xsigintayin (headwaters of Xsigintayin) see Xsigintayin
Maiziadin Lake see T'am'matsiiadin
Mat Kezie see T'am'matsiiadin
Mat-sa'-rane see Tam'matsiigogat
Maziadin and Maziadin Lake see T'am'matsiiadin
Medziaden Lake see T'am'matsiiadin
Meziadin Lake see T'am'matsiiadin
Medziadin see T'am'matsiiadin
Medziadon see T'am'matsiiadin
Muzzadden lake see T'am'matsiiadin
Nadiiloodit 153 (to each one/swim: beaver or salmon swim from one lake to other) *Brown Bear Lake (and area):* var. Ndelo.det
Nask'angaledit 140 (where/wild rose bushes) *UNGM*
Ndelo.det see Nadiiloodit
Qakspaxskit see Gaksbaxsgiit
Qum Nuck see Gwinhak
Sga'nisimgohl 111 (mountain/of flint) *Lavendar Mountain*
Sga'nisimhabasxw 163 (mountain/grassy) *UNGM:* var. Sga'nisim Habasxw
Sgathlao see Winsgahlo'
Sga'nisimluulak 77 (mountain/of ghost) *mountain area between Mount Weber and headwaters of Ginmiltkun Creek*
Sis'yun see Xsis'yun
Tal Tan Lake see T'amsuutsii'ada (Bowser Lake) in Gitksan place names
T.am.ag.angi.s see Dam'magangiist
T'amansingekw 74 (lake/where get/swans) *UNGM*

Tam-a-tsi-a'ten see T'am'matsiiadin
T'amgiil'a 121 (lake/paw or wrist) *Paw Lake*
T'amgin'apts'eek (lake/where/fillet fish) *on Nass River near, but opposite, Cranberry confluence UNGM:* var. T'amginepdza.ux
T'amginepdza.ux see T'amgin'apts'eek
T'amginlo'otsen (lake/where/elder berries) [G/N] *UNGM*
T'amgwinsgox 112 (lake/place/where fording) *Kinskuch Lake*
T'am Gitwinhlgu'l (lake/Kitwancool) *Kitwanga Lake:* var. Gitwinlku'n Lake
T'amhilin 56 (lake/lonely) *UNGM*
T'amhliloot 182 (lake/many islands) [Gy/G] *Kwinageese Lake*
T'amlilbax 73 (lake/of islands) *Sideslip Lake*
T'am'matsiiadin 126 (lake/?; according to McCullagh: "pearly water," "mother of pearl blue," pronounced "Med-zee-ah-din") *Meziadin Lake:* var. Medziadon, Maziadin, Maziadin Lake, Medziadin, Met'siadin, Met'sia.dan Lake, Muzzadden lake, Tam-a-tsi-a'ten
Tam'matsiigogat 149 (lake/?/swans) *Swan Lake:* var. Mat-sa'-rane
T'amwinluu'axit'os 115 (lake/where/in/barked/dog) *Niska Lakes*
Tchitin River see Ksit'in
Txasginax 97 (along/where/ferns) *height of land between Weber Creek and Cranberry River UNGM*
Txaslaxwiiyip 158 (along/on top/big territory [not rocky]) [Gy/G] *UNGM:* var. Txaxslaxwiyip, T'aslaxwiyi'p
Txas'tsadagat 147 (along/[where rough country]) *UNGM:* var. Txasts'adagat
Txaxslaxwiyip see Txaslaxwiiyip
Wii'laahabasxw see Wilahabasxw
Wiilaxgelt 94 (large/on where/hill) *mountain west of Weber Creek UNGM*
Wilahabasxw 99 (big/grassy area) *UNGM*
Wilbaxt'aahlgibuu see Winbaxt'aahlgibuu
Wil-k-zimelk'l-nausik see Xsi'anxts'imilixnaagets
Wil-lu-ama-gaud see Gwinamagoot
Wilp'am't'uutsxw 134 (house of/charred logs) *house site UNGM:* var. Wilp-am-'tuuts
Wil-sga-lgol see Winsgahlgu'l
Wilsgayip 66 (where/across/earth) [Gy/N] *feature on Kiteen River UNGM*
Wilukstkiwan 51 [Gy/N] *fishing station on Nass River UNGM*
Wiluugwalgan 122 (where/in/dry wood) *UNGM*
Wiluukstxawaa 50 [Gy/N] *fishing station on Nass River UNGM*
Winbaxt'aahlgibuu 68 (where/upward/sits/the wolf) [Gy/N] *UNGM:* var. Wunbaxtahlkibu
Winhat'al 10 *UNGM*
Winluu'axit'os 117 (where/in/barked/the dog) *Niska Lakes (area):* var. Win'luu'axit'os; also see Xsiwinluu'axit'os
Winluundehldehl'aks (where/meets/two rivers) *on middle Nass River UNGM*
Win-naa-skan-gymdit see Wu'nisk'angyamdit
Winsgalgol see Winsgahlgu'l
Winsgahlgu'l 72 (where/across/narrow) *former village on middle Nass River UNGM:* var. Winsgahl Ts'ilaasxw (where across narrow canyon), 'Wunsg.ahlku'l, Wunsg.ahlku'n, Win-ska-hlguu'l, Winskatkul, Wil-sga-lgol
Winsgahlo' 145 (where/across/slide) *UNGM:* var. Sgathlao
Win-ska-hlguu'l see Winsgahlgu'l
Winskatkul see Winsgahlgu'l
Woforming creek see Anxts'imilixnaagets
Wunbaxtahlkibu see Winbaxt'aahlgibuu
Wu'nidagantxw 29 (place/on/smooth) *UNGM*
Wu'nisginist 27 (place/on/pitch) *UNGM*
Wu'nisk'angyamdit 113 (where/bush/saskatoon berry) *UNGM:* var. Wun'nisk'angyamdit, Win-naa-skan-gymdit
'Wunsg.ahlku'l/Wunsg.ahlku'n see Winsgahlgu'l

Xhlgi-meda-sook see Hlgimedasoo<u>k</u>

Xsa'anxt'imi'it 87 (water/where get/kinnikinnik berry) [Gy/G] *lower Stenstrom Creek:* var. Ksa'anaxtemi.t

Xsi'andilgan 154 (water/where/beaver dams) *flows west into Nass River UNGM*

Xsi'andilgan 165 (water/where/beaver dams) *flows west into Meziadin Lake UNGM*

Xsi'angasx* 151 (water/where/wild rice [wild lily, tastes bad]) *UNGM:* var. Xsi-an-k-gasq

Xsi'anhaahl'yee 166 (water/where [grizzly]/walk along) *upper Hanna Creek*

Xsi'ansi'biins see Xsits'elasxwt

Xsi'anskee<u>x</u>s 95 (water/where/wade) *upper Cranberry River*

Xsi'ants'iikw (water/where/leaks out) *UNGM*

Xsi'anxhon 64 (water/where get/salmon) *lower Cranberry River*

Xsi'anxts'imilixnaagets 156 (water/where/beaver [eaten by]/wolverine) *Wolverine Creek:* var. An<u>x</u>tsimilixnagets, Wil-k-zimelk'l-nausik, aka Beaverlea

Xsidaniigoot 102 (water/happy/heart) *Weegett-Aluk Creeks:* var. Ksadanig.o.t

Xsigigyeenit 36 (water/above) *UNGM:* var. Ks-gi-geenit, Ksgigienit

Xsigiil'a 120 (water/paw or wrist) *Paw Creek*

Xsigintayin (water/where/?) *Kitwancool Creek*

Xsigisi'am'maldit 131 (water/along/cotton wood trees) [Gy/G] *Surveyors Creek:* var. Gisa'am'maldit

Xsigwa'angamt 96 (water/where/flint) *Weber Creek*

Xsi'gwin'aa<u>x</u>wit 93 (water/where/porcupine) *UNGM:* var. Xsigwina<u>x</u>

Xsigwinadapxw 114 (water/where/hammer) *UNGM*

Xsigwina<u>x</u> see Xsi'gwin'aa<u>x</u>wit

Xsigwinlaa<u>x</u>w (water/where/trout) *upper Kitwanga River*

Xsigwinmihlgan (water/where/burnt trees) *Ginmiltkun Creek:* see Gwinmihlgan

Xsigwinsalda 101 (water/where/slate rock) *UNGM*

Xsigwits'ilaasxwt 143 (also 98 on Map 2 inset, by error) (water/where/canyon) *Tsugwinselda Creek*

Xsigwinadapxw 114 (water/where/hammer) *UNGM*

Xsihada<u>k</u>xwt see Xsit'akxwt

Xsihlgugan 139 (water/small [willow] trees) *Calmin Creek*

Xsik'alaa'n* 128 (water/at headwaters) *UNGM*

Xsik'alaa'nhlt'a<u>x</u>* 127 (water/at head/lake) *UNGM*

Xsimaaxsxwt see Xsimaaxwsxwt

Xsimaaxwsxwt 118 (water/white or murky) *White River:* var. Xsimaaxsxwt

Xsimagangiist (water/among/fresh water mussels) *Nangeese River:* var. Mag.angis

Xsimihlhetxwt 75 (water/yellow) *Derrick Creek:* var. Ksi-mihl-etxwit, Ksimilatgut

Xsis'yun 123 (glacier) *Cambria Icefield:* var. 'Kse-s'yun

Xsit'a<u>x</u> (water/from lake) [Gy/G] *Kitwanga River:* var. Xsit'ax

Xsit'a<u>x</u> 49 (water/from lake) [Gy/N] *flows west into Nass R. near but opposite Tchitin River UNGM:* var. Ksi-tekw

Xsits'adagat 148 (water/?) *flows west into Nass River UNGM*

Xsits'elasxwt 159 (water/canyon) *Gleason and lower Moore Creeks*

Xsitxemsem 164 (river of/Txemsem) *Nass River*

Xsiwahliyansit 142 (water/old/leaves) *UNGM*

Xsiwii'aks 70 (water/big/water) *on right bank of Nass River above Cranberry confluence UNGM*

Xsiwinluu'a<u>x</u>it'os 116 (water/where/barked/the dog) *Little Paw Creek:* var. Winluua<u>x</u>it'os

Xsi'win'saagiihl'mat<u>x</u> (creek/where/lay/mountain goats) *UNGM*

Xsiyagasgiit 76 (water/down along/laying) *Cranberry River (upper two-thirds):* var. Ksiyag.askit, Ksiyagaskit

Yak-whick see La<u>x</u>wiiyip

Gitksan Place Names

Anba<u>x</u>gitwin<u>x</u> 215 (where/comes/whistling) *Mount Skowill/Oweegee Peak:* var. Mount Skowill

Andami<u>x</u>w 269 (where/to mark [seasons]) *mountain UNGM*
Andapmatx 180 (where/hunt/mountain goat) *Kologet Mountain*
Andapmatx 237 (where/hunt/mountain goat) *mountain near Canyon Lake UNGM*
Andemaul (where/fish traps) *Andimaul:* aka New Kitsegyukla
Andzoks 'Niist 247 (camp [of]/'Niist) *UNGM*
Angawtsaxw (where/shortcut) *Poison Mountain*
Anghegain see T'amangyage'en
Angyage'en see T'amangyage'en
Angyats'es (where/shortcut) *former village UNGM*
Anluubiiyoosxwt 205 (where/in/flies) *UNGM*
Ansgaxs see Xsa'anluuskee<u>x</u>s
Anyuusxw Adam 187 (cache [literally, plentiful food source] of Adam) *Adam Creek*
Athedla 292 (Tsetsaut for large intestine of moose) *UNGM:* var. Atsehlaa
Atsehlaa see Athedla
Awiijii (wind whistling: from Tsetsaut legend about wind whistling around Oweegee
  Peak) *Skowill Creek as well as name for general area:* also see Luu'xsgigeenigit Awiijii,
  Oweegee
Bagayt'sisagat 193 (among/mountain peaks) *UNGM*
Bowser Lake 229 see T'amsuutsii'ada
Chlaa mountain (Baskyala<u>x</u>ha's mountain) *mountain in Nass drainage near Canyon Lake
  UNGM*
Dam Dilch Sandon see T'amxsinihlts'enden
D'am d'oc'aks see T'amt'uutsxwhl'aks
Dam Ganhagi.'stxw see T'am Gwinhagiistxw
Dam Sabaiya see T'amsaabaya'a
<u>G</u>aldoo'o 304 ("out of way place") *Kuldo:* var. <u>G</u>aldo'o, Kuldoe, Qaldo, Kul Do
Gala<u>x</u>uuhl T'amt'uutsxwhl'aks 272 ([just] above/lake/black/water) *hillside UNGM*
Gasala<u>x</u>lo'obit 235 (where/on/rocky) *tributary of lower Canyon Creek*
Gawilmihl (burned over) *former village UNGM:* aka Old Kuldo
Geetenmaks see Gitanmaaxs
Geltsagat 298 (top of hill/sharp) *Stephen Peak*
Gisi'am'maldit see Xsigis'am'maldit
Gitangas<u>x</u> 302 (people/where/wild rice [wild lily, tastes bad]) *former village UNGM:* var.
  La<u>x</u>gitangas<u>x</u>, Kit an Gash, La<u>x</u>'angas<u>x</u>
Gitangwalk see Gitangwalkw
Gitangwalkw 144 (people/where/dry) [G/Gy] *former village UNGM:* var. Gitangwalk
Gitanmaaxs (people/where use/torch lights [to fish]) *Hazelton:* var. Geetenmaks,
  Gyitanma'kys
Gitksan-Tahltan Boundary Area 294
Gitluusek (people/?) *former village on Skeena UNGM*
Gitsegyukla see Kitsegyukla
Gits'ilaasxw (people [of]/canyon) [Ts] *Kitselas:* also see Tsemnae'usk
Gits<u>k</u>'ansnat 172 (people/bush/hawthorn) *former village near Skunsnat Lake*
Gitwanga see Gitwinga<u>x</u>
Gitwanga<u>k</u> see Gitwinga<u>x</u>
Gitwinga<u>x</u> (people/where/rabbits) *Kitwanga:* var. Kitwingach, Gitwonge', Gitwanga,
  Gyitwunga, Kitwangach, Gitwanga<u>k</u>
Gitwingol see Gitwinhlgu'l
Gitwinhlgu'l (people/where/small in numbers) [Gy] *Kitwancool* (commonly called
  Gitanyow today): var. Gitwingol, Gitwinlkul, Gitwinkul
Gitwinhlt'uutsxwhl'aks (people of/black/water) see T'amt'uutsxwhl'aks
Gitwinkul see Gitwinhlgu'l
Gitwinlkul see Gitwinhlgu'l
Gitwonge' see Gitwinga<u>x</u>
Ground Hog see Ts'aphlgwiikw
Guuhilin 280 (always lonely) *part of Slowmaldo Mountain*

Gwiis Awiijii 213 (small Awiijii) creek *UNGM*
Gwiis'xsihlgugan 251 (small/water/small/hemlock trees) *West Taylor River*
Gwinagiisxw see Gwinhagiistxw
Gwinhagiist (where/mountain alder) [G/T] *Konigus Creek*
Gwinhagiistxw (where/little shells) *Kwinageese Lake and River area:* var. T'am Gwinha-
giistxw, Xsigwinhagiistxw, Gwinagiisxw, Gwin Hagiisdxw, Konigees River, Quinageeset
Gwinsaabaya'a (where [get]/Dolly Varden) *mountain area and a campsite south of Muck-
aboo Creek UNGM*
Gwinwijix 184 (where/caribou) *mountain UNGM*
Gyahlt'in 67 (to spear/fish trap) [G/Gy/N] *Kiteen River:* var. Gilt'in, Gihlt'in, Gihltin,
Gyehl-'tin, Gyehl-'tin, Gyihlt'in, Giteen
Gyehl-'tin see Gyahlt'in
Gyihlt'in see Gyahlt'in
Gyitanma'kys see Gitanmaax
Gyitsigyuktla see Kitsegyukla
Gyitwunga see Gitwingax
Hagwilget (gentle/people) *Hagwilget*
Hlagenxwiigwiikw see Wilmaxhladokhlagenxwiigwiikw
Iskoot see Iskut
Iskut [T] *Iskut River and village:* var. Iskoot
Kaa Tsuu Tsedle ("where sockeye spawn"; a Tsetsaut name according to David
Gunanoot) [Gy] *Meziadin Lake:* see T'am'matsiiadin
K'alaanhlgiist 296 (upper/grey willow) *Slamgeesh Lake and River:* var. Qalanhlgist
K'alaanhl Luudagwigit 257 (upper/in/where/twist [zigzag]) *mountain area at head of Tay-
lor River UNGM:* aka Luudagwigit
K'alaanhl Xsi'angaxda (head of/Xsi'angaxda) see Xsi'angaxda
Kcan see Xsiyeen
Kcigonget Creek see Xsigwink'aat
Kisgaga'as 303 (people of/inland gulls) *Kisgegas village and Indian Reserve:* var. Kisgagas,
Kiskegas, Kisgigax, Kisgegas, Kisgiga'as, Kitsagas, Kishnagast
Kisgigax see Kisgaga'as
Kishnagast see Kisgaga'as
Kiskegas see Kisgaga'as
Kiskukause village see Kisgaga'as
Kispaiox see Kispiox
Kispayaks see Kispiox
Kispiox (properly, Gitanspayaxw: people/where/hiding) *Kispiox:* var. Kispayaks, Kyspyox,
Kispyox, Kis-py-aux, Kyshpyox, Kyespox
Kiteen Valley see Gyahlt'in
Kitsagas see Kisgaga'as
Kitseguecla see Kitsegyukla
Kitsegyukla (people of/Segyukla) [G] *Kitseguecla:* var. Gitsegyukla, Old Kitsegyukla, Gyit-
sigyuktla
Kit an Gash see Gitangasx
Kitwangach see Gitwingax
Kitwangar see Gitwingax
Kitwingach see Gitwingax
Klapada [T] *Klappan River:* var. Kla Pah (valley)
Konigees River see Gwinhagiistxw
Konigus River (not to be confused with Konigus Creek at head of Nass River) see Gwin-
hagiistxw
Ksa'anaxtemi.t see Xsa'anxt'imi'it
'Ksa-hl Guu-Gan see Xsihlgugan
'Ksa-Lax-oks see Xsilaxuu Ando'o
Kul Do see Galdoo'o
Kyespox see Kispiox

Kyshpyox see Kispiox
Kyspyox see Kispiox
Laghwehip, Lagh-weip, Lagh-wip see La̱xwiiyip
Lak-wi-yip see La̱xwiiyip
Laq'uyip see La̱xwiiyip
Laugh-Na-Taugh/Laugh-Ne-Taugh see La̱xdit'a̱x
La Wee Eap see La̱xwiiyip
La̱x'angasx̱ see Gitangasx̱
La̱x'anmihl (on/where/dry plateau) [?] *former village UNGM*
La̱xdit'a̱x 305 (where on/many lakes) [G] *Stephens Lake area:* var. Laugh-Ne-Taugh
La̱xgitangasx̱ see Gitangasx̱
La̱xamaawx 223 (on/meadow area) *site of Gitksan-Tsetsaut treaty at Oweegee UNGM*
La̱xbehlit (on/gentle slope) [G/Gy] *UNGM*
La̱xwiiyip (on/big/land or earth) [G/Gy] *UNGM:* former Tsetsaut territory in the vicinity of Meziadin Lake to headwaters of Stikine River: var. Laq'uyip, Lak-wi-yip, La Wee Eap, Lea,we,ape, Laghwehip, lagh-weip, lagh-wip
Lea,we,ape see La̱xwiiyip
Lipe.'itxut see Liphetxwt
Lip-ha-hut-quk see Liphetxwt
Liphetxwt 173 (by itself/standing [the mountain]) [G/Gy] *locally called Baldy Mountain UNGM:* var. Lipe.'itxut
Lipsga'nist (only/mountain) [G/Gy] *Mount Madely*
Lipsga'nist 255 (only/mountain or standing alone/mountain) *Lipsconesit Mountain*
Lo'oba'gilatso'oxs 88 (rocky/?/moccasins) *UNGM*
Lo'opguuhanak' 286 (rock/taken by/woman) *mountain UNGM*
Luudagwigit (in/where/twist [zigzag]) *mountains at source of upper Taylor River UNGM*
Luula̱xlo'obit 283 (in/upon/rocky place) *UNGM*
Luu'min Gyahlt'in 133 (inside or along/up/Gyahlt'in) [G/Gy/N] *Kiteen River:* also see Gyahlt'in
Luusilgimbaad Txemsem 259 (middle/Txemsem) *Muckaboo Creek:* aka Xsima̱xhlab-'iluustmaawxs
Luuts'abimts'imyip (in/village/under earth) [T] *former Tsetsaut village beyond Nass-Skeena headwaters UNGM:* var. Ts'imla̱xyip
Luu'xsgiigeeniget Awiijii 214 (in/upper/Awiijii) *Skowill Creek*
Mandan see Mindagan
Masxwtlo'op 197 (red/[mountain] rock) *mountain UNGM*
Mat-sa'-rane' see T'am'matsiigogat
Maxhla'anmuuxws 276 (up over/where/snow [drifts]) *mountain area UNGM*
Ma̱xhlabil'uustmaaxws 263 (over/where like/stars/on snow [sparkle]) *Muckaboo Creek*
Ma̱xhlagenxwiigwiikw see Wilma̱xhladokhlagenxwiigwiikw
Ma̱xhlala̱x'uut 206 (over/where/roast [in fire]) *UNGM*
Miin'anhlgii 281 (below/[golden eagle's] nest) *mountain UNGM*
Miinhl Ganu'aloo 200 (below/?) *UNGM*
Miinhl La̱xmihl see Miinla̱xmihl
Miinla̱xmihl 291 (below/the burn) *UNGM:* var. 'Miinlaxmihl, Miinhl-La̱x-Mihl, Miinhl La̱xmihl
'Miinlaxmihl see Miinla̱xmihl
Mindagan 306 area in the vicinity of Stevens Lake *UNGM:* var. Mun dan, Mandan
Mount Skowill see Anba̱xgitwinx̱
Mun dan see Mindagan
Naabaad Xsiluu'am'maldit 287 (runs into/water/in/cottonwood trees) *Yaza Creek*
Naadat (look [toward meadow]/sit [on side of meadow]) *UNGM*
Naala̱xts'inaasit (at/on where/slide alder patches) *height of land between Kwinageese River and Kispiox River UNGM*
Naa'ogil 192 *UNGM:* var. Naa Oogil
Naas [River] see Xsitxemsem

Neest mountain ('Niist's mountain) mountain in Nass watershed near Canyon Lake *UNGM*

Oweegee see Awiijii

Qalanhlgist see K'alaanhlgiist

Quinageeset see Gwinhagiistxw

Sa'gyoo'wilpxan 208 (move or float/log cabin) *UNGM*

Sandon Creek see Xsinihlts'enden Ando'o

Sasmihla 274 (to look up at/burn) *UNGM*

She-quin-khaat see Xsigwin<u>k</u>'aat

Shil Awa Mile Dit see Xsiluu'am'maldit

Sga'nisim Xsa'ansaksxwmoohl 275 *part of Slowmaldo Mountain UNGM*

Sgasgiit T'a<u>x</u> 219 (sideways/lake: lake at right angle to flow of creek) *lake near Bell-Irving River UNGM*

S<u>k</u>ahawagat 84 (where get/birch) *upper Stenstrom Creek*

Skowill Creek see Luu'xsgiigeeniget Awiijii

Skeena River see Xsiyeen

Stickine see Stikine

Stikine *Stikine River:* var. Stikeen, Stickine

Sto'ot Xsitxemsem 201 (beside river of/Txemsem) [G/Gy/T] *Bell-Irving River: aka West Nass River*

Sun Sik Mass see Xsa'ansaksxwmoohl

Suutsii'ada/Thuutsii'ada (murky or cloudy water: Tsetsaut language) *Bowser Lake:* see T'amsuutsii'ada

T'abeekxwhlt'a<u>x</u> 217 (round/lake) *Hodder Lake*

Tahltan [T] Tahltan *(former village at junction of Stikine and Tahltan Rivers)*

Tal Tan Lake see T'amsuutsii'ada

T'amangyage'en 240 (lake/where/chewing) *near Canyon Lake UNGM*

T'amansa'axws 249 (lake/where get/?) near *Canyon Lake UNGM*

T'amgana<u>x</u>digwanaxw 218 (lake/of bloodsuckers) *lake near Bell-Irving River UNGM*

T'am Gwinhagiistxw 174 (lake where/fresh water clam shells) *Fred Wright Lake:* var. Gwinhagiistxw, Xsigwinhagiistxw, Dam Gwanhagi.'stxw

T'amgwinsaabaya'a see T'amsaabaya'a

T'amlaala<u>x</u>uudit 176 (lake/on where/meadows or swamp) *locally known as East Bonney Lake UNGM*

T'amlaaxw 225 (lake/trout) *Todedada Lake*

T'amhliloot 182 (lake/many islands) [G/Gy] *Kwinageese Lake*

T'am'matsiigogat 149 (lake/?/swans) *Swan Lake:* var. Mat-sa'-rane'

T'amsaabaya'a 261 (lake of/Dolly Varden) *UNGM:* var. Dam Sabaiya, T'amgwinsaabaya'a

T'amsuutsii'ada 228 (lake/murky, cloudy, or silty) *Bowser Lake:* once known as Tal Tan Lake

Tamtoos forks see T'amt'uutsxwhl'aks

T'amt'uutsxwhl'aks 271 (lake/black/water) *Damdochax Lake (commonly called Blackwater Lake):* var. Gitwinhlt'uutsxwhl'aks, Wilt'uutsxwhl'aks, D'am d'oc'aks, 'Tam-'tuu'tsxw-hl-Aks, Tum to Clax Lake, Tamtoos forks (junction of Nass and Damdochax Rivers)

T'amuumxswit 270 (lake [of]/turtle case caddis) *Wiminasik [Wiiminoosikx] Lake*

T'amwiits (lake/?) [G/T] *lake at head of Konigus Creek UNGM*

T'amxsinihlts'enden 238 (lake/water/cloudy) *Canyon Lake:* var. Dam Dilch Sandon Lake

T'a'ootsip (fortified village) *rocky island in Skeena River above Kispiox UNGM*

T'aslaxwiyi'p see T<u>x</u>asla<u>x</u>wiiyip

T'axs Sgawil 221 (lake/of Sgawil) *Oweegee Lake*

T'a<u>x</u>ts'imilix 227 (lake/beaver) *Hidden Lake*

Temlaxam 169 (on/flat/prairie place) *former village UNGM:* var. Temlaxamit

T'imgesha'niidzok 289 (head [of]/camp[s]) *marker at height of land between upper Nass and Skeena Rivers at north end of Panorama Mountain UNGM*

Ts'aats'iina 131 (beaver boil: Tsetsaut language) *Surveyors Creek:* see Xsigisi'am'maldid

Ts'aphlgwiikw 285 (home [of]/marmot) *Groundhog Mountain*

Tsemnae'usk (inside/?) [Ts] *Usk:* also see Gits'ilaasxw

T'sihl-denden/Tsihl Denden see Xsi'nihlts'enden

Ts'ilaasxwmganksit (canyon/looks like/trees) *Kuldo:* aka New Kuldo; see Galdoo'o

Ts'imanluuskeexs* (inside/where/shallow water; in/place of/wading) *former village in upper Nass watershed UNGM*

Ts'imanmakhl 83 (inside/where the trail leads up) *UNGM:* var. Tsim'anmaqhl

Tsim'anmaqhl see Ts'imanmakhl

Ts'imlaxyip (inside/on/earth) see Luuts'abimts'imyip

Tum to Clax Lake see T'amtuutsxwhl'aks

Txaslaxwiiyip 158 (along/on top/big territory [not rocky]) [G/Gy] *UNGM:* var. Txaxs-laxwiyip, T'aslaxwiyi'p

Txaxslaxwiyip see Txaslaxwiiyip

Walgidisda'xw see Wilgidiksit'ax

Wilgidiksit'ax 177 (place/where/lake) *large pool on Kwinageese River UNGM:* var. Walgidisda'xw

Wilmaxhladokhlagenxwiigwiikw 260 (where/upon/makes tracks or trail of/giant/ marmot) *UNGM:* var. Wilmaxhladokhlagenx Wiigwiikw, Maxhlagenxwiigwiikw

Wilsgahlgu'l 233 (where/very narrow) *canyon on upper Nass River UNGM:* var. Winskatkul, Winsgahgu'l

Wilsganeekhlm Ho'oxs 245 (where/sounds like/hoofs [on dancing apron]/balsam tree) *tributary of Vile Creek UNGM*

Wilsgayip 300 (where/across/earth) *Martin's Flats*

Wilt'uutsxwhl'aks (where/black/water) see T'amt'uutsxwhl'aks

Wiluusgiihl An'malgwa 288 (where/in hollow/is/place [of]/cremation) *valley area at head of Nass River UNGM*

Wiluuskeexwt 301 (where/in/dark place) *UNGM*

Wisinsgiit 179 (along/ridge) *ridge near Mount Kologet UNGM*

Xadaa Agana 293 (moose/upper backbone) *Panorama Creek:* var. Agunagana

Xhlgi-meda-sook see Hlgimedasook

Xoo (Kas Xoo) 224 (grizzly creek) [G/T] *Treaty Creek*

Xsa'angyahlasxw 170 (water/where/chew [dried salmon for bait]) *UNGM:* var. Ankitlas

Xsa'angyahlts'uuts 195 (water/where/spear/birds) *Sanskisoot Creek*

Xsa'anluuskeexs (water/where/shallow) *Lorne Creek:* var. Ansgaxs

Xsa'ansaksxwmoohl 273 (water/where/wash/fish traps) *Sansixmor Creek:* var. Sun Sik Mass, Xsa'ansixmoohl

Xsa'anto'op 196 (water/where/rocky) *Santolle Creek*

Xsa'anxt'imi'it 87 (water/where get/kinnikinnik berry) [G/Gy] *lower Stenstrom Creek:* var. Ksa'anaxtemi.t

Xsa'anyam 231 (water/where/digs to bottom of pot [for best meat]) *Sanyam Creek*

Xsa'axgoot 181 (water/without/heart) *Saicote Creek:* aka Xsi'andapmatx: var. Xsa'axgo.t, Xsa'axgo't

Xsagalisa'wat see Xsigalixawit

Xsanalo'op 183 (water/where/rocky) *Shanalope Creek*

Xsanluuskeexs 248 (water/where/in/shallow) *tributary of Vile Creek UNGM*

Xsi'andapmatx see Xsa'axgoot

Xsi'andapmatx 216 (water/where/from/mountain goats) *Hodder Creek*

Xsi'andapmatx 236 (water/where/from/mountain goats) *Canyon Creek (above Canyon Lake)*

Xsi'angaxda 189 (water/where/white sand) *Kuldo Creek:* var. K'alaanhl Xsi'angaxda

Xsa'anhlamox 194 (water/where/blow [a tree] across) *O'Dwyer Creek*

Xsi'anlaagahl'hliloot 178 (water/[from] out of/[lake of] many islands) *UNGM*

Xsi'anlek'maawks 82 (water/where/?/snow slides) *UNGM*

Xsi'ansalagamdit 210 (water/where/[find] flint) *Ritchie Creek*

Xsibana 232 (water/fish trap) *UNGM*

Xsi'bagayt'sisagat 191 (water/comes from/mountain peaks) *Poison Creek*

Xsigalixawit 199 (water/flows/upriver) *Sallysout Creek:* var. Xsagalisa'wat

Xsigeltsagat 297 (water/hill/sharp [peak]) *UNGM*

Xsigenuts'ap 239 (water/[where set] deadfall) *creek near Canyon Lake UNGM*

Xsigenuts'ap 279 (water/[where set] deadfall) *Deadfall Creek*

Xsigibuu 222 (water/wolf) *UNGM*

Xsigisi'am'maldit 131 (water/along/cotton wood trees) [G/Gy] *Surveyors Creek:* var. Gisa'am'maldit

Xsiguuhilin 277 (water/[where] always/lonely) *UNGM*

Xsigwinhagiistxw 186 (water/where/fresh water clam shells) *Kwinageese River:* var. *Gwin-hagiistxw*

Xsigwink'aat 168 (water/where [placed]/walking cane) *Fiddler Creek:* var. She quin-khaat, Kcigonget

Xsigwinlaaxw (water/where/trout) [Gy] *upper Kitwanga River*

Xsigwinlikstaa't (water/where/island) *former village, UNGM*

Xsigwinwijix 185 (water/[from mountain] where/caribou) *UNGM*

Xsi'gwits'oo 80 (water/where/?) *tributary of upper Kiteen River UNGM*

Xsihis'maawnt 226 (water/[where] goose grass) *Wildfire Creek*

Xsihlgugan 253 (water of/small [willow or hemlock] trees) *Taylor River:* var. 'Ksa-hl Guu-Gan

Xsik'alidakhl 252 (water/Blue Jay) *UNGM*

Xsik'utk'unuuxs 265 (water/owl) [T] *Owl Creek*

Xsilaadamus 190 (water/[like] ladder) *Sheladamus Creek*

Xsilaadamus 230 (water/[like] ladder) *flows south into Nass River UNGM*

Xsilaalaxuudit 175 (water/on where/meadows or swamp) *Bonney Creek*

Xsilaxamaawx 220 (water/of meadow) *Oweegee Creek*

Xsilaxts'ilaasxwt 81 (water/upon/canyons) *UNGM*

Xsilax'uu (water/upon where/swamp) *Shilahou Creek*

Xsilax'uu Ando'o 267 (water/upon/swamp other side) *UNGM:* aka Xsilax'uu: var. 'Ksa'Lax-oks

Xsilaxwiiyip 262 (water/on top of/big territory) *tributary of Muckaboo Creek*

Xsiluu'alagwit 203 (water/in/flint) *UNGM*

Xsiluu'alagwit 250 (water/in/flint) *tributary of Vile Creek UNGM*

Xsiluu'am'maldit 278 (water/inside/cotton wood trees) *Slowmaldo Creek:* var. Shil Awa Mile Dit

Xsiluubiiyoosxwt 202 (water/in/insects) *Irving Creek*

Xsiluulaxleexs 244 (water/place/into/wade) *tributary of Vile Creek UNGM*

Xsiluulaxlo'obit 242 (water/inside/on rocks) *tributary of Vile Creek UNGM*

Xsiluulaxlo'obit 284 (water/inside/on rocks) *UNGM*

Xsiluumahaawit 212 (water/in/[many] porcupine) *Deltaic Creek*

Xsiluumasaawit 243 (water/into/shake) *tributary of Vile Creek UNGM*

Xsiluumaseexit 207 (water/in/spruce trees) *Spruce Creek*

Xsiluumaskeexwt 241 (water/into/where dark) *tributary of Vile Creek UNGM*

Xsiluustaalo'obit 209 (water/in/half/rocky: "rocky on one side") *Cousins Creek*

Xsiluuwitwiidit 256 (water/in which/water ouzels) *Kotsinta Creek:* var. Xsiluu Witwiidit

Xsimasxwtlo'op 198 (water/red/rock) *UNGM*

Xsimaxhlab'iluustmaawxs 266 (water/on/stars/snow [of glacier]) [G] *Muckaboo Creek:* aka Luusilgimbaad Txemsem

Xsimaxhlalax'uut 204 (water/on/height of land?) *UNGM*

Xsimiin'anhlgii 282 (water/under/[eagle's] nest) *upper Barker Creek*

Xsinihlts'enden 234 (water/like/fog or clouds) *Canyon Creek:* var. Xsinilzendin, T'sihl-danden, Tsinihl Denden, Xsi Tsinihl Denden

Xsinihlts'enden Ando'o 246 (water/like/fog or clouds/on other side) *Vile Creek:* var. Sandon Creek

Xsinilzendin see Xsinihlts'enden
Xsi's<u>k</u>ahawagat 85 (water/where get/birch) *UNGM*
Xsis<u>k</u>'ama'alt 295 (water/too big to get through [like a doorway]) *Shaslomal Creek*
Xsit'a<u>x</u> (water/from lake) [G/Gy] *Kitwanga River:* var. Xsit'ax
Xsit'uutsxwhl'aks 268 (water/black/water) *Damdochax Creek*
Xsitxemsem 164 (river of/Txemsem) *Nass River*
Xsiwiigwanks 264 (water/big/undergrund spring) [G/T] *Rochester Creek*
Xsiwiluusgiihl An'malgwa 290 (water/where/in hollow/is/place [of]/cremation) *UNGM*
Xsiwilsgayip 299 (water/where/land [between]) *Damshilgwit Creek*
Xsiwiiluudagwigit 258 (water/big/in/twist [zigzag]) *upper Taylor River*
Xsiwiluu'wa<u>x</u> 171 (water/big/basin) *Ironsides Creek*
Xsiwiiluut'aahlts'imilix 211 (water/big/sits [lives in]/beaver) *Taft Creek*
Xsiyeen (river of/mist) [G/Ts] *Skeena River:* var. Kcan

Nisga'a Place Names
Aiyansh (where/leaves) *Aiyansh (New Aiyansh):* var. Ayans, Iyennis, Ayansh
Aksgan* 13 (wet wood) *UNGM*
Anba<u>k</u>lhon see Anba<u>x</u>hlhon
Anba<u>x</u>hlhon 24 (where/come/salmon) *UNGM:* var. Anbaklhon
Angida (where/eulachon rakes) *former village UNGM*
Angwihlgolxwn 37 (where/?) *UNGM:* var. Angwihlgolxen
Ani<u>x</u>uuhl *Indian Reserve 31*
Anjoksle<u>k</u>ee ("where Le<u>k</u>ee camps") *branch of the Ksiluux that runs into small lake called La<u>x</u>ksiwasandit (see below) UNGM*
Ant<u>x</u>omiks *channel in mountainside created by Zolzap Creek UNGM;* see Ts'alts'ap
Amata'l *small spawning creek UNGM*
Anlee<u>x</u>ga'askw ("where one looks both ways") *site of large smokehouse UNGM*
Anmaxlemgan ("over and across tree") *berry ground near Kiteen River UNGM*
Anmaxslo'op* 91 (where/stands [grow]/rocks) *UNGM:* var. Anmaxslo'p
Ansewo<u>k</u>'oo<u>k</u>s [?] *UNGM*
Ansidagan *Ansedagan Creek*
Ansiwiik'il 28 *UNGM*
Anukskwiyinskw 7 ("looking down the high canyon") *camp on Nass River UNGM*
Anukswo<u>k</u> 39 ("somebody sleeping and waiting there") *camp on Nass River UNGM*
An<u>x</u>eegus<u>k</u> *mountain surrounding Vetter Peak*
An<u>x</u>oon ("where they eat salmon") *Cranberry River*
Anxsa'anskw 6 (where/haul canoe) *camp on Nass River UNGM:* var. Anxsanskw
Ayans see Aiyansh
Bowser Lake 229
Canaan *site five kilometres below Greenville on Nass River UNGM*
Dagits'in 21 *UNGM*
Ga'ahl t'een see Gyahlt'in
<u>G</u>ada'l* 33 *UNGM*
Gadiit *area toward Meziadin UNGM:* var. Kaditt
Gidiluut 42 *UNGM*
Gihltin see Gyahlt'in
Gila<u>x</u>ksip 34 ("sun bar camp") *camp on Nass River UNGM:* var. Gilaksi, kill'laugh, Cheep/Cheeap, laghsipe, Gitlaksipqu
Gilt'in see Gyahlt'in
Gingitl' ("place of spawning sockeye") *Gingit Creek/Gingietl Creek*
Gin-<u>G</u>uux River see Gwinsgox
Ginsgok see Gwinsgox
Gins-<u>G</u>uux see Gwinsgox
Gisanin an<u>x</u>eegus<u>k</u> *steep cliff between Zolzap Creek and Ksits'imelix UNGM*
Gisawilla<u>x</u>oom *valley area north of Dragon Lake UNGM*
Gisigaltkw* *UNGM*

Giswats**x** ("otter people") *Giswatz Creek*
Gitamwilks see Gitwandilix
Gitangyahlxw 47 (people/where/spear [salmon]) *camp on Nass River UNGM:* var.
Kitanqaoqu, Gitangyahlk, Gitangialqu
Gitants'alkw* 109 *UNGM:* var. Gitanzalqu, Gitzalqu, Gitanzalq
Git'anwiliks see Gitwandilix
Gitgyalk 18 (people/old?) *camp on Nass River UNGM:* var. Gitkalt
Gitka'din (people/of/[many] fish traps) *former Nisga'a village UNGM:* var. Gitxatin,
Kitxat'en, Kitkhateen
Gitksagaugasn* *UNGM*
Git-lak-damax see Gitlakdamix
Gitladamiks see Gitlakdamix
Gitlakdamiks see Gitlakdamix
Gitlakdamks see Gitlakdamix
Gitlakdamix 4 ("people on pools of water") *Aiyansh, New Aiyansh:* var. Gitlakdamks,
Gitladamiks, Gitlakdamiks, Git-lak-damax, Kit-lak-tam-aks, Kitlacdamax, Gitla**x**t'amiks,
Kit-la-toms, Kitladamax, Killaghtamax
Gitlaksipqu see Gila**x**ksip
Git-kse-'tsuutsxw see Gitxsits'uuts'xwt
Gitksidaksit 17 ("rock submerged in river") *camp on Nass River UNGM:* var. Ksidaksit
Gitksizuzqu/Gitksedzo'otsk' see Gitxsits'uuts'xwt
Gitsaksgan* 20 (people/of the raft?) *UNGM*
Gitsheoaksit see Gitxsits'uuts'xwt
Gits**k**as 41 (people/?) *UNGM:* var. Gitskas
Gitsulk (people/?) *UNGM*
Gits'yan *Gitzyon Creek*
Gitwandilix (people/"who move at certain place at certain") *former village in the vicinity of Gitlakdamixs and Aiyansh:* var. Git'anwiliks, Kit'anwi'likc
Gitwila**x**gyap* 106 (people/of/?) *former village at or near Gitlakdamixs*
Gitwinksihlxw ("people of place of lizards [salamanders]") *Canyon City:* var. Gitwinsihlxw, Kitwankci'lku, Gitwinksihlkw, Kit-whim-chis, Kitwenselco, Kit-wan-chilt
Gitwinsihlxw see Gitwinksihlxw
Gitxatin see Gitka'din
Gitxsits'uuts'xwt 23 (people/creek/[of many] birds) *camp on Nass River UNGM:* var. Gitksizuzqu, gitksedzo'otsk', Kitsizozquiot, Gitsheoaksit, Git-kse-'tsuutsxw, Gitsizutqu
Gunsguk see Gwinsgox
Gu**x**agayt *mountain UNGM*
Gwinba**x**wee'esxw 63 *Gwinkbawaueast Indian Reserve 54*
Gwindibilx 11 *UNGM*
Gwindip'win 16 *UNGM*
Gwingwiikw 38 (where/marmot) *UNGM*
Gwinhamoo**k** 9 ("place of cow parsnip") *camp on Nass River and former village UNGM:*
var. Gwinamoo**k**; see T'amgwinhamoo**k**
Gwingak* *UNGM*
Gwingilkw* *UNGM*
Gwinglank* *UNGM*
Gwinhaa**k** ("place of geese") *UNGM*
Gwinhatal *Kwinatahl River:* var. Gwinadal
Ginluula**k** ("place of ghost") *UNGM;* see Ksiginluula**k**
Gwin'mal 8 *UNGM*
Gwin'miyeen 14 *UNGM*
Gwinmoots 52 (where/rotten fish?) *UNGM*
Gwinsgox 26 (place/where fording) [N/Gy] *Kinskuch River:* var. Kinsqoik, Kinsg.o'i**x**, Gin-**G**uux River, Gunsguk, Kinsg.o.ix, Kinsgoix, Kinsgoox, Gins-**G**uux, Gins**k**uuxw
Gwinsmak 35 ("looks like a bear [camp]) *camp on Nass River UNGM*
Gwinso**k*** ("many robins there") *camp on Nass River UNGM*

Gwinstimoon 65 ("place of humpback salmon") *mountain ridge north of Mount Hoadley UNGM:* var. Gwunstim'on, Kwunstim'oon, Gwin stimoon

Gwinya'a ("place of spring salmon") *Kwinyarh Creek*

Gwunstim'on see Gwinstimoon

Gyahlt'in 67 ("seeing the fish traps") [N/Gy/G] *Kiteen River:* var. Gilt'in, Gihlt'in, Gihltin, Gyehl-'tin, Gyehl-'tin, Gyihlt'in, Giteen, Ga'ahl t'een

Gyehl-'tin see Gyahlt'in

Gyihlt'in see Gyahlt'in

Haniik'ohl 2 *about twenty-two kilometres above Greenville on Nass River UNGM:* var. Hal i colth, Al-e-quoth, Haligaulth, Haliaulth, Aliquo

Hlawut ("sharp creek") *Vetter peak*

Hlgimedasook (egg/robin) *site of robin's egg pole near Nisga'a-Gitanyow boundary UNGM:* var. Xhlgi-meda-sook

Hlginx 1 *Ishkeenickh Creek;* also see Ikshininik

Ikshininik *Ishkeenickh River and Indian Reserve*

Kalaen (from K'alaan: upper end) *Stewart-Hyder area*

Kaliaks niska' ("River of the Niska") see Xsitxemsem

K'alixaja *mountain north of Canyon City UNGM*

K'alwogn *slope of mountain UNGM*

Kaslaxanso'ox ("swampy land") *long ridge between North Seaskinnish and Nass River UNGM*

Killaghtamax see Gitlakdamix

kill'laugh, Cheep see Gilaxksip

Kinnamox Bay [N/Ts] *Kwinamass Bay:* var. Quinamass Bay

Kincolith *Kincolith:* var. Kincoleth

Kinsg.o.ix see Gwinsgox

Kinsqoik/Kinsg.o'ix see Gwinsgox

Kinuu axwt ("porcupine trap") *mountain UNGM*

Kit'anwi'likc see Gitwandilix

Kiteen Valley see Gyahlt'in

Kitimax *site in the vicinity of lower Portland Canal UNGM*

Kitkhateen see Gitka'din

Kitladamax see Gitlakdamix

Kit-lak-tam-aks see Gitlakdamix

Kit-la-toms see Gitlakdamix

Kit'anwi'likc see Gitwandilix

Kitsoohl (people/) *Kitsault*

Kitsizozquiot see Gitxsits'uuts'xwt

Kit-wan-chilt see Gitwinksihlxw

Kitwankci'lku see Gitwinksihlxw

Kitwenselco see Gitwinksihlxw

Kit-whim-chis see Gitwinksihlxw

Ksa'anmaxslo'op ("water where stands stone") *in Kiteen valley UNGM*

Ksagahlist ("water runs back up") *creek behind Canyon City UNGM*

Ksana'oot ("water of roasting") *UNGM*

Ksaxbiluust* ("waters of stars") *UNGM*

Ksewan (water/) *salmon stream on Hastings Arm*

Ksgamal see Sgamaalt

Ks-gi-geenit see Xsigigyeenit

Ksgigienit see Xsigigyeenit

Ksi an gaahl *Poupard Creek*

Ksidipk's 15 *UNGM*

Ksigakws 45 *UNGM*

Ksiginluulak ("out from Ginluulak") *Ginlulak Creek*

Ksigiselt* 32 *UNGM*

Ksi logom staahl ("out from Logom staahl") *Chigatlque Creek*

Ksiluuyim andoo ("out of alders [?] that way") *stream UNGM*

Ksiluuyim angii ("out of alders [?] this way") *Vetter Creek*
Ksi Maaksgwit 119 (water/white) *White River*
Ksi sk̲a skinis ("coming out of lodgepole pine") *North Seaskinnish Creek*
Ksi skiyt ("out of skiyt") *creek near Nass Camp UNGM*
Ksit'een ("out from fish trap") *Kseaden Creek*
Ksit'in 22 (water/fish traps) *Tchitin River*
Ksits'imelix ("out from beaver") *stream UNGM*
Ksi ts'im sto'ot *South Seaskinnish Creek*
Ksiwosan* 90 ("waters of willow") *tributary of Kiteen River (?) UNGM*
Ksk̲'eelst ("creek from peak") *tributary of Ksagahlist UNGM*
laghsipe see Gilax̲ksip
Lax̲ando'osk̲ *curve of riverbank north of Wilskiihl jayn UNGM*
Lax̲anhlo' ("on the avalanche") *riverbank west of Ginluulak UNGM*
Lax'anla'c (on/where/mountain slide) *former village of the "Kitgige'nix" UNGM*
Lax̲gadiit see Gadiit
Lax̲galts'ap 105 (on/village) *Greenville*
Lax̲gitsoohl *Alice Arm*
Lax̲ksiwasandit *small lake UNGM*
Lax̲sagat 62 (on/pine) [N/Gy] *Jackpine Mountain:* var. Lax̲-sak̲-gat
Lax̲-sak̲-gat see Lax̲sagat
Lax̲wijix 79 (on/cariboo) [N/Gy] *height of land south of Kinskuch River UNGM:* var.
　Lax̲-wijix
Lax-wijix see Lax̲wijix
Lissems (food basket) *probably lower Nass River:* aka Xsitxemsem: var. Lisems
Logom staahl ("into nettles") *Mount Hoeft*
Loot'up angidaa ("where you go to Angidaa") *riverside channel UNGM:* see Angida
Luu'k'alaanhl Gwinsgox (on/from mouth of river up/toward ferry [headwaters]) *UNGM:*
　var. Luugalaginsgoix
Luumin gwinaniis ("stream of urine") *slow-moving stream between Sand and Lava Lakes*
　UNGM
Luu'min Gyahlt'in 133 (inside or along/up/Gyahlt'in) [N/Gy/G] *Kiteen River:* also see
　Gyahlt'in
Maiziadin Lake see T'am'matsiiadin
Maziadin and Maziadin Lake see T'am'matsiiadin
Medziaden Lake see T'am'matsiiadin
Meziadin Lake see T'am'matsiiadin
Medziadin see T'am'matsiiadin
Medziadon see T'am'matsiiadin
Minluk 19 (surprise) *UNGM*
Noojit ("like a woman") *channel in mountainside created by Zolzap Creek UNGM;* see
　Ts'alts'ap
Quinamass Bay see Kinnamox Bay
Saxwhl Ts'alts'ap ("last turn of Ts'alts'ap") *site of an ancient smokehouse UNGM*
Seax see Siiaks
Sgamaalt 3 *Shumal Creek:* var. Ks-gamal, Ksgamal, Sk̲amaal
Sgarvin *UNGM*
Sgasginist 31 (on the path/pine trees) [N] *Seaskinnish Creek*
Sheak see Sii'aks
Sheax Valley see Sii'aks
Siiaks ("new water") *Tseax River:* var. Seax, Sheak, Sheax Valley
Sii'aks 104 (new/water) *camp on Nass River at confluence of Tseaxs River UNGM*
Sii t'ax̲ ("new lake" [created by the lava flow]) *Lava Lake*
Sk̲amaal see Sgamaalt
Sk̲anask̲o'odit ("bushes of thimbleberry") *site at mouth of Wegiladap Creek*
Skinak Road *possibly a trail up Chemainuk Creek UNGM*
Smailx *former Tsetsaut village on Portland Canal UNGM*

T'aam andii hat'al ("lake where they peel cedar bark") *Spencer's Lake*
T'aam ansekok.hl ("lake where they make cedar with rope") *Hoodoo Lake*
T'amginlaaxw 61 ("lake of trout") *Dragon Lake:* var. T'aam ginlaaxw
T'amginlo'otsen (lake/where/elder berries) [N/Gy] *UNGM*
T'aam gitiks yoon *Sand Lake*
T'amgwinhamook 107 (lake/where/wild celery) *Kwinamuck Lake:* var. Gwinhamook
T'amt'uutsxwhl'aks 271 (lake/black/water) [N/G] *Damdochax Lake (commonly called Blackwater Lake):* var. Gitwinhlt'uutsxwhl'aks, Wilt'uutsxwhl'aks, D'am d'oc'aks, 'Tam-'tuu'tsxw-hl-Aks
Tchitin River see Ksit'in
Ts'alts'ap *Zolzap Creek*
Ts'imanwihlist 5 (in/where/"basket net") *fish camp at Grease Harbour on Nass River UNGM:* var. Ts'im anwilis
Ts'im'axhlogast (inside/mouth/snake) *trail near Gwinsgox UNGM*
Ts'im giist *Gish Creek*
Ts'im hakwhl ("in the hook") *steep-sided valley created by Zolzap Creek UNGM;* see Ts'alts'ap
Ts'im skiyt *Mount Hoadley*
Ts'im sto'ot *Mount Priestly*
Ts'im ts'its'it *rapids at outlet of Spencer's Lake*
Wegilaxdap *Wegiladap Creek*
Wilbaxt'aahlgibuu see Winbaxt'aahlgibuu
Wildegwantkayt ("— hat") *peak of Mount Priestly*
Wilhiiskinis ("— lodgepole pine") *mouth of Amata'l UNGM*
Wilkbiwau's see Wilxbiwo'os
Wilksibaxmihl ("where fire ran out") *volcanic cone and beginning of lava flow UNGM*
Willuwitgwun masaawut *mountain peak UNGM*
Wilnak* 89 ("where against together shoot") *cabin and site UNGM:* var. Wilnaku
Wilsasaak ("it is sharp") *ridge northeast of Canyon City UNGM*
Wilsgayip 66 (?) [N/Gy] *feature on Kiteen River UNGM*
Wilskayip *low ridge east of the Tseax River UNGM*
Wilskiihl jayn ("where the Chinese man is buried") *island UNGM*
Wilukst'aas Sgawoo 12 ("where Sgawoo's mother sat") *camp on Nass River UNGM*
Wilukstkiwan 51 [Gy/N] *fishing station on Nass River UNGM*
Wiluukstxawaa 50 [N/Gy] *fishing station on Nass River UNGM*
Wiluuskihlgenix (where/in/lies/trail) *trail near Gwinsgox UNGM*
Wilxbiwo'os 44 *UNGM:* var. Wilkbiwau's
Wilyaxyaklanohl *Wilyayanooth Creek*
Winatkxw* *UNGM*
Winbaxt'aahlgibuu 68 (where/upward/sits/the wolf) [N/Gy] *UNGM:* var. Wunbaxtahlk-ibu, Wilbaxt'aahlgibuu
Wunbaxtahlkibu see Winbaxt'aahlgibuu
Wuts'idaax 40 *UNGM*
Xhlgi-meda-sook see Hlgimedasook
Xmatxhl 36 ("climbing hill with heavy pack") *camp on Nass River UNGM*
Xsi Maas Gibuu 254 (water white wolf) *Kotsinta Creek*
Xsit'ax 49 (water/from lake) [Gy/N] *flows into Nass River near but opposite Tchitin River UNGM:* var. Ksi-tekw
Xsitxemsem 164 (river of/Txemsem) *Nass River*
Xsiwii'aks 43 *on left bank of Nass River UNGM*
Xtsimenk *Chemainuk Creek*
Yagahlolo'obit ("stones come down" [a landslide]) *mountain east of Lava Lake UNGM*
Zikgan's Spring 108 *UNGM*

Glossary of Chiefs' Names

'akstox
Alaayst
Amagyet
Aminta
Anax'aus
Anhlo'o, Anhloo
Antgulilibiksxw
Atsehltaa, Atsehlaa Taa
Atxwmseex
Axdiiwiluugooda (see Axtiwiluugoodii)
Axgigii'i, axgigi
Axgwindesxw, Ax-gun desxw, Walter
    Dasque
Axmanasxw
Axmatxwmwil
Axti'anjam
Axtiwiluugoodii, Axtiiwiluugooda, Axdii-
    wiluugooda, 'Axtiwil, 'Axtiwiluu-
    goodii
Baskyalaxha, Basgyalaxa', Chlaa
Bathle, Les Bethle
Baxk'ap
Biiyoosxw, Beyosqu, Biyoosxw
Chlaa (see Baskyalaxha)
Chliem-la-ha (see Xhliimlaxha)
Dakhlemges, Deklamgeiss, deklamges'
Dalgamuukxw (see Delgamuukw)
Daniel Guno (see Gwinuu)
Daniel Skawil, Daniel Skawill, Dan
    Skawil, Dan Skewill (see Sgawil)
Deklamgeiss, deklamges' (see
    Dakhlemges)
Delgamuukw, delgamuq,
    Delgemuukw, Dalgamuukw
Diisxw
Diwen
Djogaslee, Djogoshle (see Dzogoshle)
Duubisxw

Dzogoshle, Dzogashle, Djogaslee, Djo-
    goshle, Joogaslee
Edward Spouk (see Spookw)
Edwin Haizimsqu, Edwin Hi jamusk (see
    Hayts'imsxw)
Galdudao
Galsidipxaat
Gamanuut, Simon Gun-A-Noot, Simon
    Gunanoot
Gamgaxmilmuxw, Gamgalmulmuk,
    Kamalmuk
Gamlaxyeltxw, Gamlakyeltqu, Gam-
    laxyelk, K'am-lax-yeltxw
Gamts'iwa'
Ganaawmsitak
Ganuxeex
Gayee'is, Gitkayees, Kaiyeish
Gedimgaldo'o, Geetemraldo, Gitgaldo
Geel, Geel, Qel, Kaale, Kale
Gela
Gibee'imget
Ginigla'i
Gitdumskanees
Gitgaldo (see Gedimgaldo'o)
Gla'eeyu, Gla Ee'eyiw
Gogag (see Guugaak)
Gook
Gudeex
Gu-Gaak, William Gogak (see Guugaak)
Guno, Gu-'nuu (see Gwinuu)
Gutgwinuxs
Guugaak, Gu-Gaak, William Gogak,
    Gogag
Guuhadakxw
Guxsan, Guuxsan
Gwandemexs, Gwandemes
Gwashlaa'm, Gwaas-hlaa'm, Gwasslam
Gwax Lo'op

Gwiixmaaw, Gwixmaw
Gwilaagantxw
Gwingyoo, Gwingo
Gwiniiho'osxw
Gwininitxw
Gwinuu, Kwinu, Gu-'nuu, Guno, Daniel
   Guno
Gwinyoo
Gwisgyen
Gwisilla
Gyabask
Gyalge
Gyologet (see K'yoluget)
Haa Na'ess
Hage, Hag.e
Hatchen (see Hayts'imsxw)
Haxpegwootxw
Hayts'imsxw, Hats'imsxw, Hai-jimsxw,
   Hatchen, Edwin Haizimsqu, Edwin Hi
   jamusk
Hewa
Hewin (see Tigewin)
Hlamii, Wii-hlemii
Hleek
Hlengwax, Hlegwax
Hlewa'nst
Hlidax, Hlidux
Joogaslee (see Dzogoshle)
Kaale, Kale (see Geel)
KAKQUE (see Kyeexw)
Kamalmuk (see Gamgaxmilmuxw)
K'am-lax-yeltxw (see Gamlaxyeltxw)
K'eexkw (see Kyeexw)
Koluget (see K'yoluget)
Kotsinta
Ksdiyaawak, Kstyawk
Ksemgaakhl
Ksemgitgigyeenix
Ksemguneekxw, Ksemguneq
Ksemxsan, Ksem-xsaan, Ksim Xsaan
Kstyawk (see Ksdiyaawak)
Ksu
Kwa'amhon
Kwiiyeehl
Kwinu (see Gwinuu)
Kwunaxhat
Kxw-hliiyeemlaxa (see Xhliimlaxha)
Kyeexw, K'yee-xaxw, KAKQUE, K'eexkw
K'yoluget, K'yologet, Gyologet, Koluqet
Laats
Laganitsxw, Laknitsk, Lagaxnitsxw
Legenetta (see Liginihla)
Lelt, Lalt
Levi (Dangeli)
Ligigalwil
Liginihla, Legenetta

Loochore, Lucharn (see Luuxhon)
Luskayok, Luuskayok
Luus
Luutkudziiwus
Luuxhon, Luu-xhoon, Lux,on, Loochore,
   Lucharn
Maas Gibuu, Muskaboo
Madeegam Gyamk
Maksqum Lags
Malii, 'Malii, Mali
Manesk (see Minee'eskw)
Meluulak, Mo-loo-loch
Minee'eskw, Meneesk, Menesk, Manesk
Muskaboo (see Maas Gibuu)
Naagan, Nagan
Nagusts'ikatsa
Nane Na-Qua-On
Nawis
Neatsqua (see Niitsw)
Neek't
Neest (see 'Niist)
'niaxsqaks
Niik'yap
Niisangwadiksxw, Niis Angwadikskw
Niis-hlak-Gan-us
'Niist, Neest
Niisyok, Peter Nisyok
Niitsxw, Neastqua
Nikateen
Niskinwatk
No'nes
Noxs Diigyet
Noxs Din
Noxs Skawil (see Sgawil)
Pa'atneexhl
Peter Nisyok (see Niisyok)
Pete Tashoots (see Taashuuts)
Peter Wilizqu (see 'Wiilitsxw)
Qel (see Geel)
Sagawan
Samilyaan, Sum-mil-yan
Saniik
Semedik (see Simediik)
Sgat'iin, Sgat'iin, Skat'iin, Sqatin, Sco-
   dain, Scoteen, Scot-tein, Sgadi.n,
   Skat'iin, Skat'een
Sgawil, Skawil, Skawil, Skawill, Skowill,
   Noxs Skawil (see also Daniel Skawil)
Sidook
Simediik, Semedik
Simon Gun-A-Noot, Simon Gunanoot
   (see Gamanuut)
Sindihl
Singewin, Sin-Gi-win
Skat'iin, Skat'een (see Sgat'iin)
Skawil, Skawill, Skowill (see Sgawil)

Spookw, Edward Spouk
Sqatin (see Sgat'iin)
Sum-mil-yan (see Samilyaan)
Suwiiguus
Taas Aguun
Taashuuts, Tashuuts, Pete Tashoots
Tiba
Tigewin, Hewin
Tok, Tok
T'ooxens
Ts'iigwa
'Tsii-wa,Ts'iiwa, Wa'a
Ts'imgwanks
Txa'anlaxhatxw, Txanlaxhatk
Txaldedaw
Txawok
Wa'a (see Ts'iwa'a)
Wememnassac (see Wiiminoosikx)
Wi tax-ha-yetsxw (see Wudaxhayetsxw)
Wialax (see Wii'a'lax)
Wigademxskaak (see Wiigadimxsgaak)
Wii Goobil (see Wiigoob'l)
Wii Muugwiluxsxw
Wii Nak
Wii'a'lax, Wialax
Wiibowax
Wiigadimxsgaak, Wiigetim Skaak, Wigademxskaak
Wiigoob'l, Wii Goobil, Wiigoobil
Wii-hlemii (see Hlamii)

Wiik'aax
Wiilaxha
'Wiilitsxw, Wiilitsxw, WI-LIZQU, Wilits, Henry Willitzqu, Peter Wilizqu
Wiiminoosikx, Wiiminoosik, 'Wiiminoosikx, Wii-minoosi'kx, Wememnassac, Wimanosak, Wimenozek
'Wiixa, 'Wii-xa'a, 'Wiixa, Wixe, Wiixa
Wiiyagadeets, Yack-o-Dades
Wilits (see 'Wiilitsxw)
Wi-Lizqu
William Gogag (see Guugaak)
wimanosak, Wimenozek (see Wiiminoosikx)
Wist'is
Wi-tax-ha-yetsxw (see Wudaxhayetsxw)
Wixe (see 'Wiixa)
Wogalwil
Wo'os Sa'lo'op
Wudaxhayetsxw, Wudaxayets, Wi tax-ha-yetsxw, Wi-tax-ha-yetsxw
Xgwooyemtxw
Xhliimlaxha, Xhliemlaxa, Kxw-hliiyeemlaxa, Chliem-la-ha
Xskiigmlaxha, Xsgiigmlaxha, Xsgiigamlaxha, Xskiigemlaxha
Yack-o-Dades (see Wiiyagadeets)
Yanukws, Yankws, yenkws
Yaxyak
Zaloo

Bibliography

Published Sources

Abbott, D., ed. *The World Is as Sharp as a Knife: An Anthology in Honour of Wilson Duff.* Victoria: BCPM 1981

Barbeau, Marius. "The Poor Man's Trail." *Canadian Geographical Journal* 9,1 (1934): 3-13

–. *Totem Poles: Volume 1, According to Crests and Topics.* National Museum of Canada, Bulletin 119, Anthropological Series no. 30. Ottawa: National Museum of Canada 1950

–. "Tsimshian Songs." *Publications of the American Ethnological Society* 18 (1951): 97-280

Berger, Thomas. "Wilson Duff and Native Land Claims." In Abbott, *Sharp as a Knife*, 49-64.

Boas, Franz. "The Ts'ets'a'ut (the Tinneh Tribe of Portland Inlet). Report on the Northwestern Tribes of Canada," 35-48. *British Association for the Advancement of Science, 65th Report*, v. 10. London 1895

–. "Traditions of the Ts'ets'a'ut" *Journal of American Folk-Lore* 9,35 (1897): 17-48

Boas, Franz, and Earle Pliny. "Ts'ets'aut, an Athapaskan Language from Portland Canal, British Columbia." *International Journal of American Linguistics* 3,1 (1924): 1-35

British Columbia. *Papers Relating to the Commission Appointed to Enquire into the State and Condition of the Indians of the North-West Coast of British Columbia.* Victoria: Government Printer 1888

–. *Report of Conferences between the Provincial Government and Indian Delegates from Fort Simpson and Naas River.* Victoria: Government Printer 1887

Canada. DIA. *Annual Report.* Ottawa: Queen's Printer 1898

Canada. House of Parliament and Senate. "Special Joint Committee of the Senate and House of Commons Appointed to Inquire into the Claims of the Allied Tribes of British Columbia, as Set Forth in Their Petition Submitted to Parliament in 1926; Report and Evidence." *Journals of the Senate of Canada* (first session of the sixteenth Parliament) (1926-7): appendix

Chismore, G. "From the Nass to the Skeena." *Overland Monthly* 6 (1885): 449-58

Collison, William H. *In the Wake of the War Canoe.* London: Seeley, Service 1915

"Constitution of the Indian Settlement of Aiyansh." *Trail Cruiser: Aiyansh Mission Magazine* 1,2 (1917): 15-18

Cove, John. "A Detailed Inventory of the Barbeau Northwest Coast Files." National Museum of Man, Mercury Series, Canadian Centre for Folk Culture Studies, Paper No. 54. Ottawa: National Museum of Man 1985

Cox, Constance. "Simon Gun-a-Noot: The Authentic Story." *Native Voice* (Special Edition 1958): 34-7

Dawson, George M. "Report on an Exploration of the Yukon District, N.W.T. and Adjacent Northern Part of British Columbia." *Geological Survey of Canada, Annual Report, 1887-1888.* Montreal: GSC 1889. 7-277

Derrick, Mae, ed. *Adaawhl Gitanyaaw.* Kitwancool, BC: Kitwancool Indian Band 1978

Duff, Wilson, ed. *Histories, Territories and Laws of the Kitwancool.* Anthropology in BC, Memoir No. 4. Victoria: BCPM 1959

–. "Tsetsaut." In Helm, *Subarctic*, 454-7

Emmons, George T. "The Tahltan Indians." *University of Pennsylvania Museum, Anthropological Publication* 4,1 (1911)

Emmons, G.T., and F. de Laguna. *The Tlingit Indians.* Vancouver: Douglas and McIntyre 1991

FIBC. *The Nishga Petition to His Majesty's Privy Council: A Record of Interviews with the Government of Canada together with Related Documents.* N.p.: FIBC 1915. Copy at BCA

Galois, Robert. "Colonial Encounters: The Worlds of Arthur Wellington Clah, 1855-1881." *BC Studies* 115/116 (Autumn/Winter 1997-8): 105-47

–. "The History of the Upper Skeena Region, 1850 to 1927." *Native Studies Review* 9,2 (1993-4): 113-83

–. "The Indian Rights Association, Native Protest Activity and the Land Question in British Columbia, 1913-1916." *Native Studies Review* 8,2 (1992): 1-34

Gentilcore, R., ed. *Historical Atlas of Canada: The Land Transformed, 1800-1891.* Toronto: University of Toronto Press 1993

Gough, B. *Gunboat Frontier: British Maritime Authority and Northwest Coast Indians, 1846-90.* Vancouver: UBC Press 1984

Gunanoot, Fred. "The Story of Simon P. Gunanoot." *Native Voice* (July 1947): 15

Hall, Ralph. *Pioneer Goldseekers of the Omineca.* Victoria: Morriss Publishing 1994

Halpin, Marjorie. "William Beynon, Ethnographer: Tsimshian, 1888-1958." In M. Liberty, ed., *American Indian Intellectuals*, 141-56. Proceedings of the American Ethnological Society, 1976. St. Paul: West Publishing 1978

Helm, June, ed. *Subarctic: Handbook of North American Indians.* Vol. 6. Washington: Smithsonian Institution 1981

Hurley, Maisie. "Biography of Ronald Campbell-Johnstone." *Native Voice* (1953): 3

Jenness, Diamond. "The Sekani Indians of British Columbia." National Museum of Canada Bulletin 84, Anthropological Series 20. Ottawa: National Museum of Canada 1937

Leech, Peter J. "The Pioneer Telegraph Survey of British Columbia." *BC Mining Record* (Aug. 1899): 17-26

MacDonald, George, and Richard Inglis. "Skeena River Prehistory." National Museum of Man, Mercury Series, Archaeological Survey Papers 87. Ottawa: National Museum of Man 1979

Malloch, G.S. "Reconnaissance on the Upper Skeena River, between Hazelton and the Groundhog Coal-Field, British Columbia." Canada, Sessional Paper 26. Ottawa: Queen's Printer 1912

McCullagh, James B. "Autumn Leaves." *Aiyansh Notes* (1907-9), continued as *North British Columbia News* (1909-10)

–. "Ignis. A Parable of the Great Lava Plain in the Valley of Eternal Bloom." Aiyansh, BC, 1918 (copy at BCA)

Marsden, Susan, and Robert Galois. "The Tsimshian, the Hudson's Bay Company, and the Geopolitics of the Northwest Coast Fur Trade, 1787-1840." *Canadian Geographer* 39,2 (1995): 169-83

Moss, Madonna, and Jon M. Erlandson. "Forts, Refuge Rocks, and Defensive Sites: The Antiquity of Warfare along the North Pacific Coast of North America." *Arctic Anthropology* 29,2 (1992): 73-90

Neering, Rosemary. *Continental Dash: The Russian American Telegraph.* Ganges, BC: Horsdal and Schubart 1989

NTC. *Nisga'a: People of the Mighty River.* New Aiyansh, BC: NTC 1992

–. *Lock Stock and Barrel: Nisga'a Ownership Statement.* New Aiyansh, BC: NTC 1995

Patterson, E. Palmer. *Mission on the Nass.* Waterloo: Eulachon Press 1982

Raunet, D. *Without Surrender, without Consent: A History of the Nishga Land Claims.* Vancouver: Douglas and McIntyre 1984

Robertson, W. Fleet. "Notes on a Trip to Dease Lake and to the Groundhog Coalfield." *British Columbia, Minister of Mines, Annual Report* (1912): K65-94

Sapir, Edward. "A Sketch of the Social Organization of the Nass River Indians." *Geological Survey of Canada, Museum Bulletin 19, Anthropological Series 7* (1915): 1-30

Scott, Robert N. "Indians Living on and Near the Boundary between British Columbia and the Russian-American Territory Recently Ceded to the United States." *Annual Report of the United States Commissioner of Indian Affairs for the Year 1869,* 563-4. Washington, DC: Government Printing Office 1870

Selwyn, A.R. "Summary Report on the Operations of the Geological Survey for the Year 1893." *Geological Survey of Canada, Annual Report 7.* Ottawa: Queen's Printer 1894.

Shotridge, Louis. "A Visit to the Tsimshian Indians: The Skeena River (Continued)." *University of Pennsylvania Museum Journal* 10,3 (1919): 117-48

Tennant, Paul. *Aboriginal Peoples and Politics: The Indian Land Question in British Columbia, 1849-1989.* Vancouver: UBC Press 1990

Tharp, James. "The Position of the Tsetsaut among Northern Athapaskans." *International Journal of American Linguistics* 38,1 (1972): 14-25

Wi-lizqu, and J.B. McCullagh. "An Indian Feud." *North British Columbia News* July 1925: 171-4

Manuscript Sources

Adlam, Robert G. "The Structural Basis of Tahltan Society." PhD diss., University of Toronto, 1985

Archer, David. "Results of the Prince Rupert Dating Project." Victoria: BC Heritage Trust 1992

Barbeau, Marius C., and William Beynon. Northwest Coast Files (BF Series), 1915-59. Ottawa: CMC

Barbeau, M., and W. Beynon. "The Gwenhoot of Alaska: In Search of a Bounteous Land." Ottawa: Folklore Division, CMC, c. 1950

–. "Raven Clan Outlaws of the North Pacific Coast." Ottawa: Folklore Division, CMC, c. 1950

–. "Temlarh'am: The Land of Plenty on the North Pacific Coast." Ottawa: Folklore Division, CMC, c. 1950

–. "Wolf Clan Invaders from the Northern Plateaux among the Tsimsyans." Ottawa: Folklore Division, CMC, c. 1950

Beynon, William. Manuscripts. Columbia University, c. 1939. Ann Arbor, MI: University Microfilms International

British Columbia. Attorney General. Correspondence Inward. GR 429, BCA

–. Department of Fish and Wildlife. Traplines. GR 1085, BCA

–. Department of Lands. Correspondence Inward. 1871-83, GR 868, BCA

–. Premier. Correspondence. GR 441, BCA

–. Provincial Police. Correspondence. GR 55, BCA

–. Provincial Secretary. Correspondence. GR 526, BCA

–. Royal Commission on Forestry (1955). Proceedings. GR 668, BCA

–. Supreme Court. *Delgamuukw v. The Queen.* Proceedings at Trial, Exhibits, Affidavits, Commission Evidence, Final Argument, 1986-1990. GA, Hazelton, BC

–. Surveys and Lands Branch. Correspondence. 0 Series, GR 991, BCA

–. Colonial Secretary. Correspondence Inward, 1859-70. GR 1392, BCA

Callbreath, Grant, and Cook. Letterbooks, 1878-98. Hubbel Collection, University of Washington. Microfilm 1132, UBC

Campbell-Johnston, Amy, and Ronald Campbell-Johnston. "With the Mystic Totem Pole People and Other Episodes" and "The Story of the Totem" (1908-12). Copy in possession of Neil J. Sterritt

Canada. DIA. Babine Agency. Letterbooks. NAC, RG 10, vols. 1583-9

–. –. Black Series. NAC, RG 10

–. –. Central Registry Files. NAC, RG 10, vols. 7780, 7786

–. –. Deputy Superintendent General. Letterbooks. NAC, RG 10, vol. 1128

–. –. Indian Reserve Commission. Letterbooks, 1876-1910. NAC, RG 10, vols. 1275-6

–. –. Office of the Indian Commissioner for British Columbia. Correspondence. NAC, RG 10, vols. 10872, 11041, 11298

–. Department of Oceans and Fisheries. Records Pertaining to British Columbia. NAC, RG 23. Microfilm R5474, UBC

–. Governor General. Correspondence from the Colonial Office. NAC, RG 7

–. Privy Council Office. Orders-in-Council. NAC, RG 2

–. Supreme Court of Canada. *Calder* v. *Attorney General of British Columbia.* Reasons for Judgement, 31 Jan. 1973

Canada, and British Columbia. Royal Commission on Indian Affairs, 1913-16, Babine and Nass Agencies Hearings. Transcripts prepared by Union of BC Indian Chiefs. Originals in NAC, RG 10, vol. 11024, files AH 1, AH 8, microfilm T 3961, 3963. Copies at UBCSC

–. –. Correspondence and Documents. Vol. 11020, file 518; 11022, file 560A; 11023, file 600; 11026, file SNA-2; microfilms T 3957, 3959, 3960, 3965

Clah, Arthur Wellington. Diaries and Papers. 70 vols. WMS, Amer 140, Wellcome Institute, London. Microfilm at NAC

Collison, H.A. "Teeming Waters." F/3/C 49, BCA

Conway, Edward. Letterbook, 1865-6. J/I/C76.2, BCA

Corsiglia, John. "The Nisga'a and Their Neighbours." Ayuukhl Nishga Land Ownership and Occupancy Study, c. 1987. NTC, Aiyansh, BC

Cybulski, Jerome. "Context of Human Remains from the Lachane Site, GbTo33. Ottawa: Manuscript on file, Library Documents Section (Archaeology), CMC

Dangeli, Reginald. "Tsetsaut History: The Forgotten Tribe of Southern-Southeast Alaska." Alaska Historical Commission, Studies in History, Juneau, 1985

Duff, Wilson. Files. UBCMAA

–. Papers. GA, Hazelton, and also GR 2809, BCA

Emmons, G.T. Papers. In Newcombe Family Papers. Add. mss. 1077, vol. 62, file 56, BCA

Fedje, Daryl. "Millennial Tides and Shifting Shores: A Gwaii Haanas Story and Its Implications for Coastal Archaeology." Unpublished manuscript on file at Parks Canada, Victoria, 1998

Gardiner, James A. Diaries, 27 May-19 Aug., 20 Aug.-21 Sept. 1875. Add. mss. 440, BCA

Great Britain. Privy Council Office. Original Correspondence. PC 8/1240, file 111,098

Humphrey, William. Diary, 11 Mar.-26 Aug. 1874. E/C/H881, BCA

Kitwancool chiefs. Kitwancool Research Submission to Minister of Indian Affairs, 1978

Loring, Richard. Papers (Transcripts). MG 29/C/21, NAC

–. Letter to R.E. Gosnell, librarian, Provincial Assembly, Victoria, BC, 5 September 1896. BCA

McKay, J.W. Papers. Add. mss. 2735, BCA

McNeary, Stephen. "The Traditional Economic and Social Life of the Niska of British Columbia." Report submitted to CMC, Ottawa, 1974

–. "Where Fire Came Down: Social and Economic Life of the Niska." Ph.D. diss., Bryn Mawr College, 1976

Manson, Donald. "Journal of a Trip up the Naas River." B 201/a/1, HBCA

Marsden, Susan. "Defending the Mouth of the Skeena: Perspectives on Tsimshian Tlingit Relations." Paper presented at the 29th Annual Meeting of the Canadian Archaeological Association, Halifax, 1996

Morison, Charles F. "Reminiscences of the Early Days of British Columbia 1862-1870 by a Pioneer of the North West Coast." Ed. J.W. Morison. Add. mss. 424, BCA

O'Reilly, P. Diary, 1881. Microfilm 12A, BCA

Thompson, G.E. Duplicate Reports, 1866-7 [re COT exploration in 1867 in the Skeena, Nass, and Stikine regions]. Colony of British Columbia, Department of Lands and Works. Herald Street Collection, GR 1069, file I 143, BCA

Woods, Helen. Diary, 1880. Add. mss. 773, BCA

Maps

Great Britain. Admiralty. Admiralty Chart 2190, "Nass Bay." Hydrographic Office, London, 1872

Shotridge, Louis. Kitwancool Map. Photograph no. 14952, University of Pennsylvania, Philadelphia

Tapes

Guédon, Marie-Françoise Tapes. VII-C-58T and VII-C-60T. Recorded in collaboration with Chris Harris and Polly Sargent, 1973. CMC collection, Ottawa

Index

Neil J. Sterritt, Madeegam Gyamk, was research director for the Gitksan in the 1970s, president of the Gitksan-Wet'suwet'en Tribal Council from 1981 to 1987, an expert witness in the *Delgamuukw* case, and has worked extensively at the national level on constitutional issues. He has learned the territories first hand and on the land from hereditary chiefs and matriarchs beginning as a child and continuing into the present. **Susan Marsden** has researched the oral history and indigenous system of land tenure of Northwest Coast First Nations since the 1970s, especially during the preparation for *Delgamuukw* v. *The Queen*, and was an expert witness in the *Delgamuukw* case. **Robert Galois** is associated with the Geography Department at UBC, has published numerous articles on Aboriginal issues, and was an expert witness in the *Delgamuukw* case. **Peter Grant** has worked in the Gitksan community since 1978 and was one of the lead lawyers in *Delgamuukw*. He is currently a partner in the legal firm Hutchins, Soroka and Grant. **Richard Overstall** has spent nearly twenty years working with the Gitksan on Aboriginal issues. He played a major role in framing the research for the *Delgamuukw* case.

Set in Stone by Brenda and Neil West, BN Typographics West

Printed and bound in Canada by Friesens

Copy editor: Dallas Harrison

Proofreader: Joanne Richardson

Indexer: Patricia Buchanan

Cartographer: Eric Leinberger